Hell's Paradise

JIGOKURAKU

STORY AND ART BY
YUJI KAKU

HELL'S

PARADISE

JIGOKURAKU

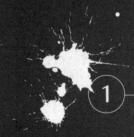

1

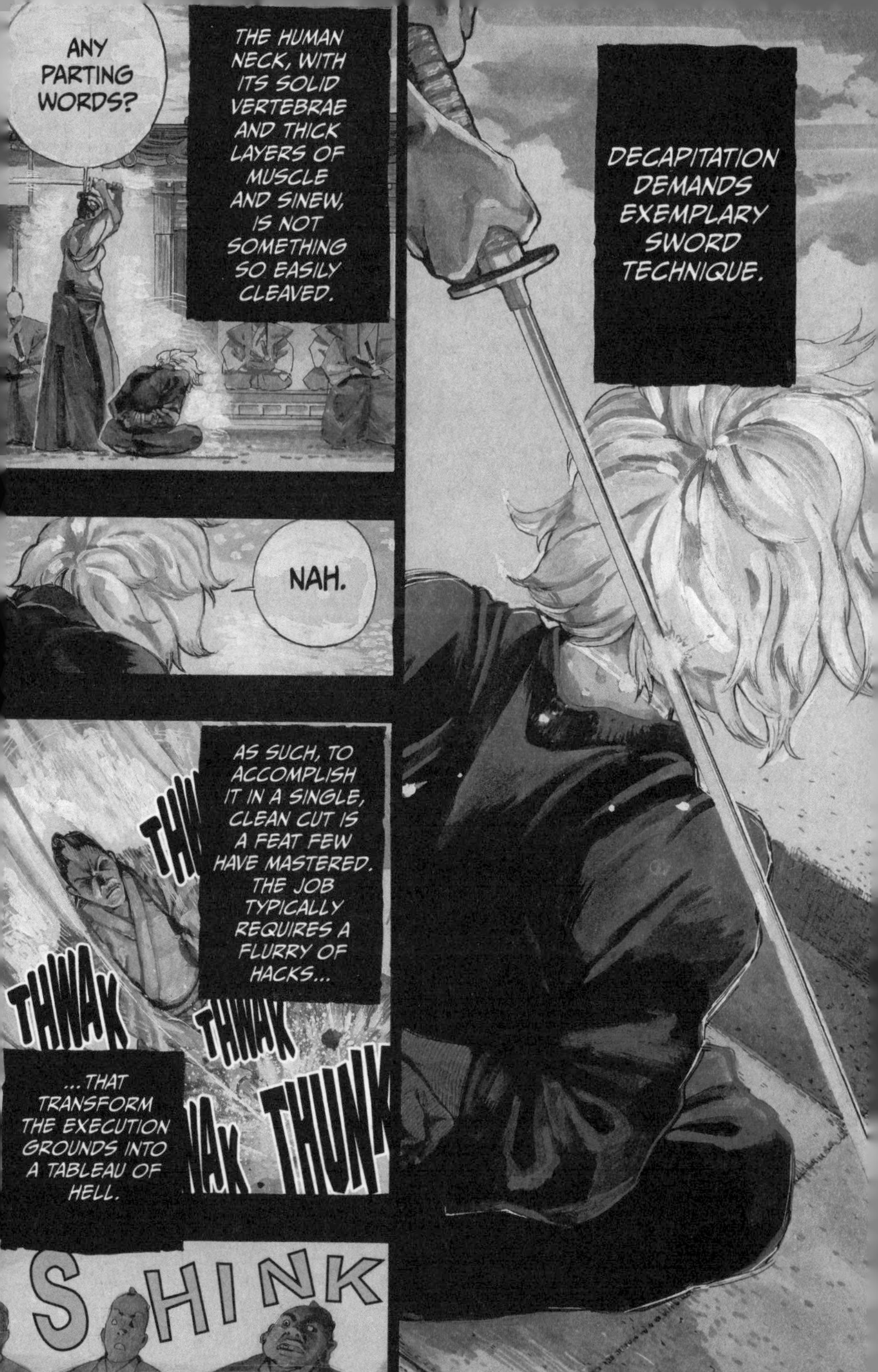
DECAPITATION DEMANDS EXEMPLARY SWORD TECHNIQUE.
THE HUMAN NECK, WITH ITS SOLID VERTEBRAE AND THICK LAYERS OF MUSCLE AND SINEW, IS NOT SOMETHING SO EASILY CLEAVED.
ANY PARTING WORDS?
NAH.
AS SUCH, TO ACCOMPLISH IT IN A SINGLE, CLEAN CUT IS A FEAT FEW HAVE MASTERED. THE JOB TYPICALLY REQUIRES A FLURRY OF HACKS...
THWAK
THWAK
THUNK
...THAT TRANSFORM THE EXECUTION GROUNDS INTO A TABLEAU OF HELL.
SHINK

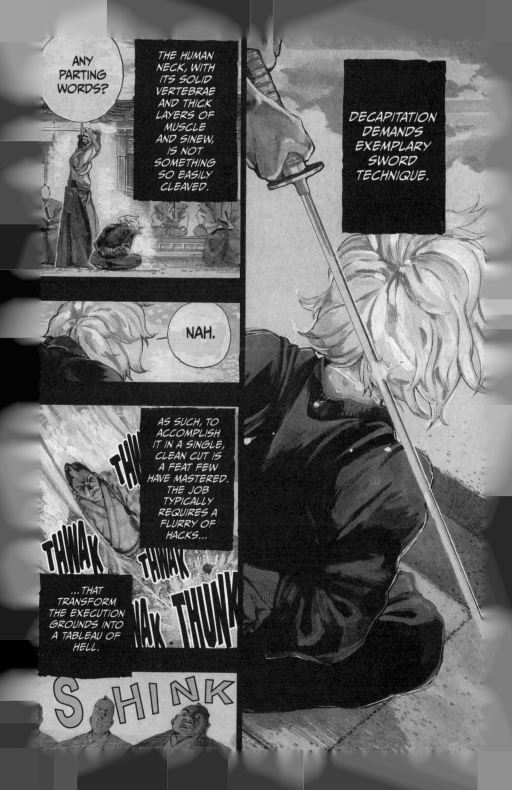

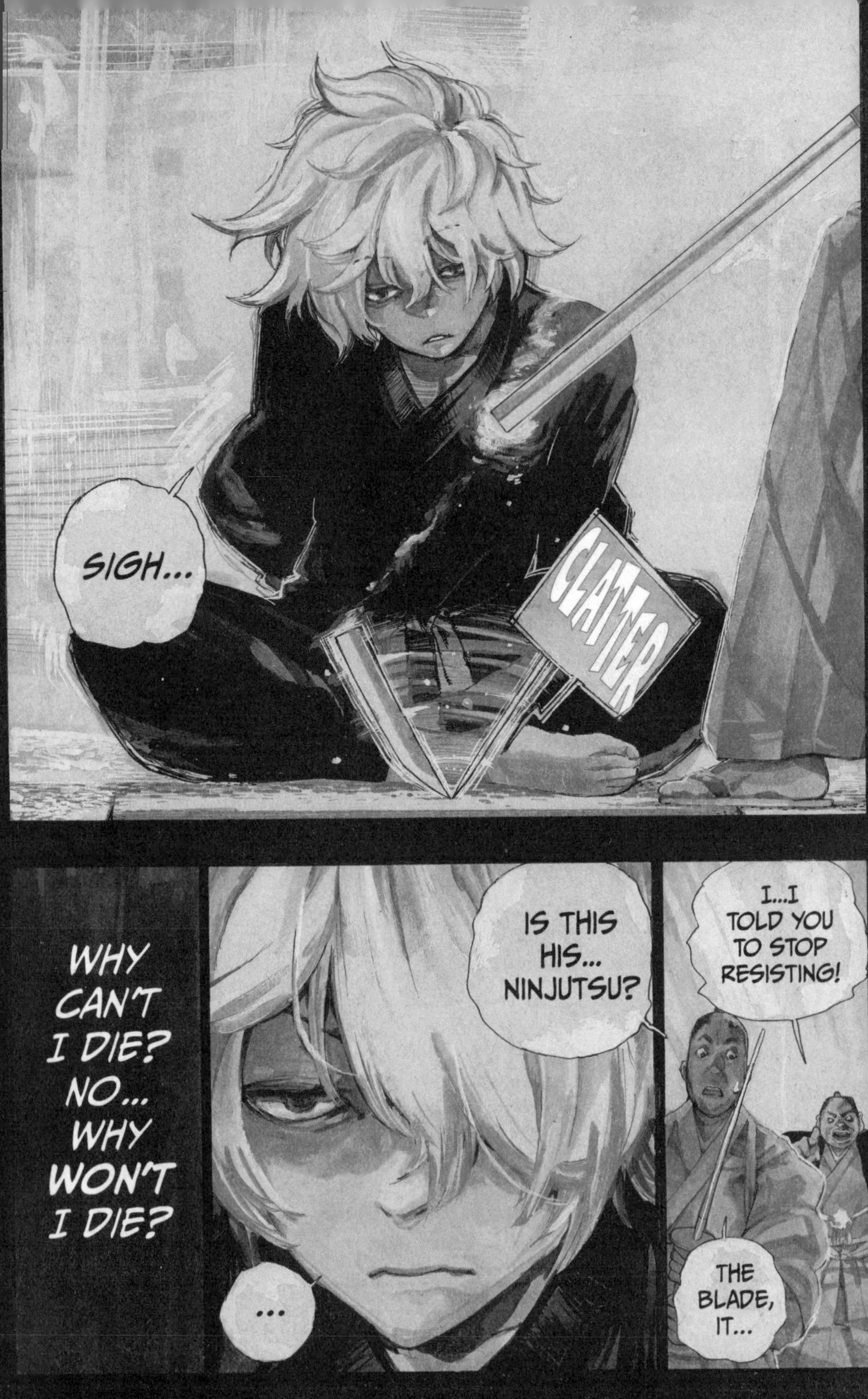
SIGH...
CLATTER
I...I TOLD YOU TO STOP RESISTING!
THE BLADE, IT...
IS THIS HIS... NINJUTSU?
...
WHY CAN'T I DIE? NO... WHY WON'T I DIE?

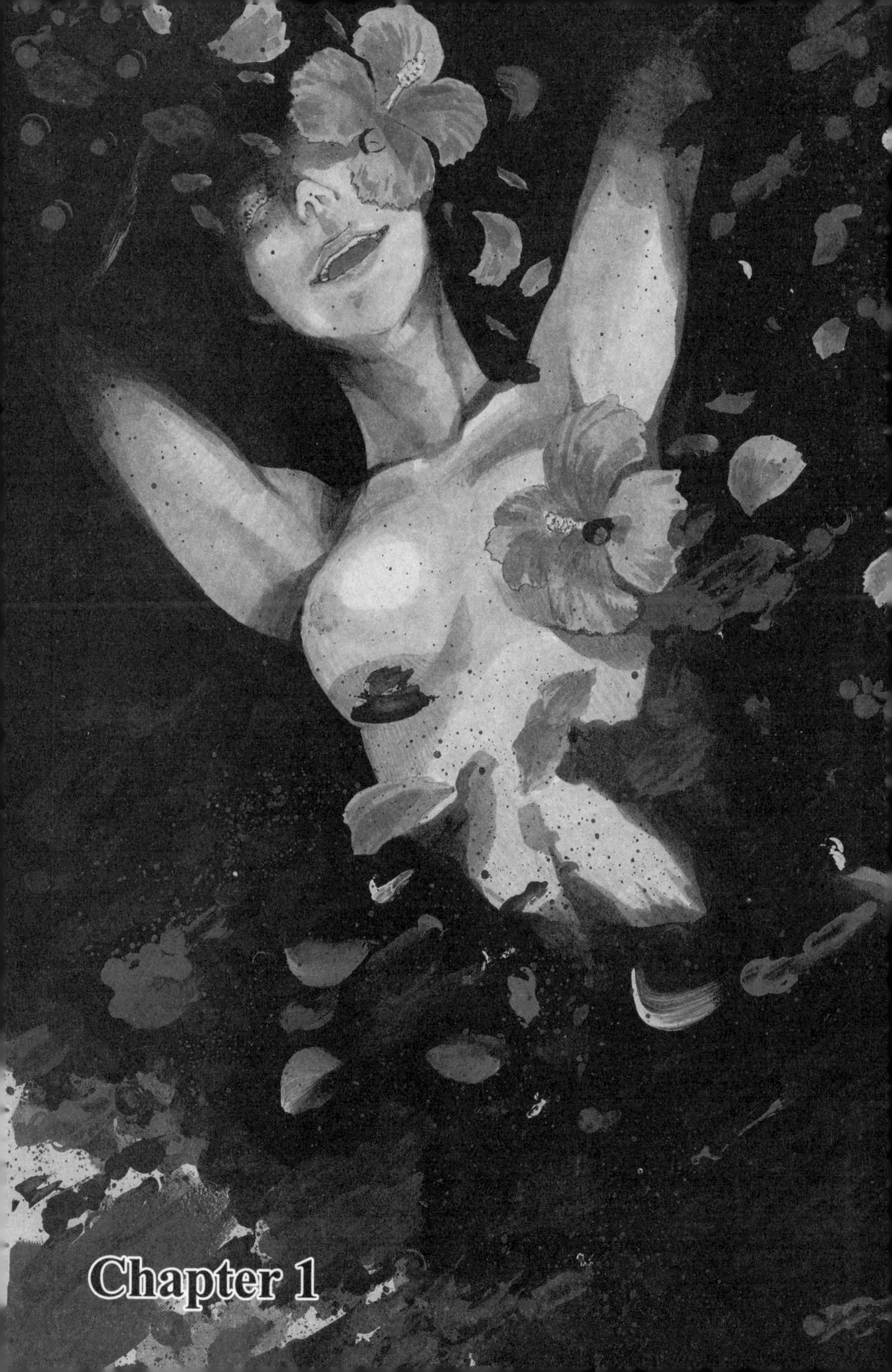

Chapter 1

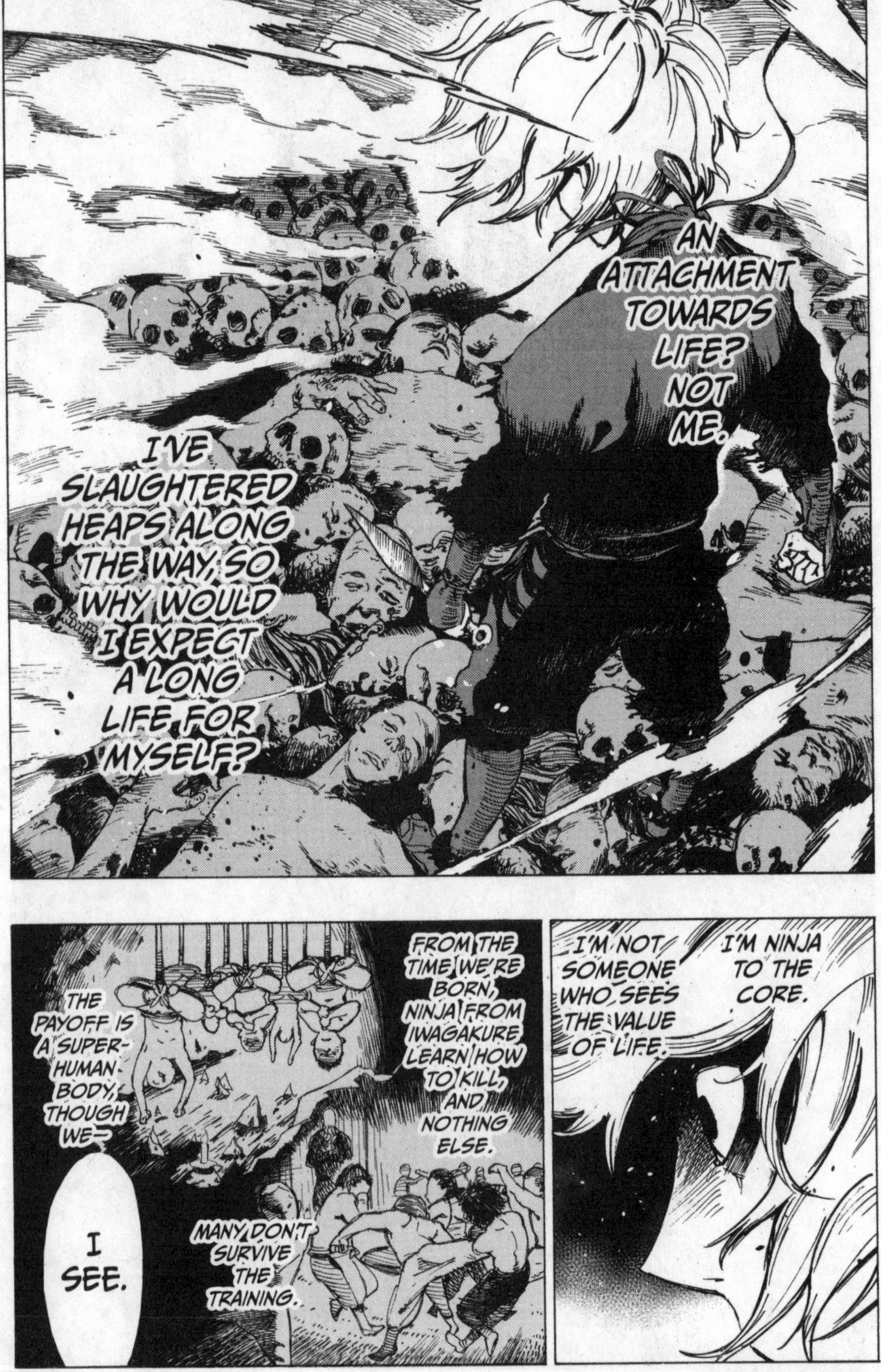
AN ATTACHMENT TOWARDS LIFE? NOT ME.
I'VE SLAUGHTERED HEAPS ALONG THE WAY, SO WHY WOULD I EXPECT A LONG LIFE FOR MYSELF?
I'M NINJA TO THE CORE.
I'M NOT SOMEONE WHO SEES THE VALUE OF LIFE.
FROM THE TIME WE'RE BORN, NINJA FROM IWAGAKURE LEARN HOW TO KILL, AND NOTHING ELSE.
THE PAYOFF IS A SUPER-HUMAN BODY, THOUGH WE—
MANY DON'T SURVIVE THE TRAINING.
I SEE.

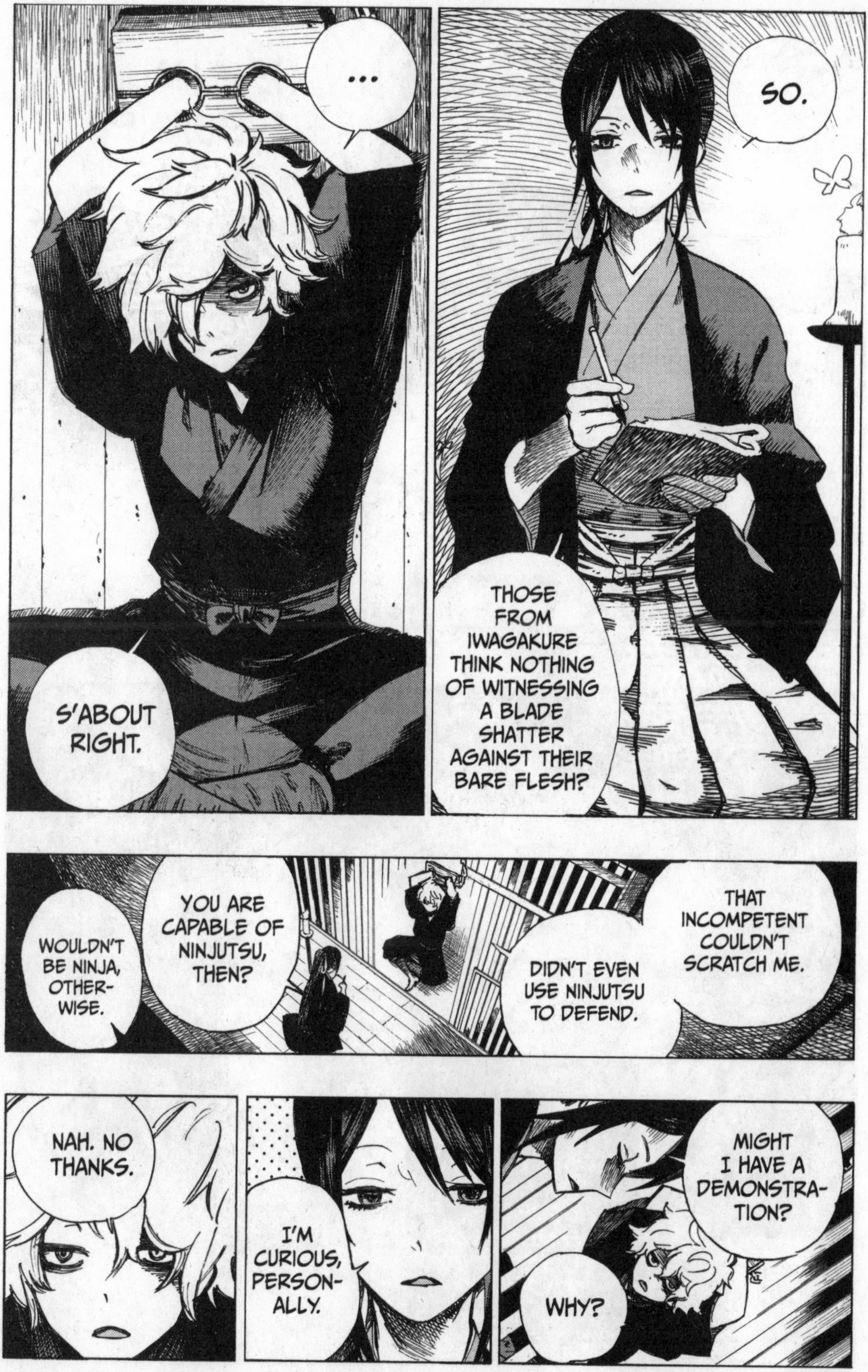
SO.
THOSE FROM IWAGAKURE THINK NOTHING OF WITNESSING A BLADE SHATTER AGAINST THEIR BARE FLESH?
...
S'ABOUT RIGHT.
THAT INCOMPETENT COULDN'T SCRATCH ME.
DIDN'T EVEN USE NINJUTSU TO DEFEND.
YOU ARE CAPABLE OF NINJUTSU, THEN?
WOULDN'T BE NINJA, OTHER-WISE.
MIGHT I HAVE A DEMONSTRA-TION?
WHY?
I'M CURIOUS, PERSON-ALLY.
NAH. NO THANKS.

HE SHALL BE BURNED AT THE STAKE!!

...

EXECUTION BY FLAME WAS ORIGINALLY CONCEIVED OF AS AN APPROPRIATE PUNISHMENT FOR ARSONISTS.

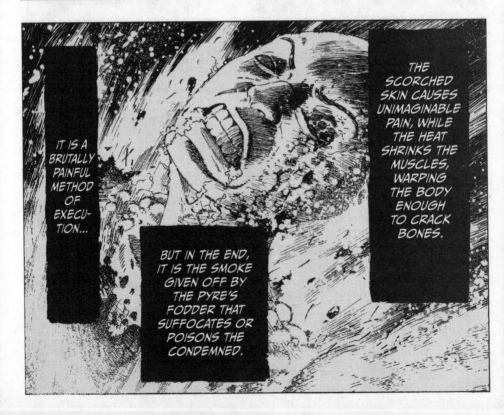

THE SCORCHED SKIN CAUSES UNIMAGINABLE PAIN, WHILE THE HEAT SHRINKS THE MUSCLES, WARPING THE BODY ENOUGH TO CRACK BONES.

IT IS A BRUTALLY PAINFUL METHOD OF EXECUTION...

BUT IN THE END, IT IS THE SMOKE GIVEN OFF BY THE PYRE'S FODDER THAT SUFFOCATES OR POISONS THE CONDEMNED.

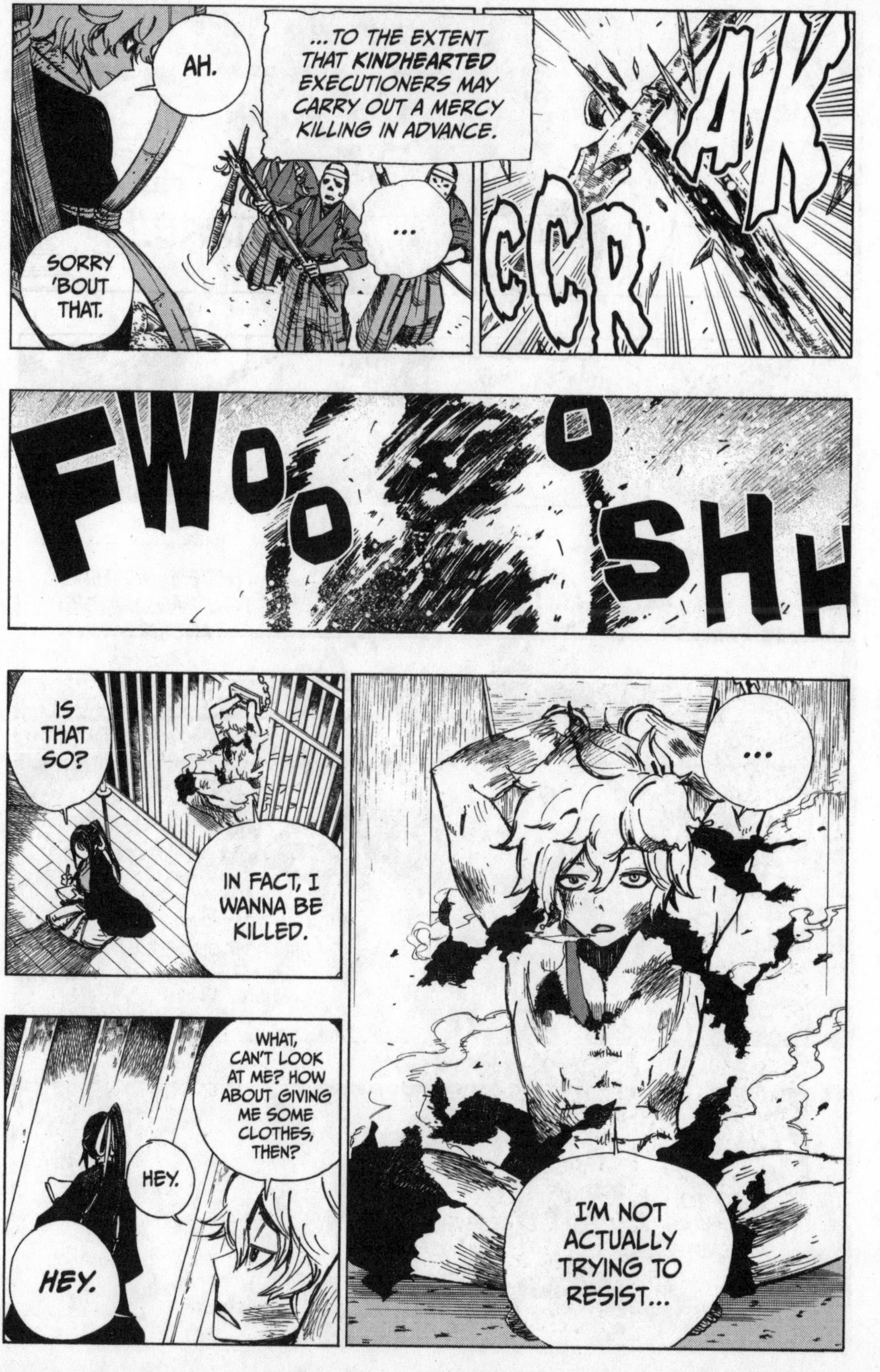
CCRAK
...TO THE EXTENT THAT KINDHEARTED EXECUTIONERS MAY CARRY OUT A MERCY KILLING IN ADVANCE.
...
AH.
SORRY 'BOUT THAT.
FWOOOSHH
...
I'M NOT ACTUALLY TRYING TO RESIST...
IS THAT SO?
IN FACT, I WANNA BE KILLED.
WHAT, CAN'T LOOK AT ME? HOW ABOUT GIVING ME SOME CLOTHES, THEN?
HEY.
HEY.

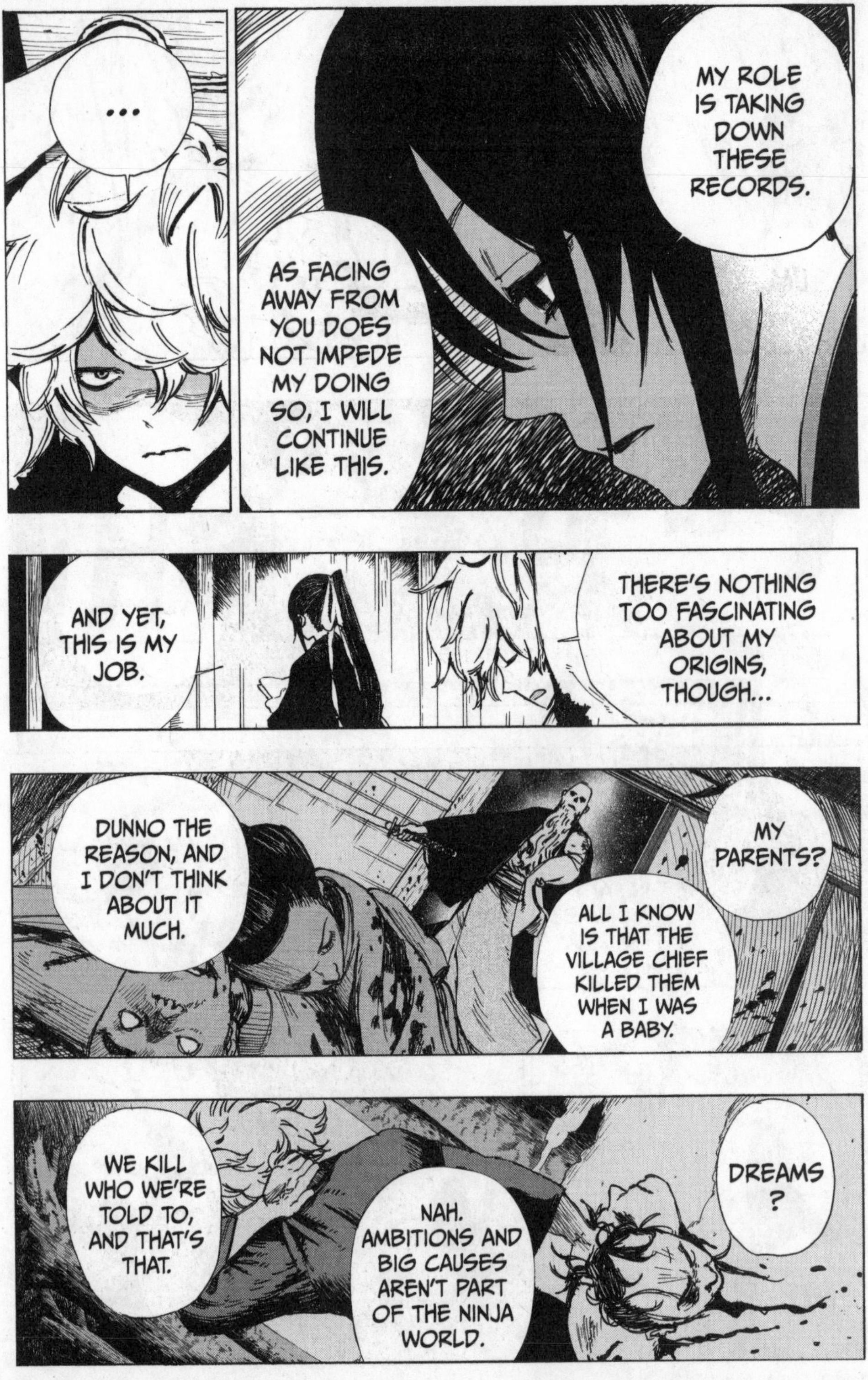
MY ROLE IS TAKING DOWN THESE RECORDS.
AS FACING AWAY FROM YOU DOES NOT IMPEDE MY DOING SO, I WILL CONTINUE LIKE THIS.
...
THERE'S NOTHING TOO FASCINATING ABOUT MY ORIGINS, THOUGH...
AND YET, THIS IS MY JOB.
MY PARENTS?
ALL I KNOW IS THAT THE VILLAGE CHIEF KILLED THEM WHEN I WAS A BABY.
DUNNO THE REASON, AND I DON'T THINK ABOUT IT MUCH.
DREAMS?
NAH. AMBITIONS AND BIG CAUSES AREN'T PART OF THE NINJA WORLD.
WE KILL WHO WE'RE TOLD TO, AND THAT'S THAT.

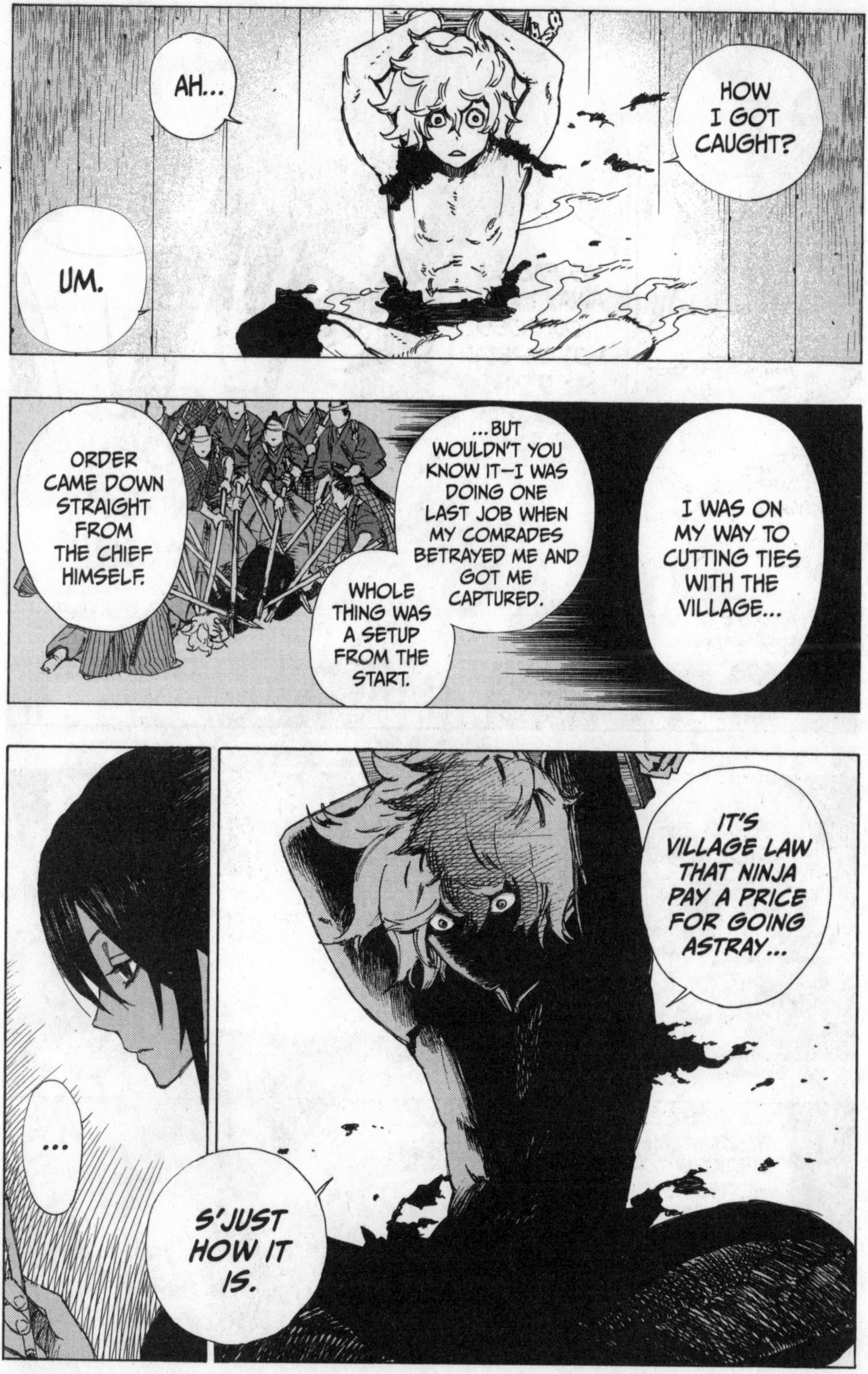
HOW I GOT CAUGHT?
AH...
UM.
I WAS ON MY WAY TO CUTTING TIES WITH THE VILLAGE...
...BUT WOULDN'T YOU KNOW IT—I WAS DOING ONE LAST JOB WHEN MY COMRADES BETRAYED ME AND GOT ME CAPTURED.
WHOLE THING WAS A SETUP FROM THE START.
ORDER CAME DOWN STRAIGHT FROM THE CHIEF HIMSELF.
IT'S VILLAGE LAW THAT NINJA PAY A PRICE FOR GOING ASTRAY...
S'JUST HOW IT IS.
...

WHY'D I CUT AND RUN, YOU'RE ASKING?

AND?

HE SHALL BE TORN ASUNDER BY OXEN!!

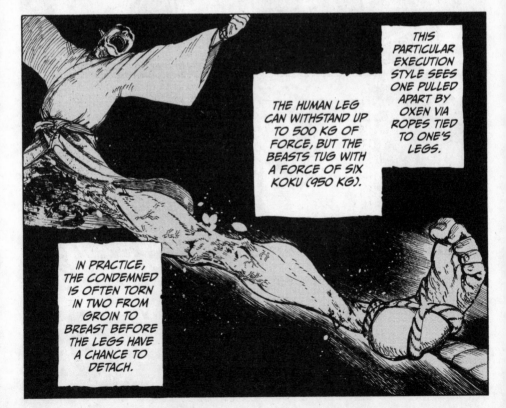

THIS PARTICULAR EXECUTION STYLE SEES ONE PULLED APART BY OXEN VIA ROPES TIED TO ONE'S LEGS.

THE HUMAN LEG CAN WITHSTAND UP TO 500 KG OF FORCE, BUT THE BEASTS TUG WITH A FORCE OF SIX KOKU (950 KG).

IN PRACTICE, THE CONDEMNED IS OFTEN TORN IN TWO FROM GROIN TO BREAST BEFORE THE LEGS HAVE A CHANCE TO DETACH.

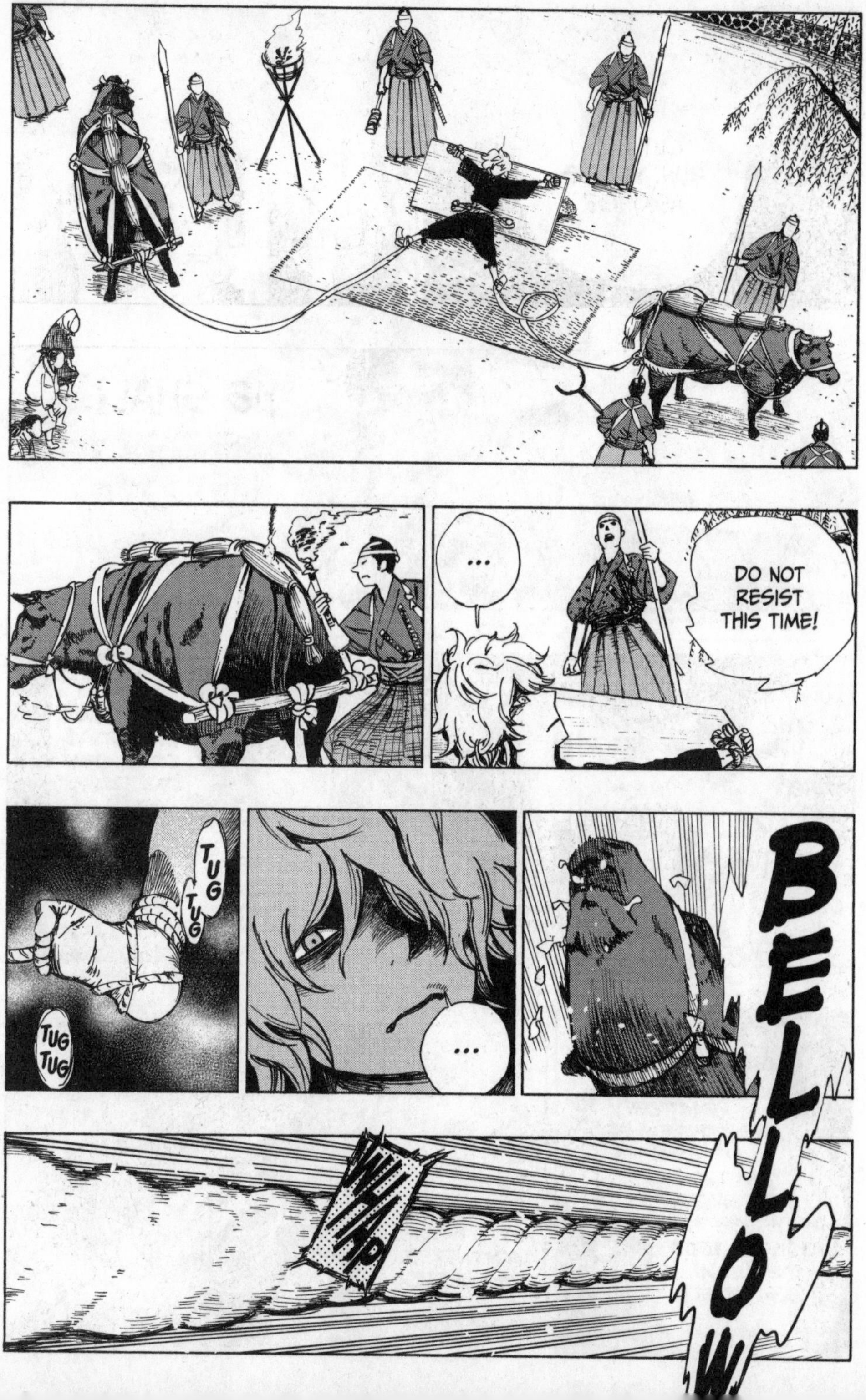
DO NOT RESIST THIS TIME!
...
BELLOW
...
TUG TUG
TUG TUG
WHAP

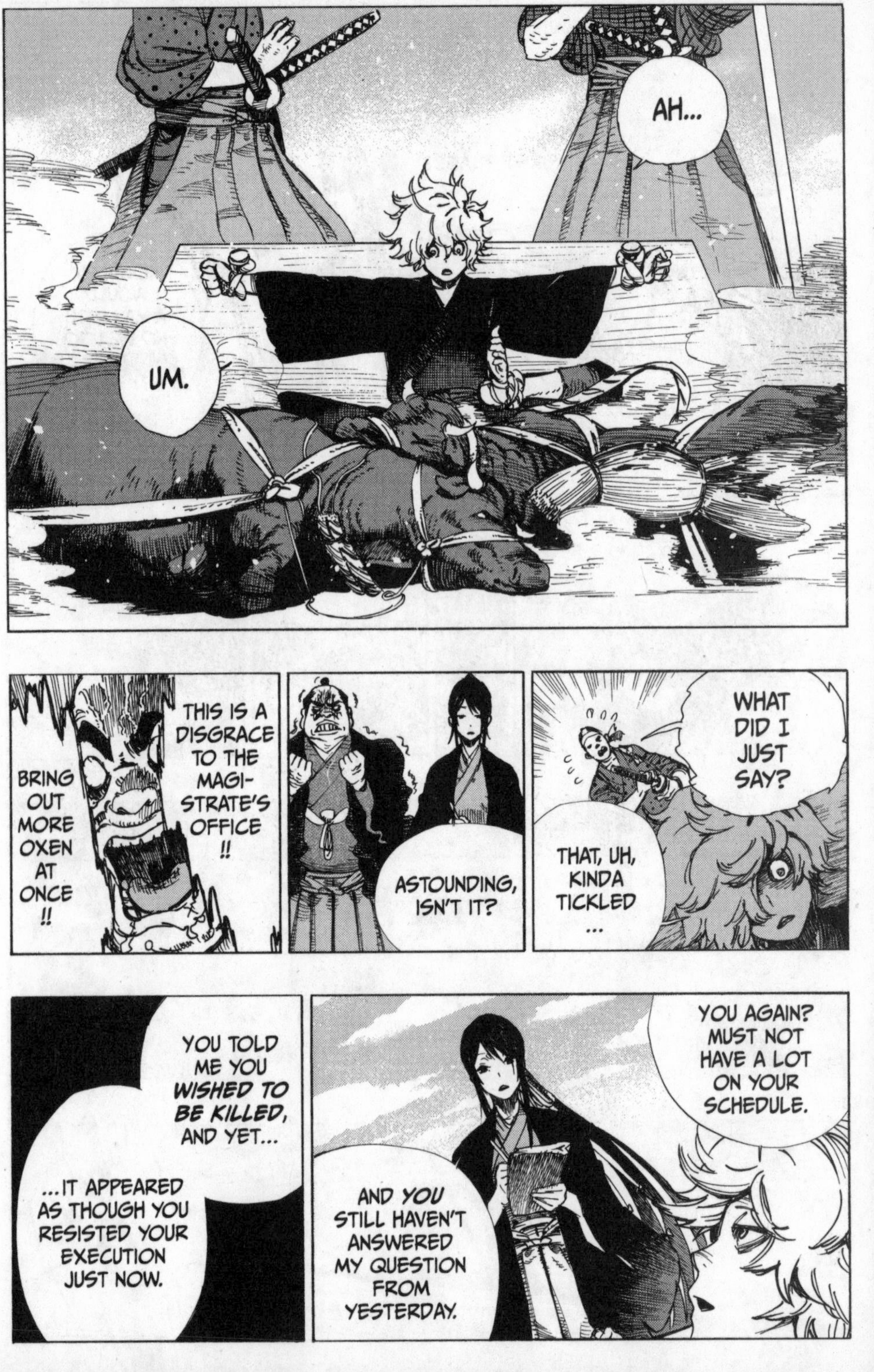
AH...
UM.
WHAT DID I JUST SAY?
THAT, UH, KINDA TICKLED ...
ASTOUNDING, ISN'T IT?
THIS IS A DISGRACE TO THE MAGI-STRATE'S OFFICE !!
BRING OUT MORE OXEN AT ONCE !!
YOU AGAIN? MUST NOT HAVE A LOT ON YOUR SCHEDULE.
AND *YOU* STILL HAVEN'T ANSWERED MY QUESTION FROM YESTERDAY.
YOU TOLD ME YOU *WISHED TO BE KILLED*, AND YET...
...IT APPEARED AS THOUGH YOU RESISTED YOUR EXECUTION JUST NOW.

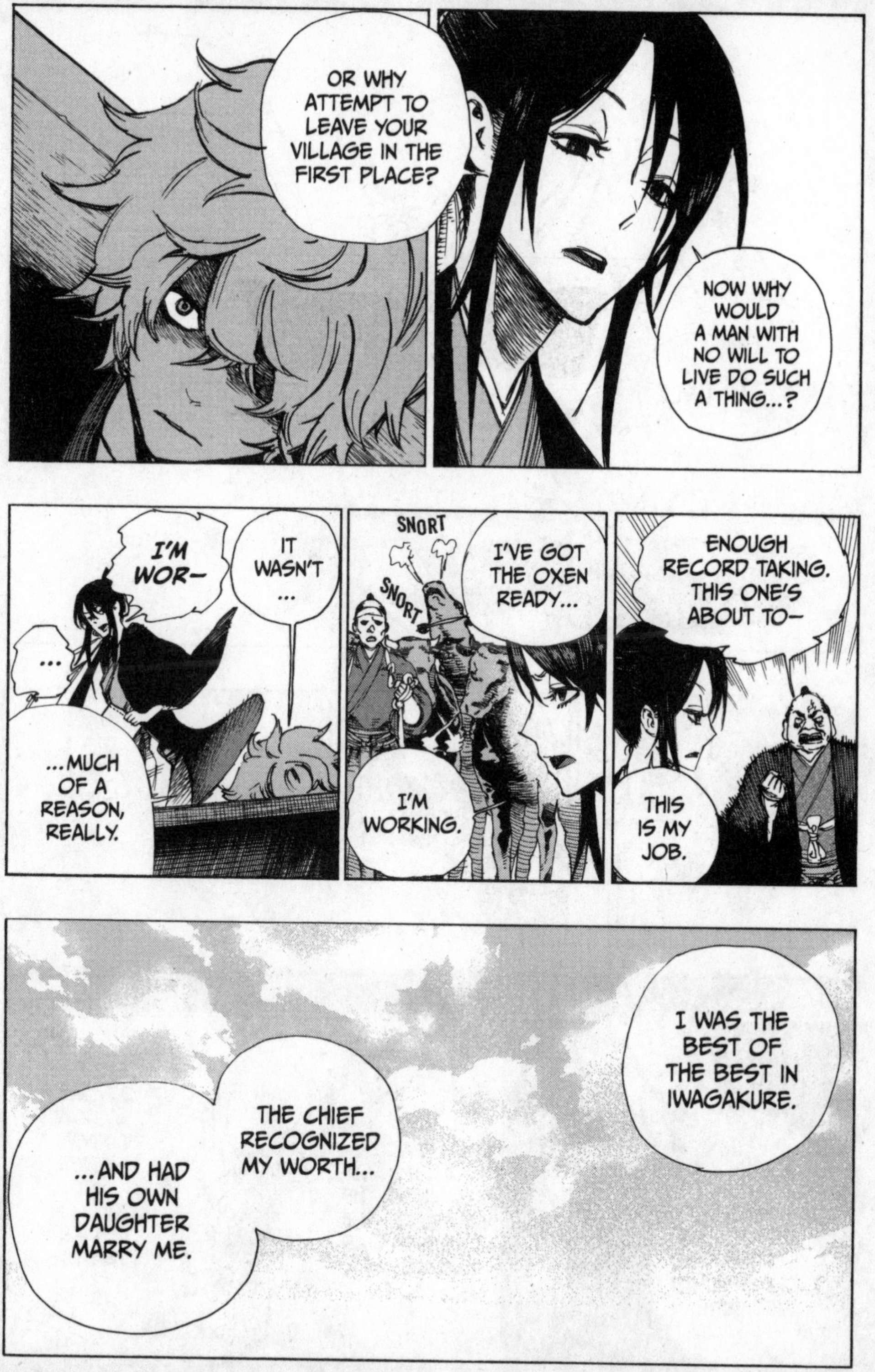
NOW WHY WOULD A MAN WITH NO WILL TO LIVE DO SUCH A THING...?
OR WHY ATTEMPT TO LEAVE YOUR VILLAGE IN THE FIRST PLACE?
ENOUGH RECORD TAKING. THIS ONE'S ABOUT TO–
THIS IS MY JOB.
SNORT
SNORT
I'VE GOT THE OXEN READY...
I'M WORKING.
I'M WOR–
IT WASN'T ...
...
...MUCH OF A REASON, REALLY.
I WAS THE BEST OF THE BEST IN IWAGAKURE.
THE CHIEF RECOGNIZED MY WORTH...
...AND HAD HIS OWN DAUGHTER MARRY ME.

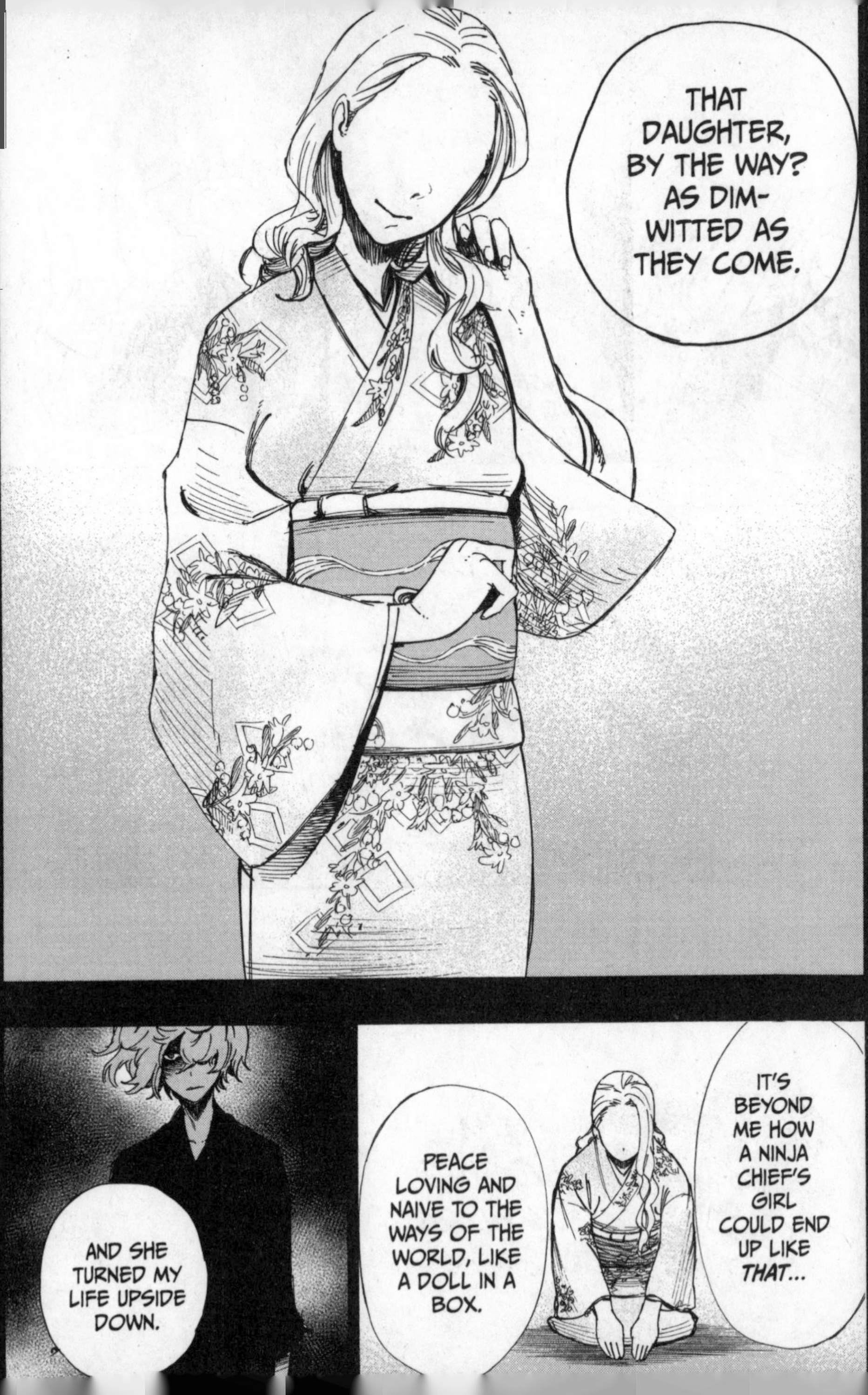
THAT DAUGHTER, BY THE WAY? AS DIM-WITTED AS THEY COME.
IT'S BEYOND ME HOW A NINJA CHIEF'S GIRL COULD END UP LIKE *THAT*...
PEACE LOVING AND NAIVE TO THE WAYS OF THE WORLD, LIKE A DOLL IN A BOX.
AND SHE TURNED MY LIFE UPSIDE DOWN.

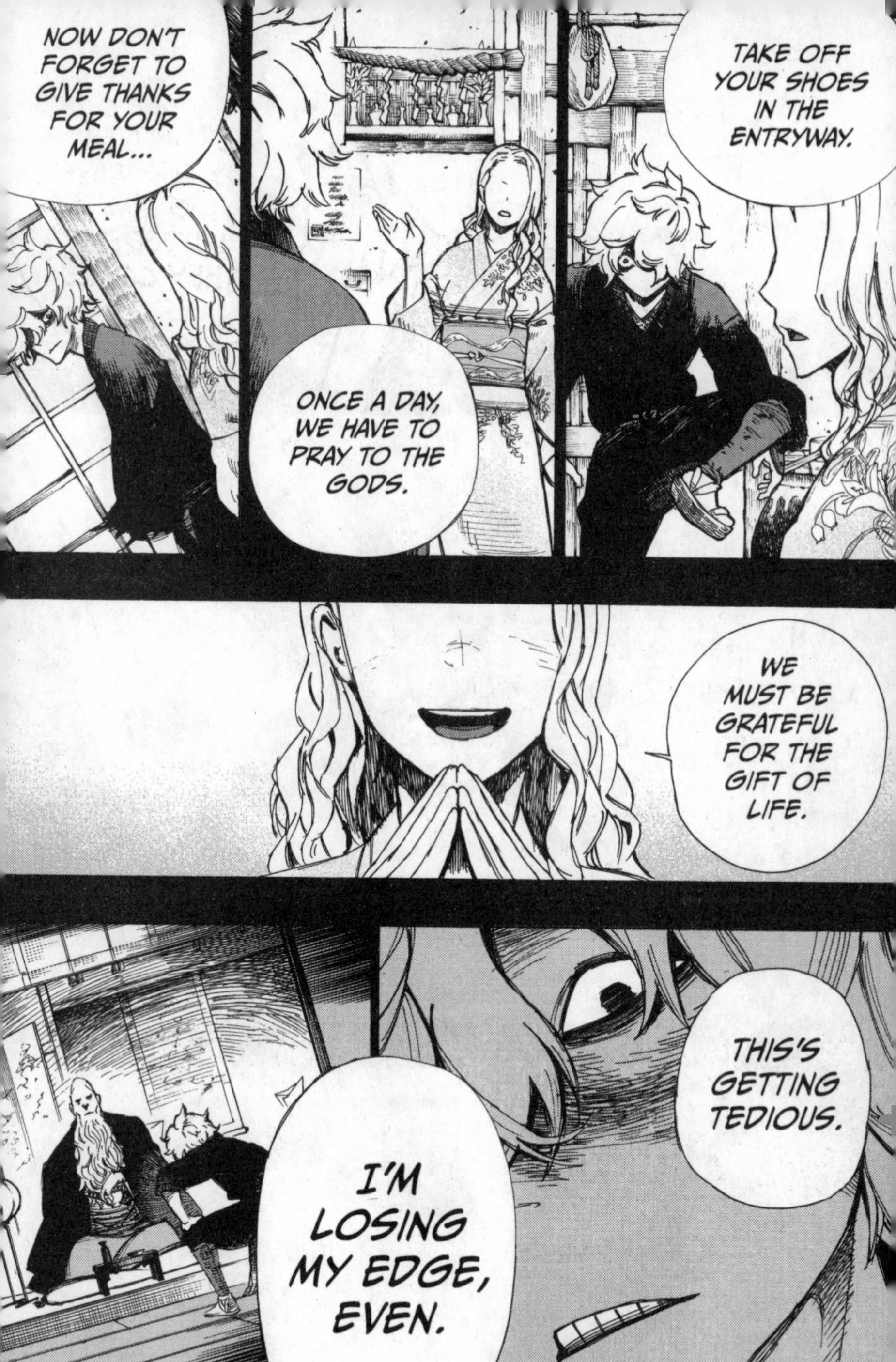
TAKE OFF YOUR SHOES IN THE ENTRYWAY.
ONCE A DAY, WE HAVE TO PRAY TO THE GODS.
NOW DON'T FORGET TO GIVE THANKS FOR YOUR MEAL...
WE MUST BE GRATEFUL FOR THE GIFT OF LIFE.
THIS'S GETTING TEDIOUS.
I'M LOSING MY EDGE, EVEN.

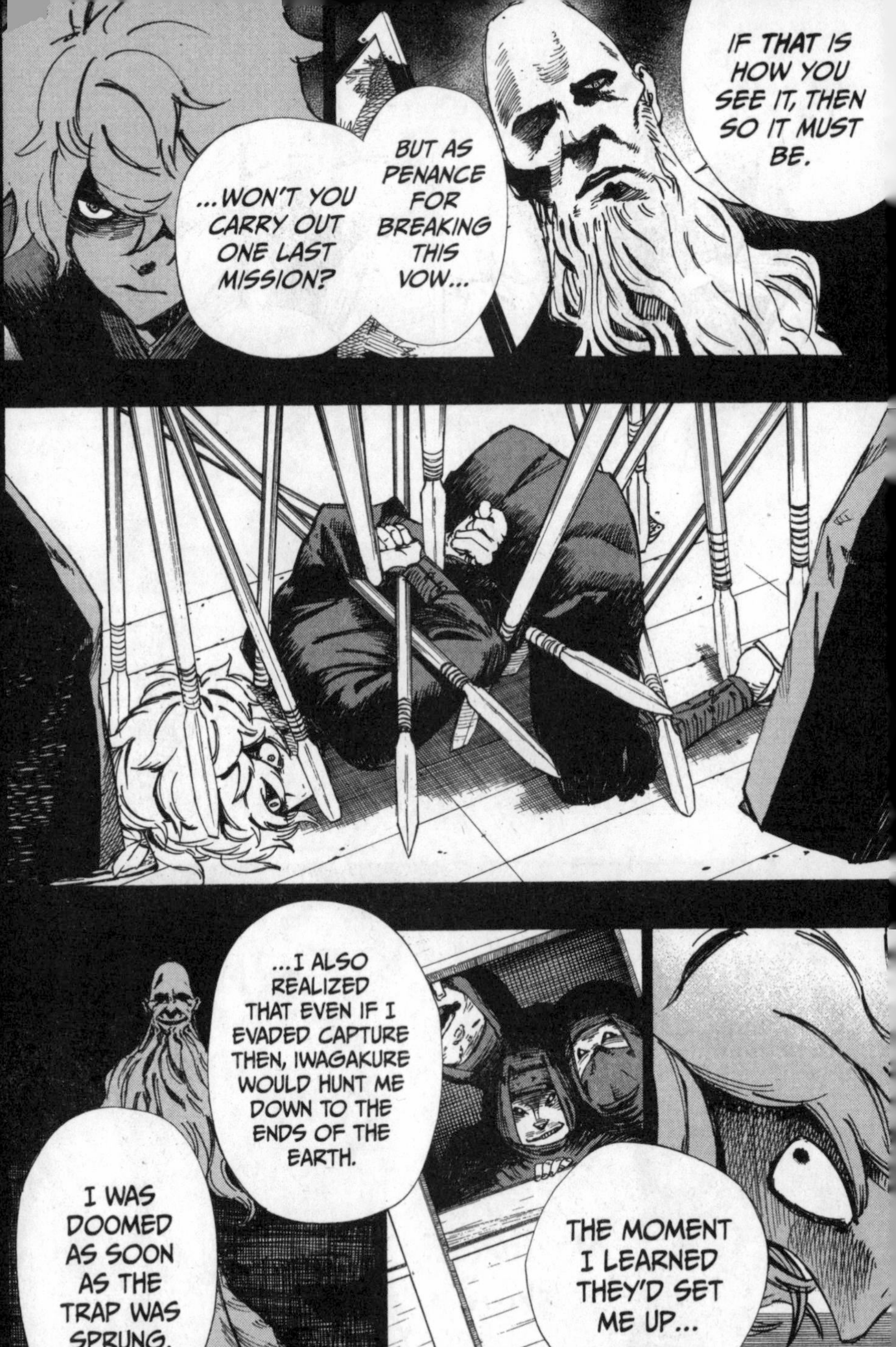
IF THAT IS HOW YOU SEE IT, THEN SO IT MUST BE.
BUT AS PENANCE FOR BREAKING THIS VOW...
...WON'T YOU CARRY OUT ONE LAST MISSION?
THE MOMENT I LEARNED THEY'D SET ME UP...
...I ALSO REALIZED THAT EVEN IF I EVADED CAPTURE THEN, IWAGAKURE WOULD HUNT ME DOWN TO THE ENDS OF THE EARTH.
I WAS DOOMED AS SOON AS THE TRAP WAS SPRUNG.

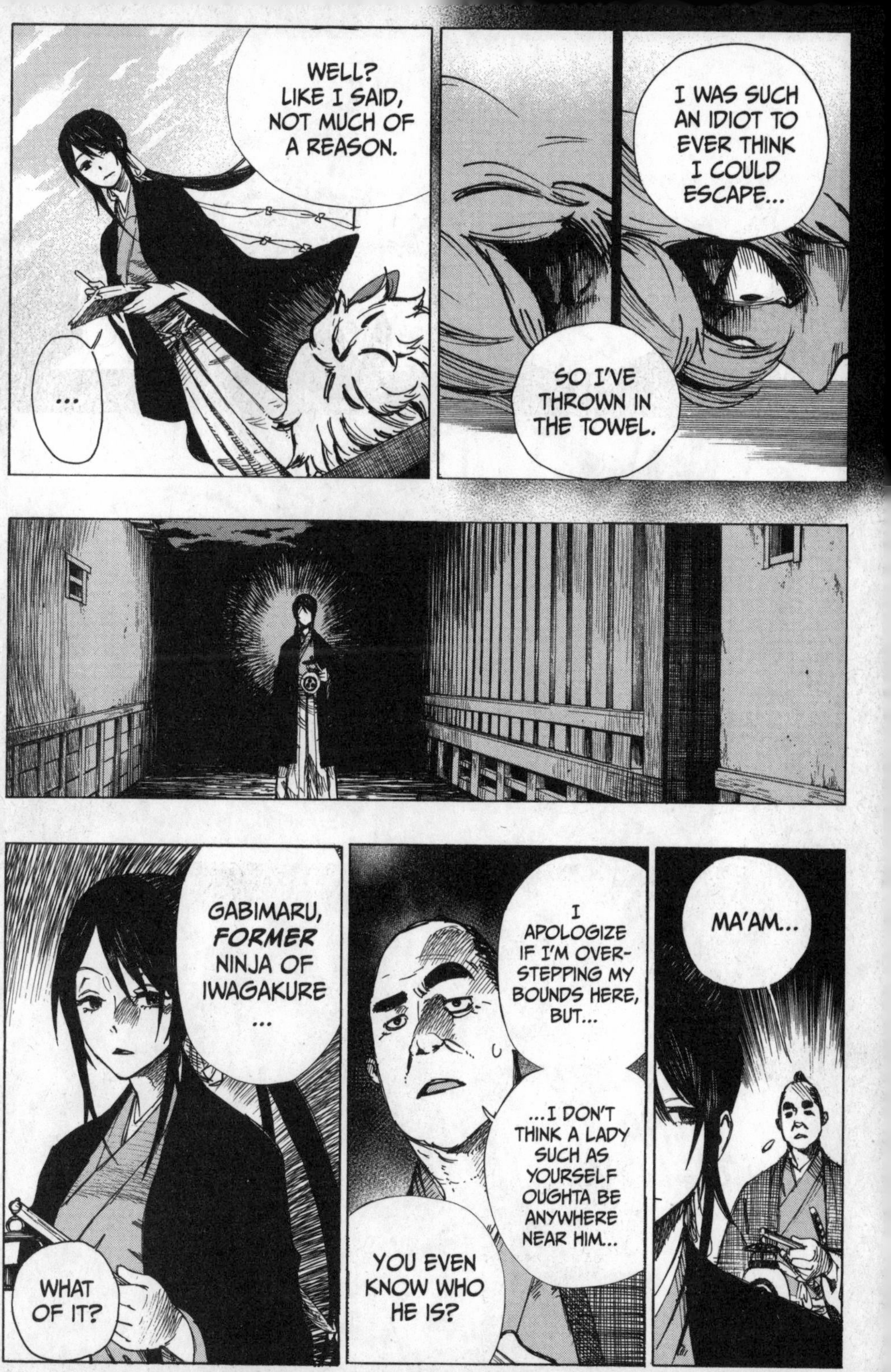
I WAS SUCH AN IDIOT TO EVER THINK I COULD ESCAPE...
SO I'VE THROWN IN THE TOWEL.
WELL? LIKE I SAID, NOT MUCH OF A REASON.
...
MA'AM...
I APOLOGIZE IF I'M OVER-STEPPING MY BOUNDS HERE, BUT...
...I DON'T THINK A LADY SUCH AS YOURSELF OUGHTA BE ANYWHERE NEAR HIM...
YOU EVEN KNOW WHO HE IS?
GABIMARU, *FORMER* NINJA OF IWAGAKURE ...
WHAT OF IT?

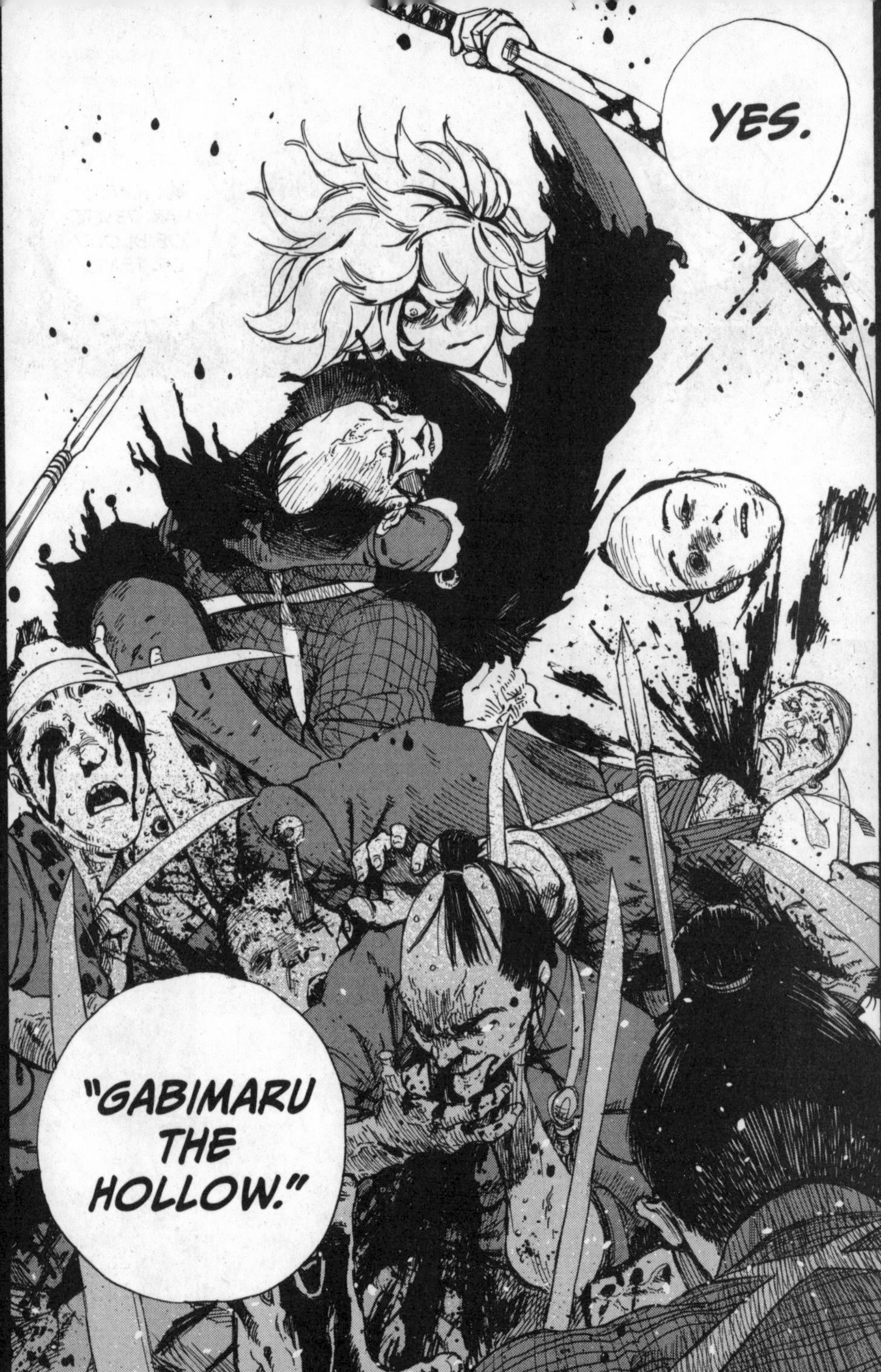
YES.
"GABIMARU THE HOLLOW."

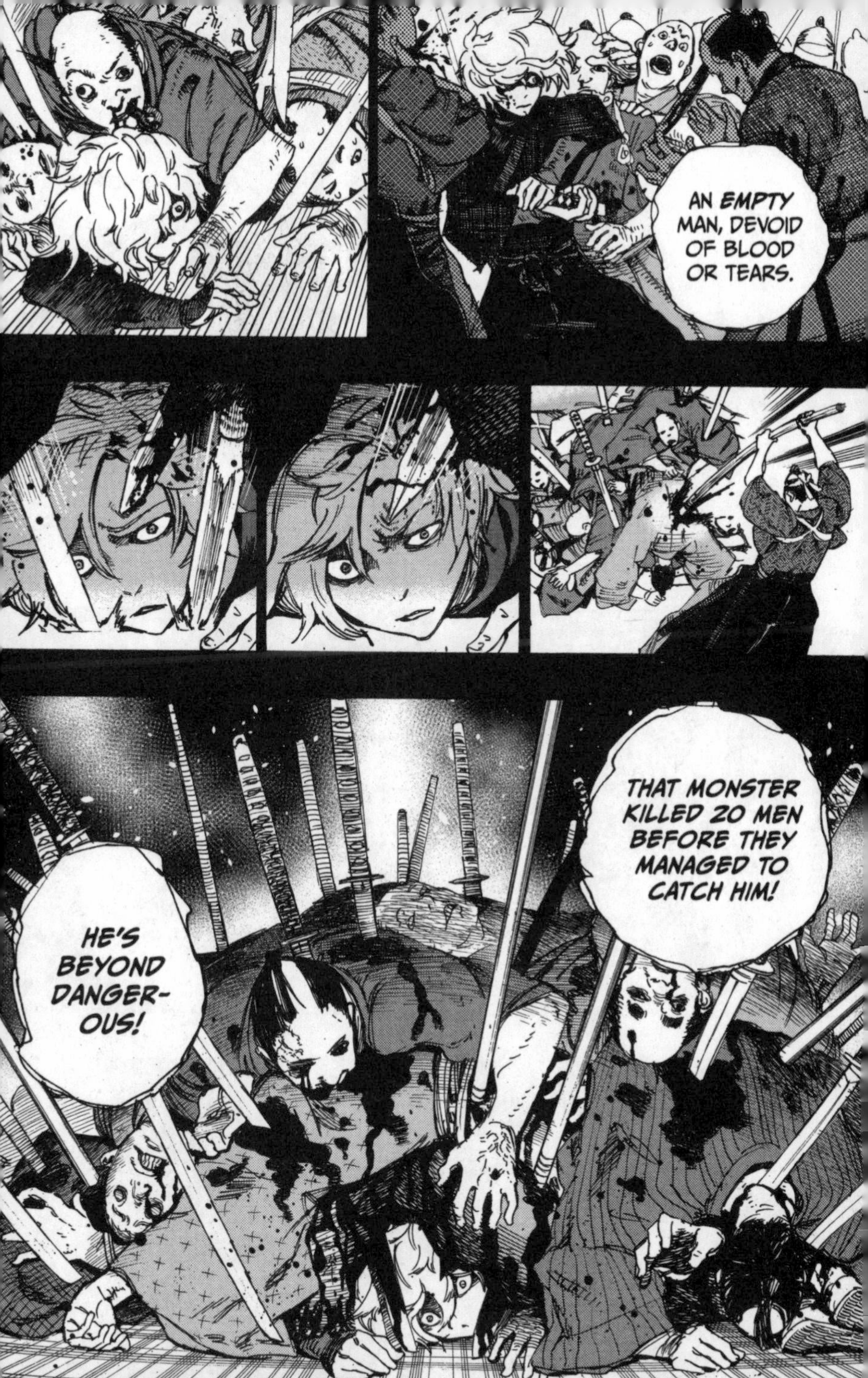
AN EMPTY MAN, DEVOID OF BLOOD OR TEARS.
THAT MONSTER KILLED 20 MEN BEFORE THEY MANAGED TO CATCH HIM!
HE'S BEYOND DANGER-OUS!

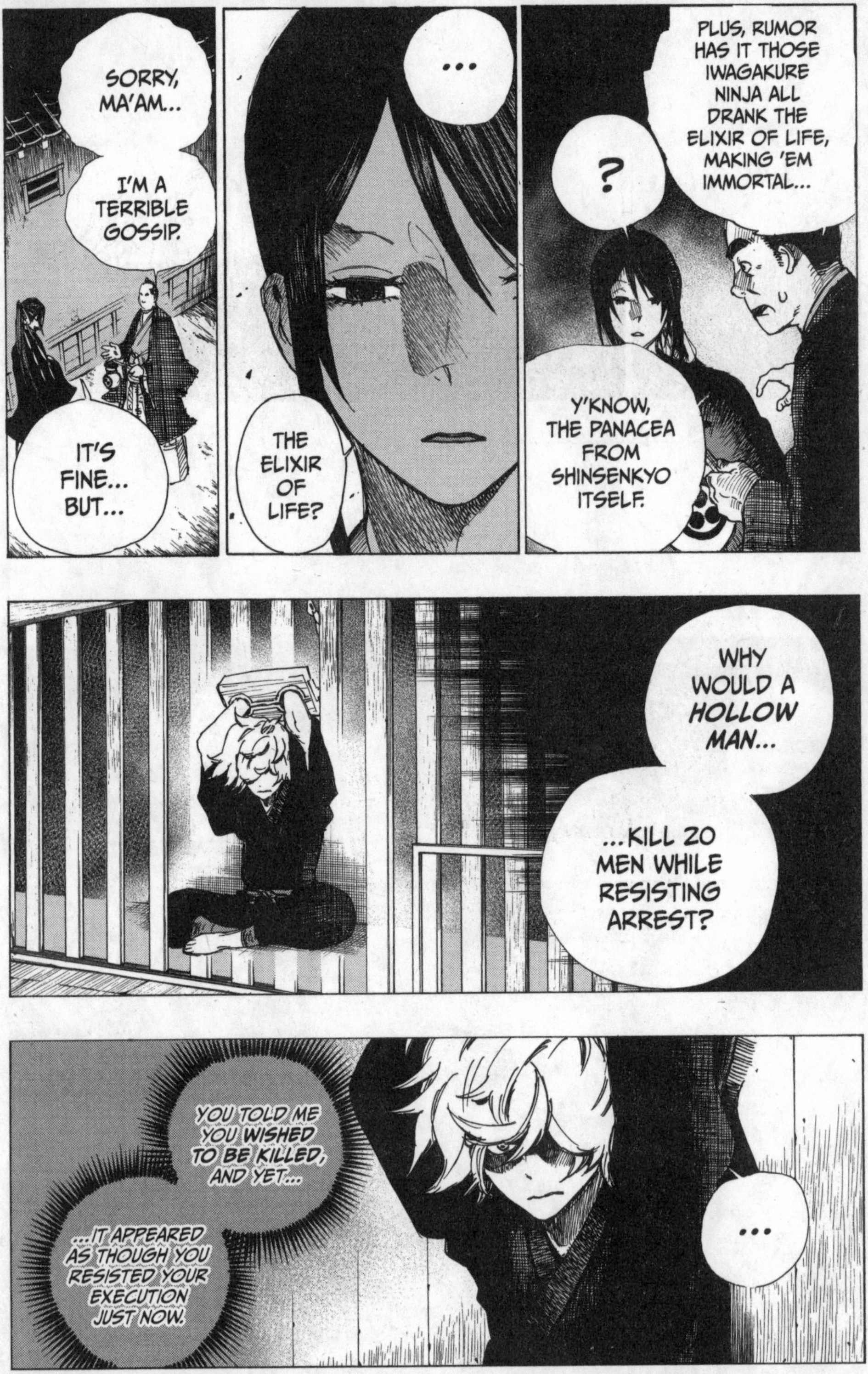
PLUS, RUMOR HAS IT THOSE IWAGAKURE NINJA ALL DRANK THE ELIXIR OF LIFE, MAKING 'EM IMMORTAL...
?
Y'KNOW, THE PANACEA FROM SHINSENKYO ITSELF.
...
THE ELIXIR OF LIFE?
SORRY, MA'AM...
I'M A TERRIBLE GOSSIP.
IT'S FINE... BUT...
WHY WOULD A *HOLLOW MAN*...
...KILL 20 MEN WHILE RESISTING ARREST?
...
YOU TOLD ME YOU **WISHED** TO BE KILLED, AND YET...
...IT APPEARED AS THOUGH YOU RESISTED YOUR EXECUTION JUST NOW.

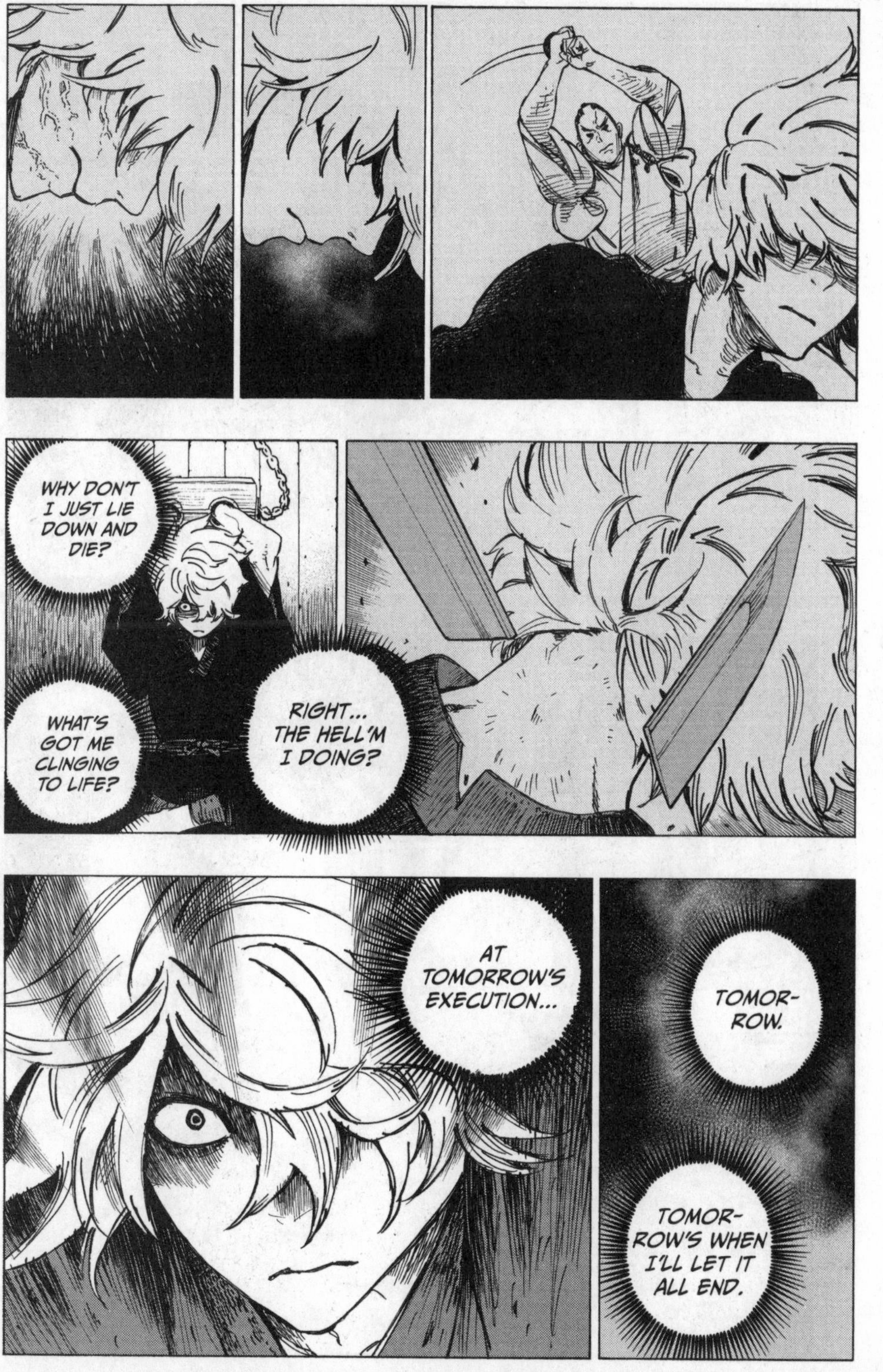
WHY DON'T I JUST LIE DOWN AND DIE?
RIGHT... THE HELL'M I DOING?
WHAT'S GOT ME CLINGING TO LIFE?
TOMOR-ROW.
TOMOR-ROW'S WHEN I'LL LET IT ALL END.
AT TOMORROW'S EXECUTION...

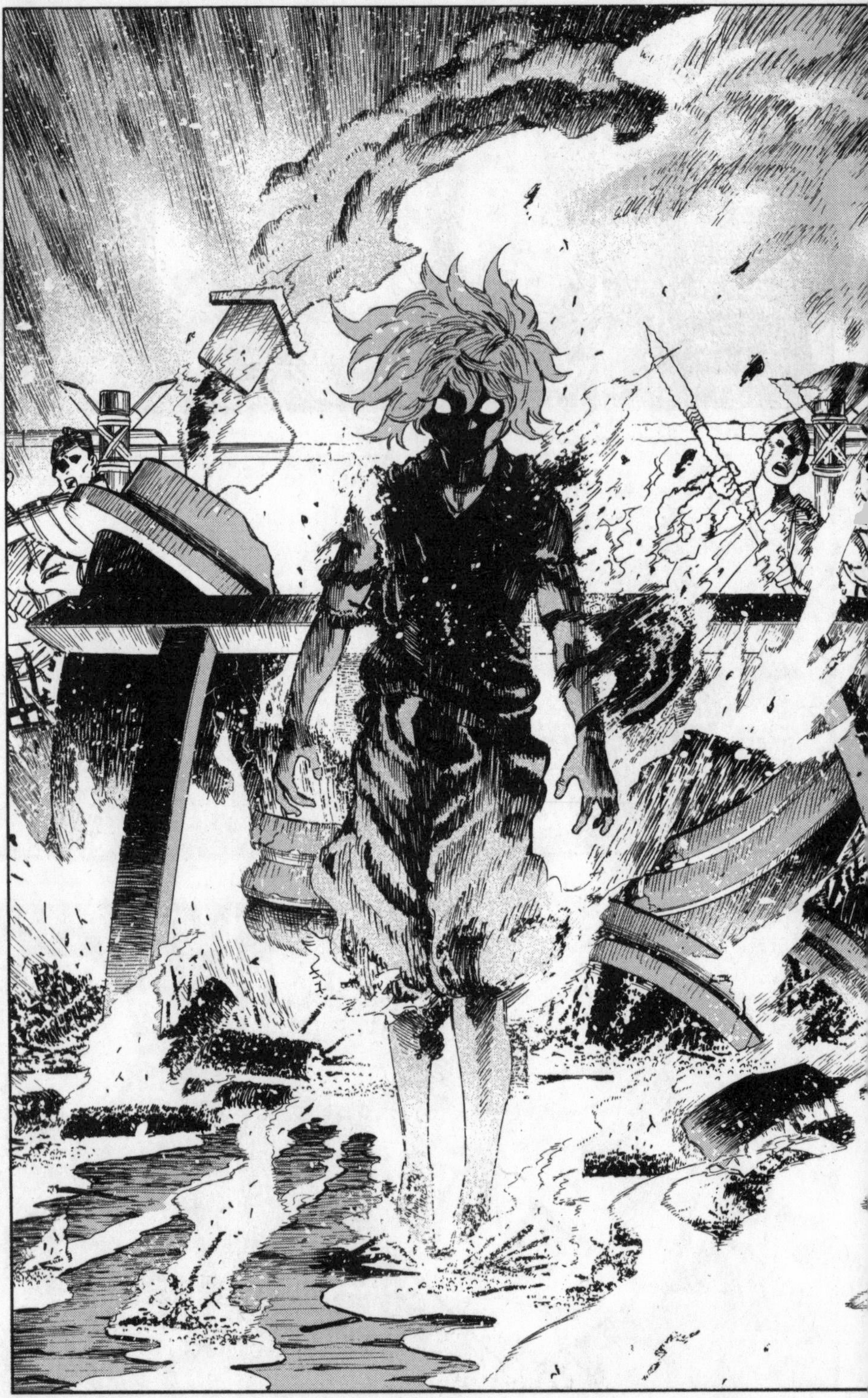

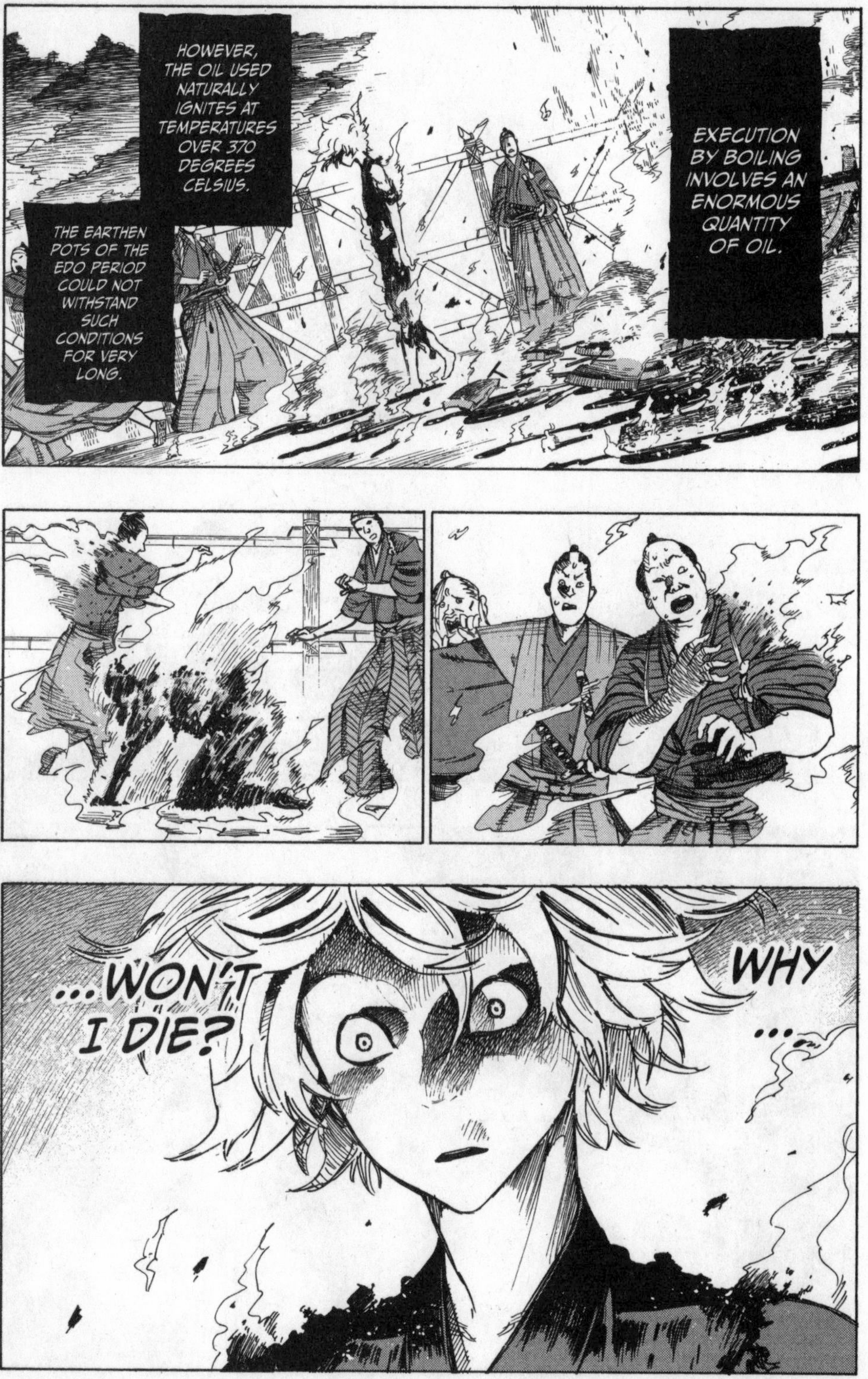
EXECUTION BY BOILING INVOLVES AN ENORMOUS QUANTITY OF OIL.
HOWEVER, THE OIL USED NATURALLY IGNITES AT TEMPERATURES OVER 370 DEGREES CELSIUS.
THE EARTHEN POTS OF THE EDO PERIOD COULD NOT WITHSTAND SUCH CONDITIONS FOR VERY LONG.
WHY
...
...WON'T I DIE?

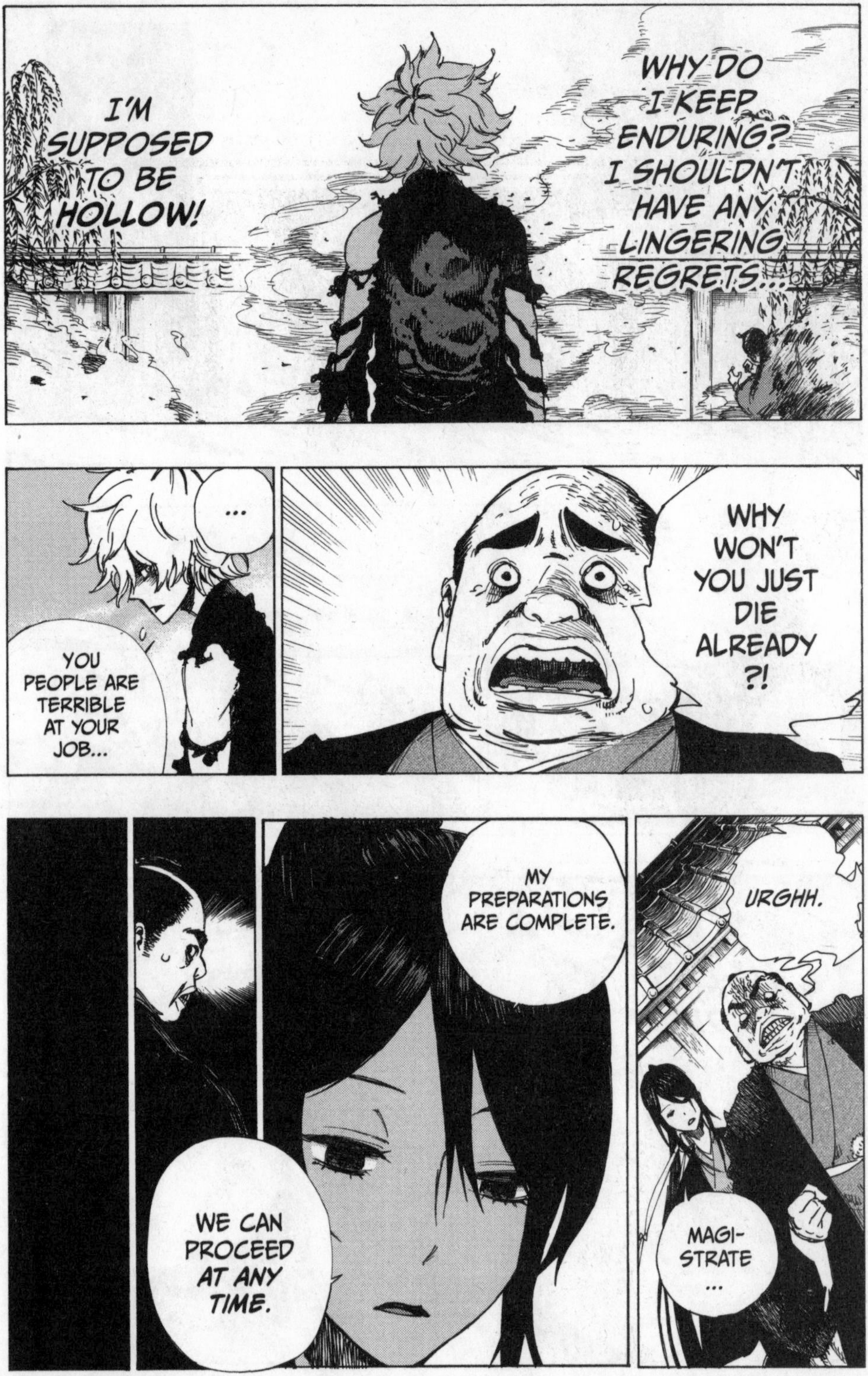
WHY DO I KEEP ENDURING? I SHOULDN'T HAVE ANY LINGERING REGRETS...
I'M SUPPOSED TO BE HOLLOW!
WHY WON'T YOU JUST DIE ALREADY?!
...
YOU PEOPLE ARE TERRIBLE AT YOUR JOB...
URGHH.
MAGISTRATE...
MY PREPARATIONS ARE COMPLETE.
WE CAN PROCEED AT ANY TIME.

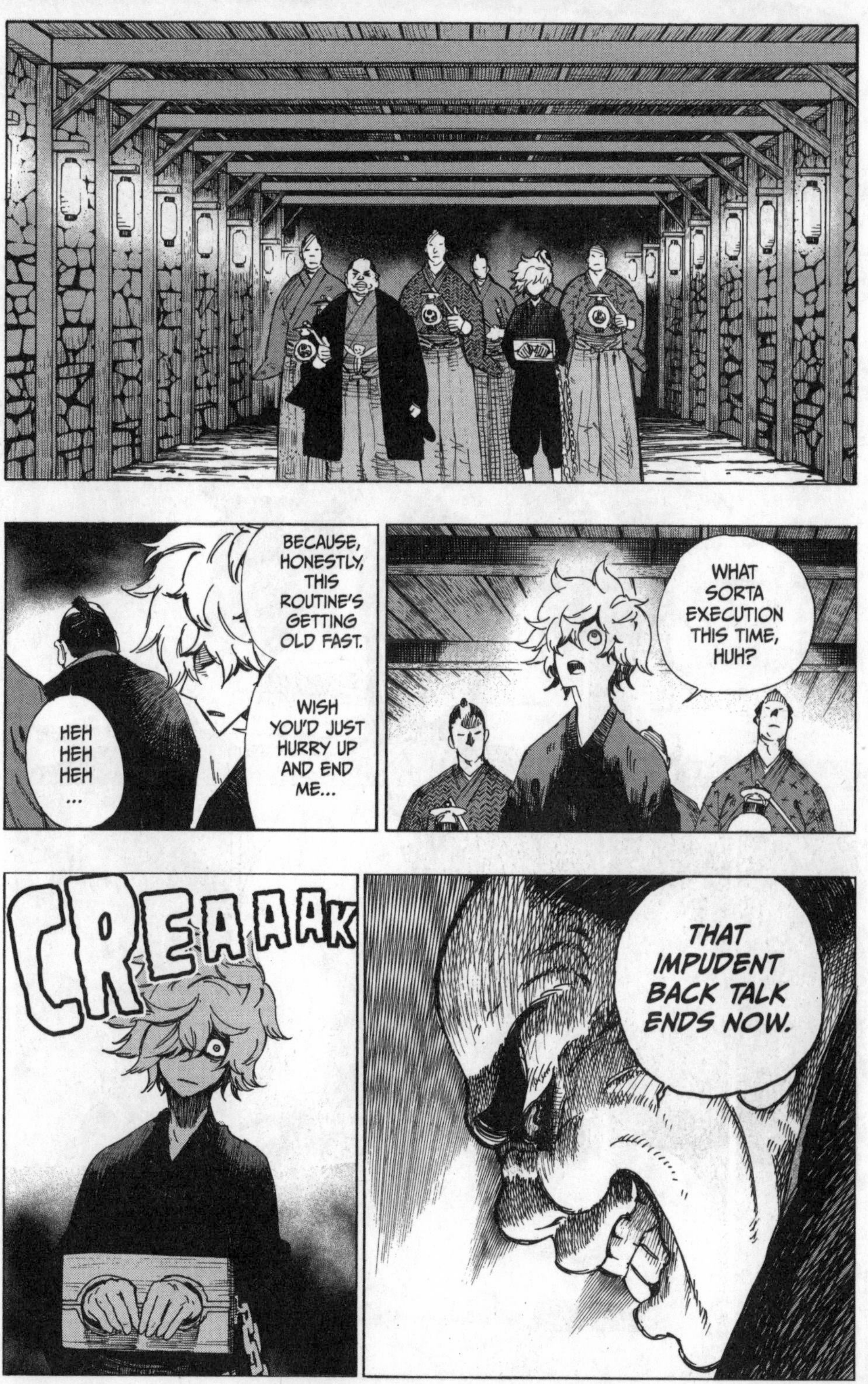
WHAT SORTA EXECUTION THIS TIME, HUH?
BECAUSE, HONESTLY, THIS ROUTINE'S GETTING OLD FAST.
WISH YOU'D JUST HURRY UP AND END ME...
HEH HEH HEH ...
THAT IMPUDENT BACK TALK ENDS NOW.
CREAAAK

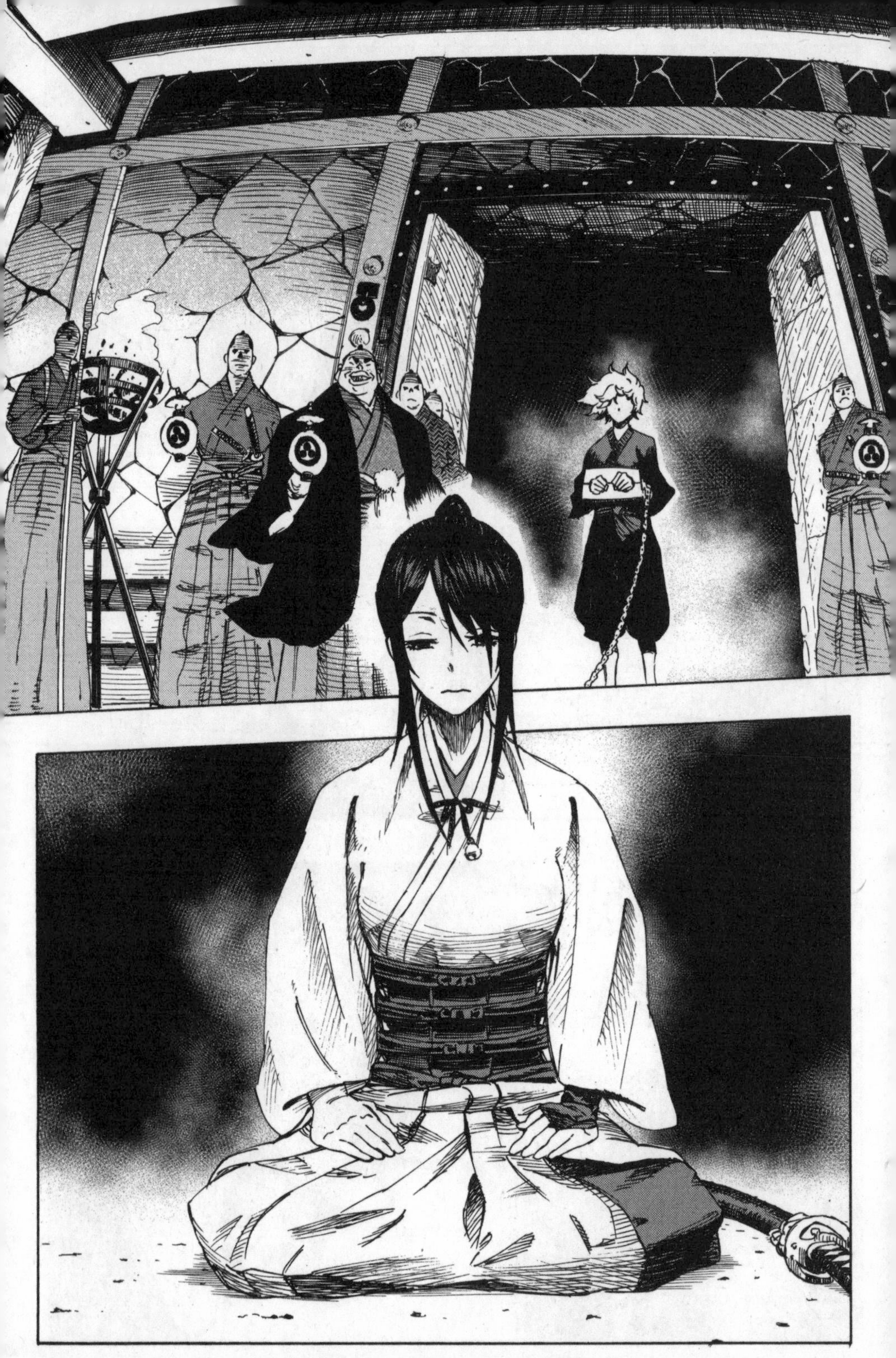

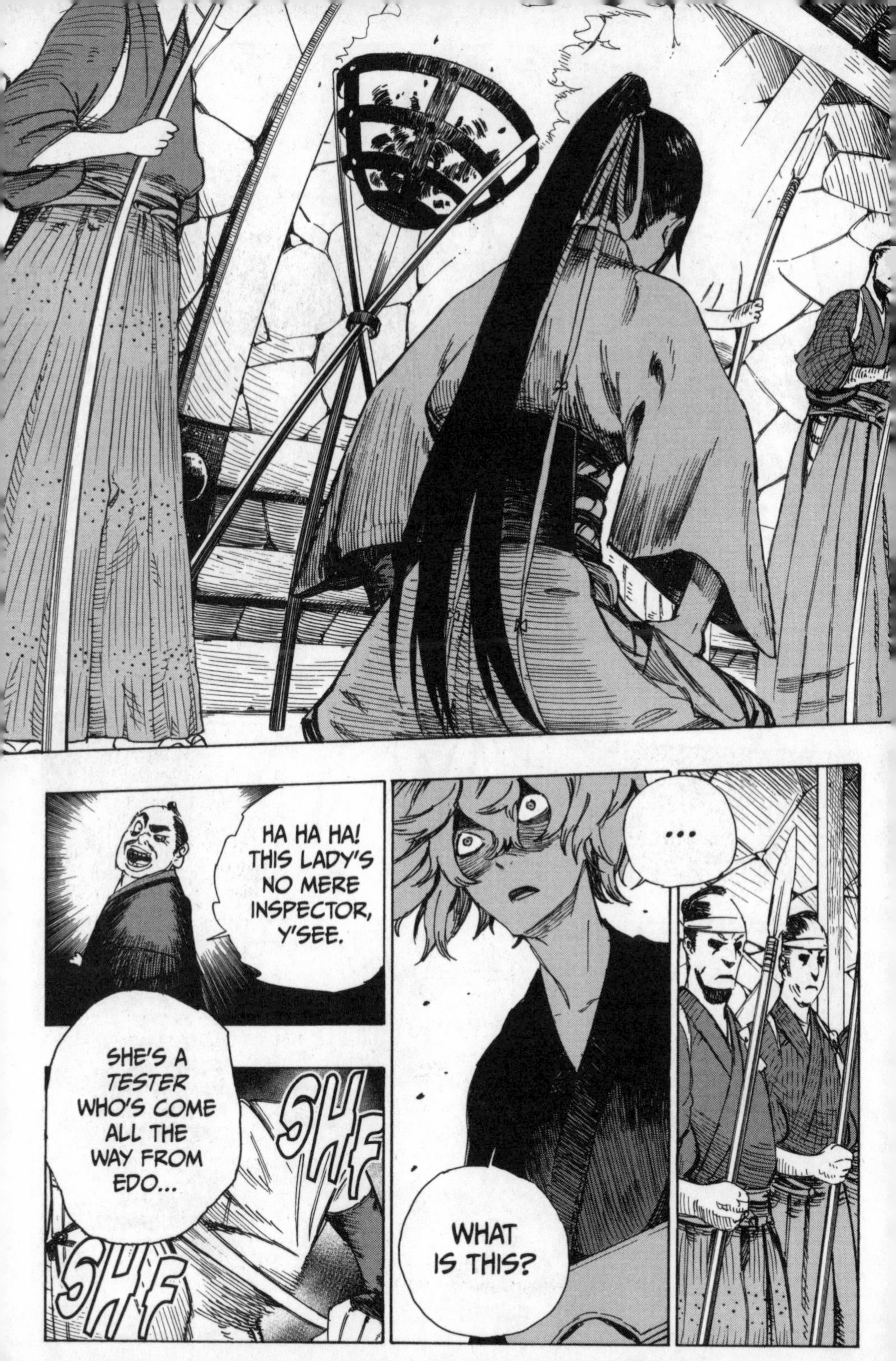
...
WHAT IS THIS?
HA HA HA! THIS LADY'S NO MERE INSPECTOR, Y'SEE.
SHE'S A TESTER WHO'S COME ALL THE WAY FROM EDO...
SHF
SHF

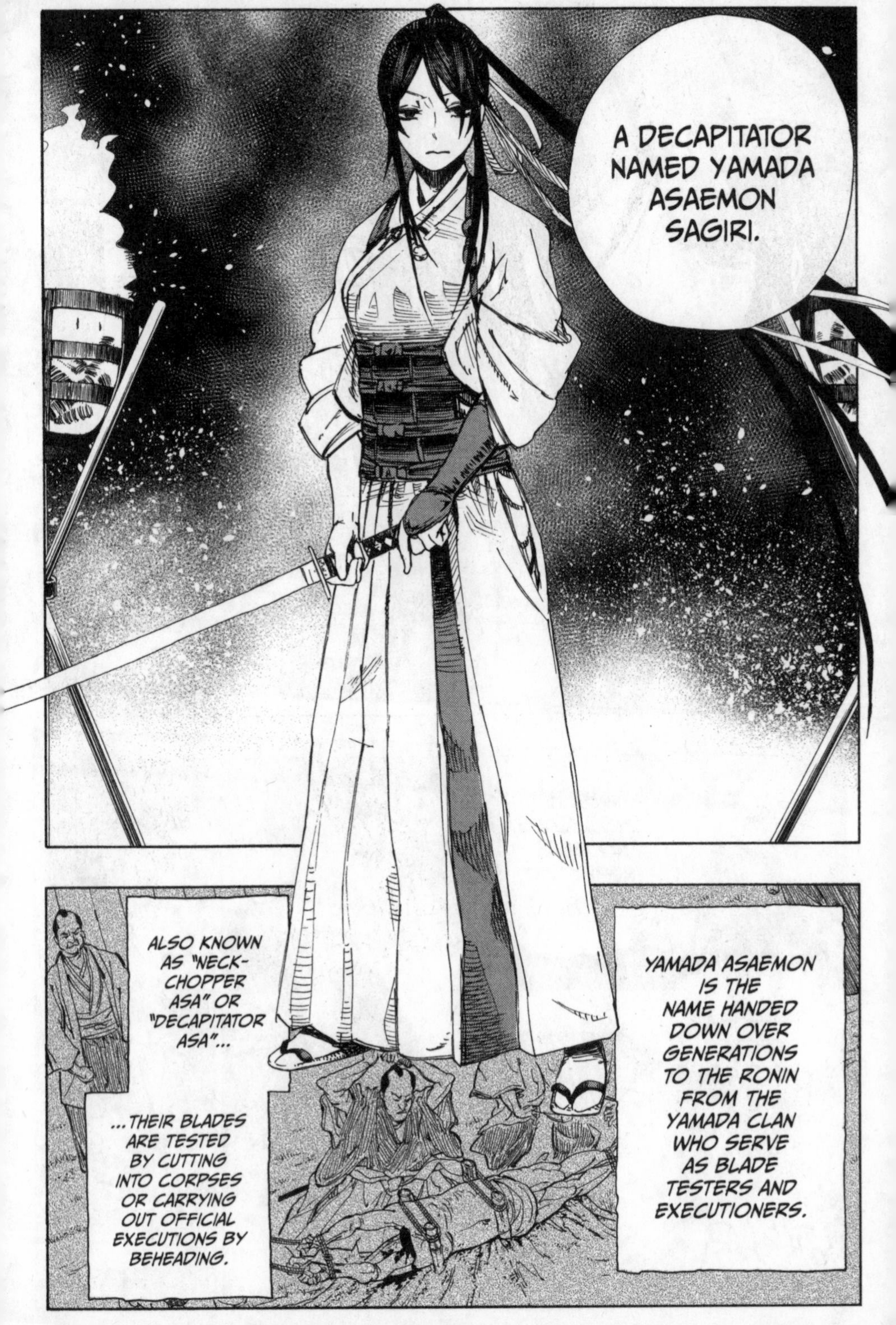
A DECAPITATOR NAMED YAMADA ASAEMON SAGIRI.
YAMADA ASAEMON IS THE NAME HANDED DOWN OVER GENERATIONS TO THE RONIN FROM THE YAMADA CLAN WHO SERVE AS BLADE TESTERS AND EXECUTIONERS.
ALSO KNOWN AS "NECK-CHOPPER ASA" OR "DECAPITATOR ASA"...
...THEIR BLADES ARE TESTED BY CUTTING INTO CORPSES OR CARRYING OUT OFFICIAL EXECUTIONS BY BEHEADING.

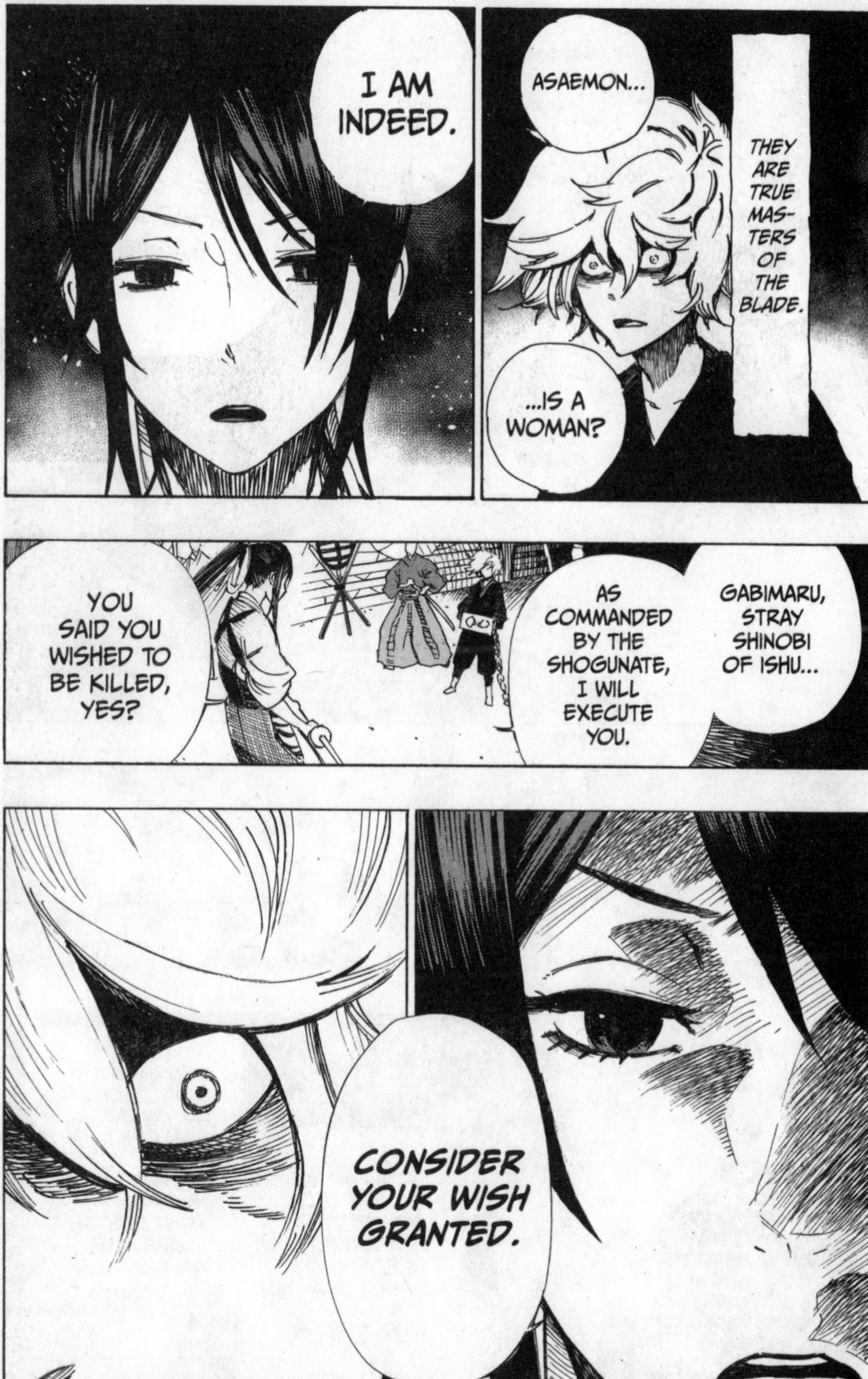
THEY ARE TRUE MASTERS OF THE BLADE.
ASAEMON...
...IS A WOMAN?
I AM INDEED.
GABIMARU, STRAY SHINOBI OF ISHU...
AS COMMANDED BY THE SHOGUNATE, I WILL EXECUTE YOU.
YOU SAID YOU WISHED TO BE KILLED, YES?
CONSIDER YOUR WISH GRANTED.

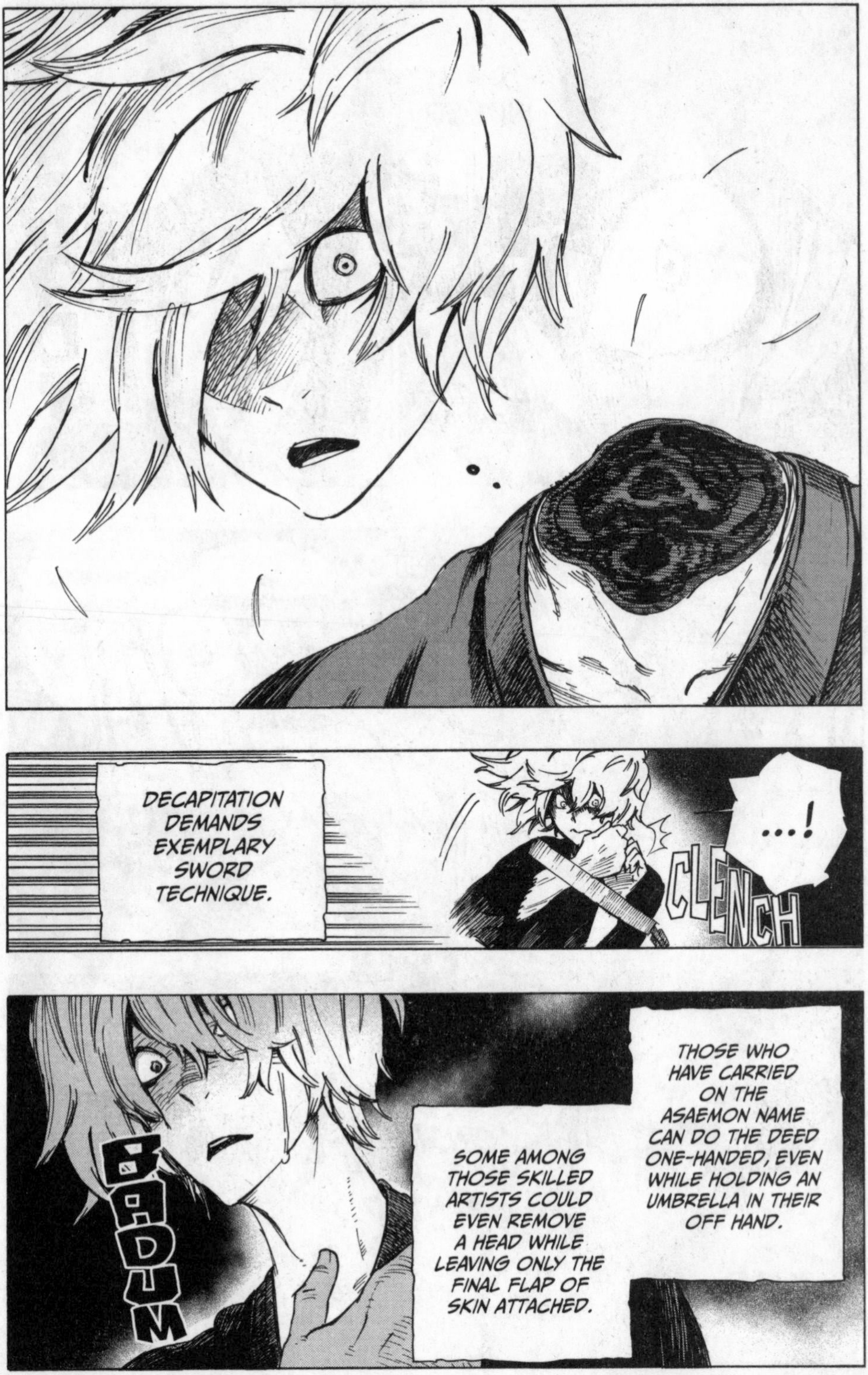
...!
CLENCH
DECAPITATION DEMANDS EXEMPLARY SWORD TECHNIQUE.
THOSE WHO HAVE CARRIED ON THE ASAEMON NAME CAN DO THE DEED ONE-HANDED, EVEN WHILE HOLDING AN UMBRELLA IN THEIR OFF HAND.
SOME AMONG THOSE SKILLED ARTISTS COULD EVEN REMOVE A HEAD WHILE LEAVING ONLY THE FINAL FLAP OF SKIN ATTACHED.
BADUM

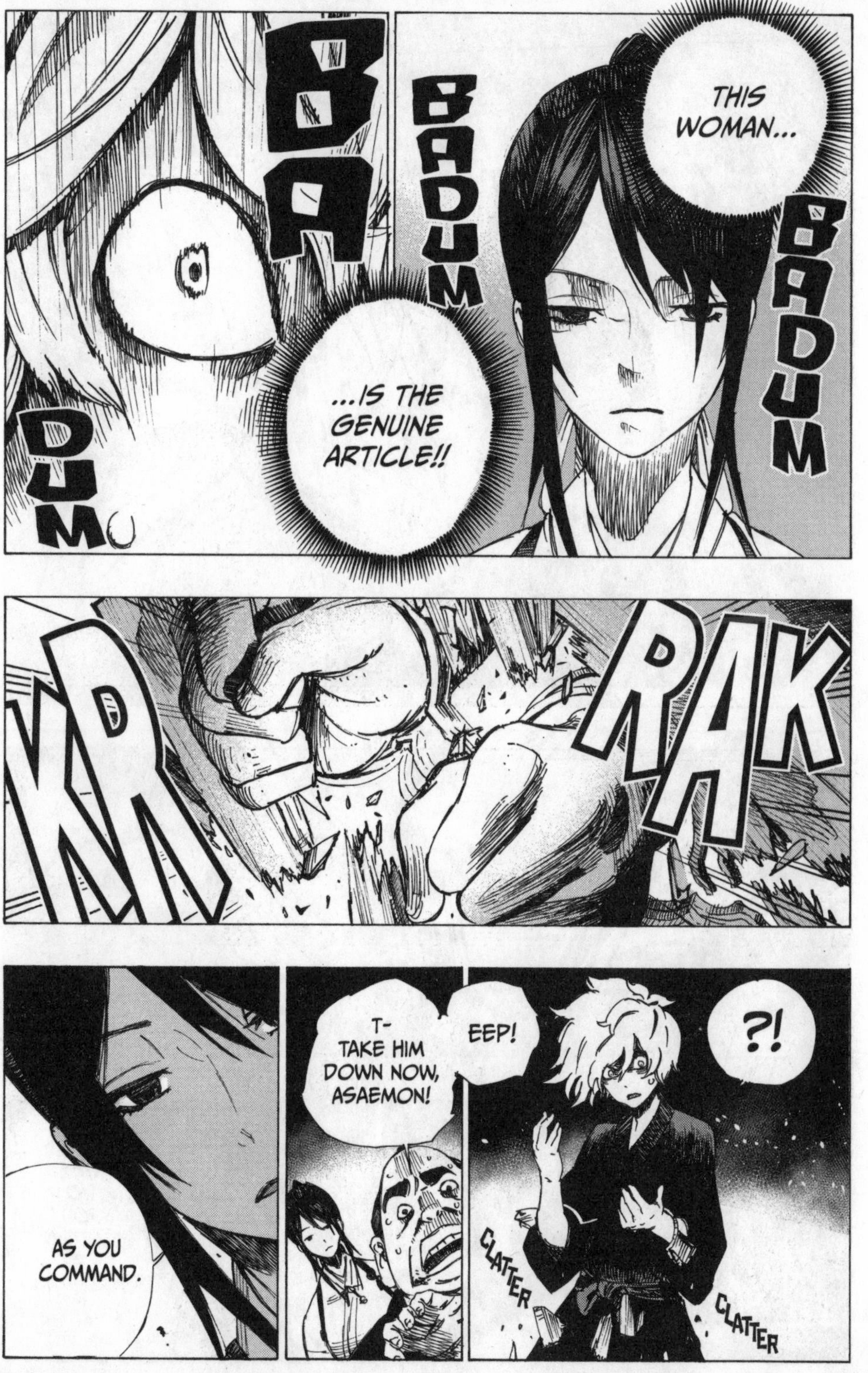
THIS WOMAN...
BADUM
BADUM
...IS THE GENUINE ARTICLE!!
BA
DUM
KRRAK
?!
CLATTER
CLATTER
EEP!
T- TAKE HIM DOWN NOW, ASAEMON!
AS YOU COMMAND.

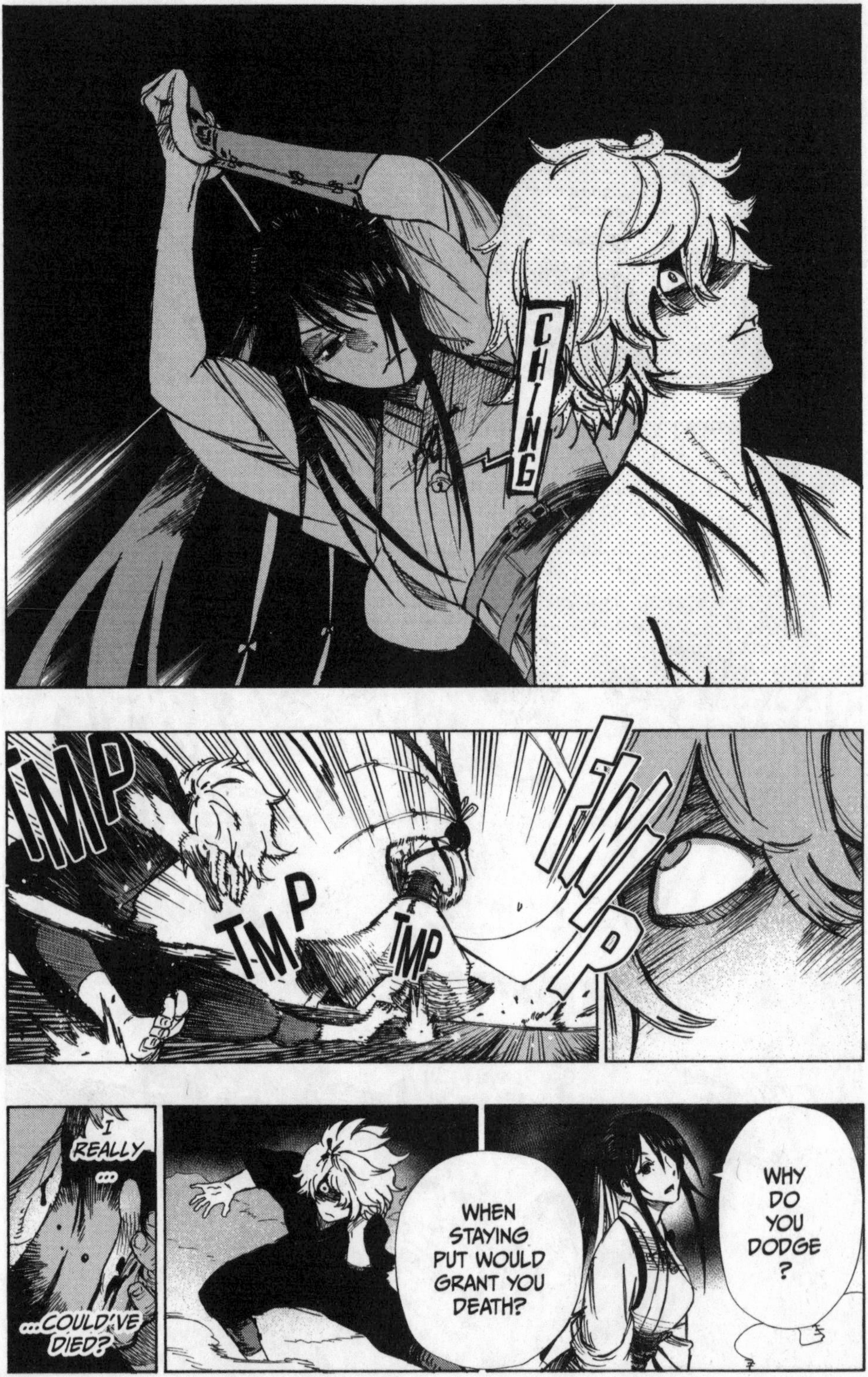
CHING
FWIP
TMP
TMP
WHY DO YOU DODGE?
WHEN STAYING PUT WOULD GRANT YOU DEATH?
I REALLY ...
...COULD'VE DIED?

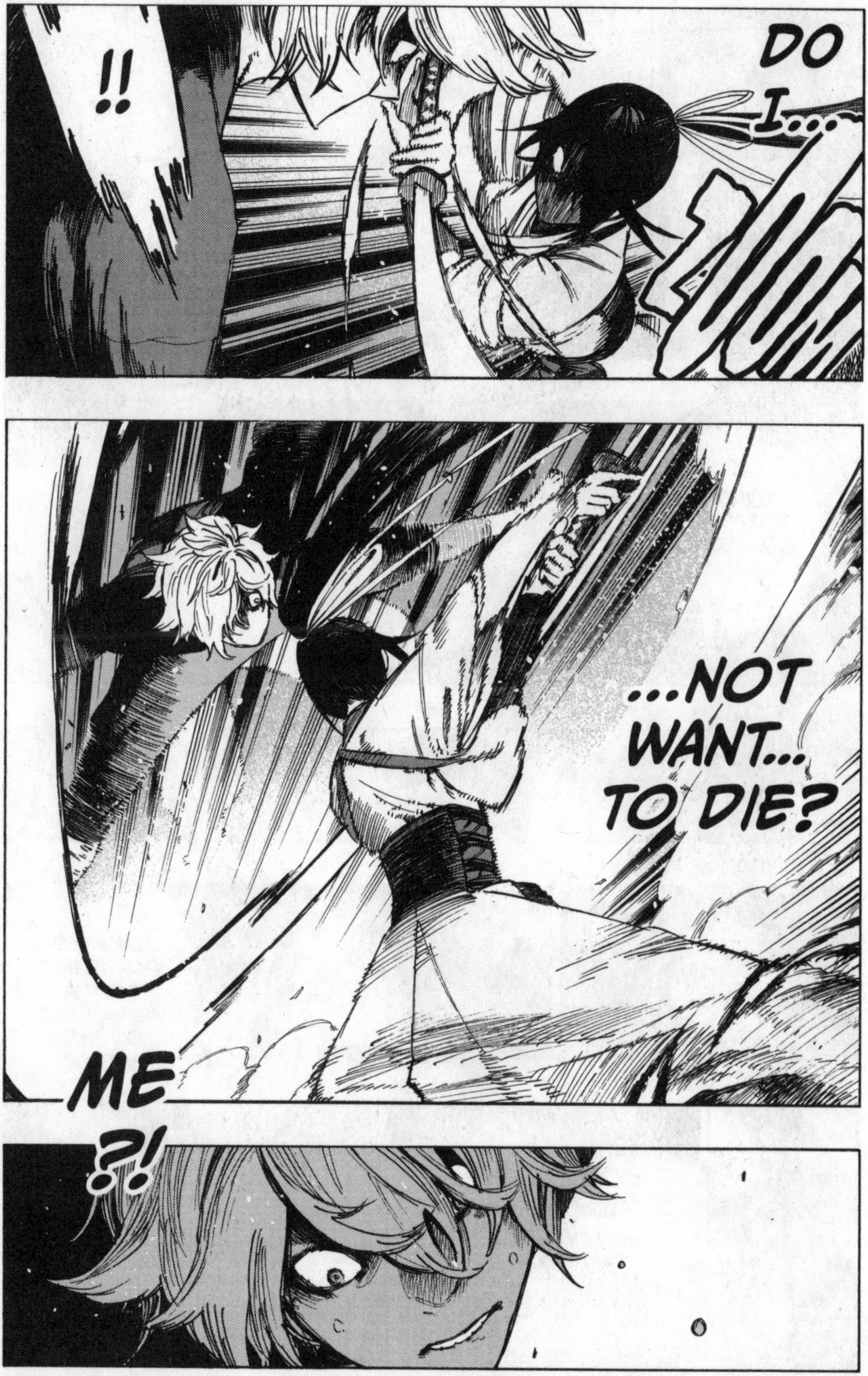
DO I...
!!
...NOT WANT... TO DIE?
ME
?!

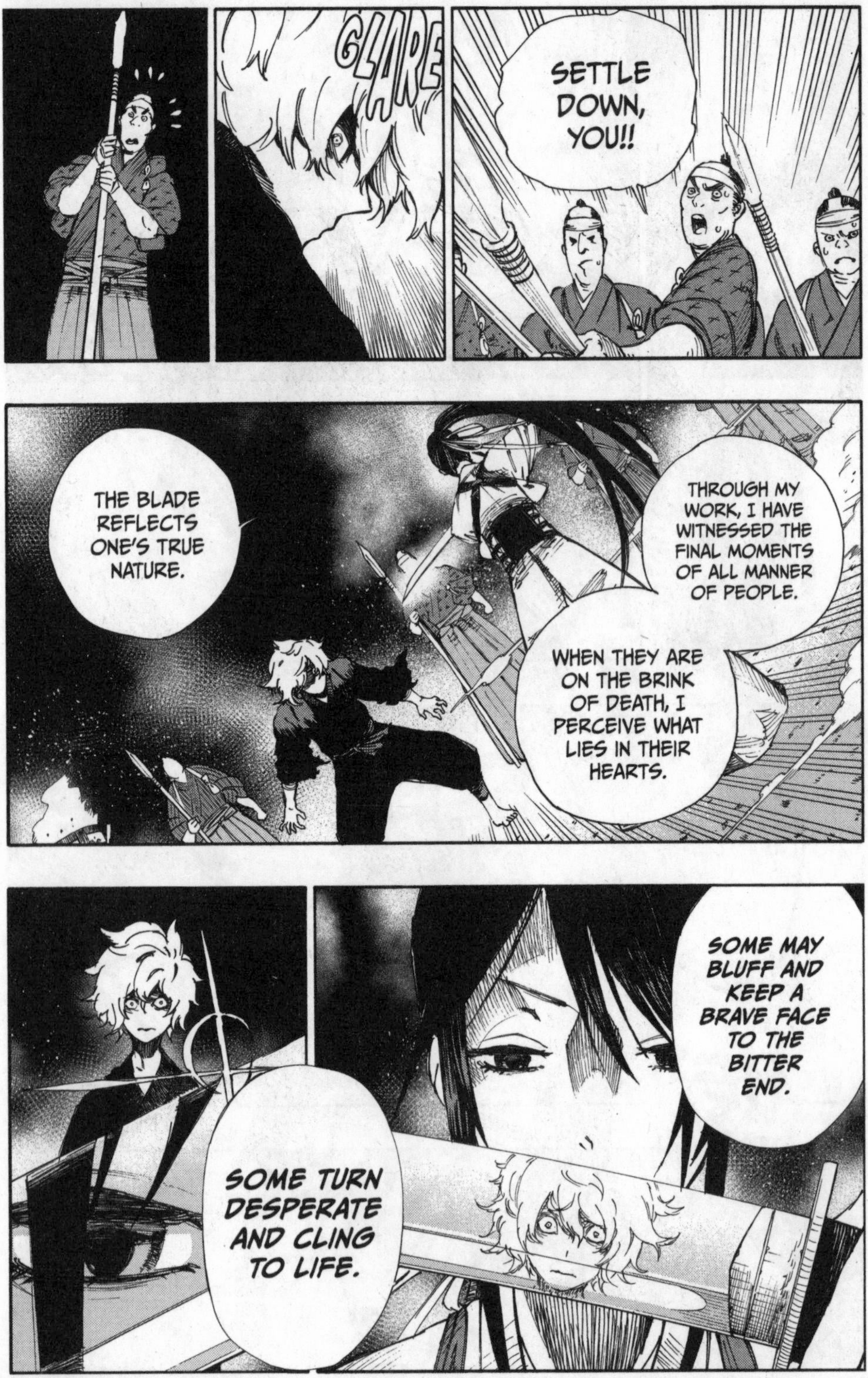
SETTLE DOWN, YOU!!
GLARE
THROUGH MY WORK, I HAVE WITNESSED THE FINAL MOMENTS OF ALL MANNER OF PEOPLE.
WHEN THEY ARE ON THE BRINK OF DEATH, I PERCEIVE WHAT LIES IN THEIR HEARTS.
THE BLADE REFLECTS ONE'S TRUE NATURE.
SOME MAY BLUFF AND KEEP A BRAVE FACE TO THE BITTER END.
SOME TURN DESPERATE AND CLING TO LIFE.

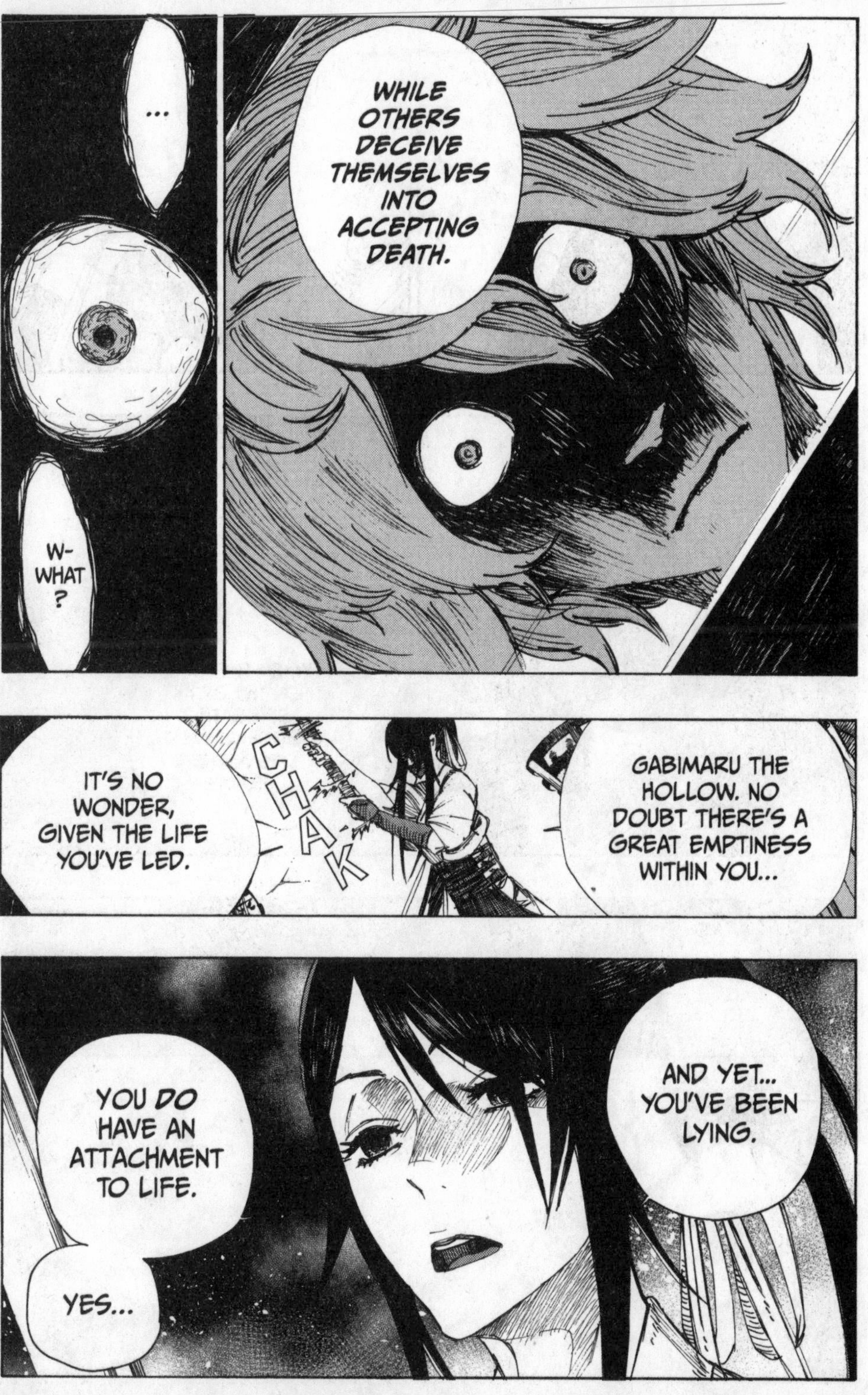
WHILE OTHERS DECEIVE THEMSELVES INTO ACCEPTING DEATH.
...
W-WHAT?
GABIMARU THE HOLLOW. NO DOUBT THERE'S A GREAT EMPTINESS WITHIN YOU...
CHAK
IT'S NO WONDER, GIVEN THE LIFE YOU'VE LED.
AND YET... YOU'VE BEEN LYING.
YOU DO HAVE AN ATTACHMENT TO LIFE.
YES...

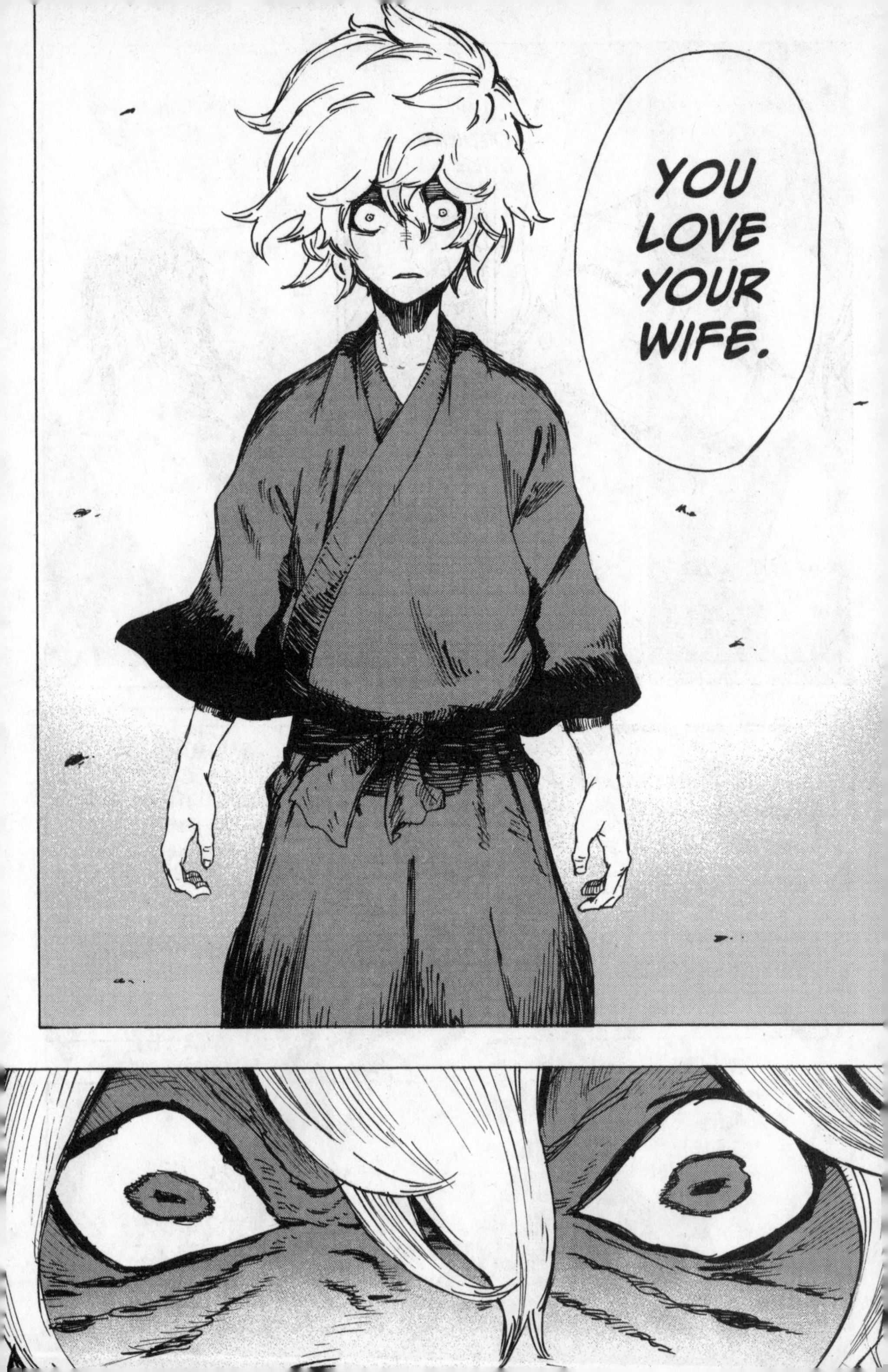
YOU LOVE YOUR WIFE.

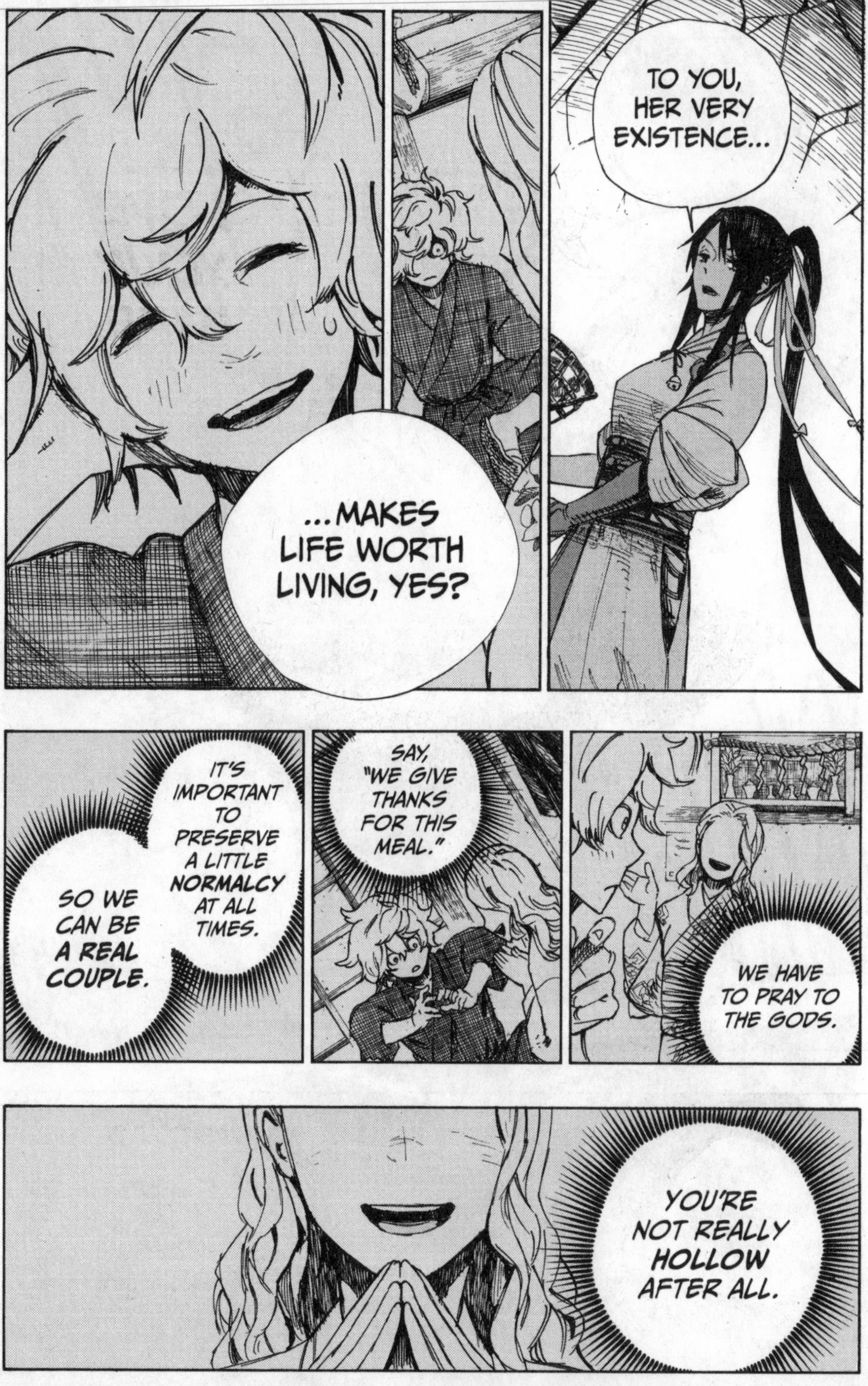
TO YOU, HER VERY EXISTENCE...
...MAKES LIFE WORTH LIVING, YES?
WE HAVE TO PRAY TO THE GODS.
SAY, "WE GIVE THANKS FOR THIS MEAL."
IT'S IMPORTANT TO PRESERVE A LITTLE NORMALCY AT ALL TIMES.
SO WE CAN BE A REAL COUPLE.
YOU'RE NOT REALLY HOLLOW AFTER ALL.

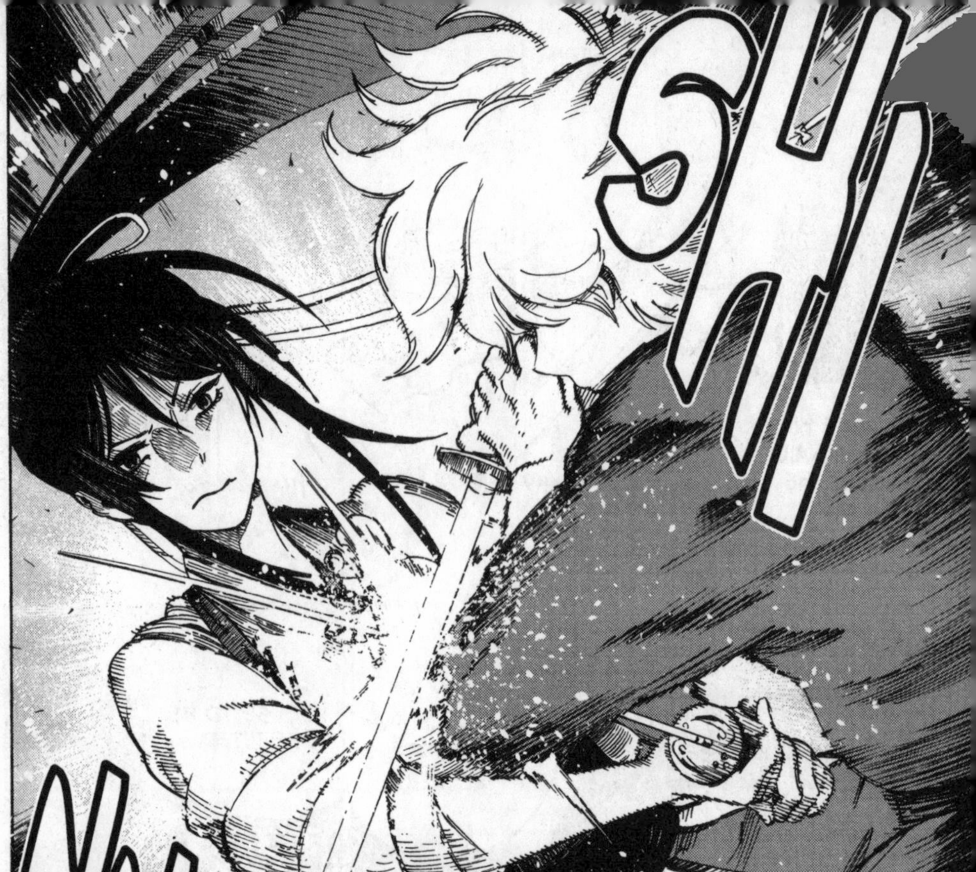
SHI
NNG
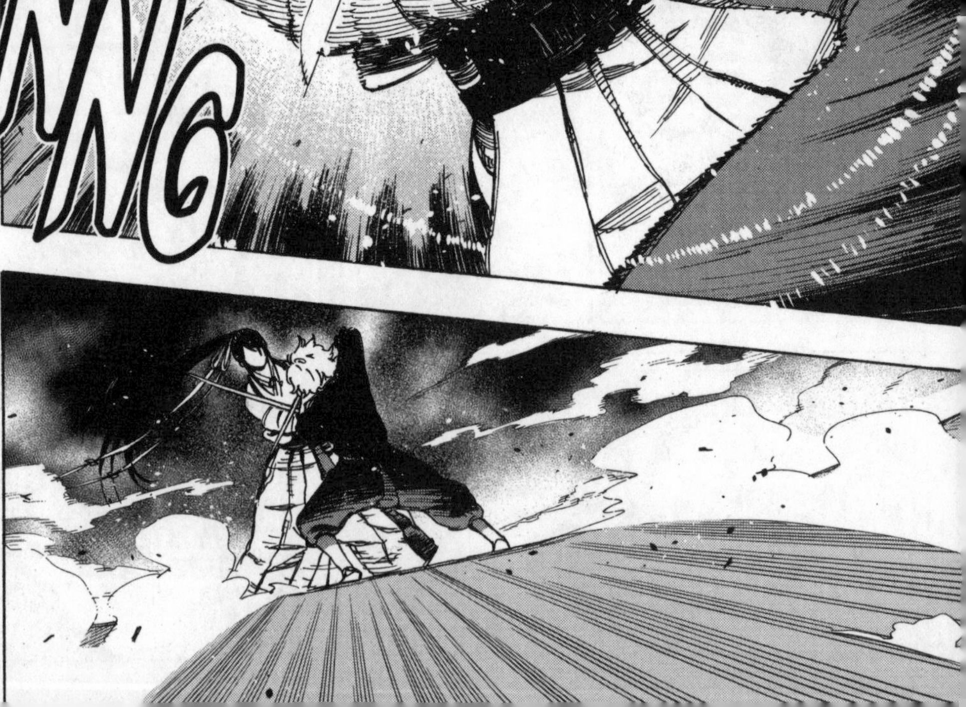

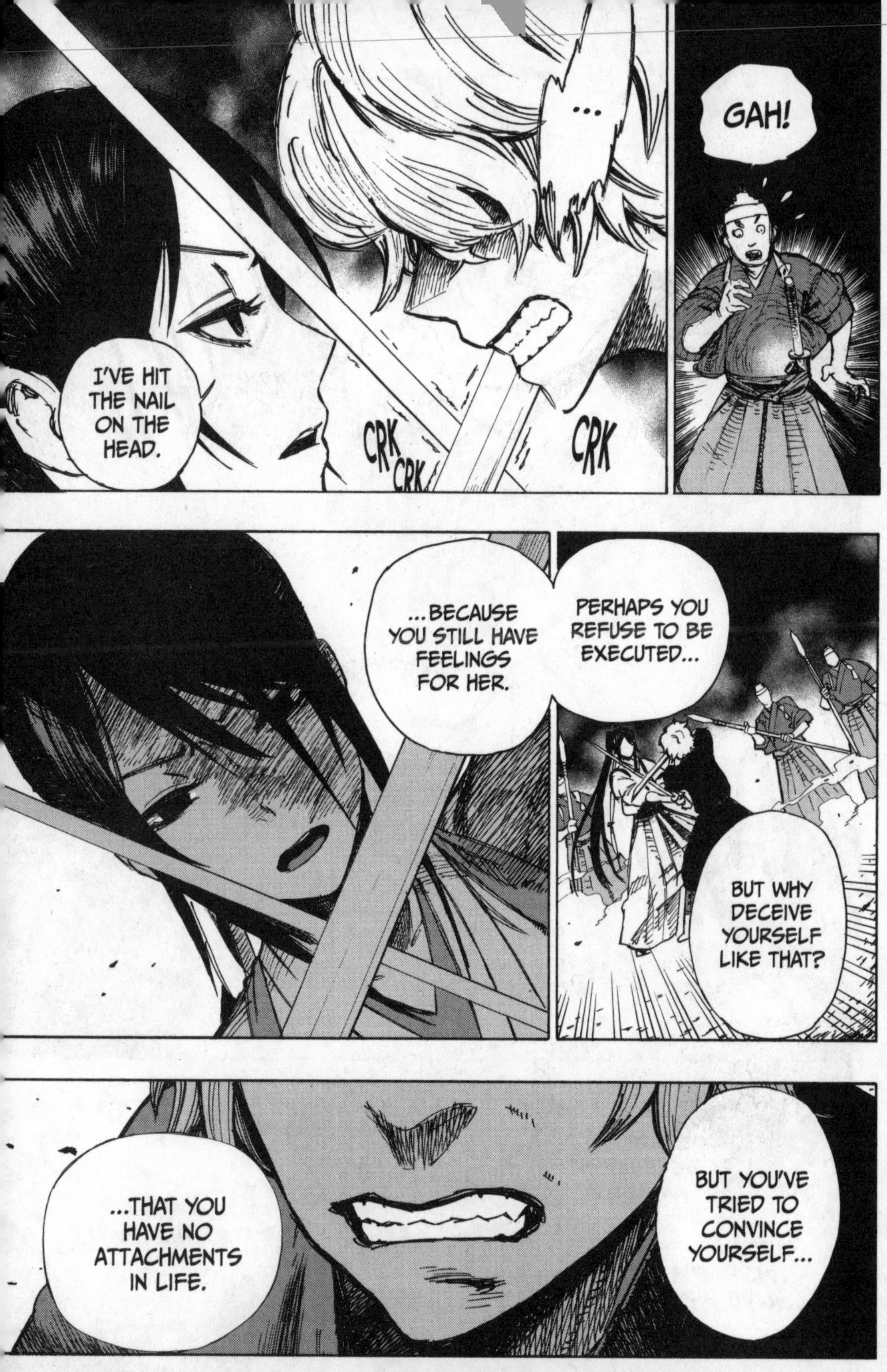
GAH!
...
CRK
CRK CRK
I'VE HIT THE NAIL ON THE HEAD.
PERHAPS YOU REFUSE TO BE EXECUTED...
...BECAUSE YOU STILL HAVE FEELINGS FOR HER.
BUT WHY DECEIVE YOURSELF LIKE THAT?
BUT YOU'VE TRIED TO CONVINCE YOURSELF...
...THAT YOU HAVE NO ATTACHMENTS IN LIFE.

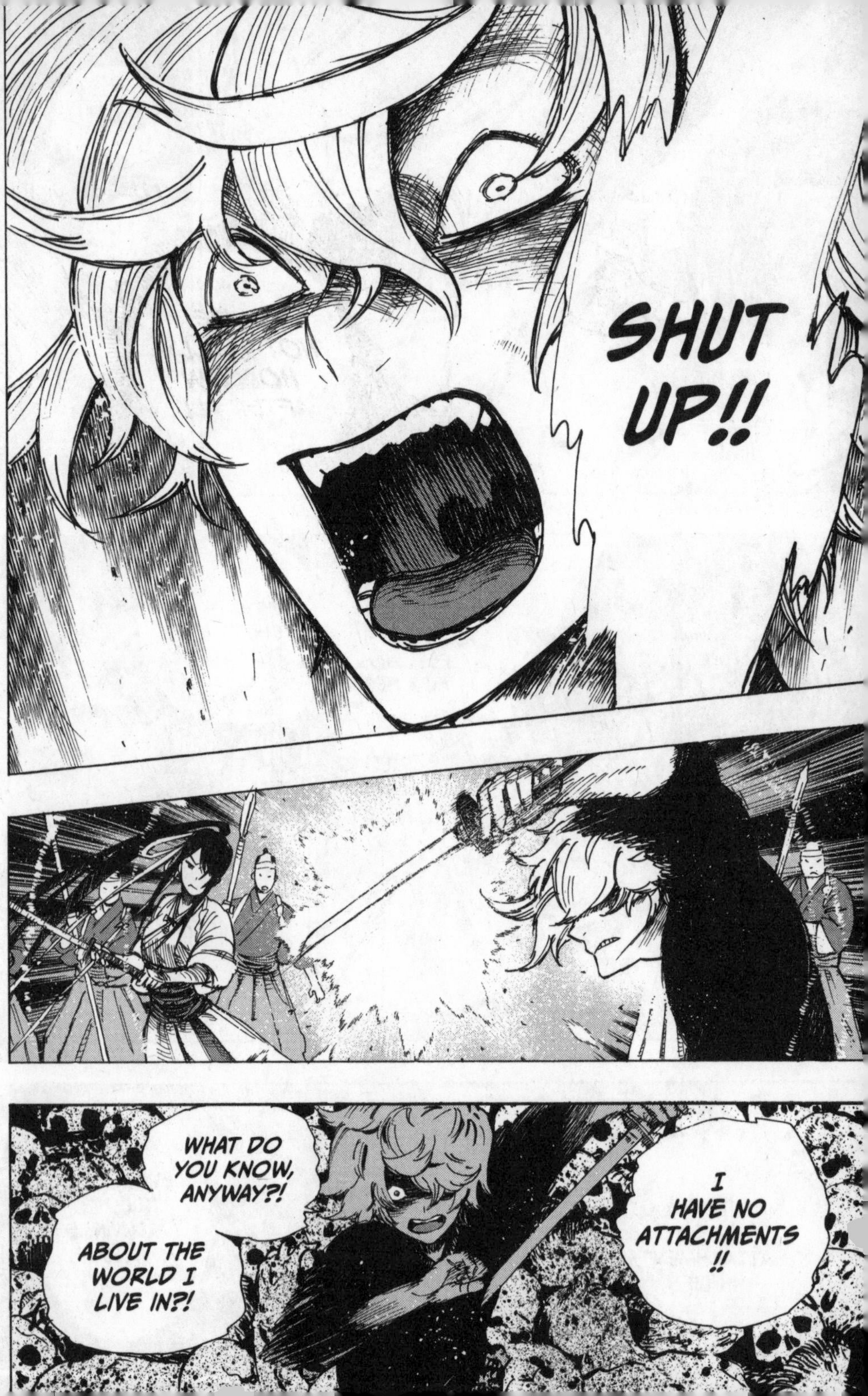
SHUT UP!!
I HAVE NO ATTACHMENTS!!
WHAT DO YOU KNOW, ANYWAY?!
ABOUT THE WORLD I LIVE IN?!

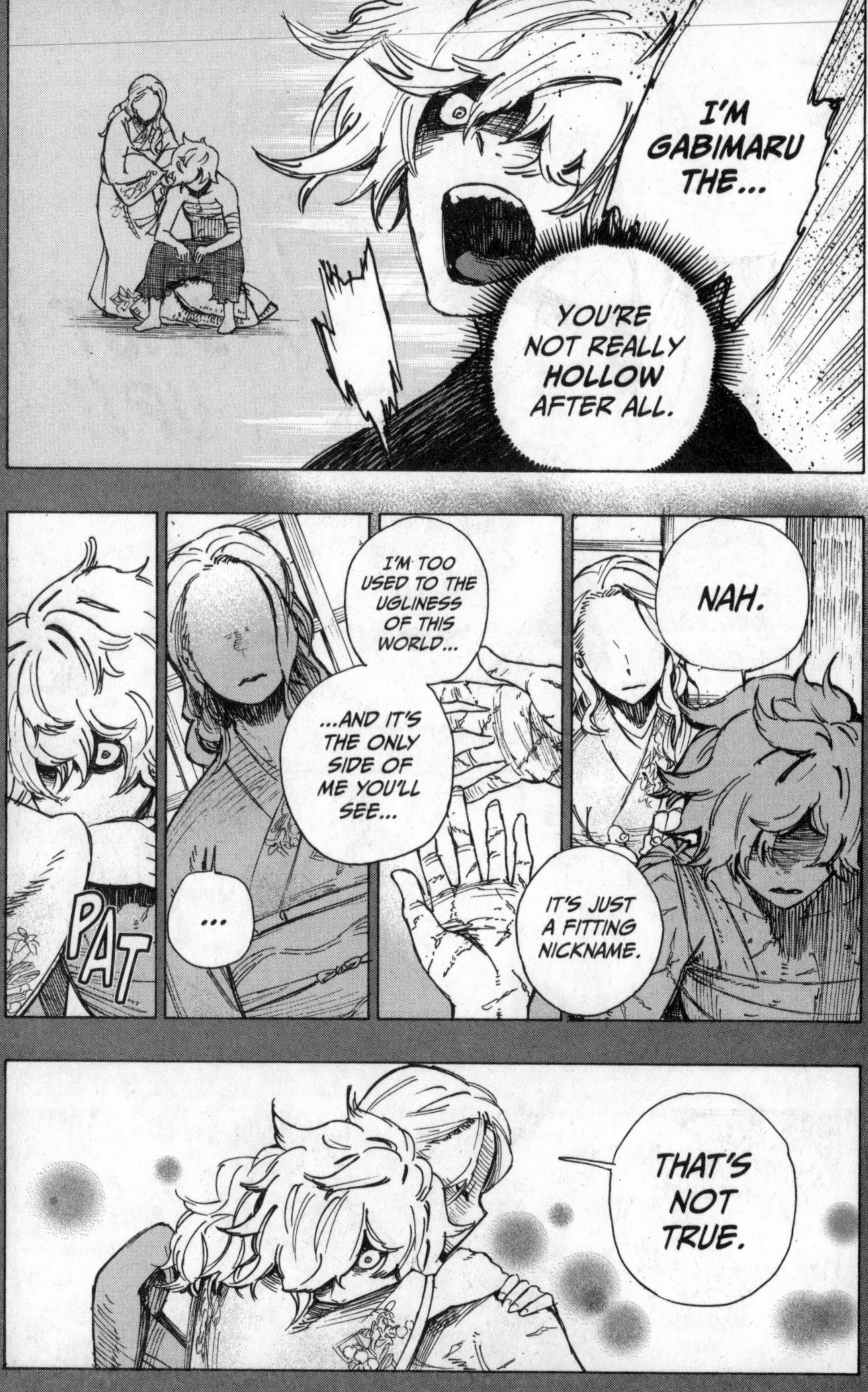
I'M GABIMARU THE...
YOU'RE NOT REALLY HOLLOW AFTER ALL.
NAH.
IT'S JUST A FITTING NICKNAME.
I'M TOO USED TO THE UGLINESS OF THIS WORLD...
...AND IT'S THE ONLY SIDE OF ME YOU'LL SEE...
...
PAT
THAT'S NOT TRUE.

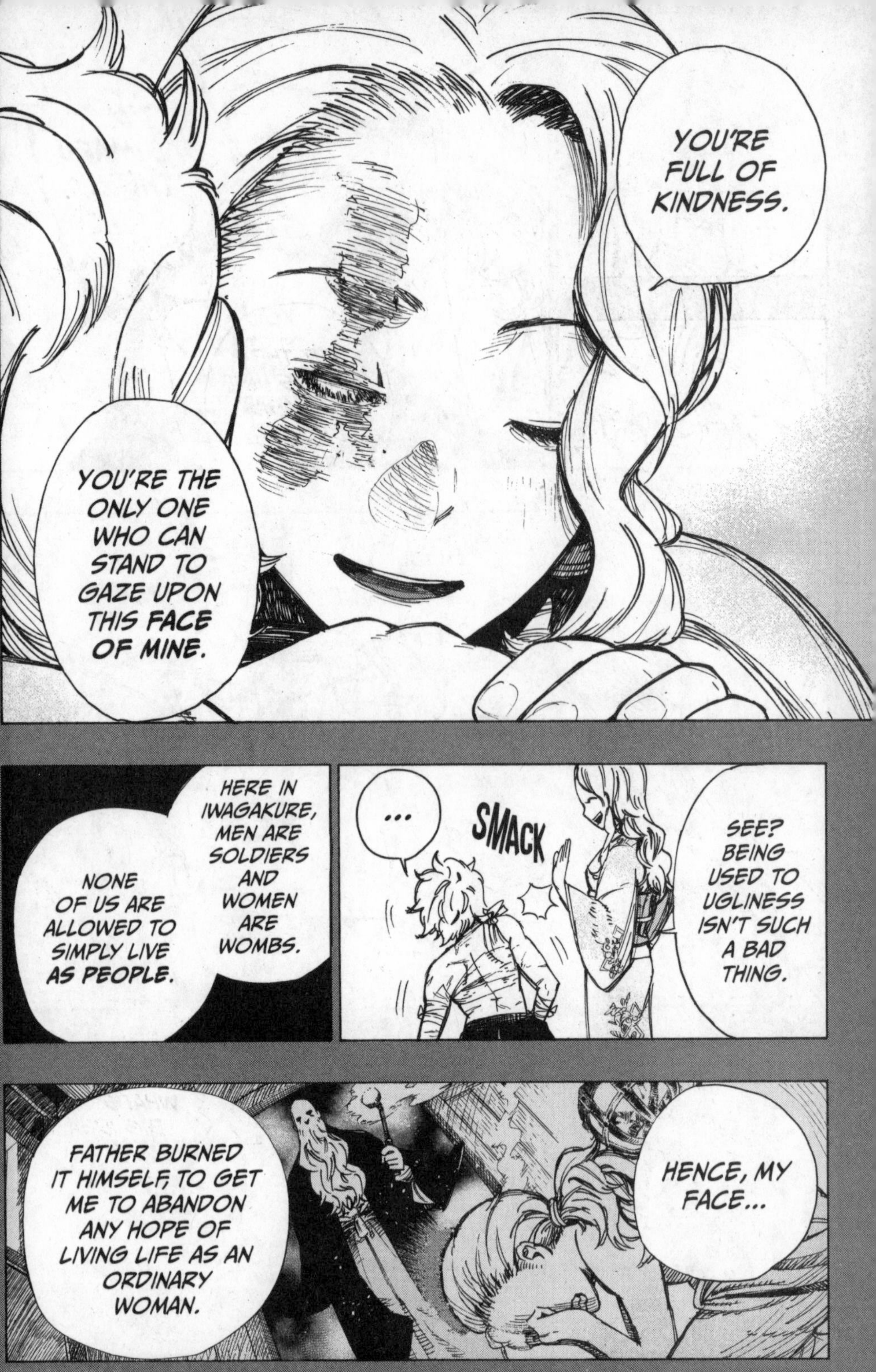
YOU'RE FULL OF KINDNESS.
YOU'RE THE ONLY ONE WHO CAN STAND TO GAZE UPON THIS FACE OF MINE.
SEE? BEING USED TO UGLINESS ISN'T SUCH A BAD THING.
...
SMACK
HERE IN IWAGAKURE, MEN ARE SOLDIERS AND WOMEN ARE WOMBS.
NONE OF US ARE ALLOWED TO SIMPLY LIVE AS PEOPLE.
HENCE, MY FACE...
FATHER BURNED IT HIMSELF, TO GET ME TO ABANDON ANY HOPE OF LIVING LIFE AS AN ORDINARY WOMAN.

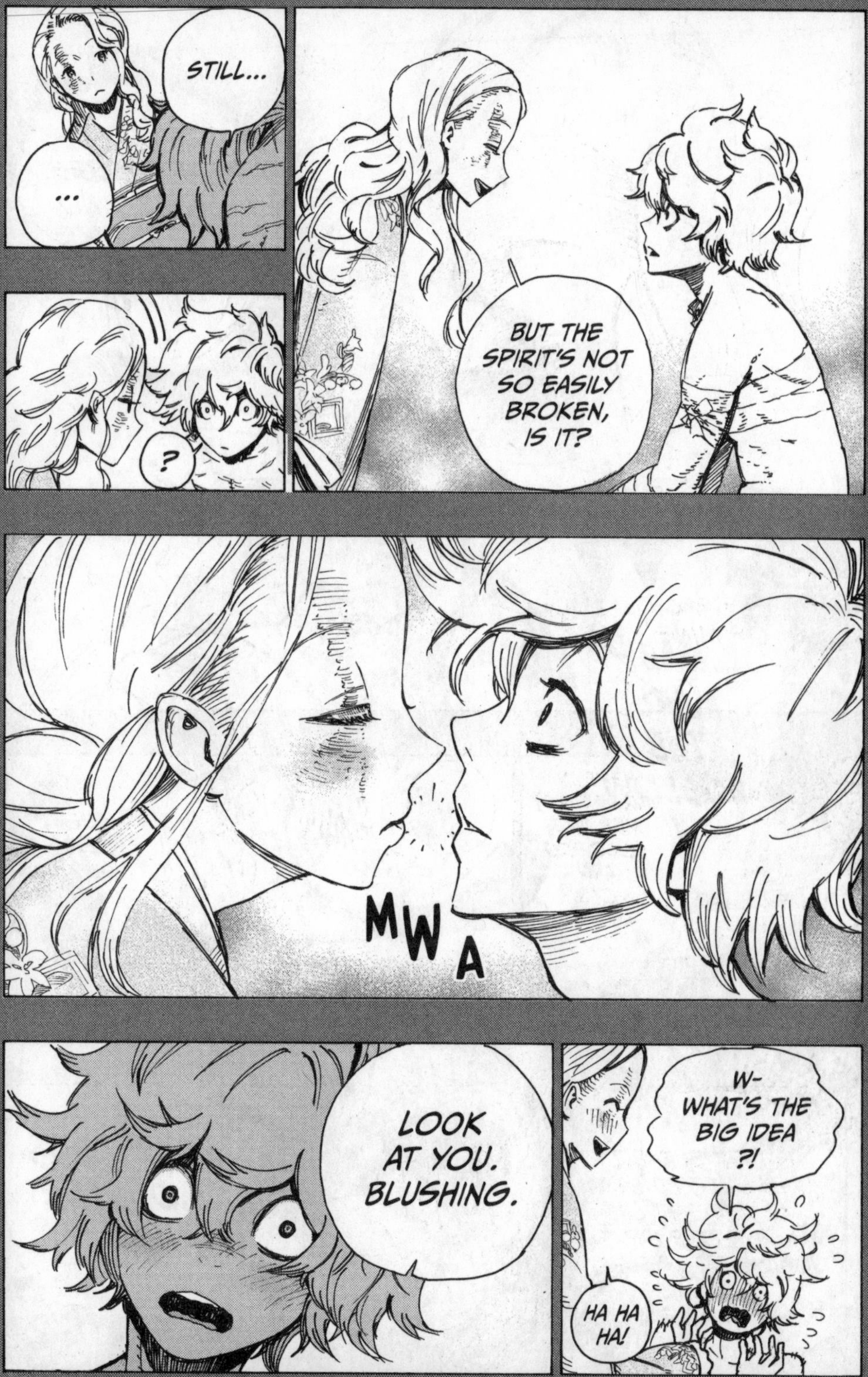
STILL...
...
?
BUT THE SPIRIT'S NOT SO EASILY BROKEN, IS IT?
MWA
LOOK AT YOU. BLUSHING.
W- WHAT'S THE BIG IDEA ?!
HA HA HA!

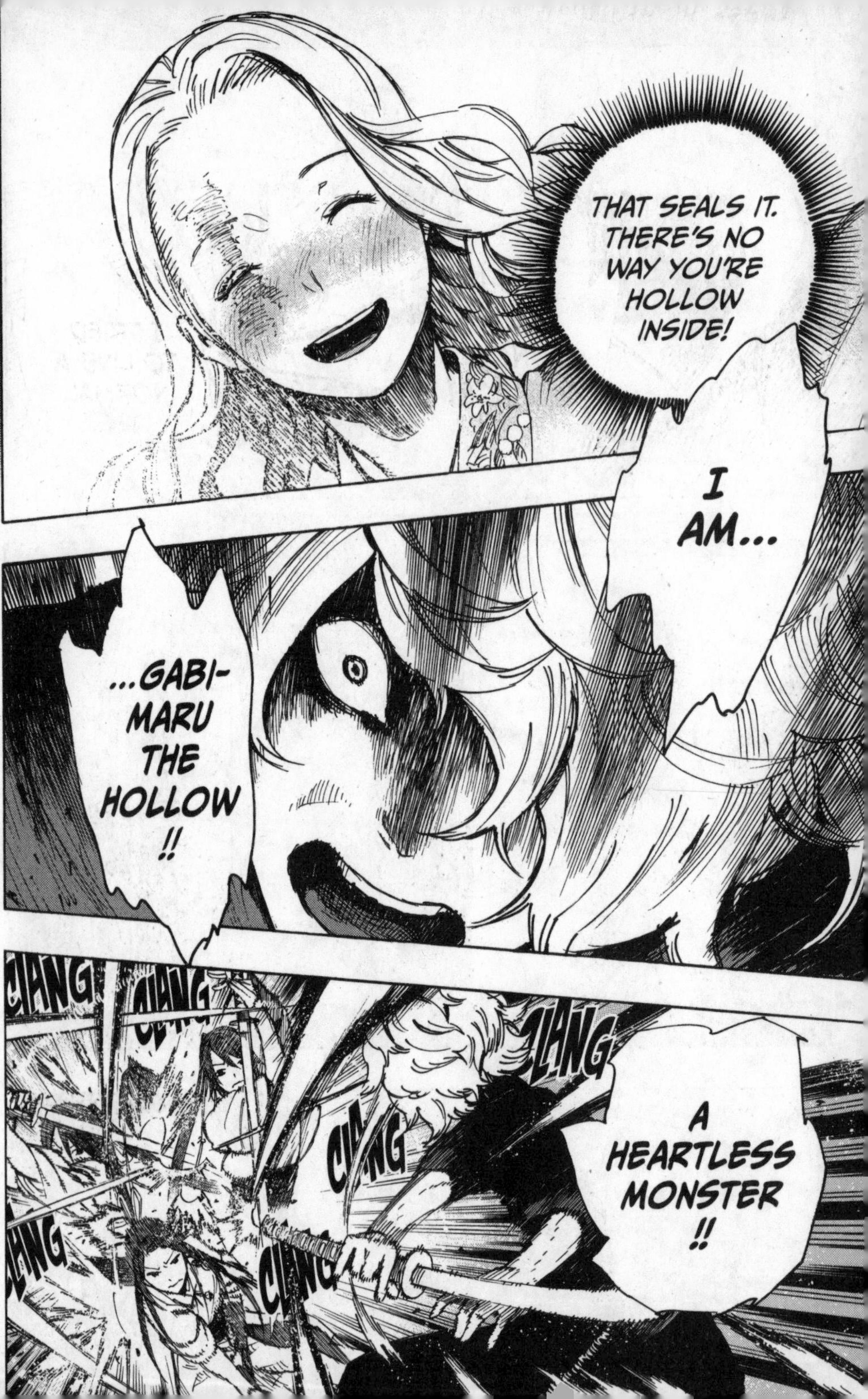
THAT SEALS IT. THERE'S NO WAY YOU'RE HOLLOW INSIDE!
I AM...
...GABI-MARU THE HOLLOW !!
CLANG
A HEARTLESS MONSTER !!
CLANG
CLANG
CLANG
CLANG
CLANG
CLANG
CLANG

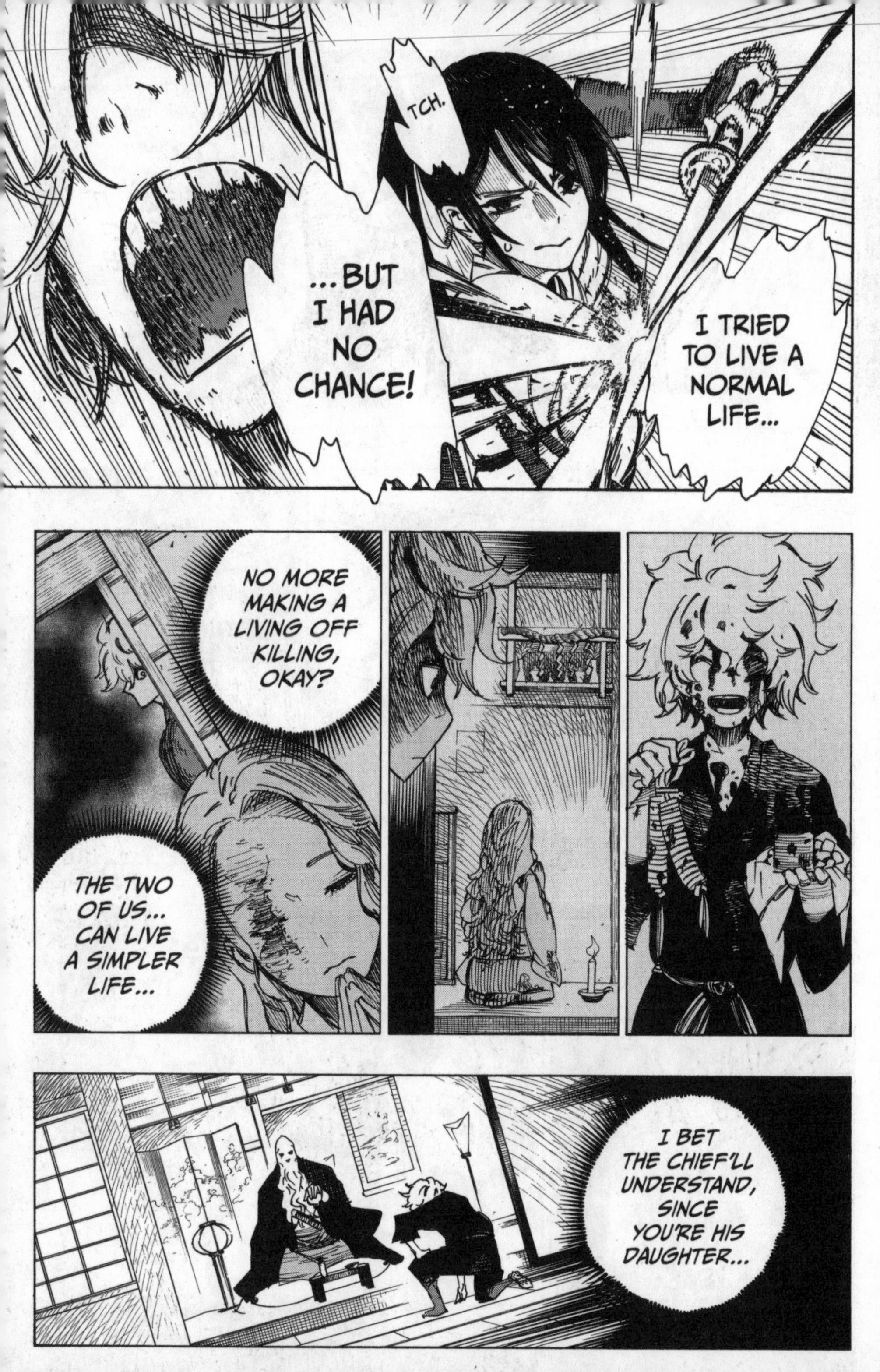
I TRIED TO LIVE A NORMAL LIFE...
...BUT I HAD NO CHANCE!
TCH.
NO MORE MAKING A LIVING OFF KILLING, OKAY?
THE TWO OF US... CAN LIVE A SIMPLER LIFE...
I BET THE CHIEF'LL UNDERSTAND, SINCE YOU'RE HIS DAUGHTER...

I WON'T HAVE TO KILL ANYONE.

LIVING SOMEWHERE PEACEFUL...

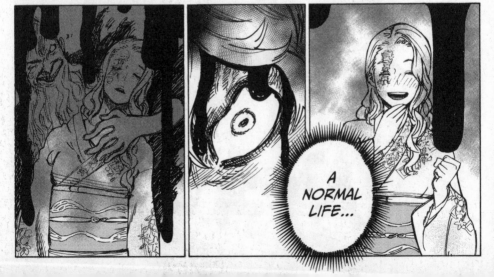

A NORMAL LIFE...

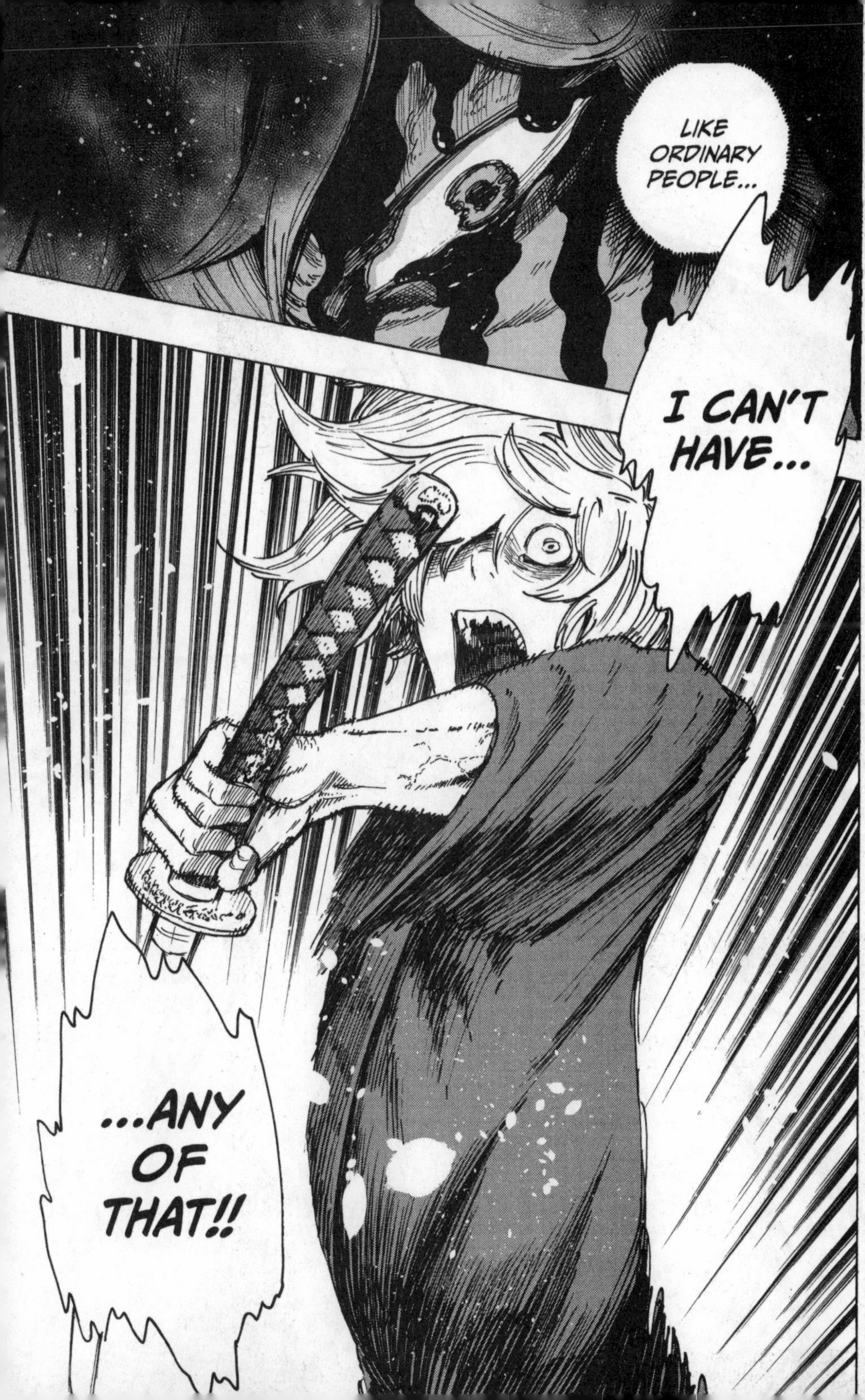
LIKE ORDINARY PEOPLE...
I CAN'T HAVE...
...ANY OF THAT!!

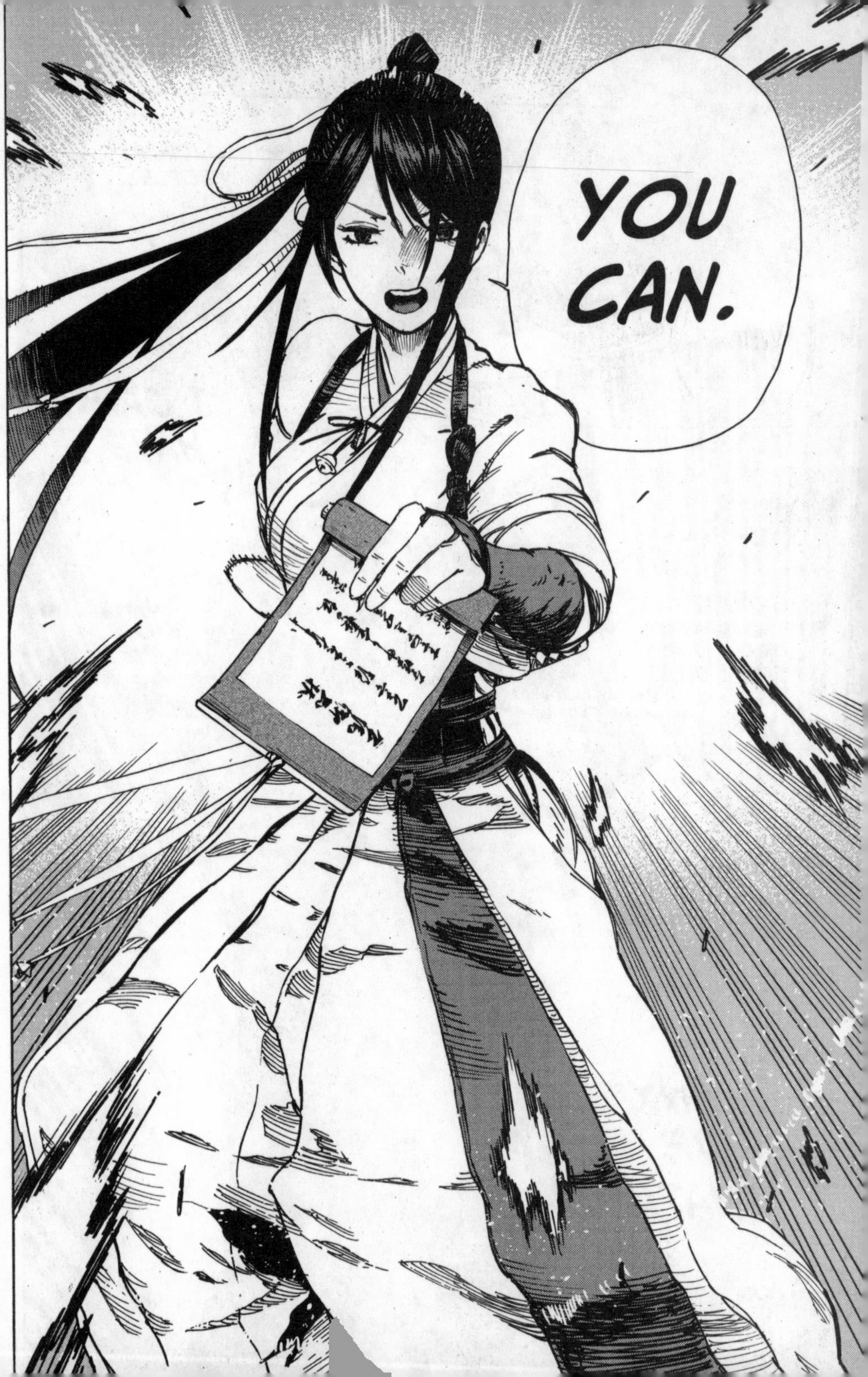
YOU CAN.

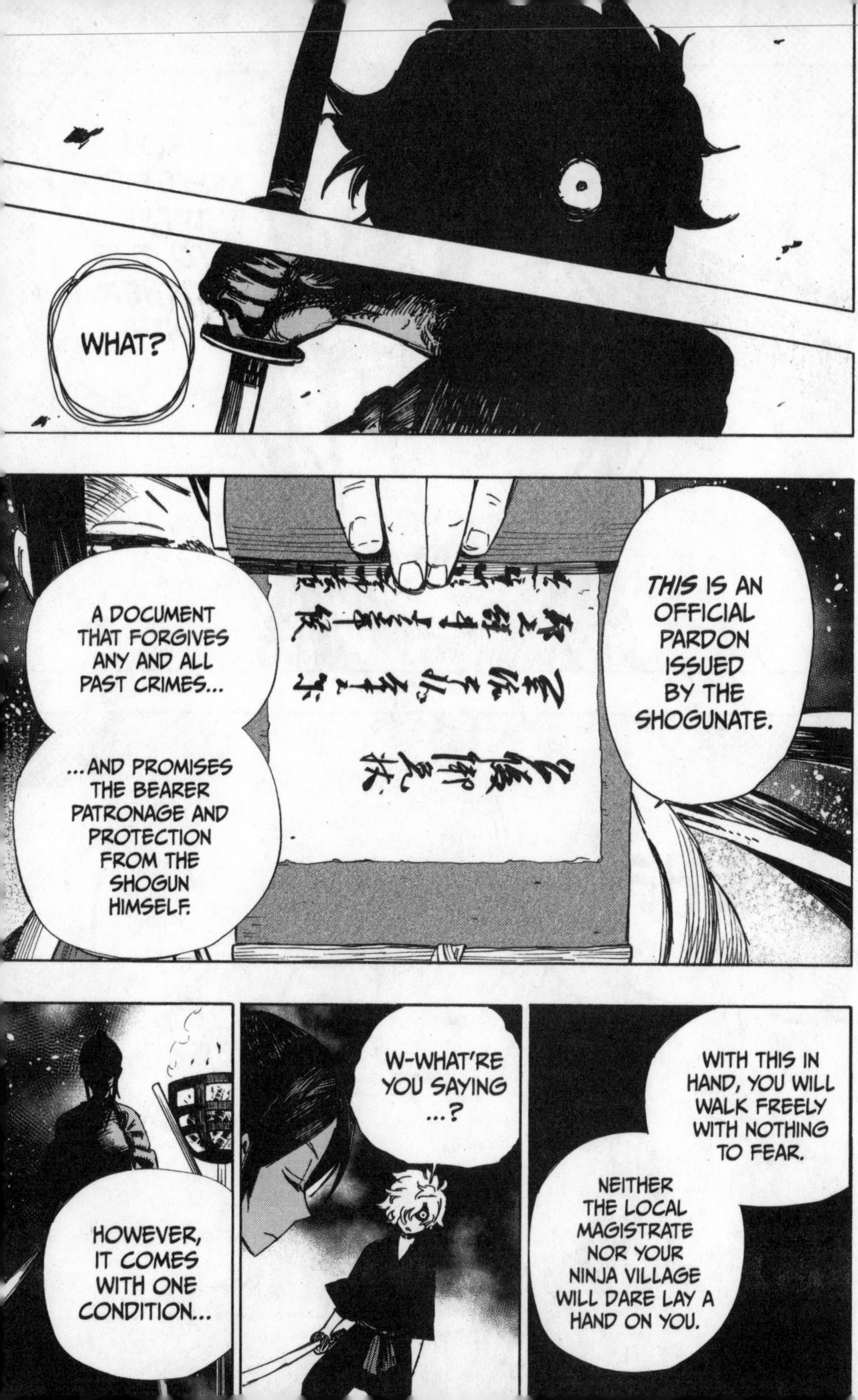
WHAT?
THIS IS AN OFFICIAL PARDON ISSUED BY THE SHOGUNATE.
A DOCUMENT THAT FORGIVES ANY AND ALL PAST CRIMES...
...AND PROMISES THE BEARER PATRONAGE AND PROTECTION FROM THE SHOGUN HIMSELF.
WITH THIS IN HAND, YOU WILL WALK FREELY WITH NOTHING TO FEAR.
NEITHER THE LOCAL MAGISTRATE NOR YOUR NINJA VILLAGE WILL DARE LAY A HAND ON YOU.
W-WHAT'RE YOU SAYING ...?
HOWEVER, IT COMES WITH ONE CONDITION...

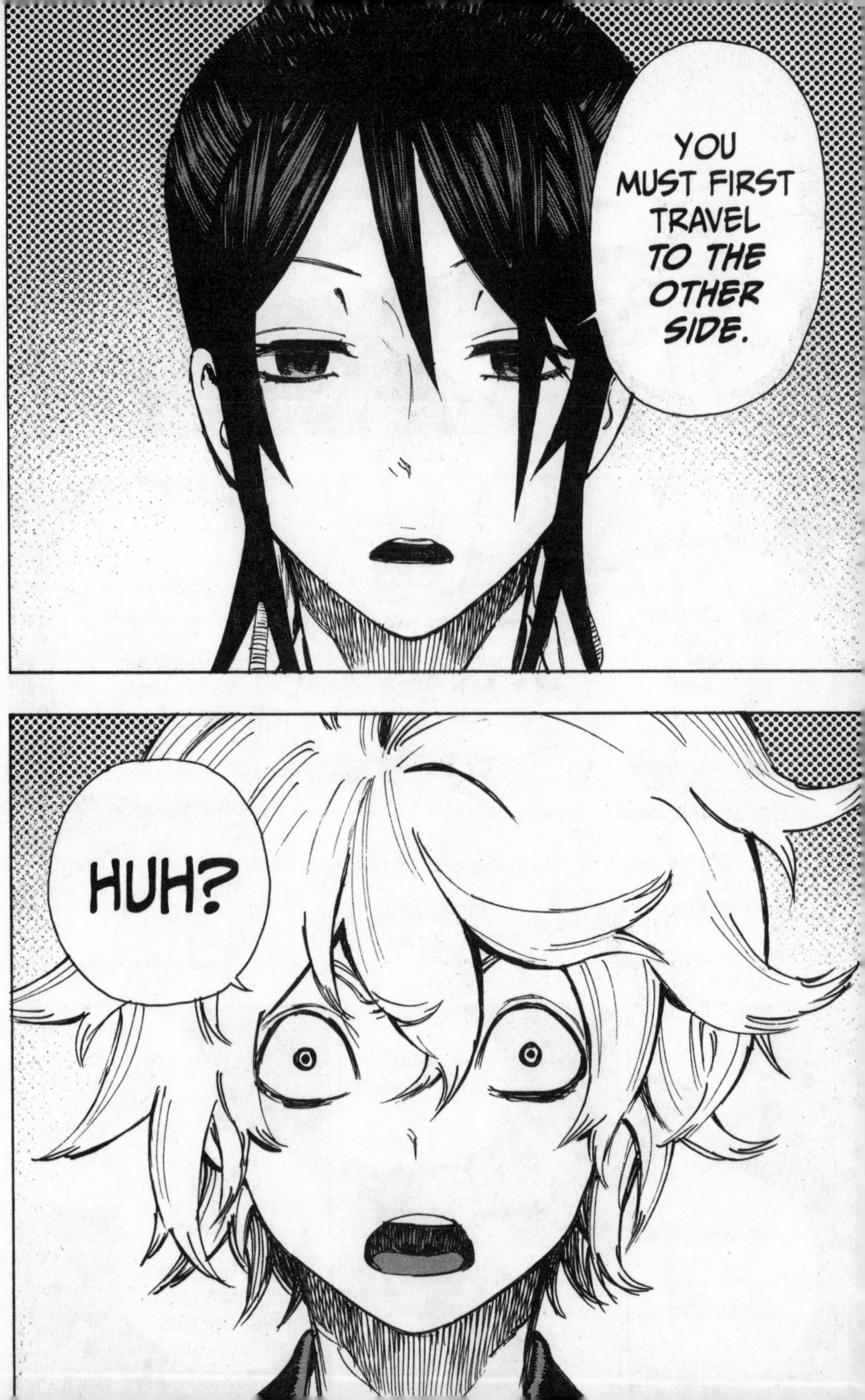
YOU MUST FIRST TRAVEL TO THE OTHER SIDE.
HUH?

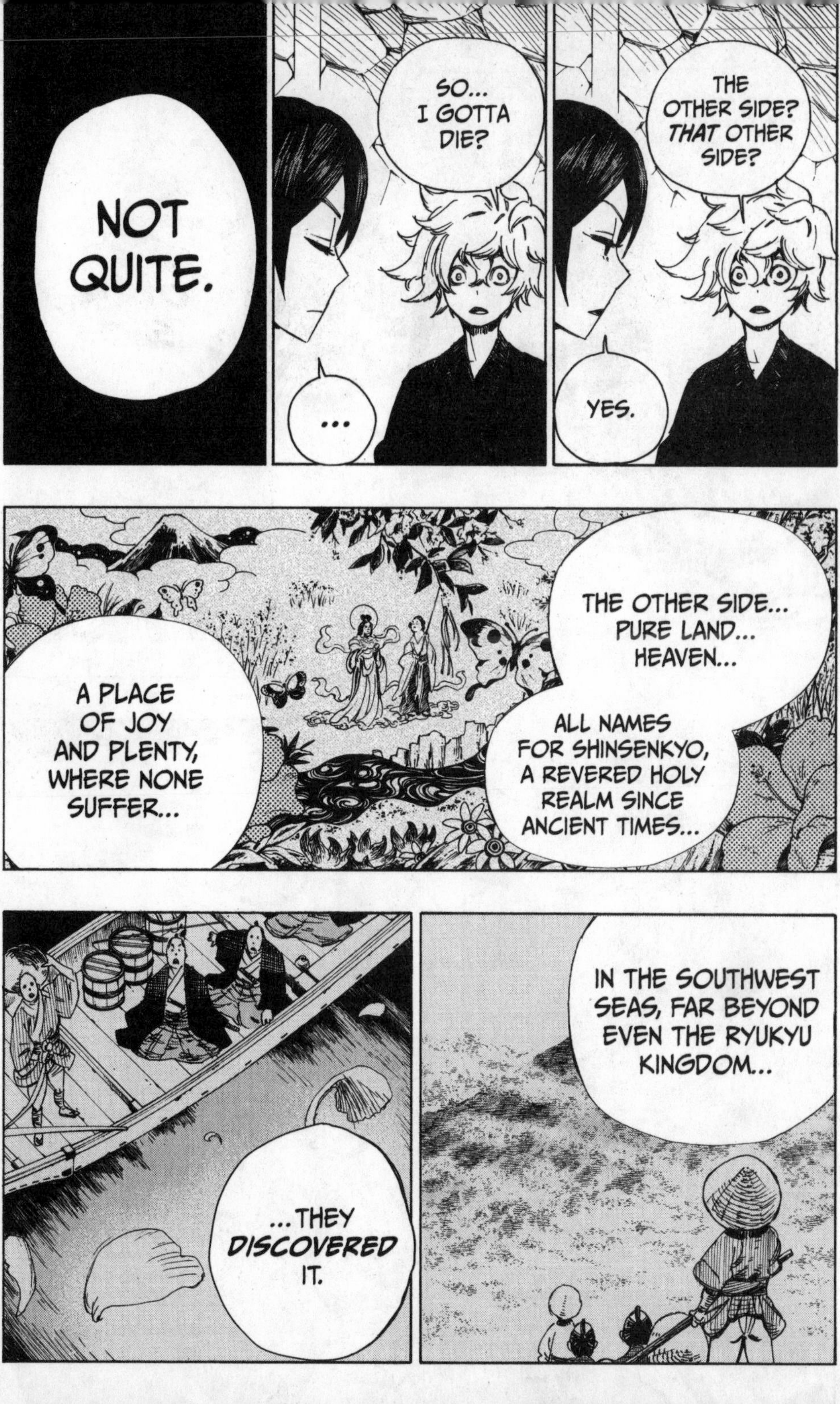
THE OTHER SIDE? *THAT* OTHER SIDE?
YES.
SO... I GOTTA DIE?
...
NOT QUITE.
THE OTHER SIDE... PURE LAND... HEAVEN...
ALL NAMES FOR SHINSENKYO, A REVERED HOLY REALM SINCE ANCIENT TIMES...
A PLACE OF JOY AND PLENTY, WHERE NONE SUFFER...
IN THE SOUTHWEST SEAS, FAR BEYOND EVEN THE RYUKYU KINGDOM...
...THEY *DISCOVERED* IT.

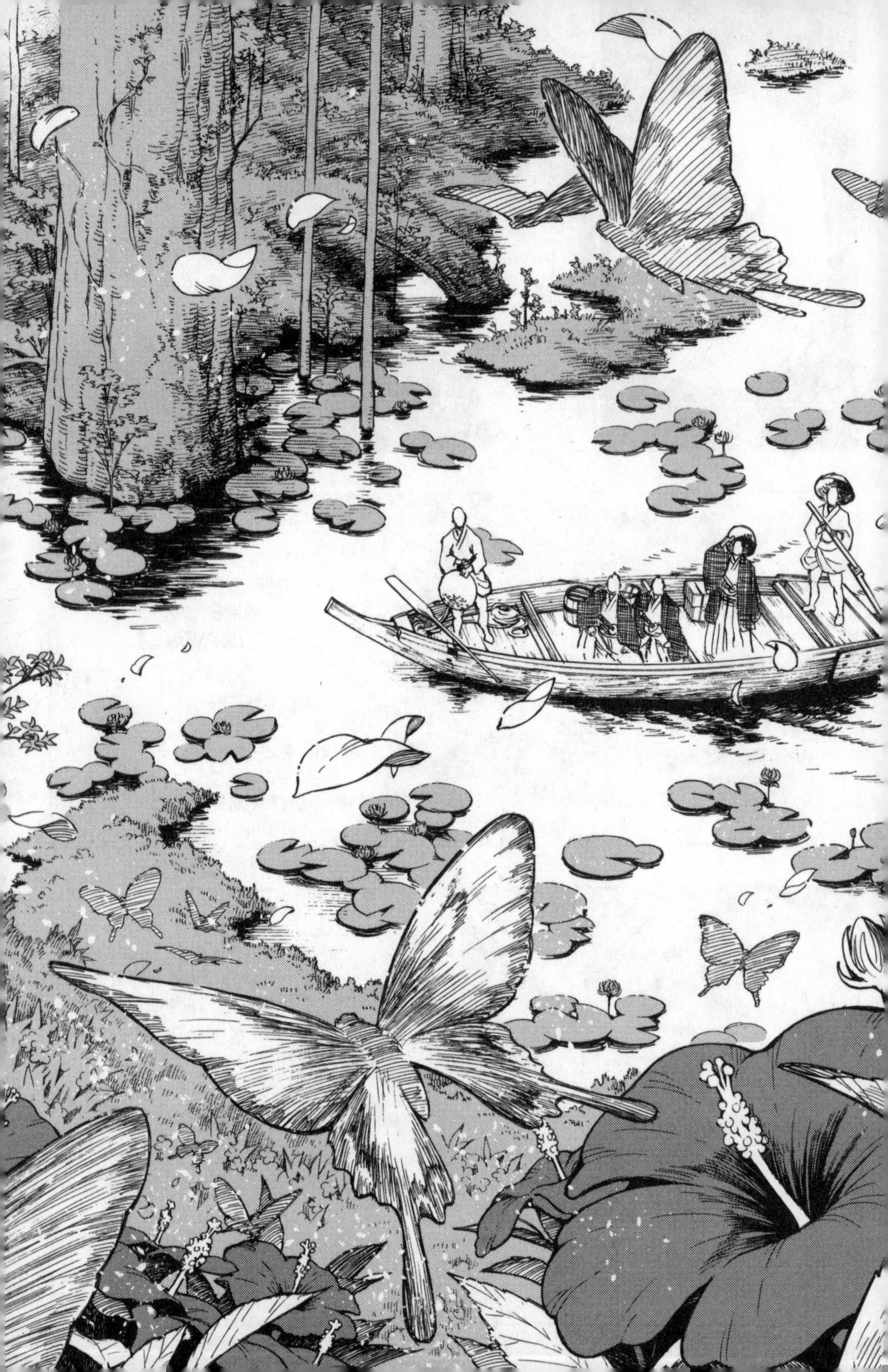

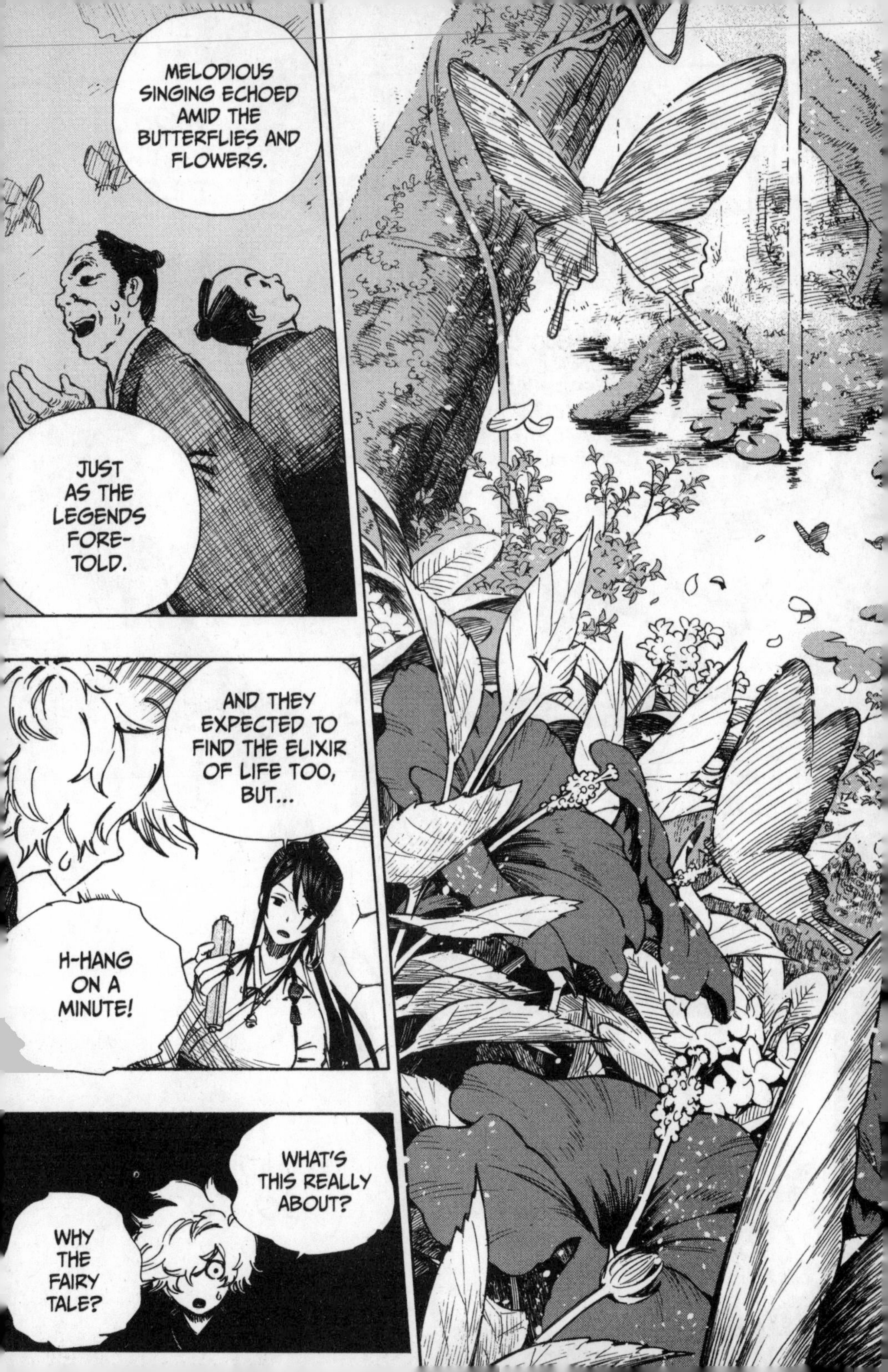
MELODIOUS SINGING ECHOED AMID THE BUTTERFLIES AND FLOWERS.
JUST AS THE LEGENDS FORE-TOLD.
AND THEY EXPECTED TO FIND THE ELIXIR OF LIFE TOO, BUT...
H-HANG ON A MINUTE!
WHAT'S THIS REALLY ABOUT?
WHY THE FAIRY TALE?

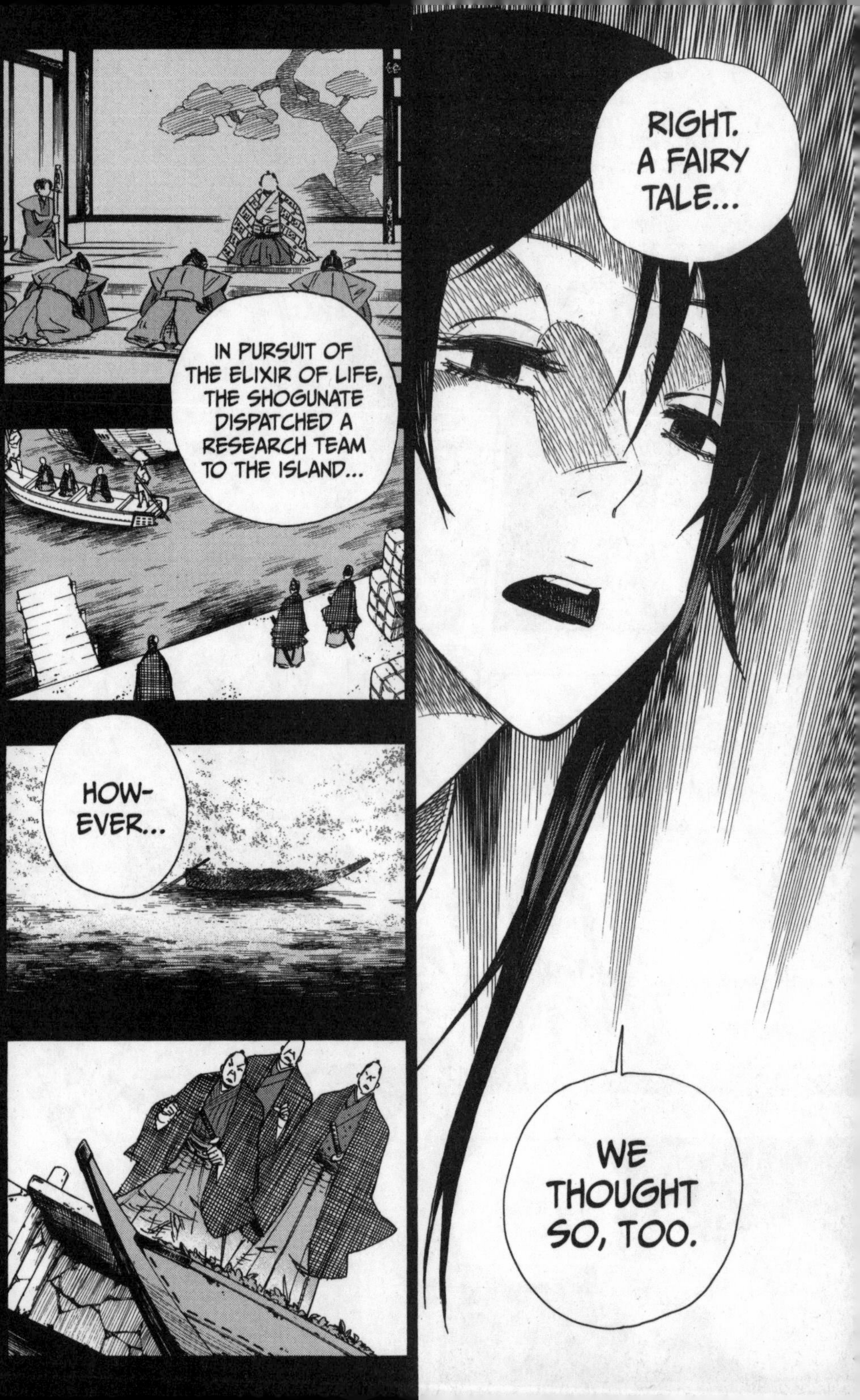
RIGHT. A FAIRY TALE...
WE THOUGHT SO, TOO.
IN PURSUIT OF THE ELIXIR OF LIFE, THE SHOGUNATE DISPATCHED A RESEARCH TEAM TO THE ISLAND...
HOW-EVER...

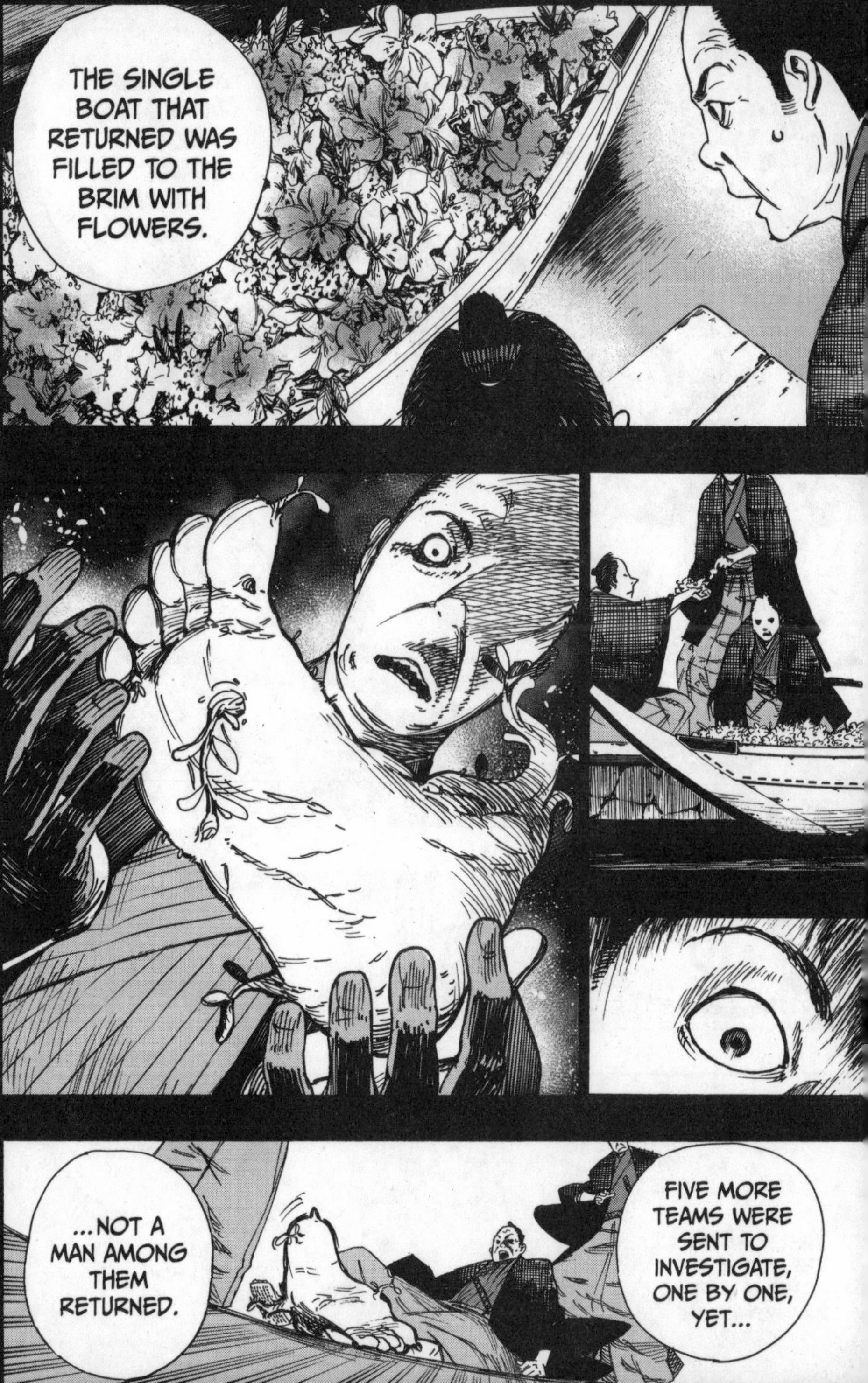
THE SINGLE BOAT THAT RETURNED WAS FILLED TO THE BRIM WITH FLOWERS.
FIVE MORE TEAMS WERE SENT TO INVESTIGATE, ONE BY ONE, YET...
...NOT A MAN AMONG THEM RETURNED.

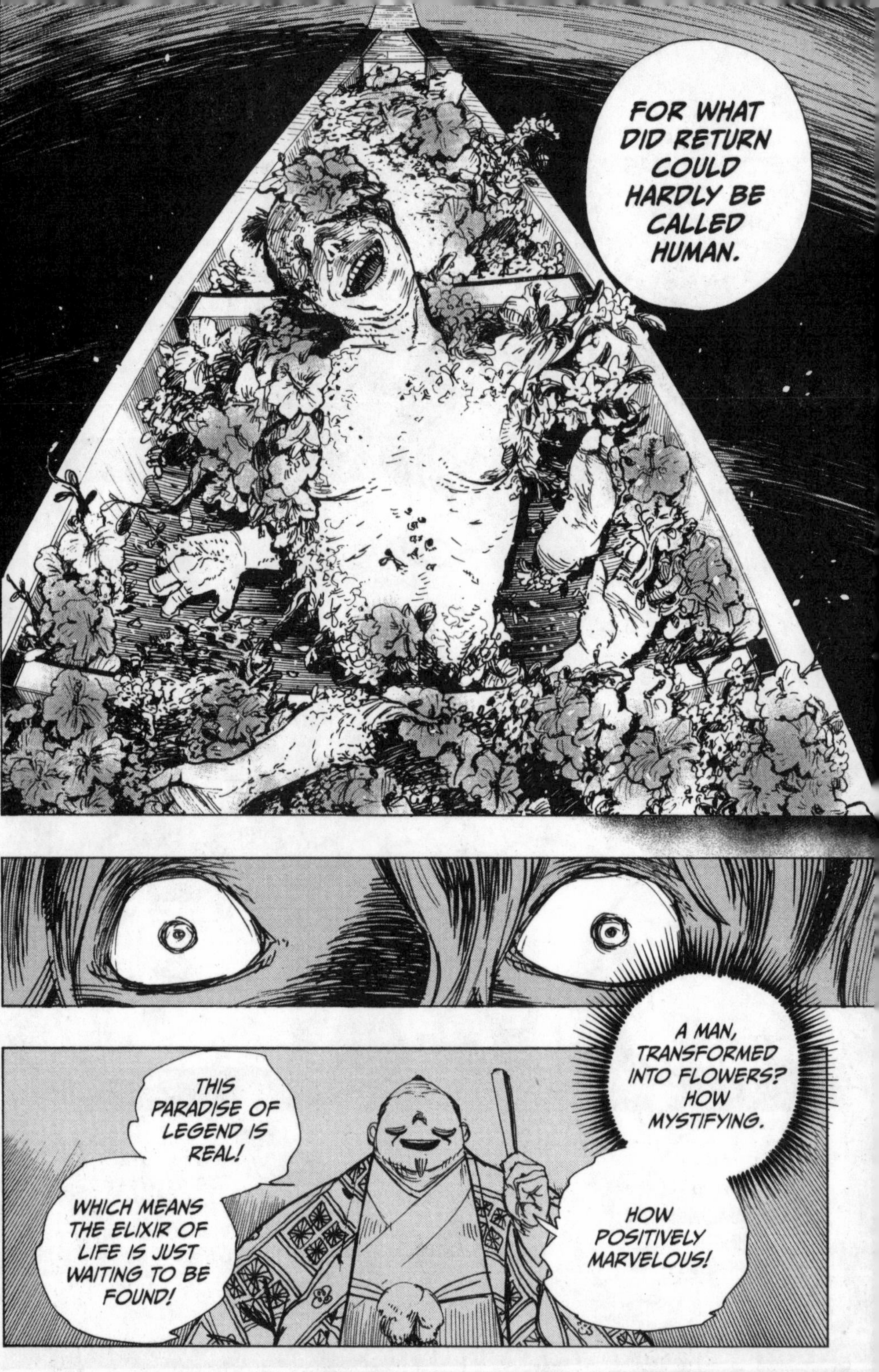
FOR WHAT DID RETURN COULD HARDLY BE CALLED HUMAN.
A MAN, TRANSFORMED INTO FLOWERS? HOW MYSTIFYING.
HOW POSITIVELY MARVELOUS!
THIS PARADISE OF LEGEND IS REAL!
WHICH MEANS THE ELIXIR OF LIFE IS JUST WAITING TO BE FOUND!

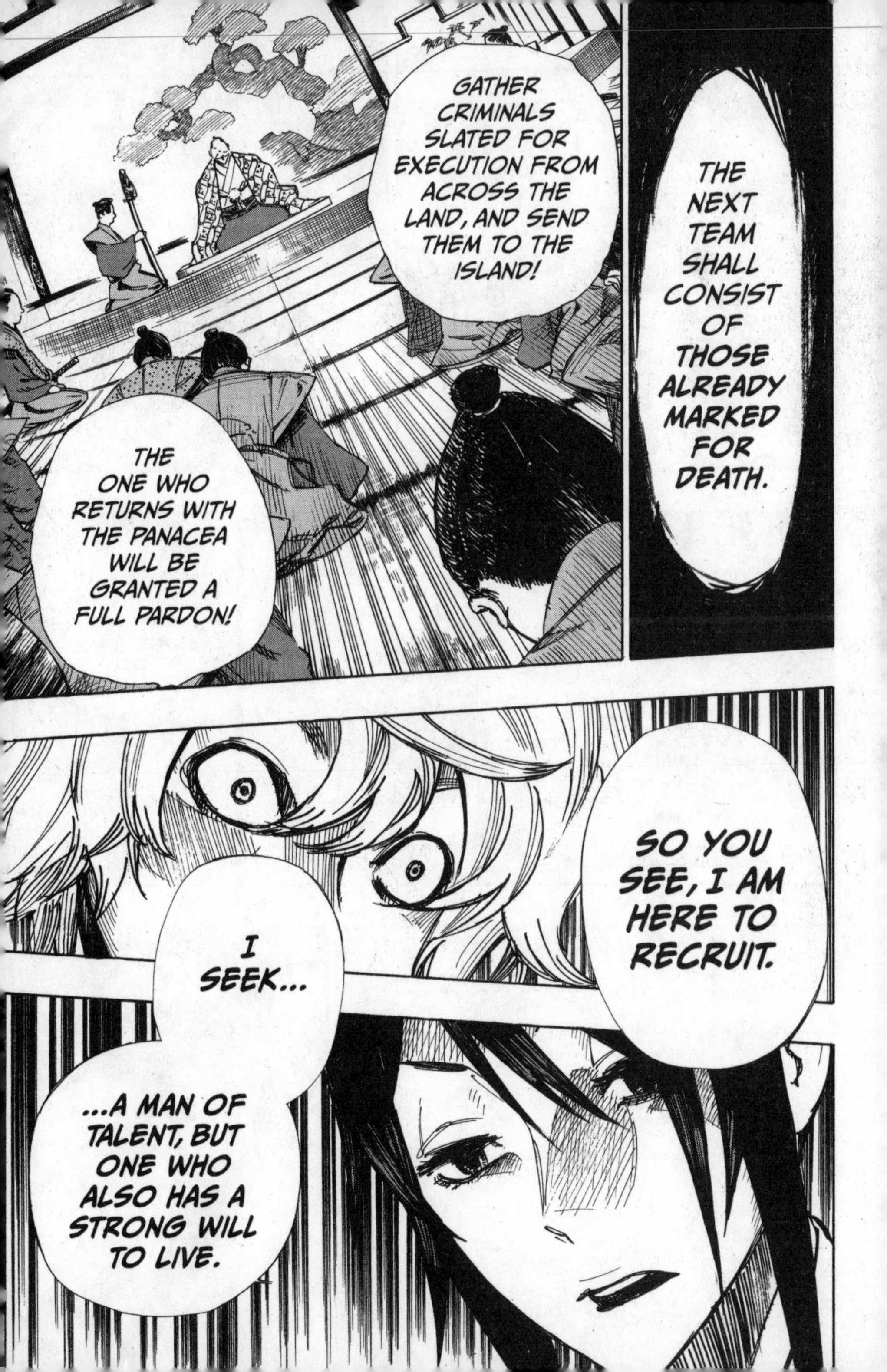
THE NEXT TEAM SHALL CONSIST OF THOSE ALREADY MARKED FOR DEATH.
GATHER CRIMINALS SLATED FOR EXECUTION FROM ACROSS THE LAND, AND SEND THEM TO THE ISLAND!
THE ONE WHO RETURNS WITH THE PANACEA WILL BE GRANTED A FULL PARDON!
SO YOU SEE, I AM HERE TO RECRUIT.
I SEEK...
...A MAN OF TALENT, BUT ONE WHO ALSO HAS A STRONG WILL TO LIVE.

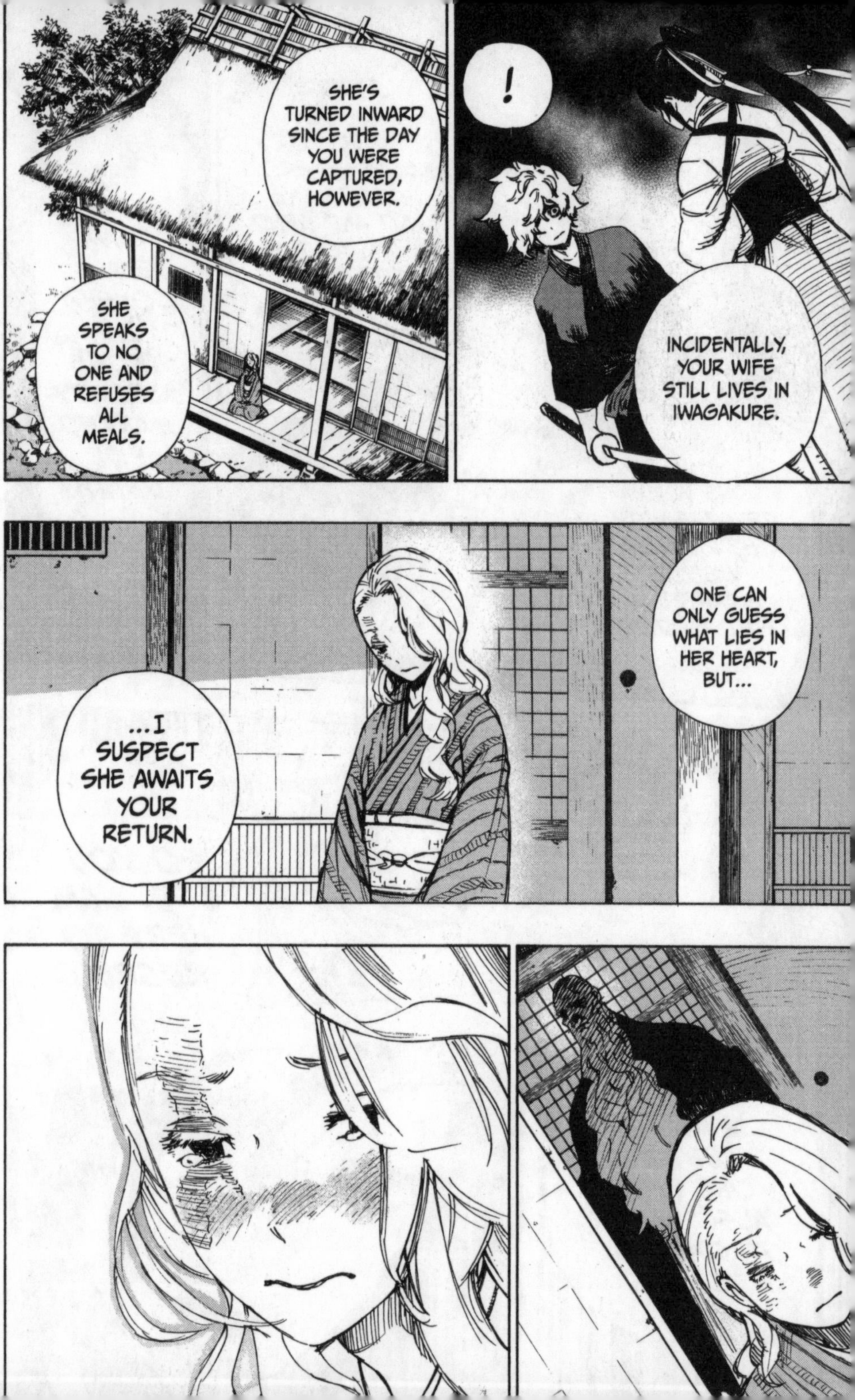
INCIDENTALLY, YOUR WIFE STILL LIVES IN IWAGAKURE.
!
SHE'S TURNED INWARD SINCE THE DAY YOU WERE CAPTURED, HOWEVER.
SHE SPEAKS TO NO ONE AND REFUSES ALL MEALS.
ONE CAN ONLY GUESS WHAT LIES IN HER HEART, BUT...
...I SUSPECT SHE AWAITS YOUR RETURN.

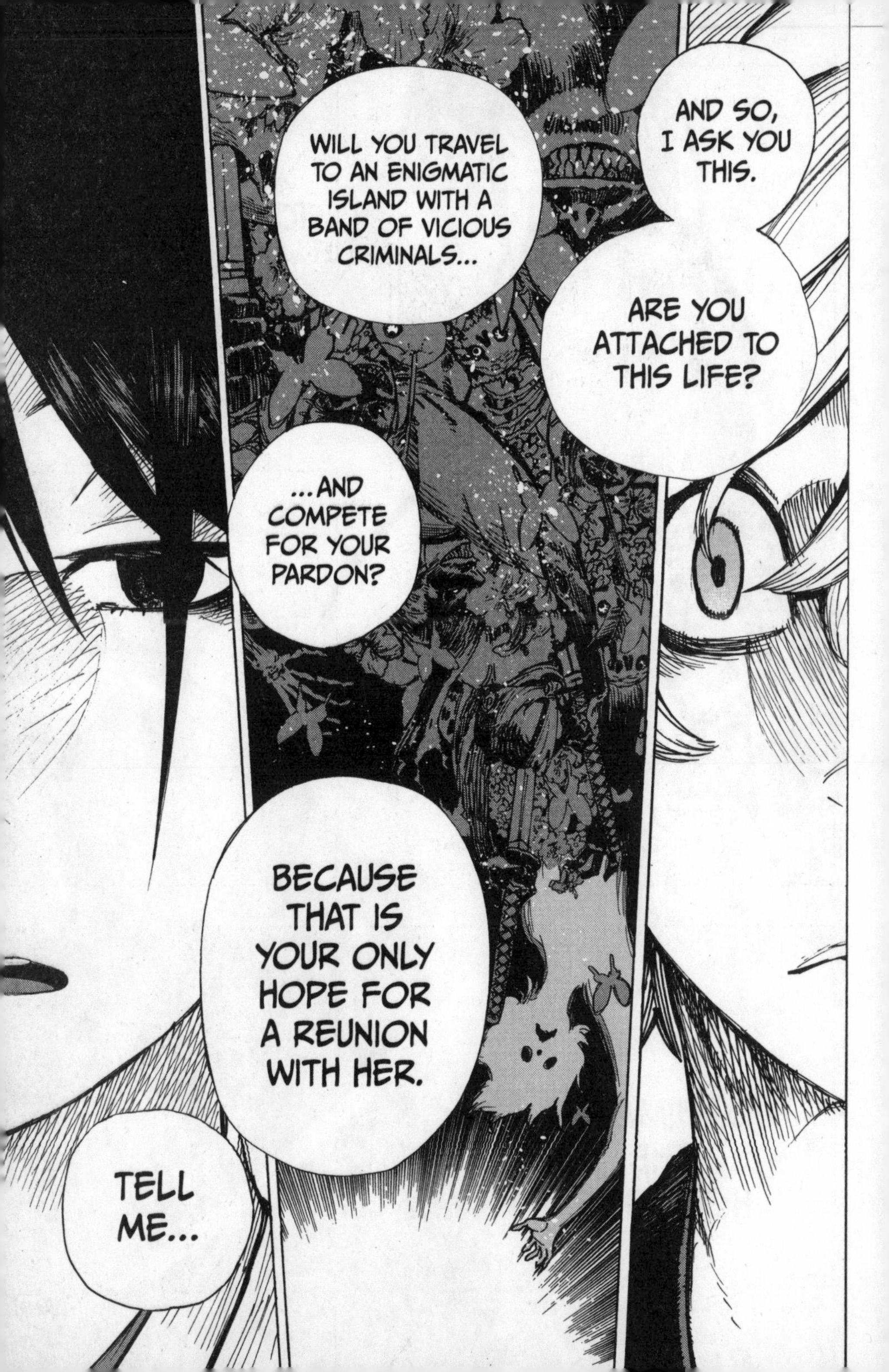
AND SO, I ASK YOU THIS.
ARE YOU ATTACHED TO THIS LIFE?
WILL YOU TRAVEL TO AN ENIGMATIC ISLAND WITH A BAND OF VICIOUS CRIMINALS...
...AND COMPETE FOR YOUR PARDON?
BECAUSE THAT IS YOUR ONLY HOPE FOR A REUNION WITH HER.
TELL ME...

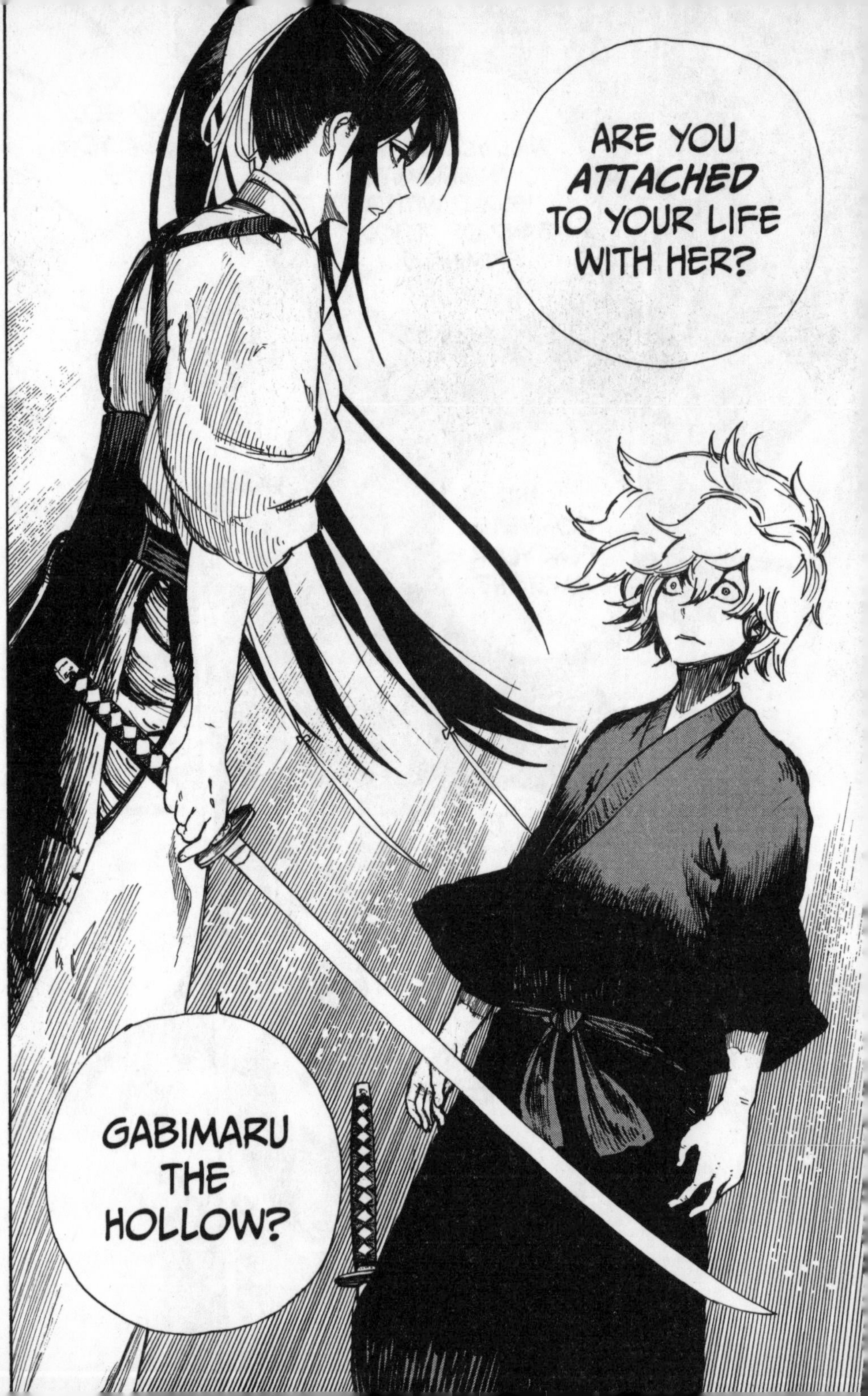
ARE YOU *ATTACHED* TO YOUR LIFE WITH HER?
GABIMARU THE HOLLOW?

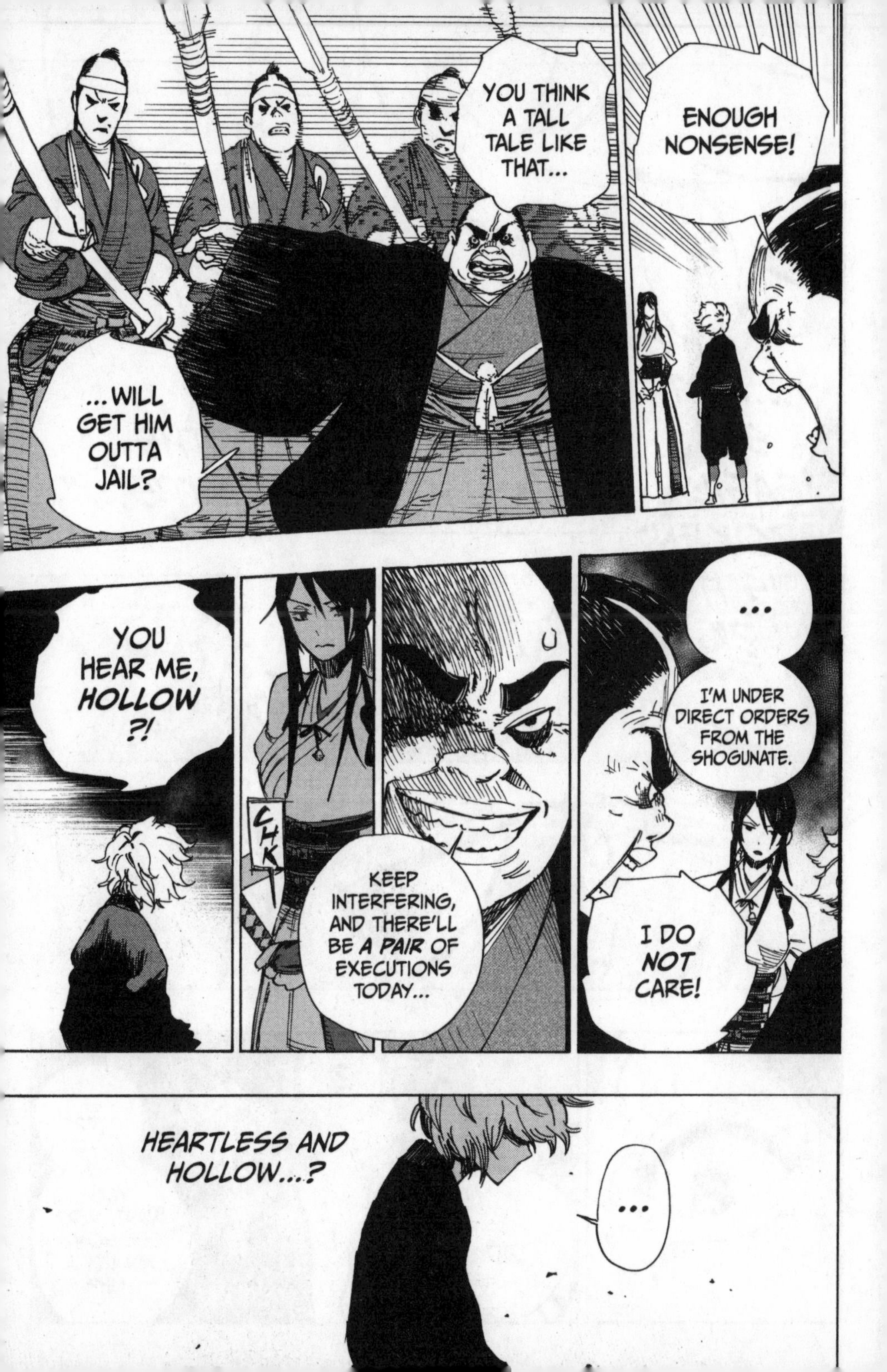
ENOUGH NONSENSE!
YOU THINK A TALL TALE LIKE THAT...
...WILL GET HIM OUTTA JAIL?
...
I'M UNDER DIRECT ORDERS FROM THE SHOGUNATE.
I DO NOT CARE!
KEEP INTERFERING, AND THERE'LL BE A PAIR OF EXECUTIONS TODAY...
CHK
YOU HEAR ME, HOLLOW?!
...
HEARTLESS AND HOLLOW...?

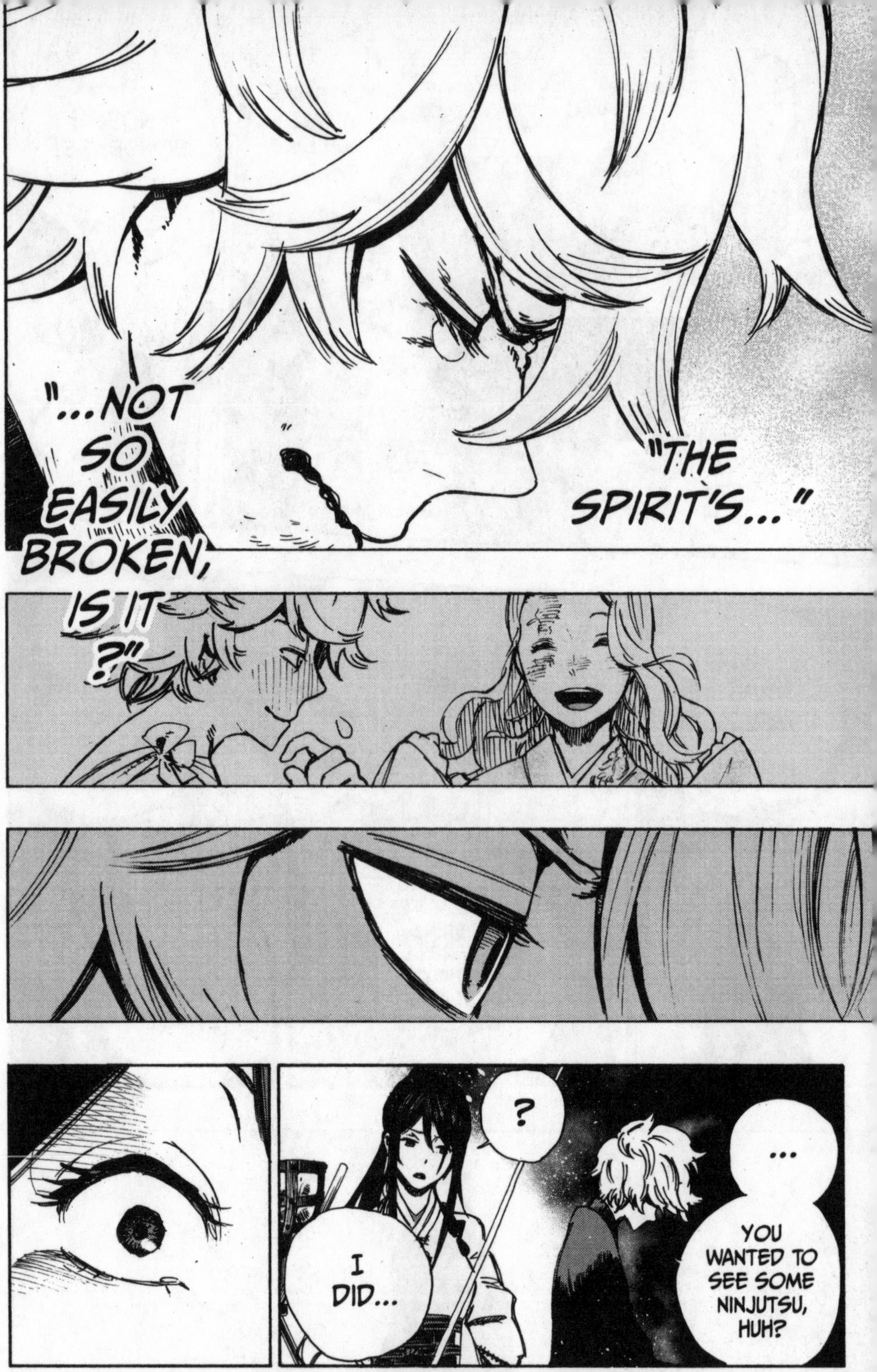
"THE SPIRIT'S..."
"...NOT SO EASILY BROKEN, IS IT?"
...
?
YOU WANTED TO SEE SOME NINJUTSU, HUH?
I DID...

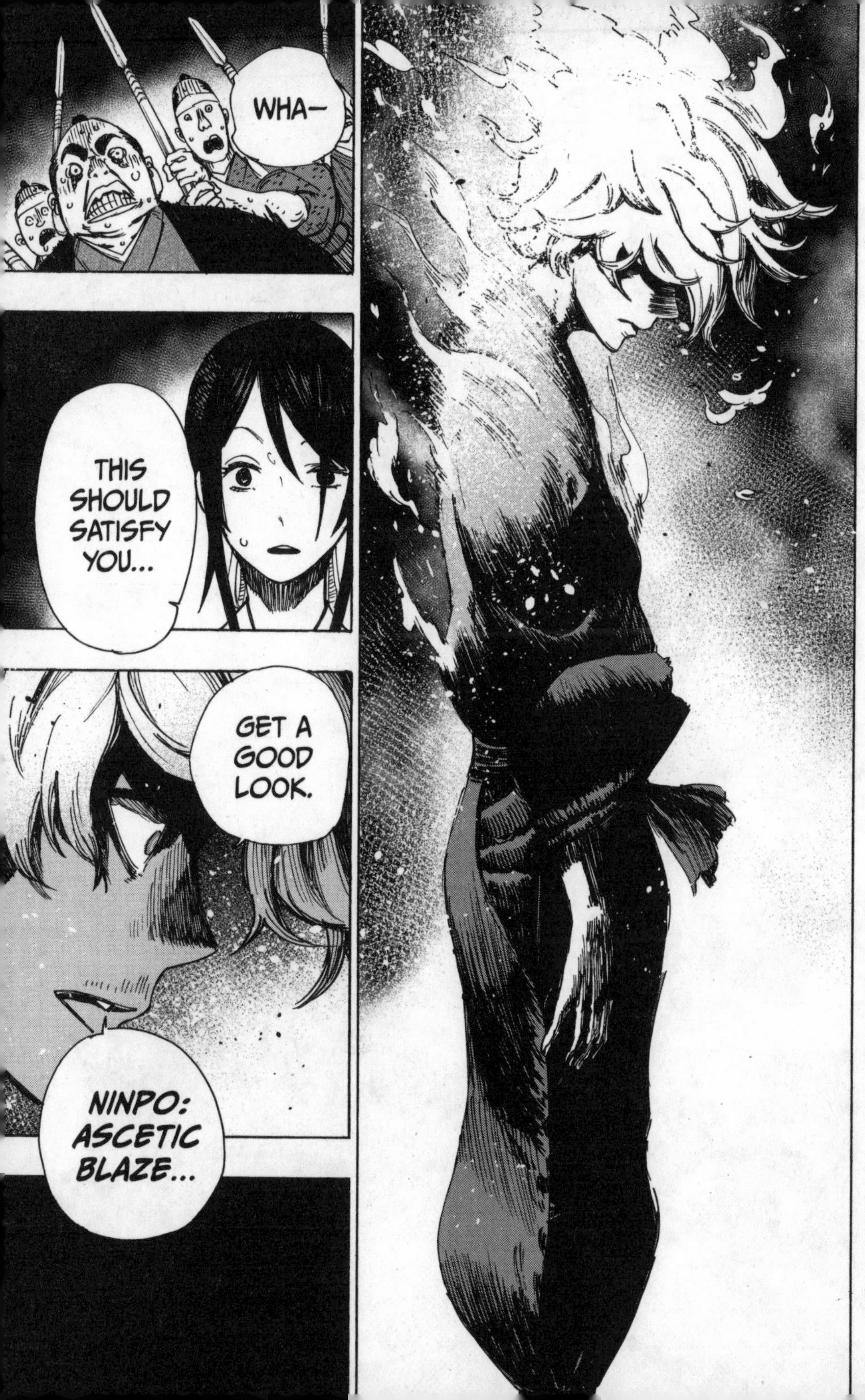
WHA-
THIS SHOULD SATISFY YOU...
GET A GOOD LOOK.
NINPO: ASCETIC BLAZE...

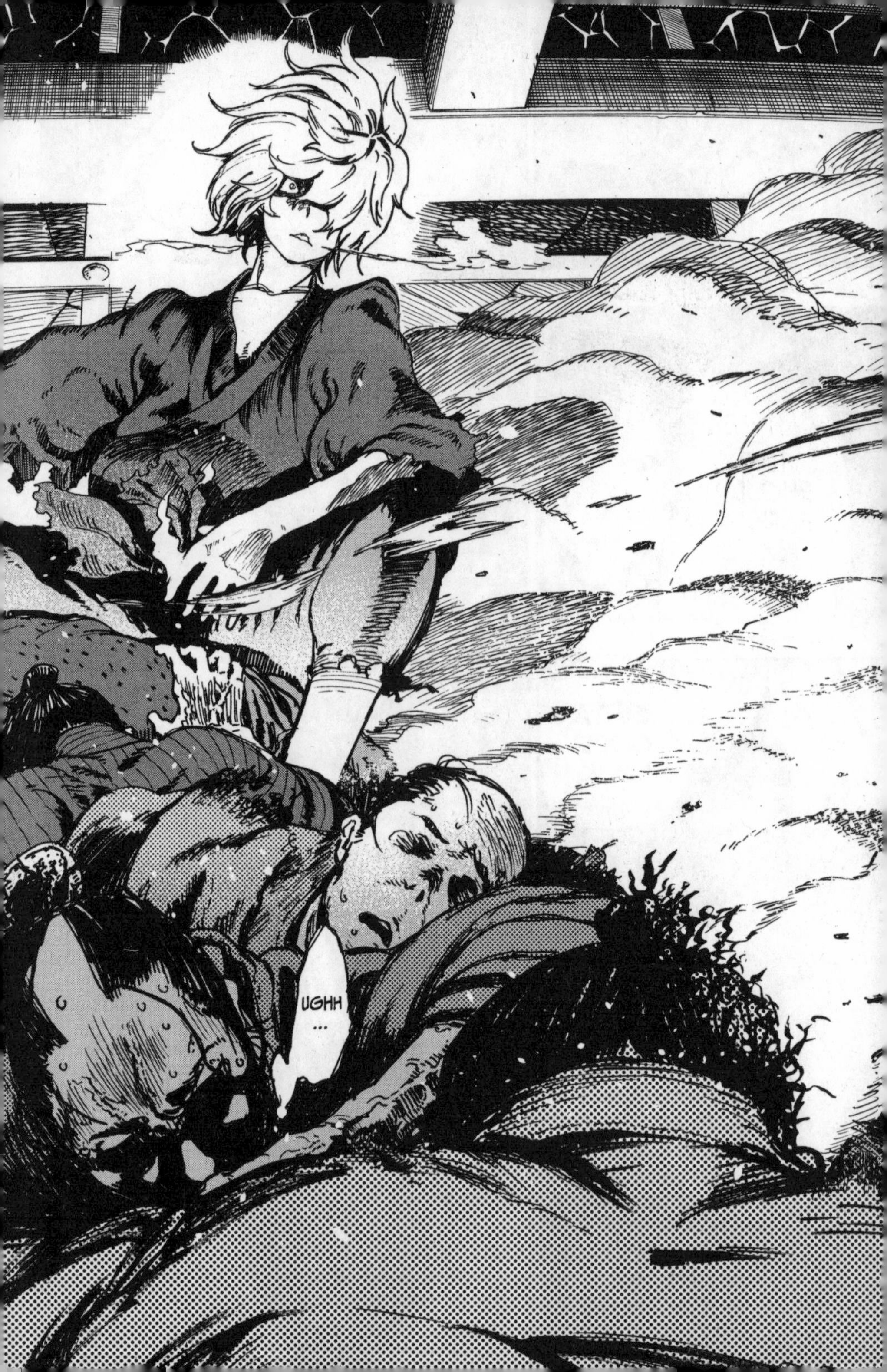
UGHH ...

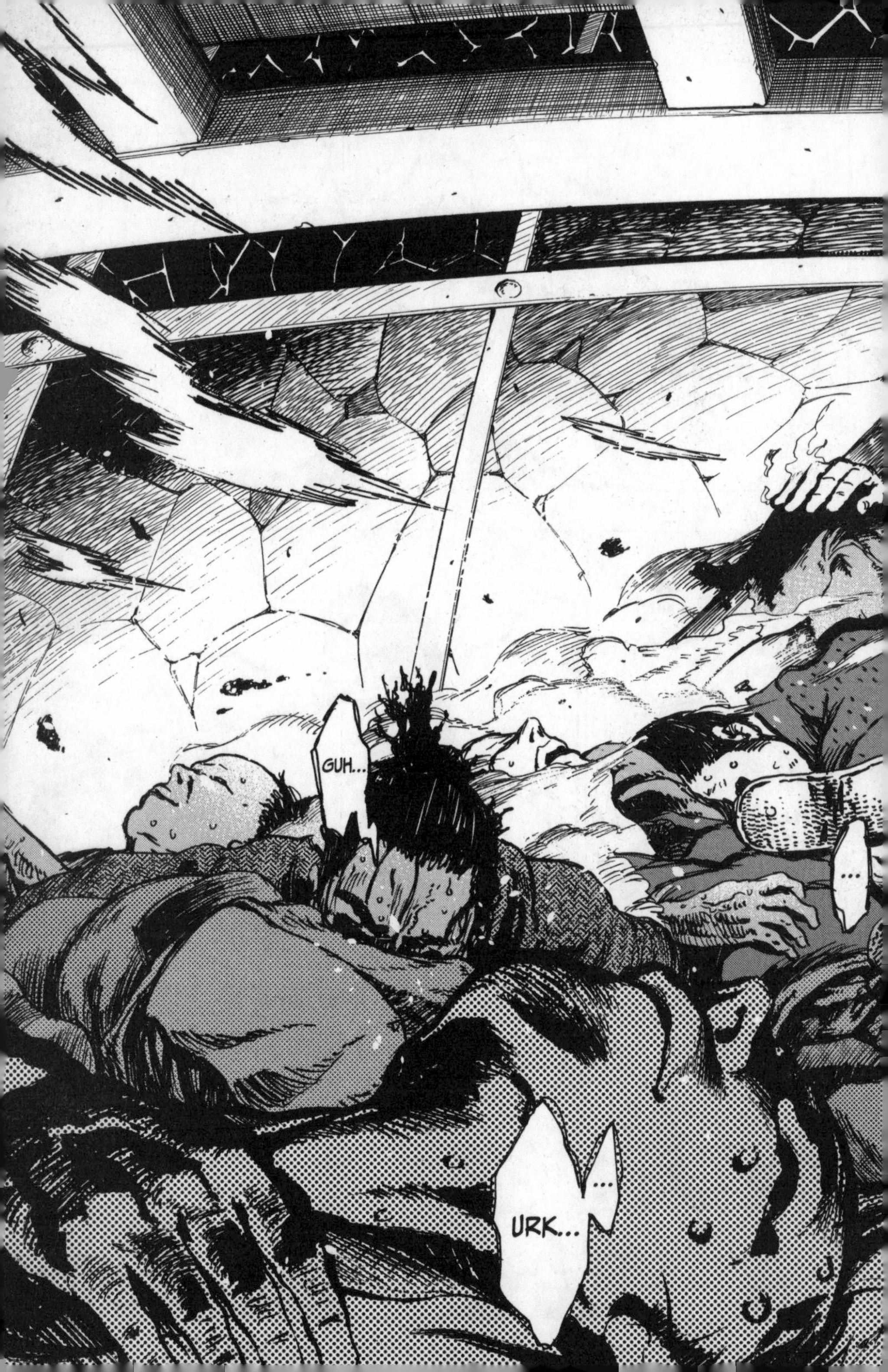
...
GUH...
...
URK...

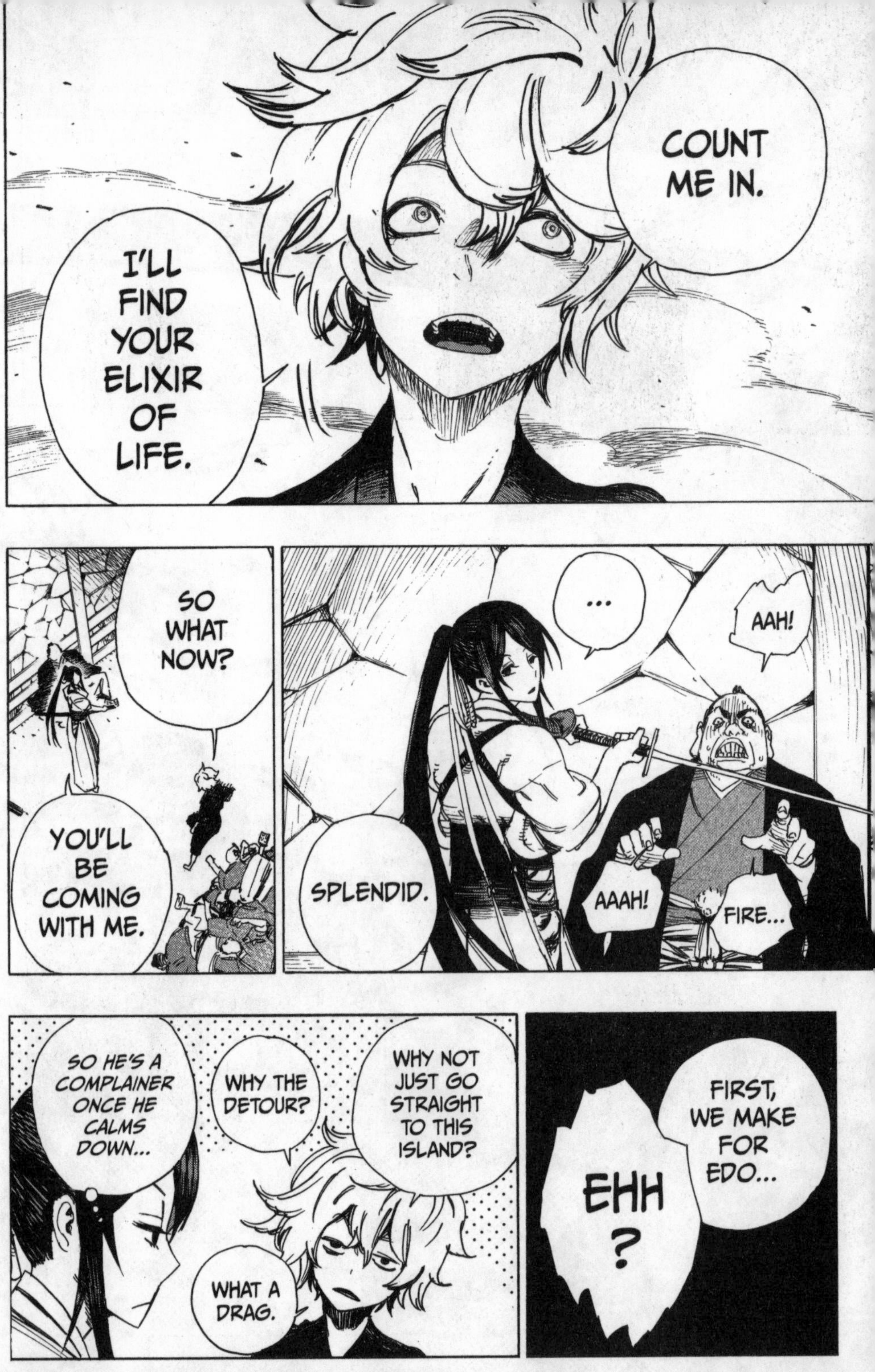
COUNT ME IN.
I'LL FIND YOUR ELIXIR OF LIFE.
AAH!
...
FIRE...
AAAH!
SPLENDID.
SO WHAT NOW?
YOU'LL BE COMING WITH ME.
FIRST, WE MAKE FOR EDO...
EHH?
WHY NOT JUST GO STRAIGHT TO THIS ISLAND?
WHY THE DETOUR?
SO HE'S A COMPLAINER ONCE HE CALMS DOWN...
WHAT A DRAG.

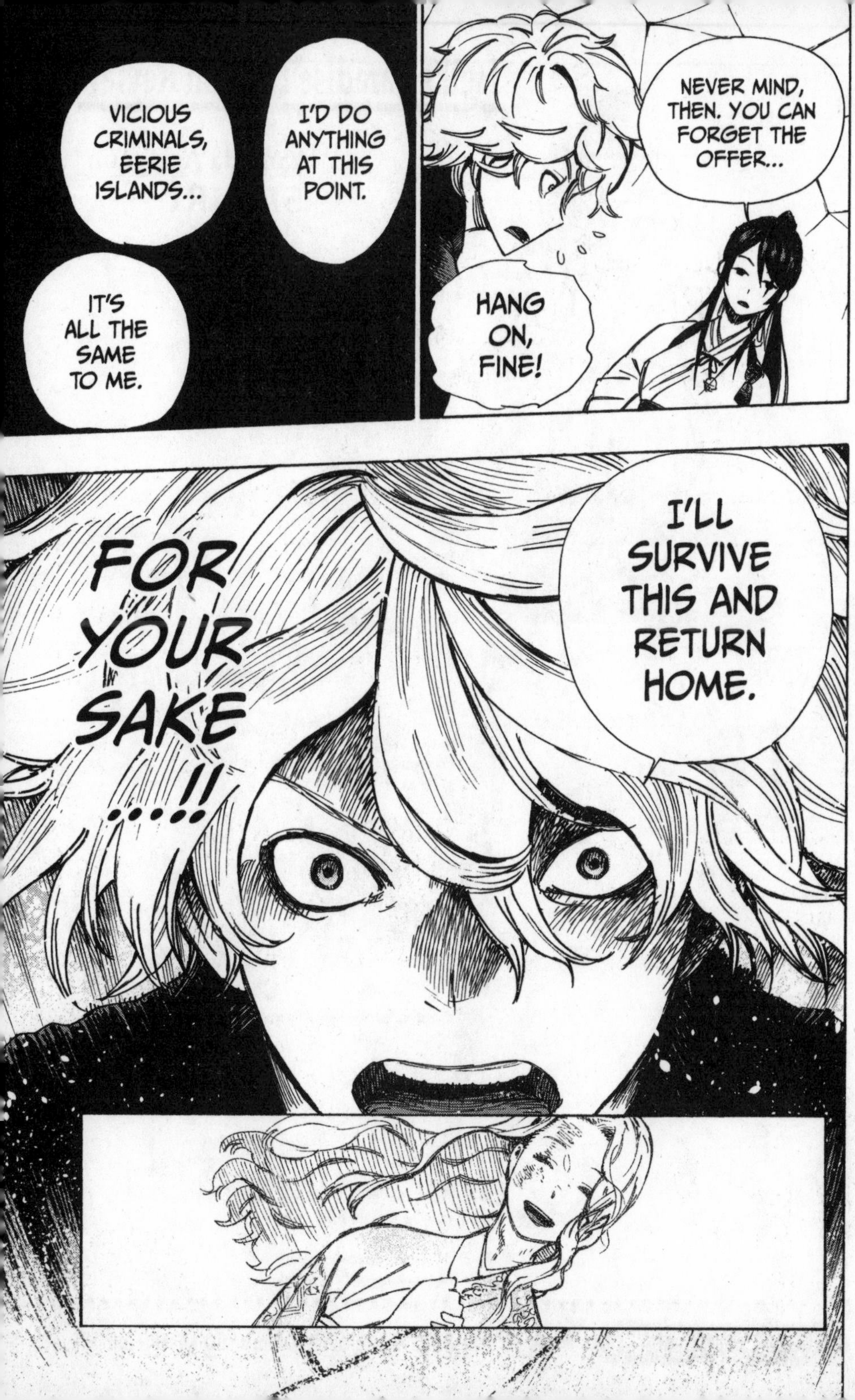
NEVER MIND, THEN. YOU CAN FORGET THE OFFER...
HANG ON, FINE!
I'D DO ANYTHING AT THIS POINT.
VICIOUS CRIMINALS, EERIE ISLANDS...
IT'S ALL THE SAME TO ME.
I'LL SURVIVE THIS AND RETURN HOME.
FOR YOUR SAKE....!!

Hell's Paradise Fashion Review

Yamada Asaemon
SAGIRI

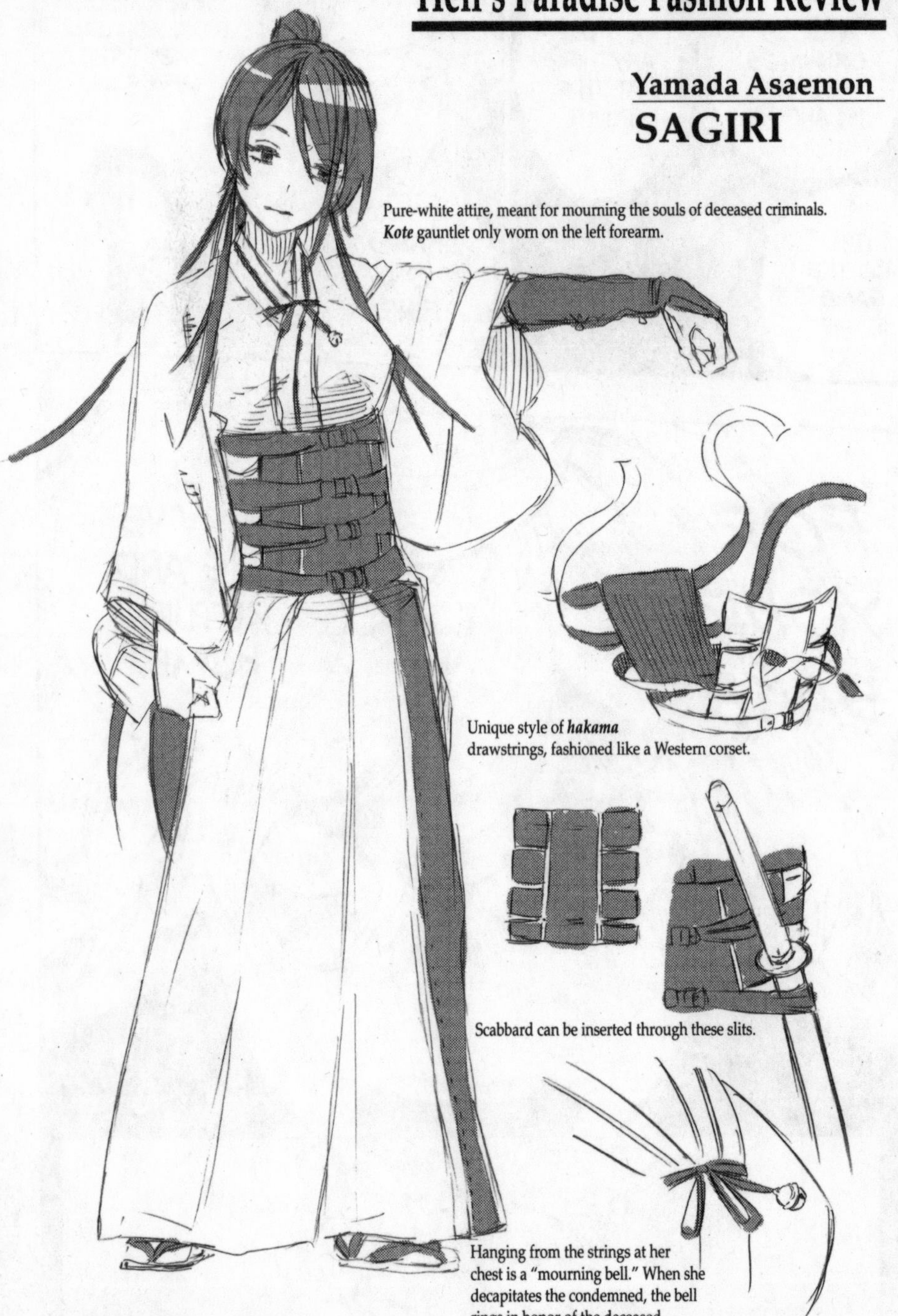

Pure-white attire, meant for mourning the souls of deceased criminals.
Kote gauntlet only worn on the left forearm.
Unique style of *hakama* drawstrings, fashioned like a Western corset.
Scabbard can be inserted through these slits.
Hanging from the strings at her chest is a "mourning bell." When she decapitates the condemned, the bell rings in honor of the deceased.

EVALUATION ► CHIC SAMURAI CHICK ★★☆ MIXING IT UP WITH THE HAKAMA DRAWSTRINGS ADDS A TOUCH OF FEMININITY.

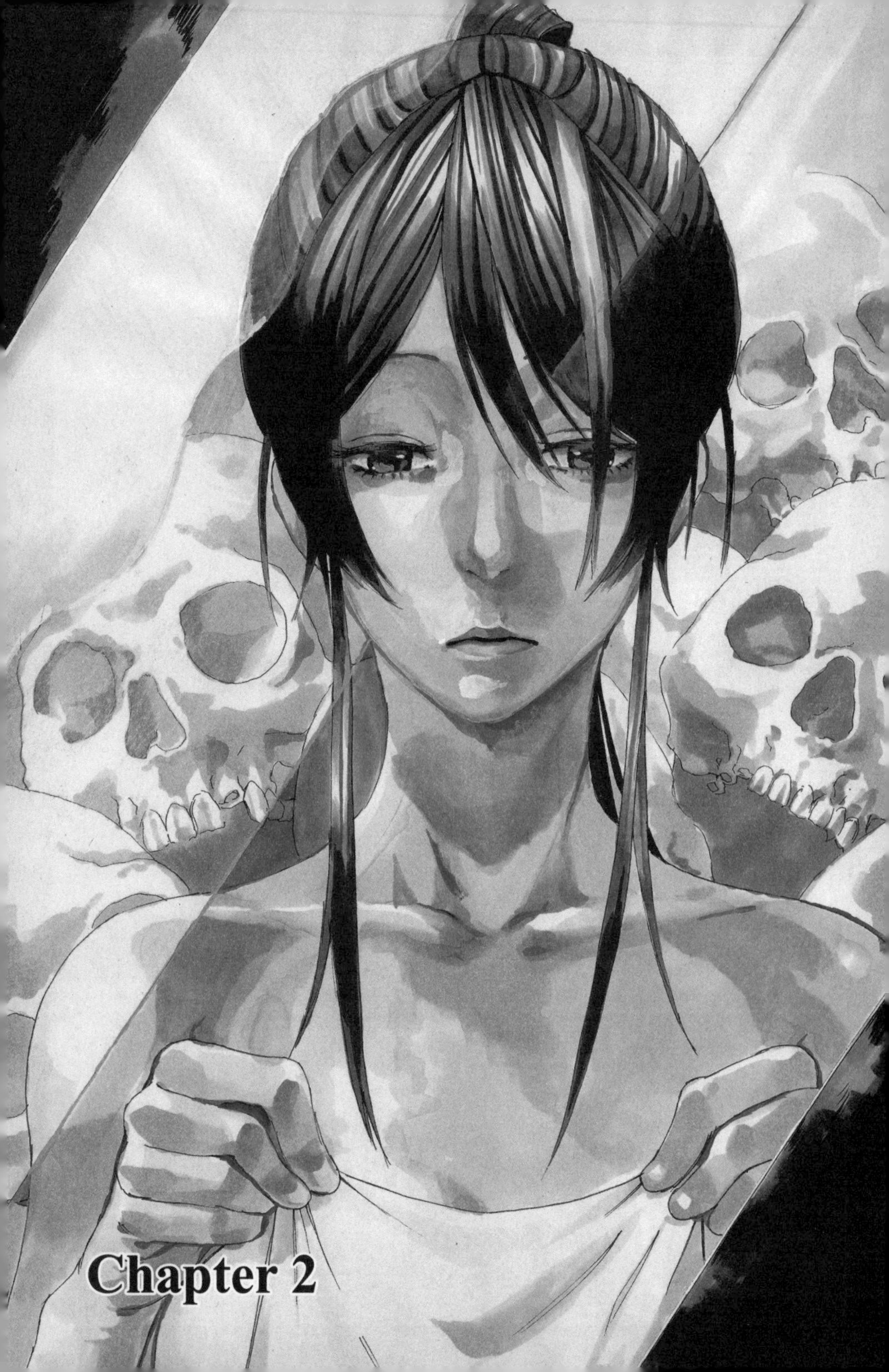

Chapter 2

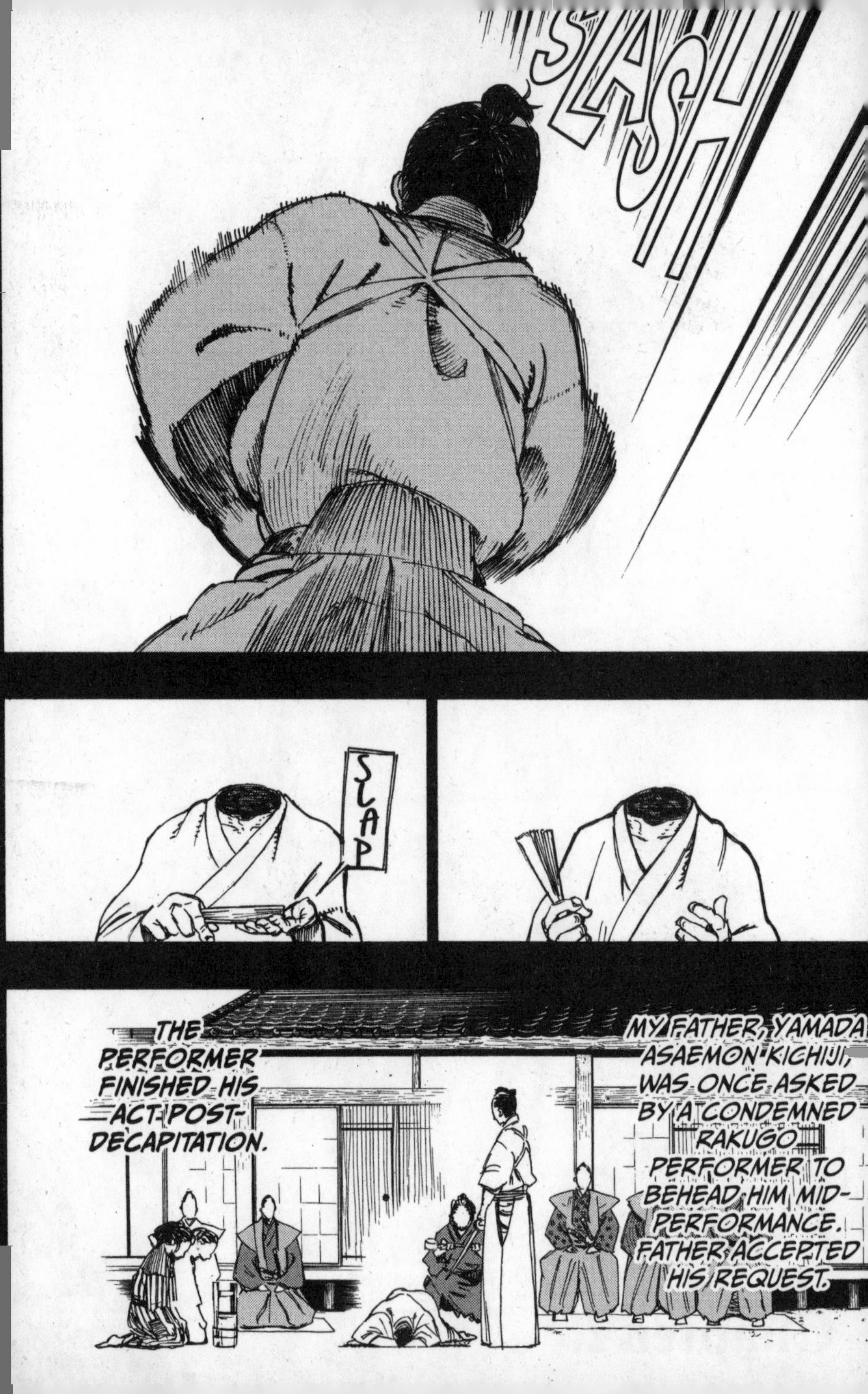
SLASH
SLAP
MY FATHER, YAMADA ASAEMON KICHIJI, WAS ONCE ASKED BY A CONDEMNED RAKUGO PERFORMER TO BEHEAD HIM MID-PERFORMANCE. FATHER ACCEPTED HIS REQUEST.
THE PERFORMER FINISHED HIS ACT POST-DECAPITATION.

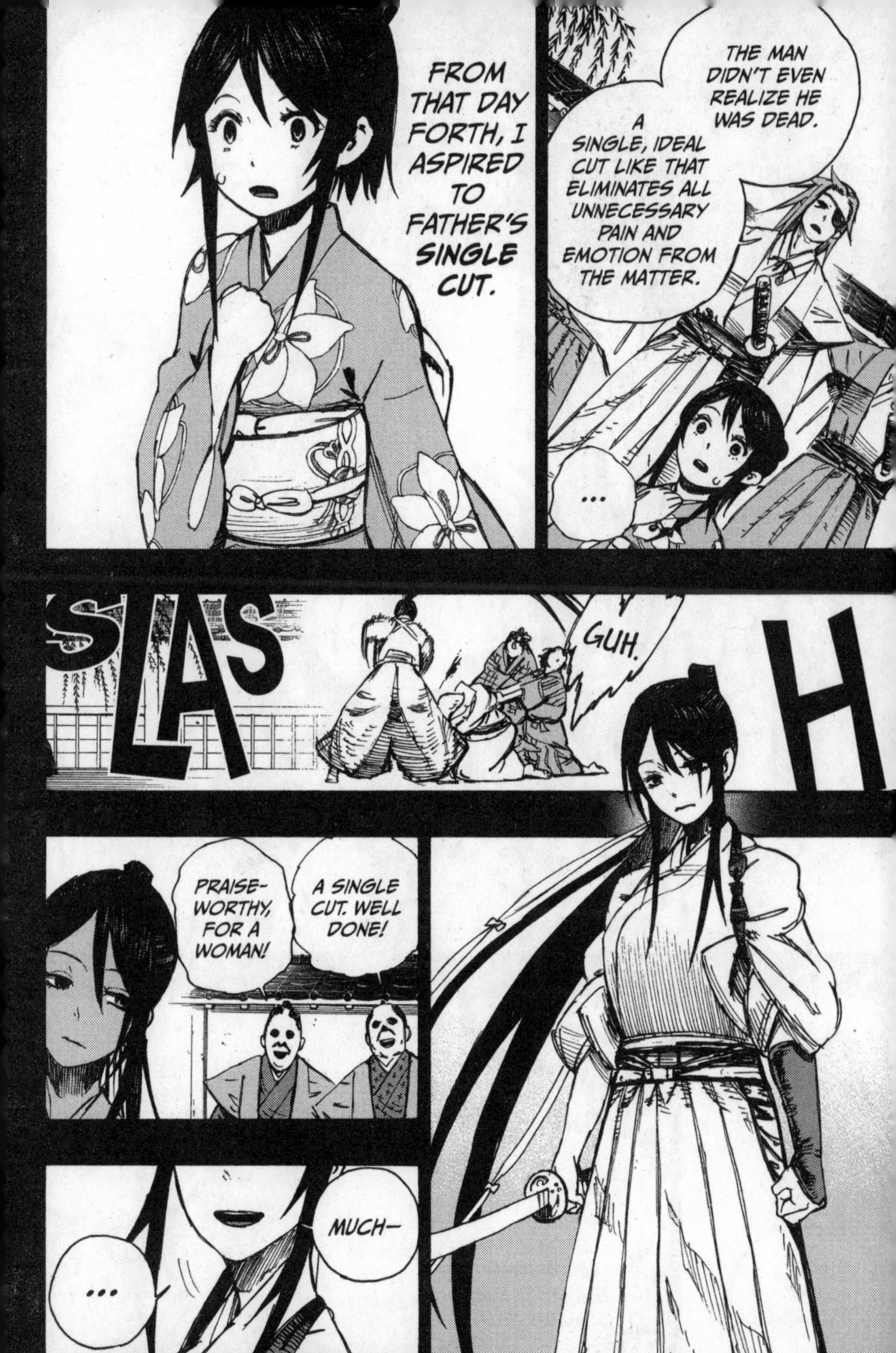
THE MAN DIDN'T EVEN REALIZE HE WAS DEAD.
A SINGLE, IDEAL CUT LIKE THAT ELIMINATES ALL UNNECESSARY PAIN AND EMOTION FROM THE MATTER.
...
FROM THAT DAY FORTH, I ASPIRED TO FATHER'S SINGLE CUT.
SLASH
GUH.
A SINGLE CUT. WELL DONE!
PRAISE-WORTHY, FOR A WOMAN!
MUCH—
...

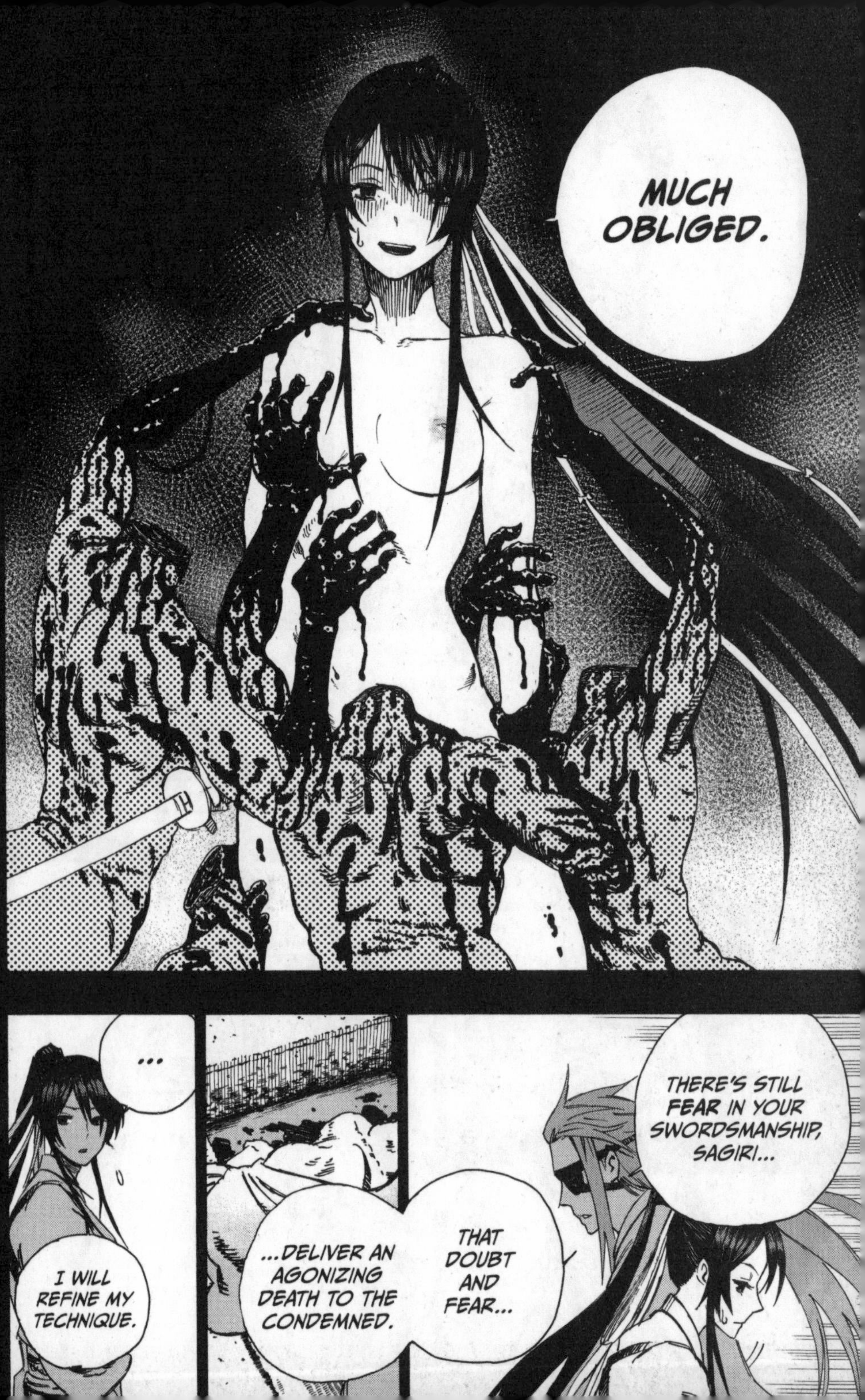
MUCH OBLIGED.
THERE'S STILL FEAR IN YOUR SWORDSMANSHIP, SAGIRI...
THAT DOUBT AND FEAR...
...DELIVER AN AGONIZING DEATH TO THE CONDEMNED.
...
I WILL REFINE MY TECHNIQUE.

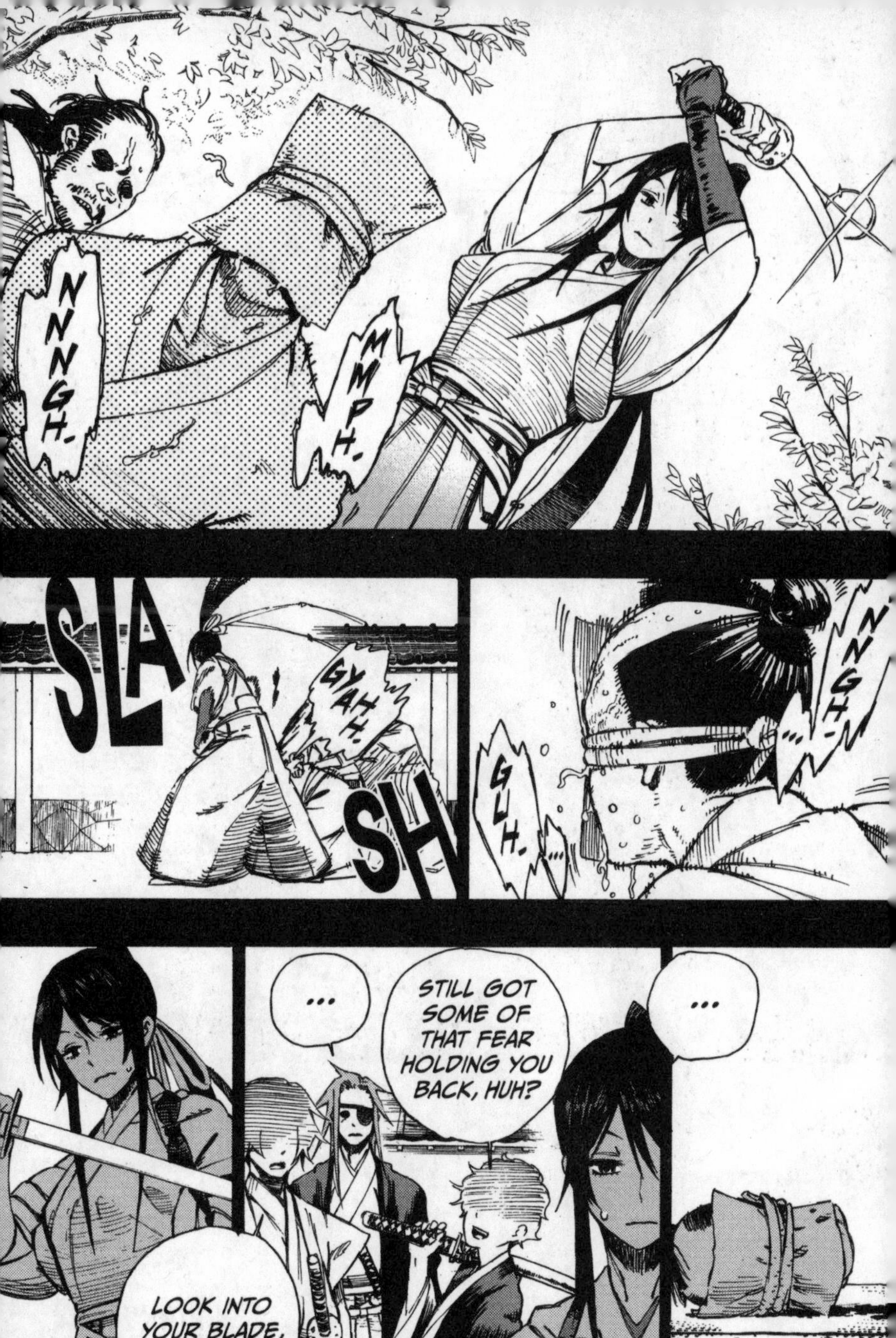
MMMPH-
NNNGH-
NNNGH-...
GUH-...
GYAHH.
SLA
SH
...
STILL GOT SOME OF THAT FEAR HOLDING YOU BACK, HUH?
...
LOOK INTO YOUR BLADE, SAGIRI.

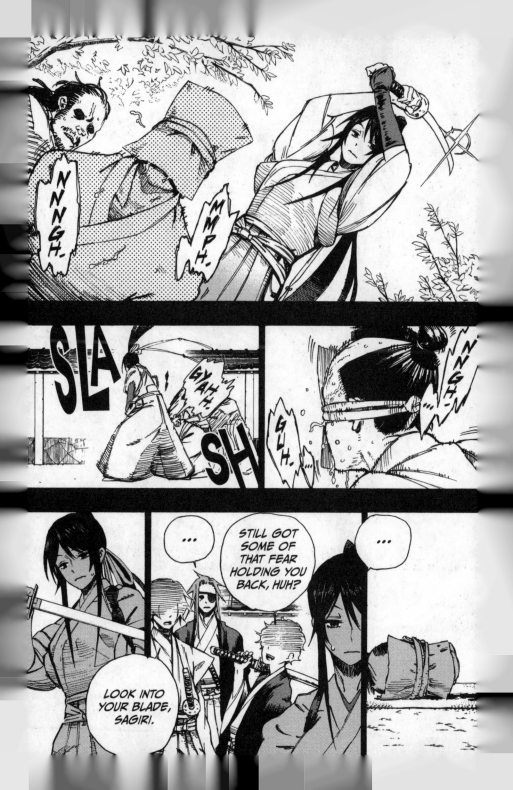

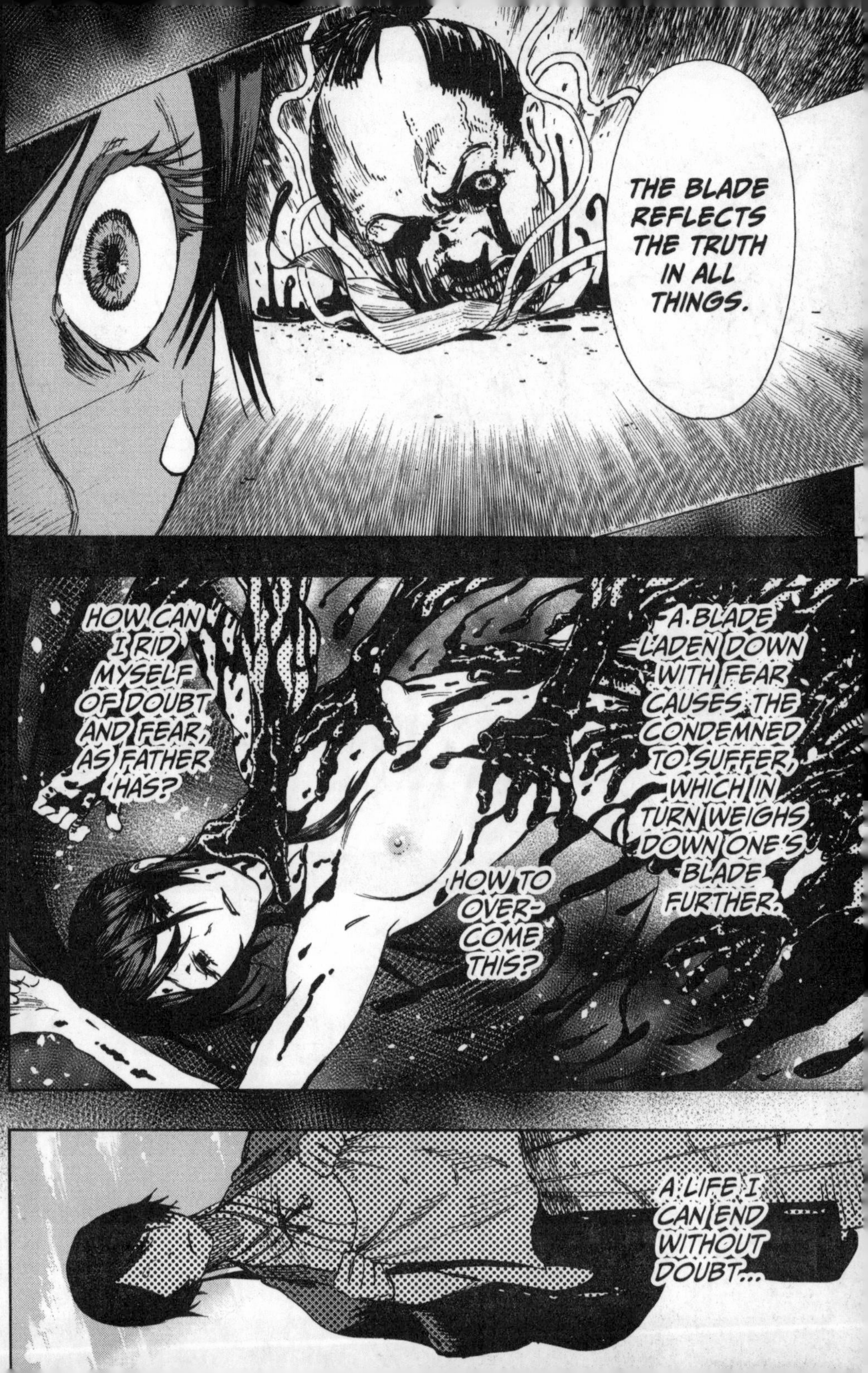
THE BLADE REFLECTS THE TRUTH IN ALL THINGS.
A BLADE LADEN DOWN WITH FEAR CAUSES THE CONDEMNED TO SUFFER, WHICH IN TURN WEIGHS DOWN ONE'S BLADE FURTHER.
HOW CAN I RID MYSELF OF DOUBT AND FEAR, AS FATHER HAS?
HOW TO OVER-COME THIS?
A LIFE I CAN END WITHOUT DOUBT...

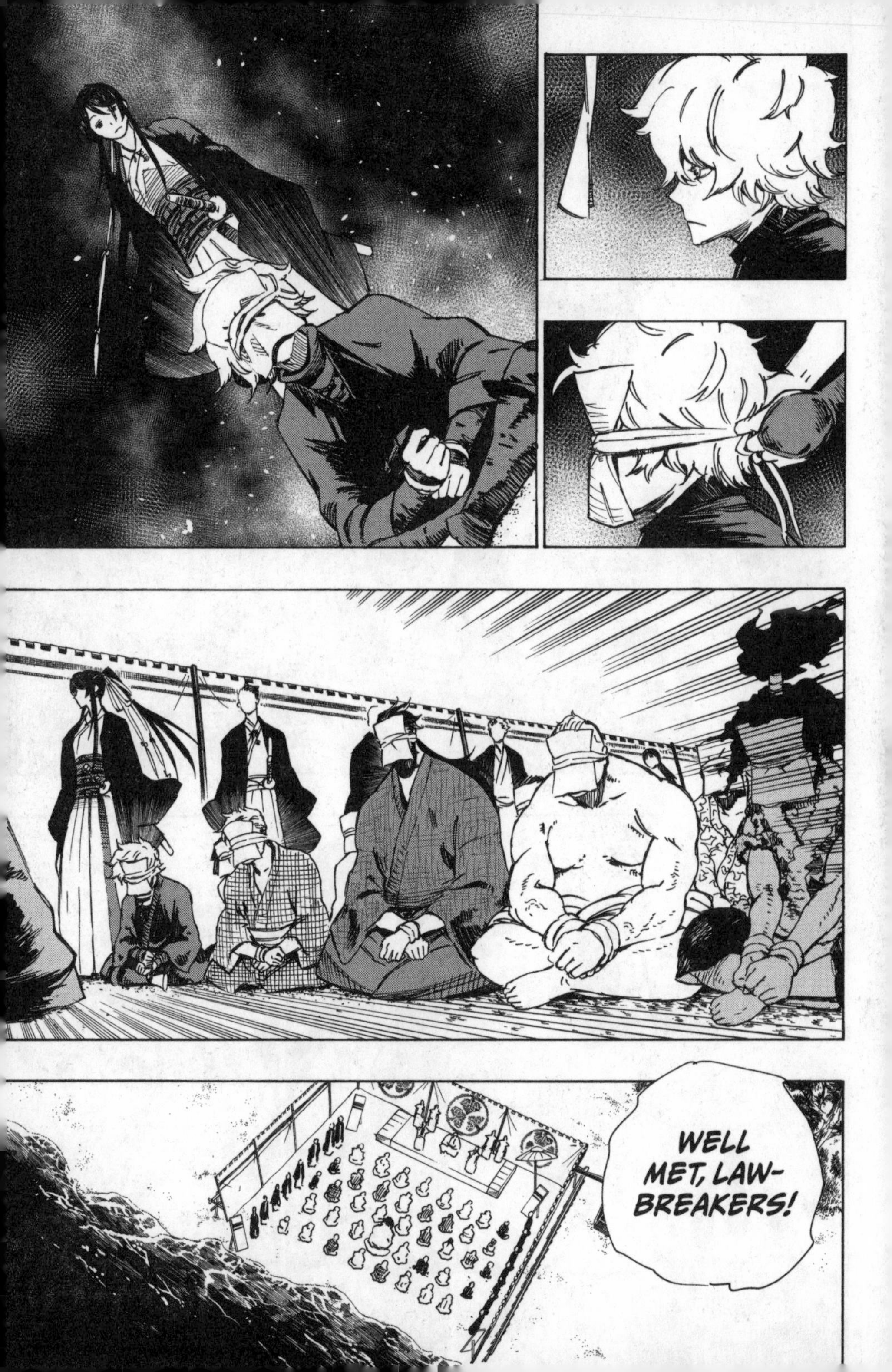
WELL MET, LAW-BREAKERS!

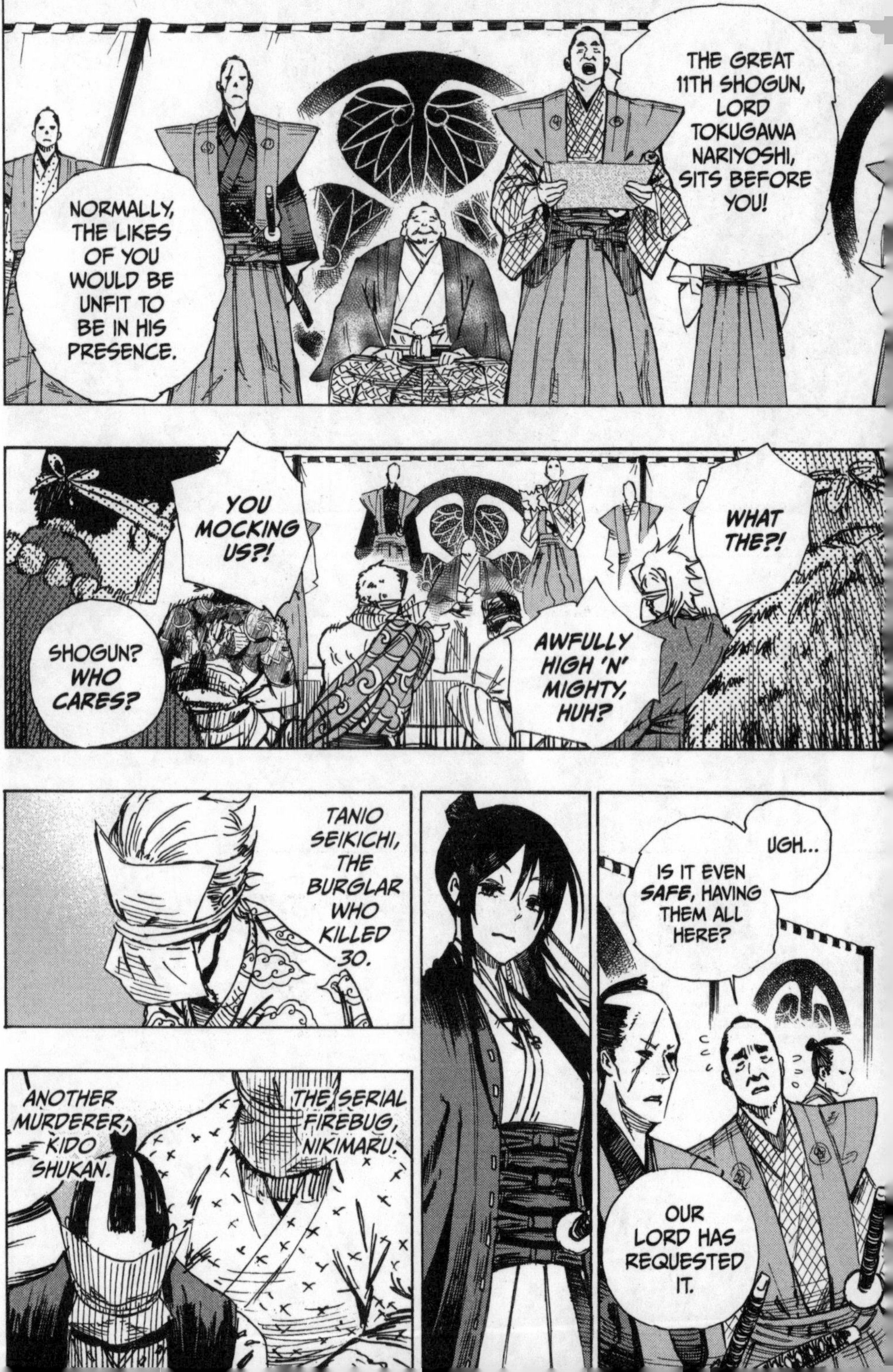
THE GREAT 11TH SHOGUN, LORD TOKUGAWA NARIYOSHI, SITS BEFORE YOU!
NORMALLY, THE LIKES OF YOU WOULD BE UNFIT TO BE IN HIS PRESENCE.
WHAT THE?!
AWFULLY HIGH 'N' MIGHTY, HUH?
YOU MOCKING US?!
SHOGUN? WHO CARES?
UGH...
IS IT EVEN SAFE, HAVING THEM ALL HERE?
OUR LORD HAS REQUESTED IT.
TANIO SEIKICHI, THE BURGLAR WHO KILLED 30.
THE SERIAL FIREBUG, NIKIMARU.
ANOTHER MURDERER, KIDO SHUKAN.

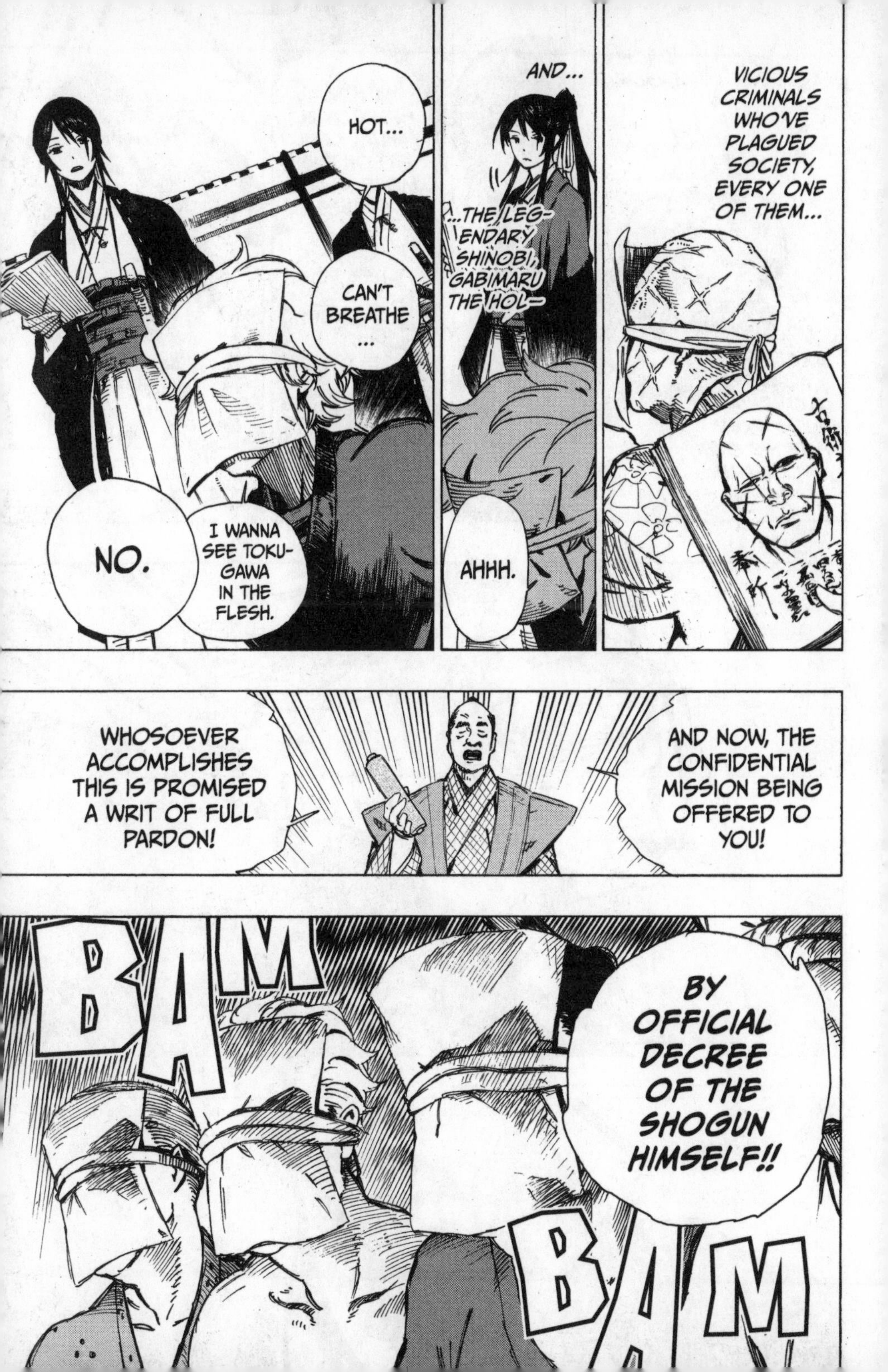
VICIOUS CRIMINALS WHO'VE PLAGUED SOCIETY, EVERY ONE OF THEM...
AND...
...THE LEGENDARY SHINOBI, GABIMARU THE HOL–
AHHH.
HOT...
CAN'T BREATHE ...
I WANNA SEE TOKUGAWA IN THE FLESH.
NO.
AND NOW, THE CONFIDENTIAL MISSION BEING OFFERED TO YOU!
WHOSOEVER ACCOMPLISHES THIS IS PROMISED A WRIT OF FULL PARDON!
BY OFFICIAL DECREE OF THE SHOGUN HIMSELF!!
BAM
BAM

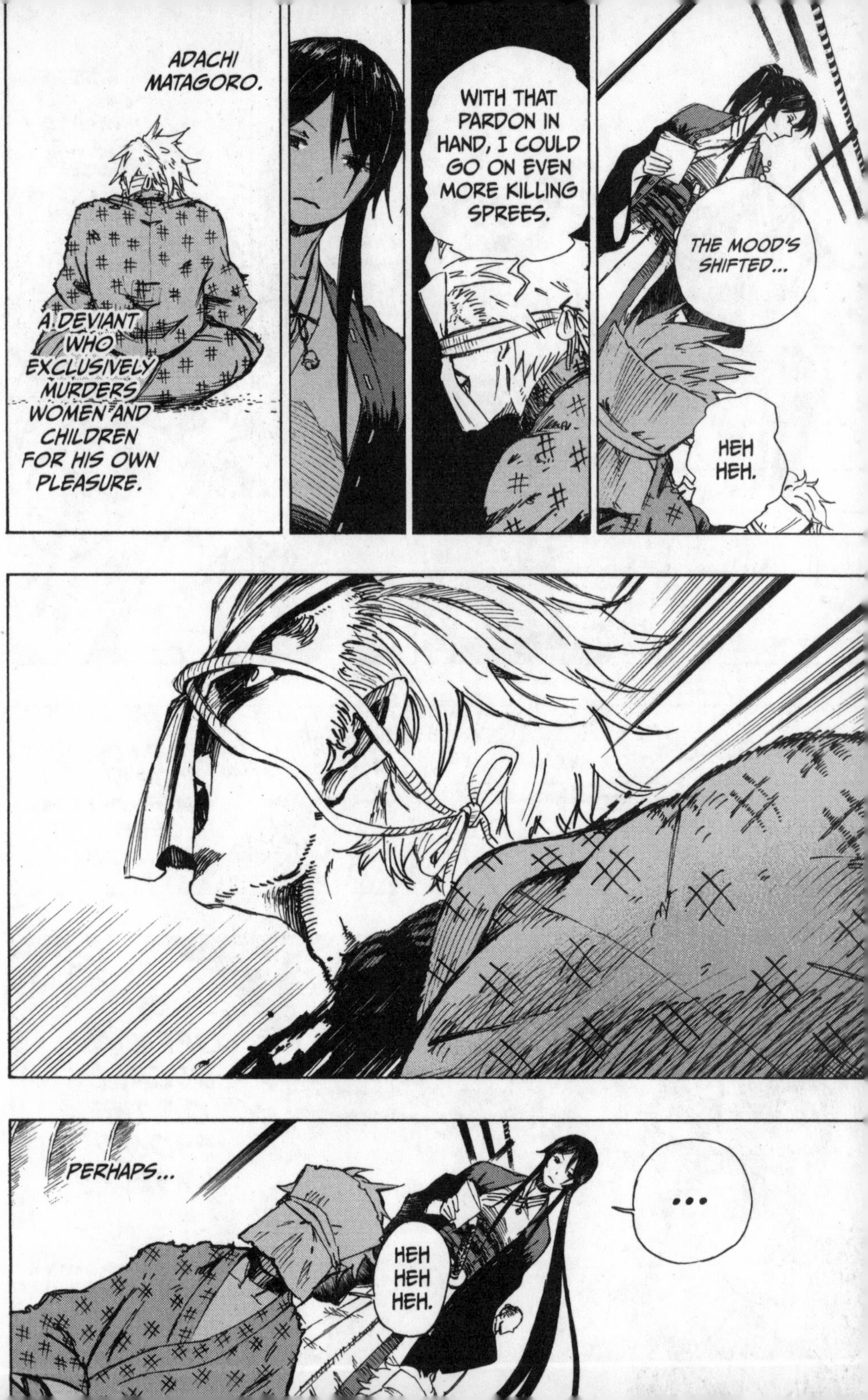

THE MOOD'S SHIFTED...
HEH HEH.
WITH THAT PARDON IN HAND, I COULD GO ON EVEN MORE KILLING SPREES.
ADACHI MATAGORO.
A DEVIANT WHO EXCLUSIVELY MURDERS WOMEN AND CHILDREN FOR HIS OWN PLEASURE.
...
HEH HEH HEH.
PERHAPS...

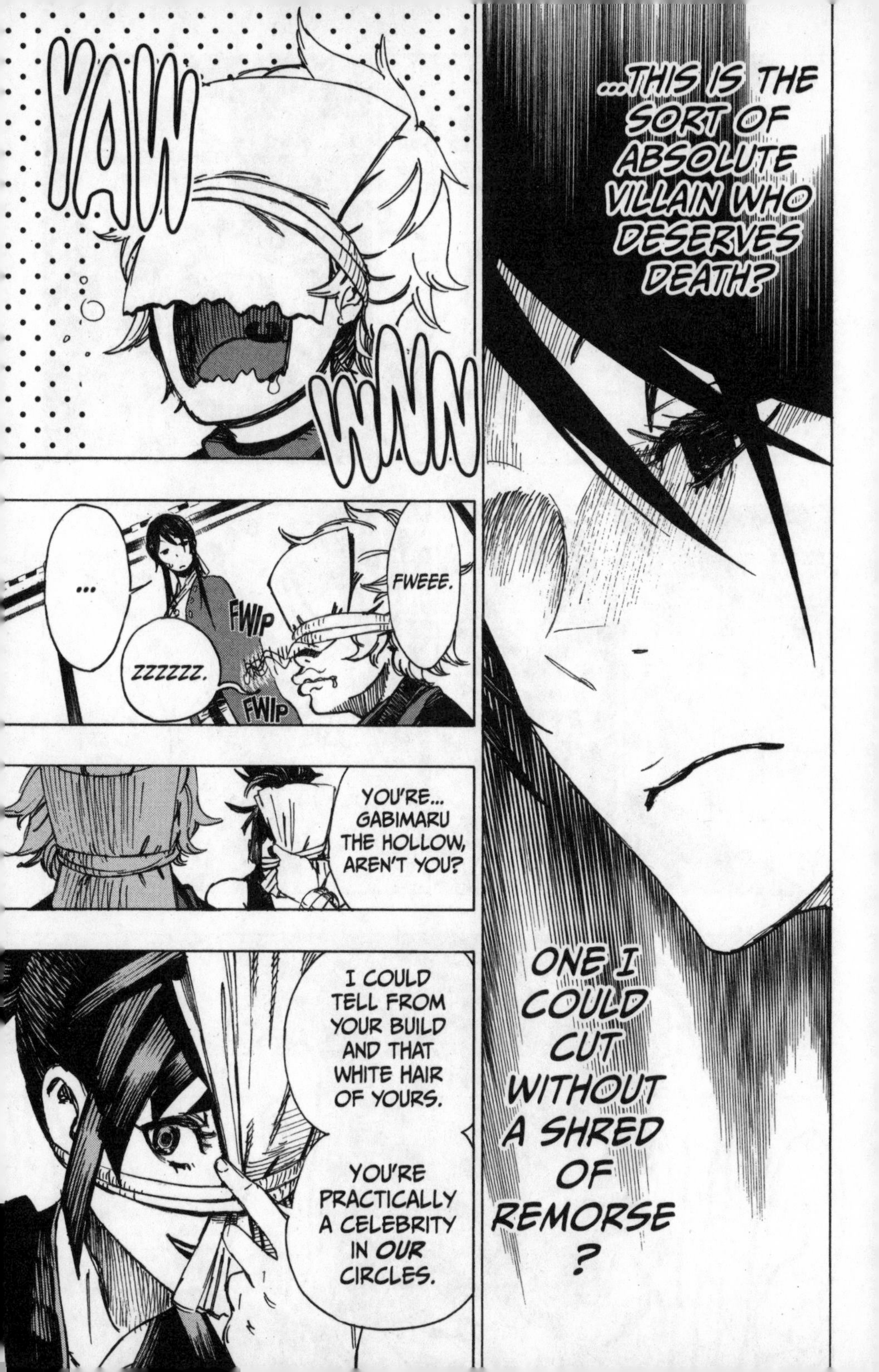
...THIS IS THE SORT OF ABSOLUTE VILLAIN WHO DESERVES DEATH?
ONE I COULD CUT WITHOUT A SHRED OF REMORSE ?
YAW
WNN
FWEEE.
...
FWIP
ZZZZZZ.
FWIP
YOU'RE... GABIMARU THE HOLLOW, AREN'T YOU?
I COULD TELL FROM YOUR BUILD AND THAT WHITE HAIR OF YOURS.
YOU'RE PRACTICALLY A CELEBRITY IN *OUR* CIRCLES.

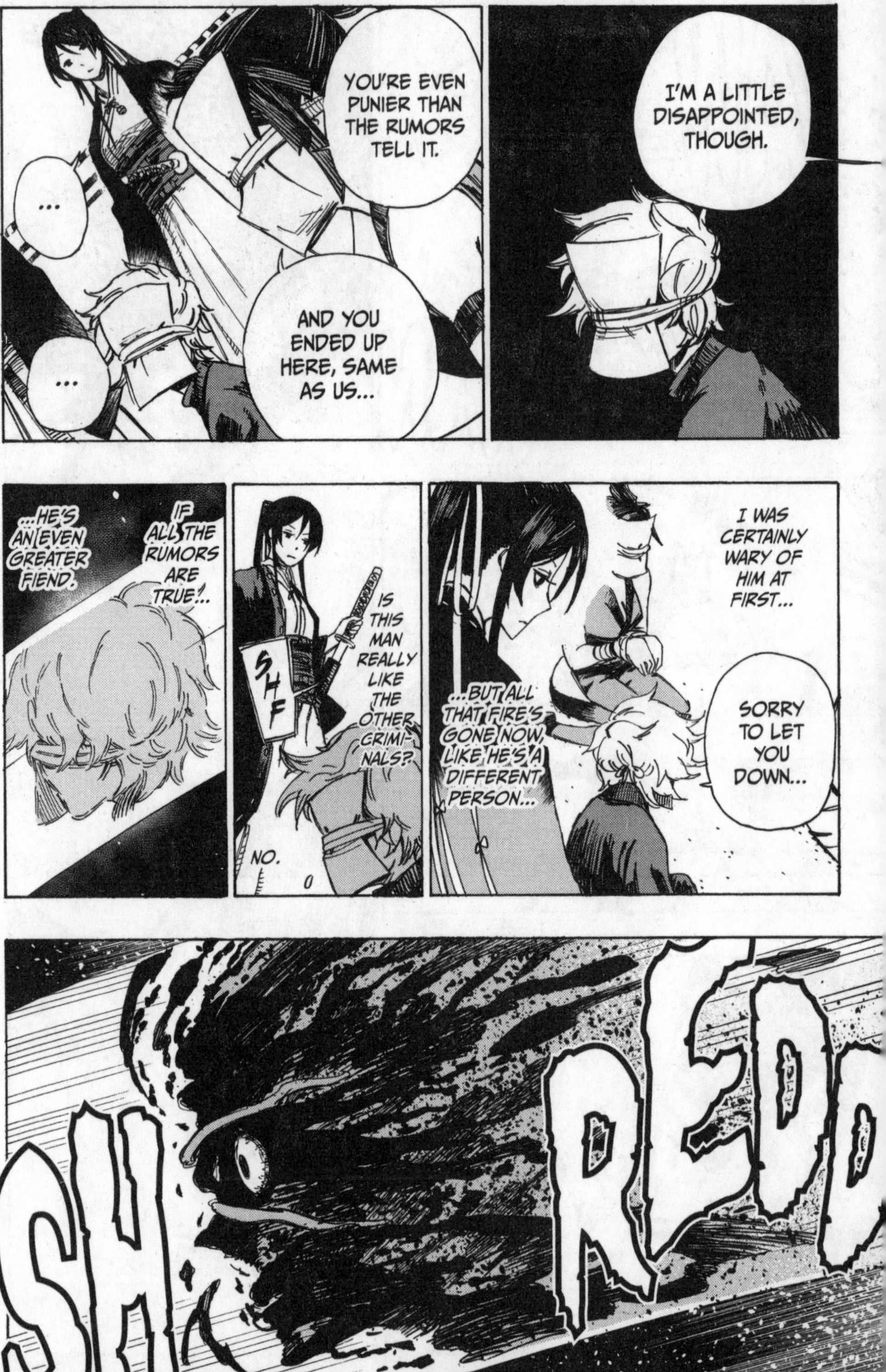
I'M A LITTLE DISAPPOINTED, THOUGH.
YOU'RE EVEN PUNIER THAN THE RUMORS TELL IT.
...
AND YOU ENDED UP HERE, SAME AS US...
...
I WAS CERTAINLY WARY OF HIM AT FIRST...
SORRY TO LET YOU DOWN...
...BUT ALL THAT FIRE'S GONE NOW, LIKE HE'S A DIFFERENT PERSON...
IS THIS MAN REALLY LIKE THE OTHER CRIMINALS?
SHF
NO.
IF ALL THE RUMORS ARE TRUE...
...HE'S AN EVEN GREATER FIEND.
SHREDD

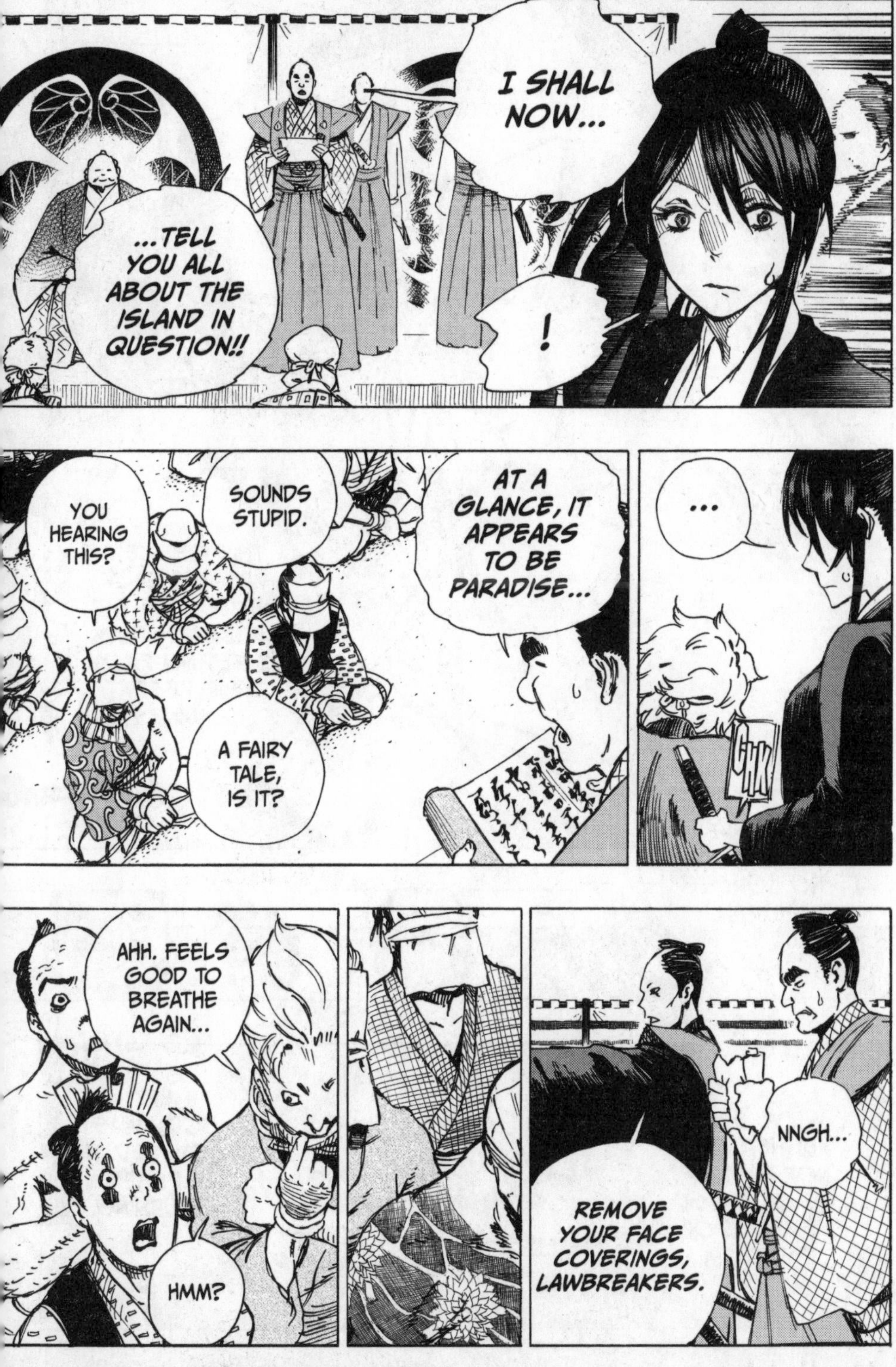
I SHALL NOW...
...TELL YOU ALL ABOUT THE ISLAND IN QUESTION!!
!
...
CHK
AT A GLANCE, IT APPEARS TO BE PARADISE...
SOUNDS STUPID.
YOU HEARING THIS?
A FAIRY TALE, IS IT?
NNGH...
REMOVE YOUR FACE COVERINGS, LAWBREAKERS.
AHH. FEELS GOOD TO BREATHE AGAIN...
HMM?

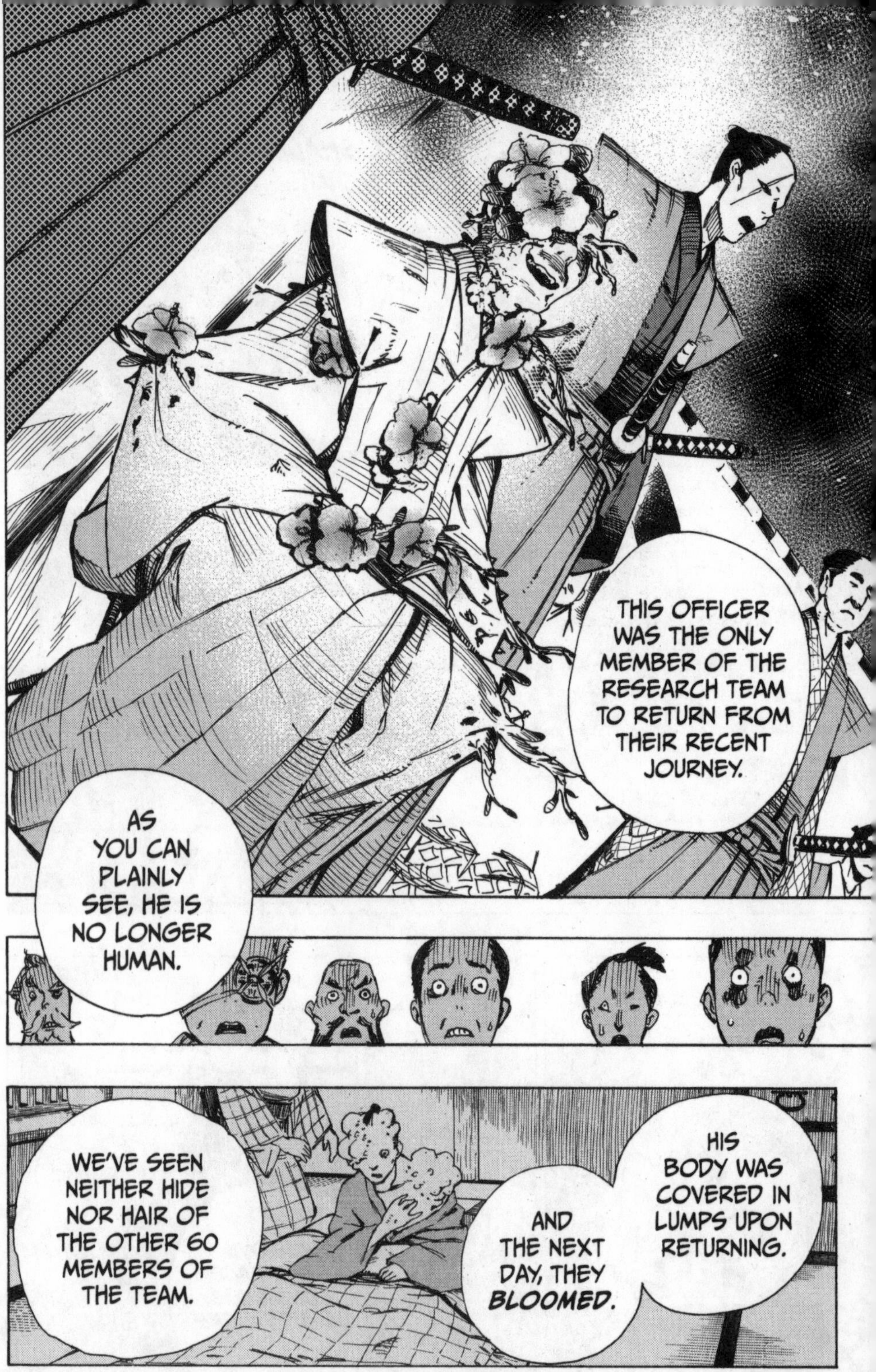
THIS OFFICER WAS THE ONLY MEMBER OF THE RESEARCH TEAM TO RETURN FROM THEIR RECENT JOURNEY.
AS YOU CAN PLAINLY SEE, HE IS NO LONGER HUMAN.
HIS BODY WAS COVERED IN LUMPS UPON RETURNING.
AND THE NEXT DAY, THEY *BLOOMED*.
WE'VE SEEN NEITHER HIDE NOR HAIR OF THE OTHER 60 MEMBERS OF THE TEAM.

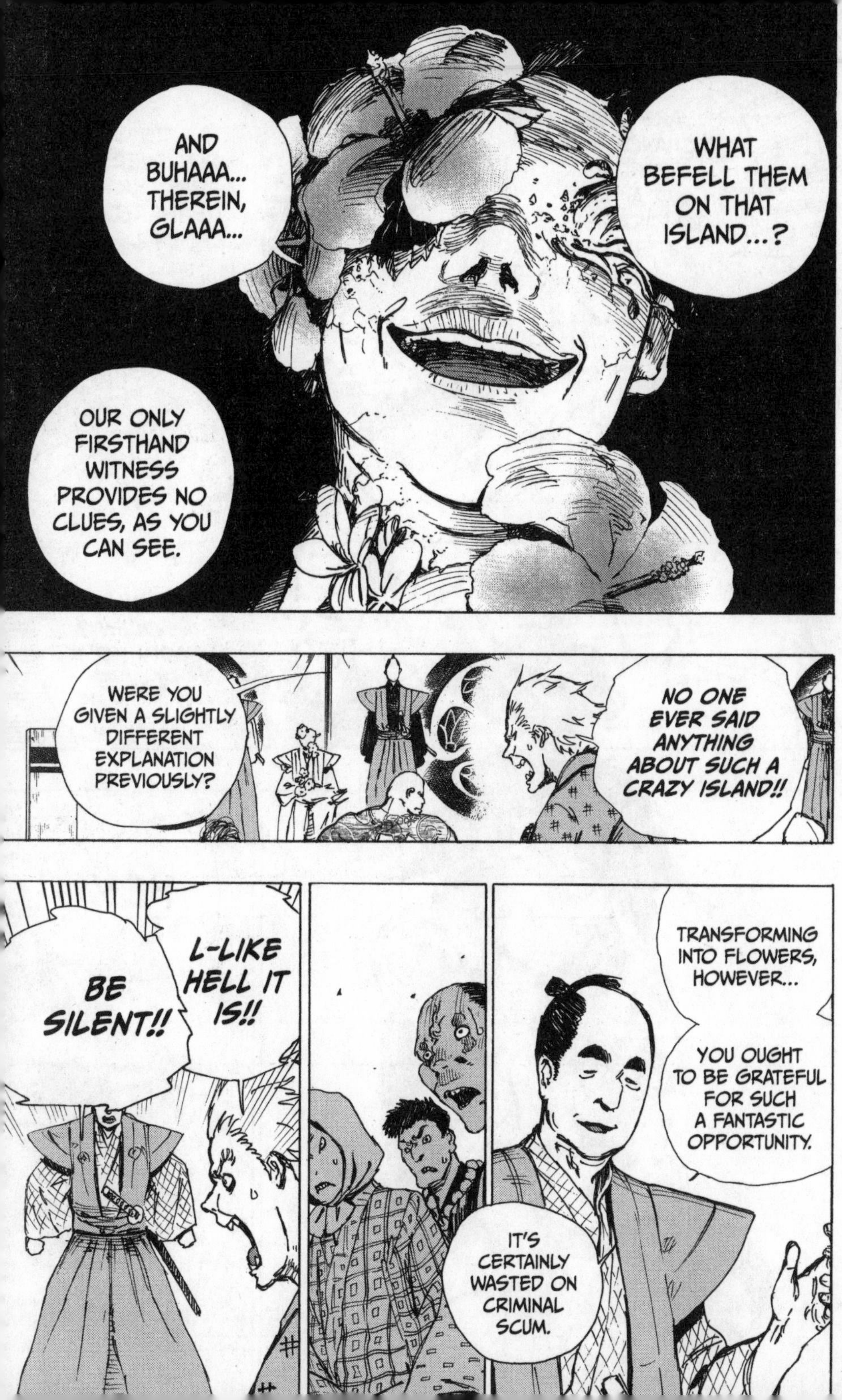
WHAT BEFELL THEM ON THAT ISLAND...?
AND BUHAAA... THEREIN, GLAAA...
OUR ONLY FIRSTHAND WITNESS PROVIDES NO CLUES, AS YOU CAN SEE.
NO ONE EVER SAID ANYTHING ABOUT SUCH A CRAZY ISLAND!!
WERE YOU GIVEN A SLIGHTLY DIFFERENT EXPLANATION PREVIOUSLY?
TRANSFORMING INTO FLOWERS, HOWEVER...
YOU OUGHT TO BE GRATEFUL FOR SUCH A FANTASTIC OPPORTUNITY.
IT'S CERTAINLY WASTED ON CRIMINAL SCUM.
L-LIKE HELL IT IS!!
BE SILENT!!

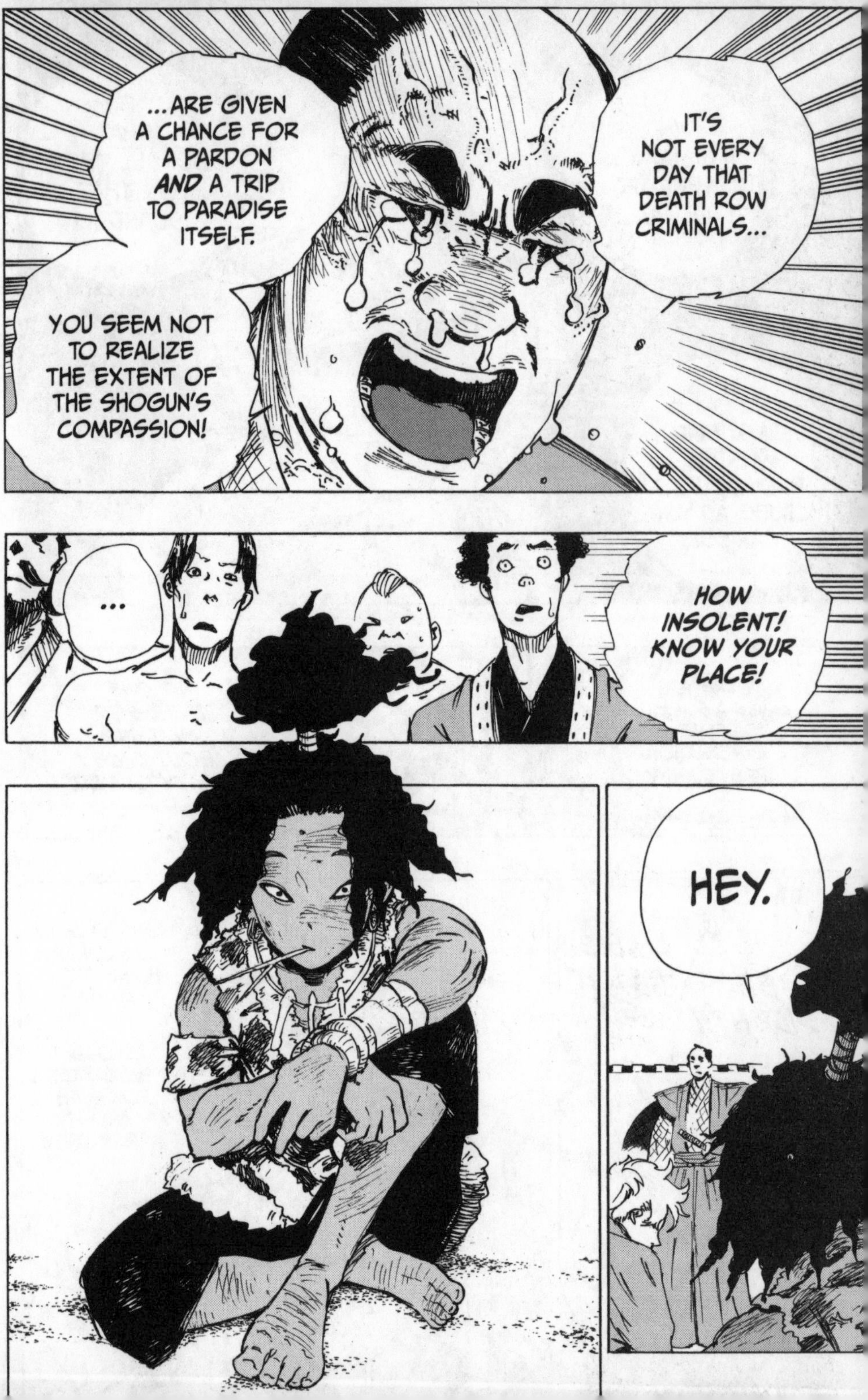
IT'S NOT EVERY DAY THAT DEATH ROW CRIMINALS...
...ARE GIVEN A CHANCE FOR A PARDON *AND* A TRIP TO PARADISE ITSELF.
YOU SEEM NOT TO REALIZE THE EXTENT OF THE SHOGUN'S COMPASSION!
HOW INSOLENT! KNOW YOUR PLACE!
...
HEY.

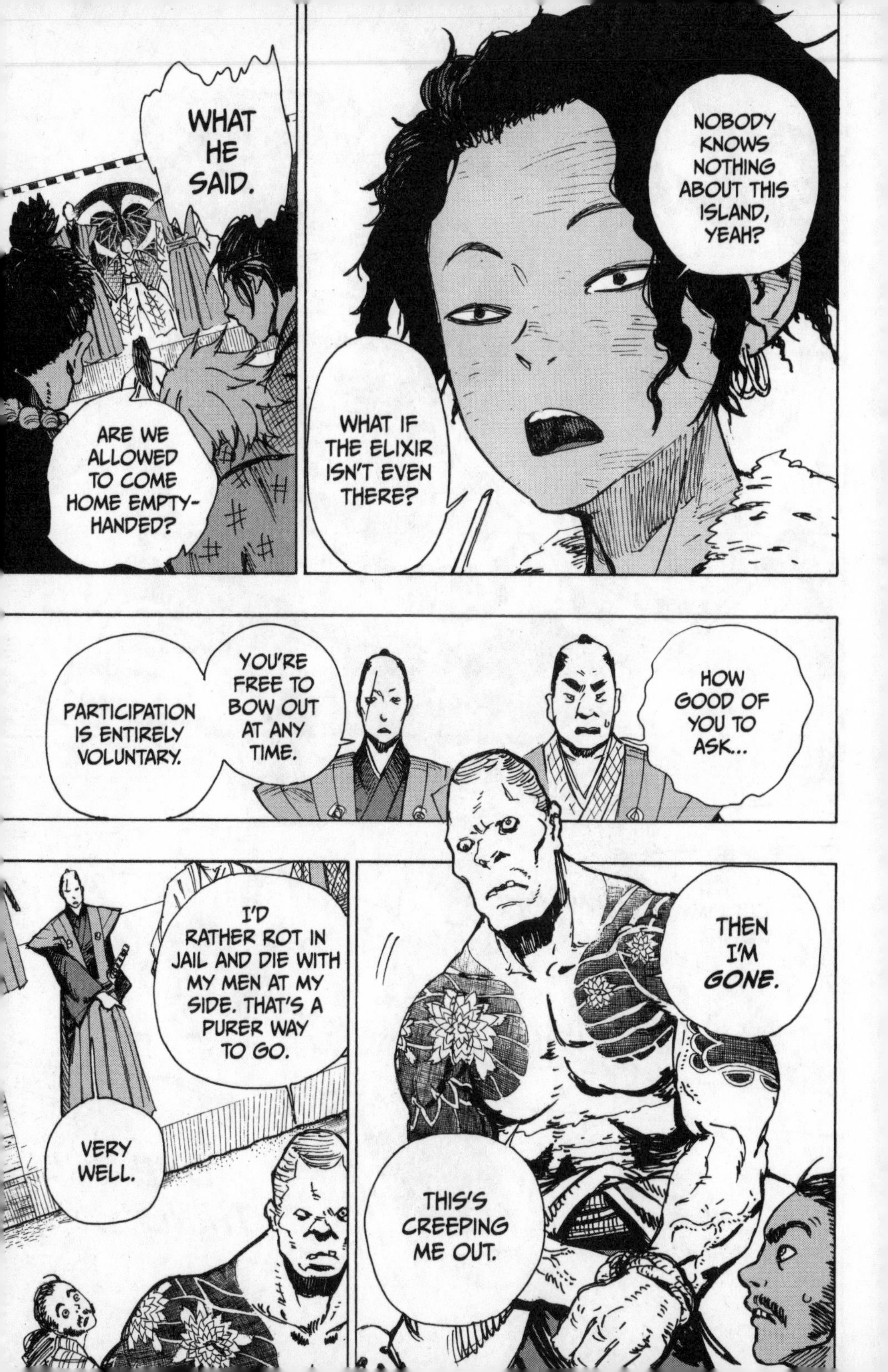
NOBODY KNOWS NOTHING ABOUT THIS ISLAND, YEAH?
WHAT IF THE ELIXIR ISN'T EVEN THERE?
WHAT HE SAID.
ARE WE ALLOWED TO COME HOME EMPTY-HANDED?
HOW GOOD OF YOU TO ASK...
YOU'RE FREE TO BOW OUT AT ANY TIME.
PARTICIPATION IS ENTIRELY VOLUNTARY.
THEN I'M *GONE*.
THIS'S CREEPING ME OUT.
I'D RATHER ROT IN JAIL AND DIE WITH MY MEN AT MY SIDE. THAT'S A PURER WAY TO GO.
VERY WELL.

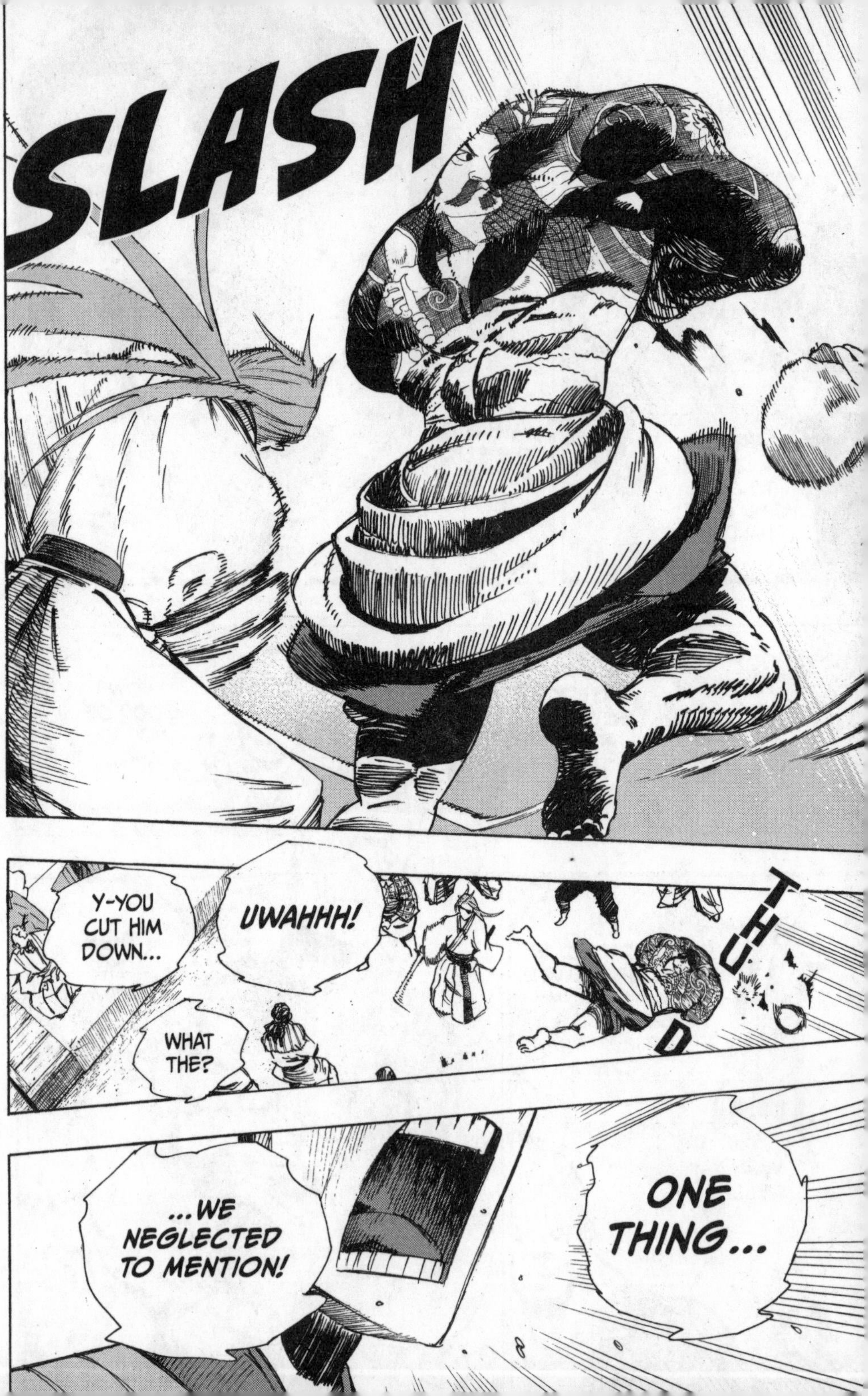
SLASH
THUD
UWAHHH!
Y-YOU CUT HIM DOWN...
WHAT THE?
ONE THING...
...WE NEGLECTED TO MENTION!

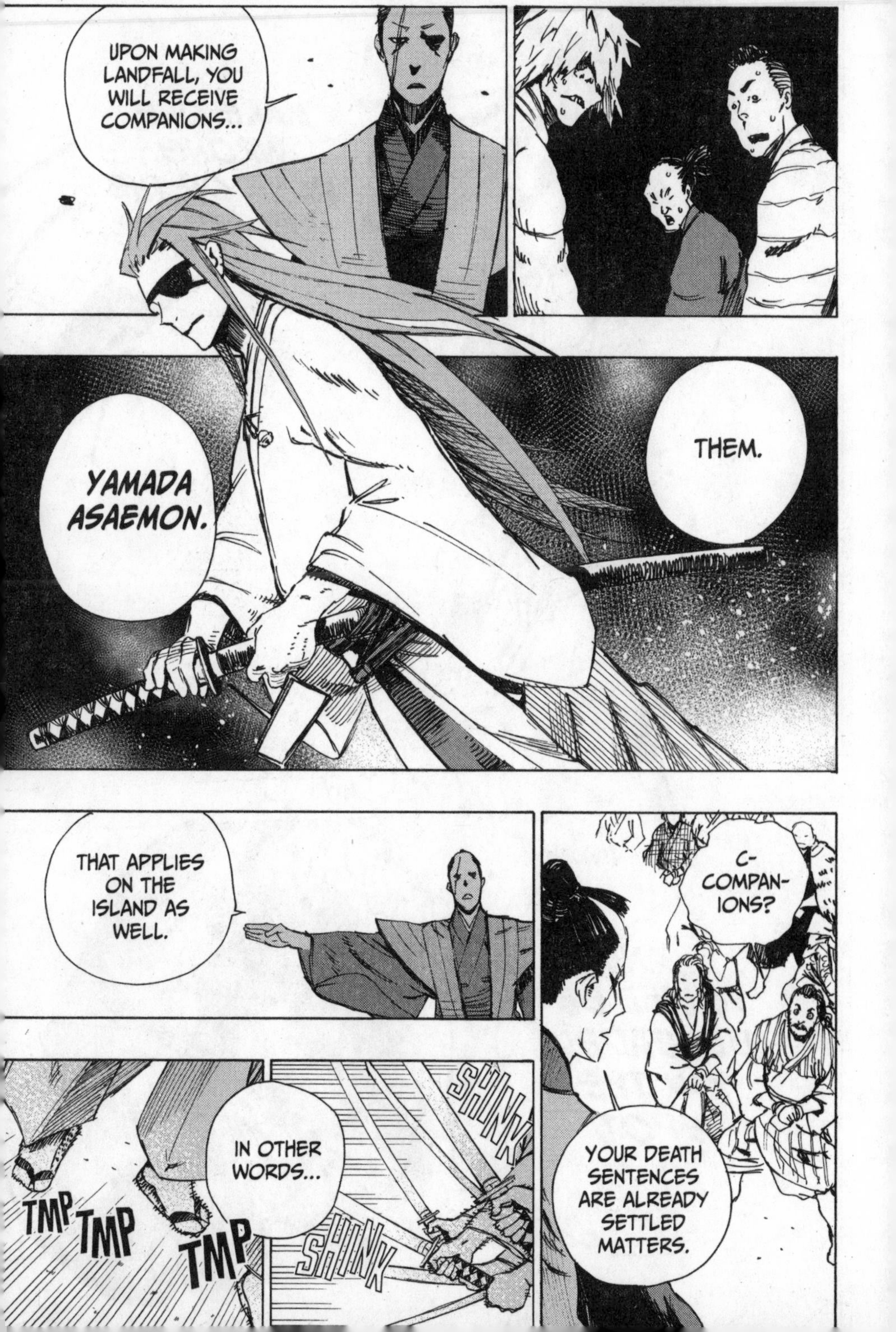
UPON MAKING LANDFALL, YOU WILL RECEIVE COMPANIONS...
THEM.
YAMADA ASAEMON.
C-COMPANIONS?
YOUR DEATH SENTENCES ARE ALREADY SETTLED MATTERS.
THAT APPLIES ON THE ISLAND AS WELL.
SHINK
IN OTHER WORDS...
SHINK
TMP TMP
TMP

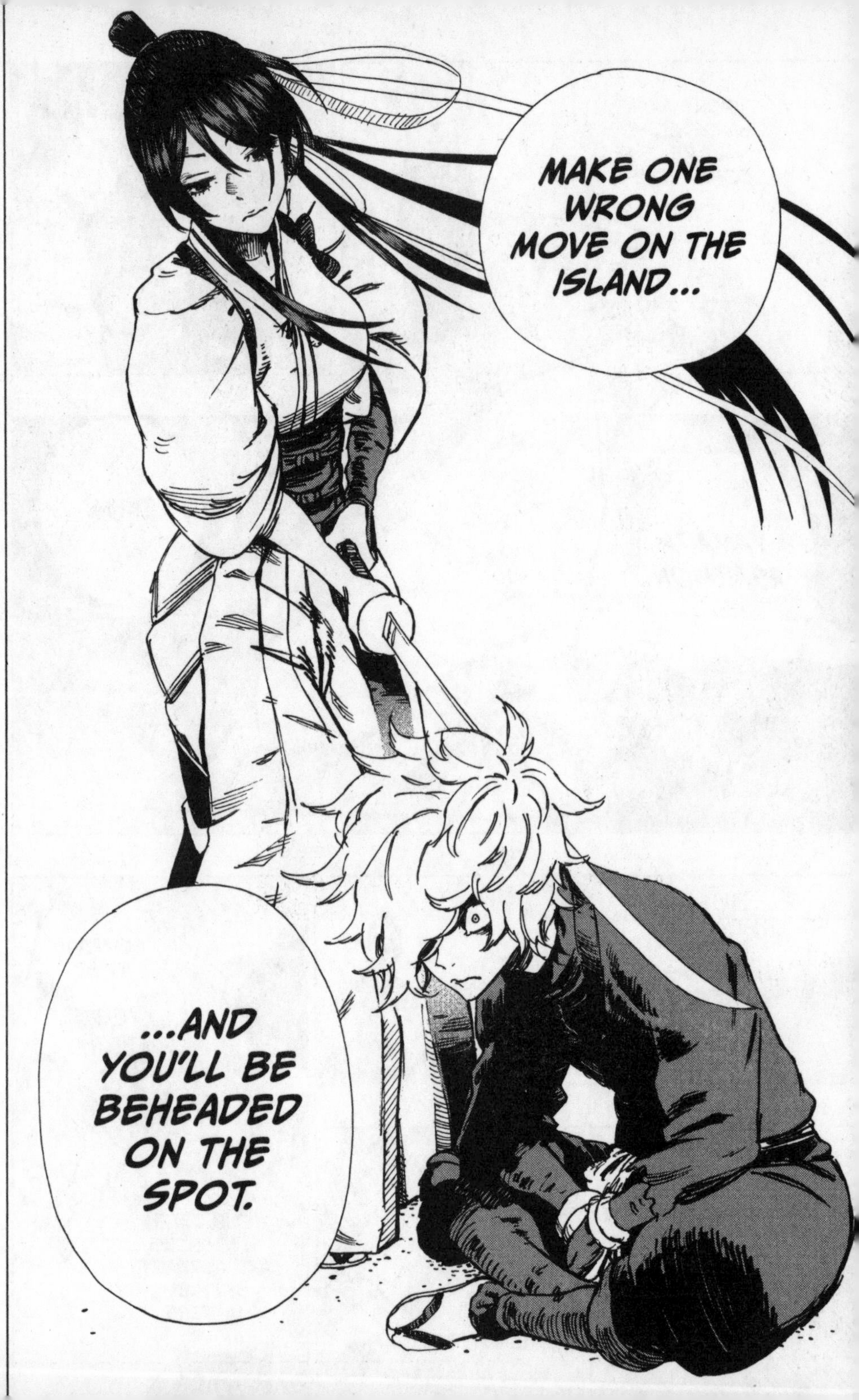
MAKE ONE WRONG MOVE ON THE ISLAND...
...AND YOU'LL BE BEHEADED ON THE SPOT.

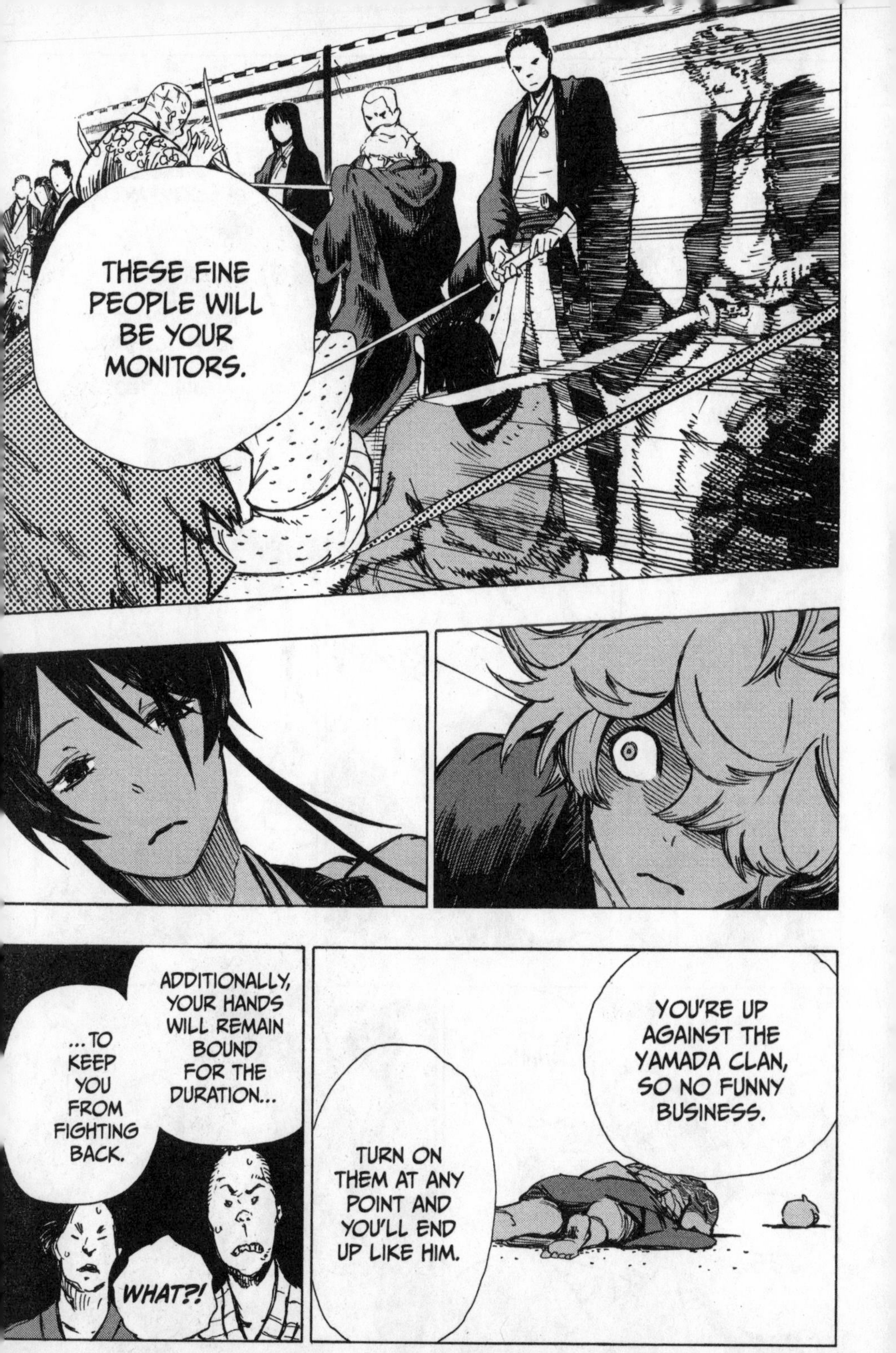
THESE FINE PEOPLE WILL BE YOUR MONITORS.
YOU'RE UP AGAINST THE YAMADA CLAN, SO NO FUNNY BUSINESS.
TURN ON THEM AT ANY POINT AND YOU'LL END UP LIKE HIM.
ADDITIONALLY, YOUR HANDS WILL REMAIN BOUND FOR THE DURATION...
...TO KEEP YOU FROM FIGHTING BACK.
WHAT?!

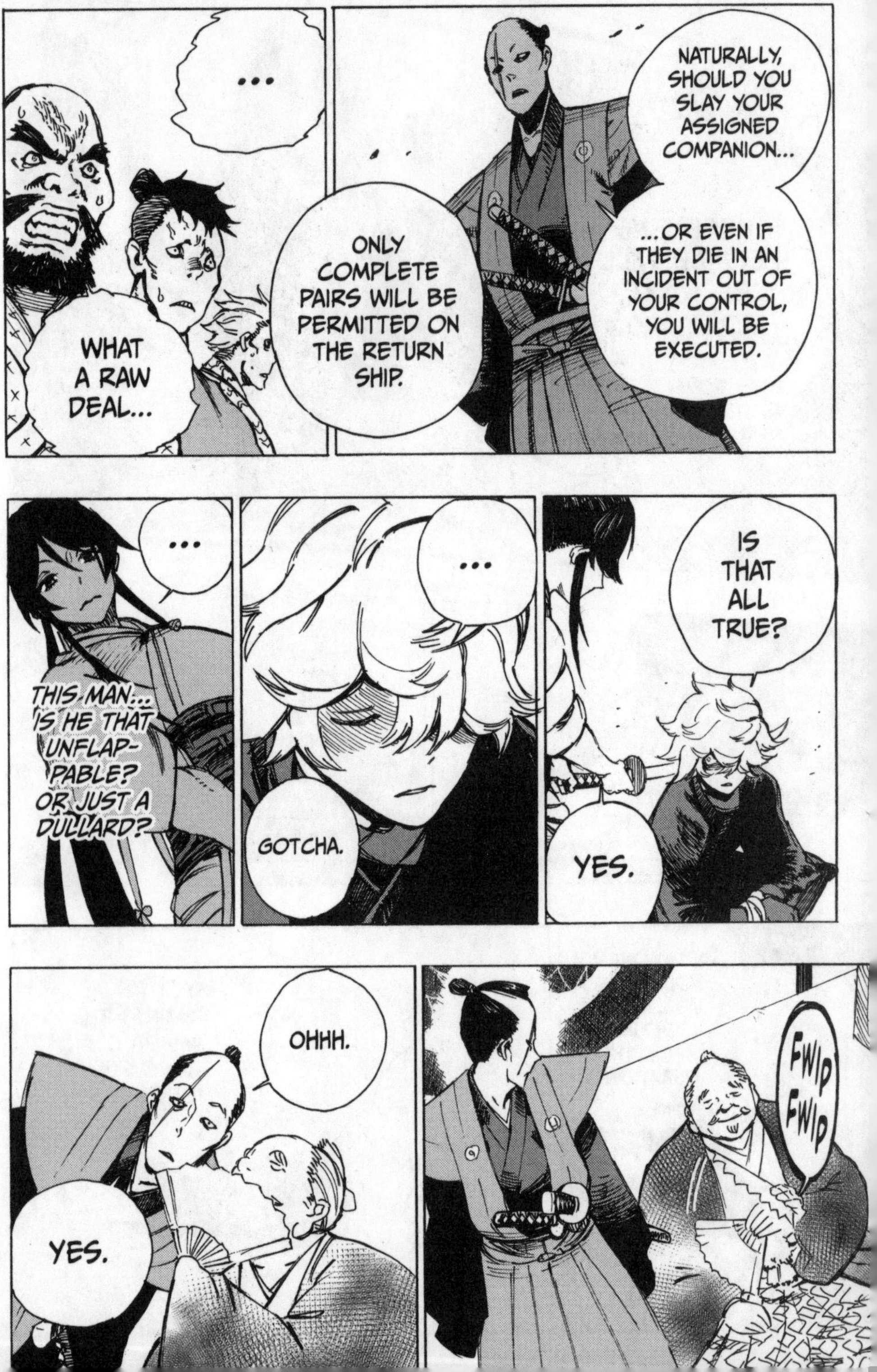
NATURALLY, SHOULD YOU SLAY YOUR ASSIGNED COMPANION...
...OR EVEN IF THEY DIE IN AN INCIDENT OUT OF YOUR CONTROL, YOU WILL BE EXECUTED.
ONLY COMPLETE PAIRS WILL BE PERMITTED ON THE RETURN SHIP.
...
WHAT A RAW DEAL...
IS THAT ALL TRUE?
YES.
...
GOTCHA.
...
THIS MAN... IS HE THAT UNFLAP-PABLE? OR JUST A DULLARD?
FWIP FWIP
OHHH.
YES.

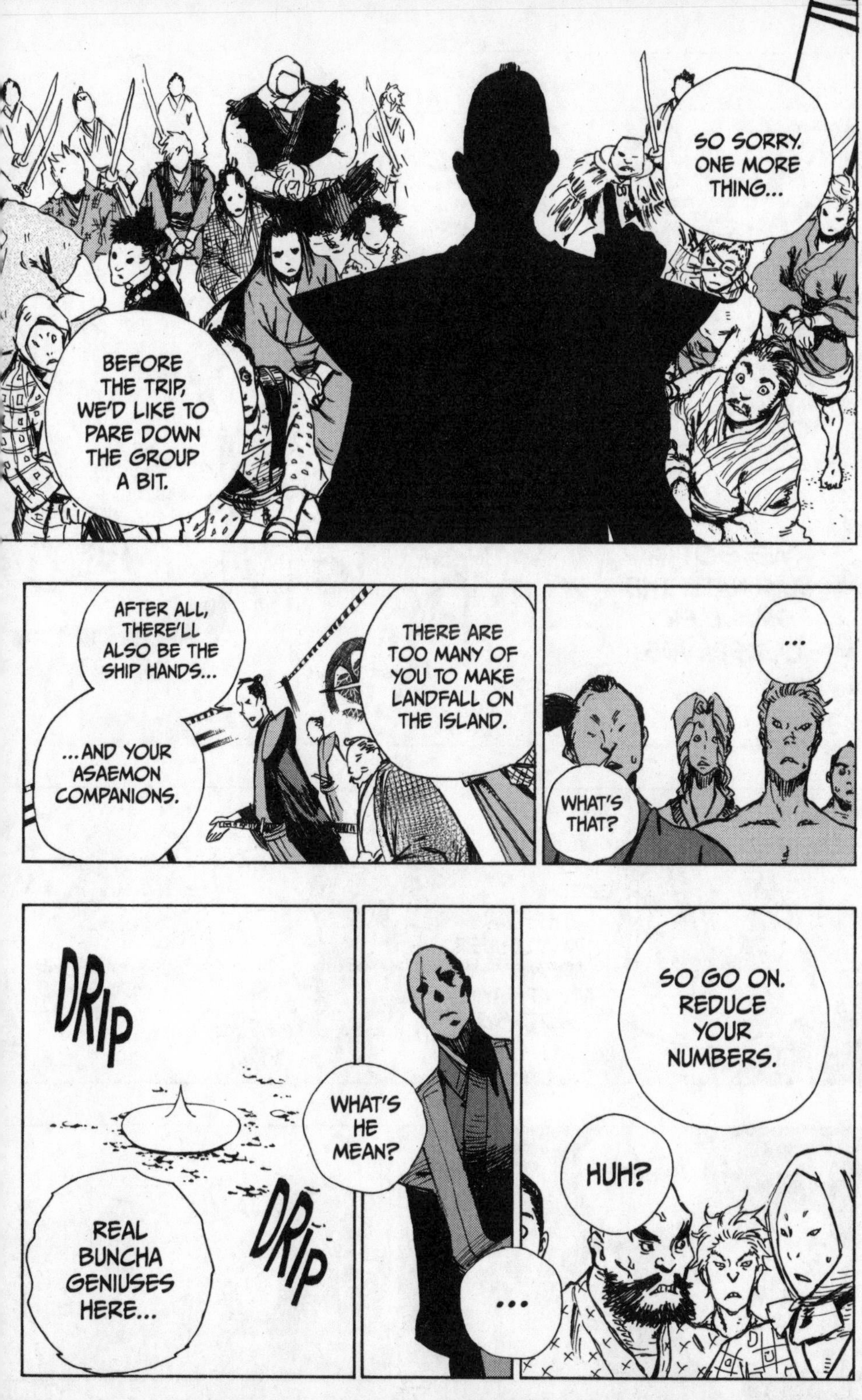
SO SORRY. ONE MORE THING...
BEFORE THE TRIP, WE'D LIKE TO PARE DOWN THE GROUP A BIT.
...
WHAT'S THAT?
THERE ARE TOO MANY OF YOU TO MAKE LANDFALL ON THE ISLAND.
AFTER ALL, THERE'LL ALSO BE THE SHIP HANDS...
...AND YOUR ASAEMON COMPANIONS.
SO GO ON. REDUCE YOUR NUMBERS.
HUH?
...
WHAT'S HE MEAN?
DRIP
DRIP
REAL BUNCHA GENIUSES HERE...

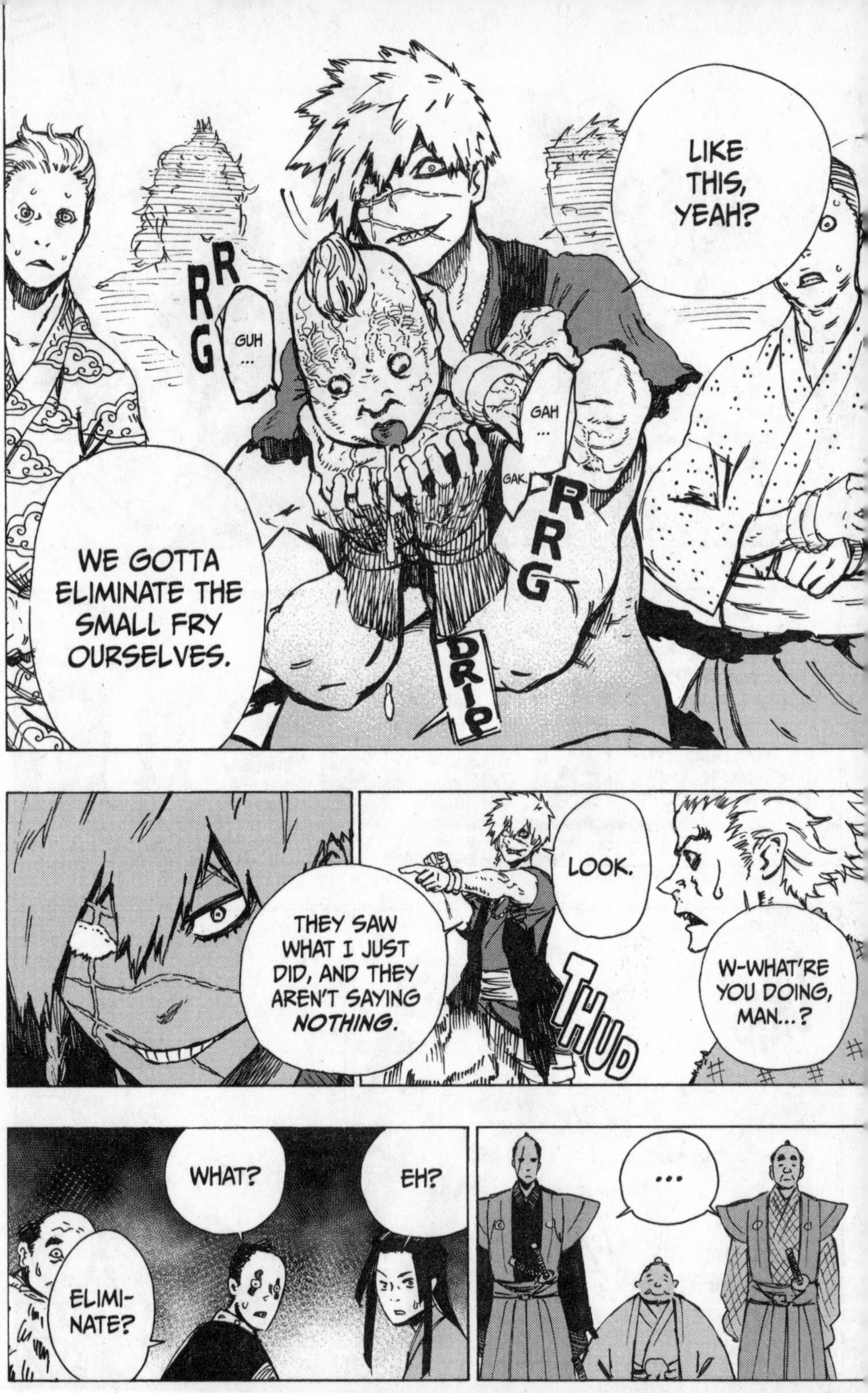
LIKE THIS, YEAH?
RRG
GUH ...
GAH ...
GAK.
RRRG
WE GOTTA ELIMINATE THE SMALL FRY OURSELVES.
DRIP
LOOK.
W-WHAT'RE YOU DOING, MAN...?
THUD
THEY SAW WHAT I JUST DID, AND THEY AREN'T SAYING *NOTHING*.
...
EH?
WHAT?
ELIMI-NATE?

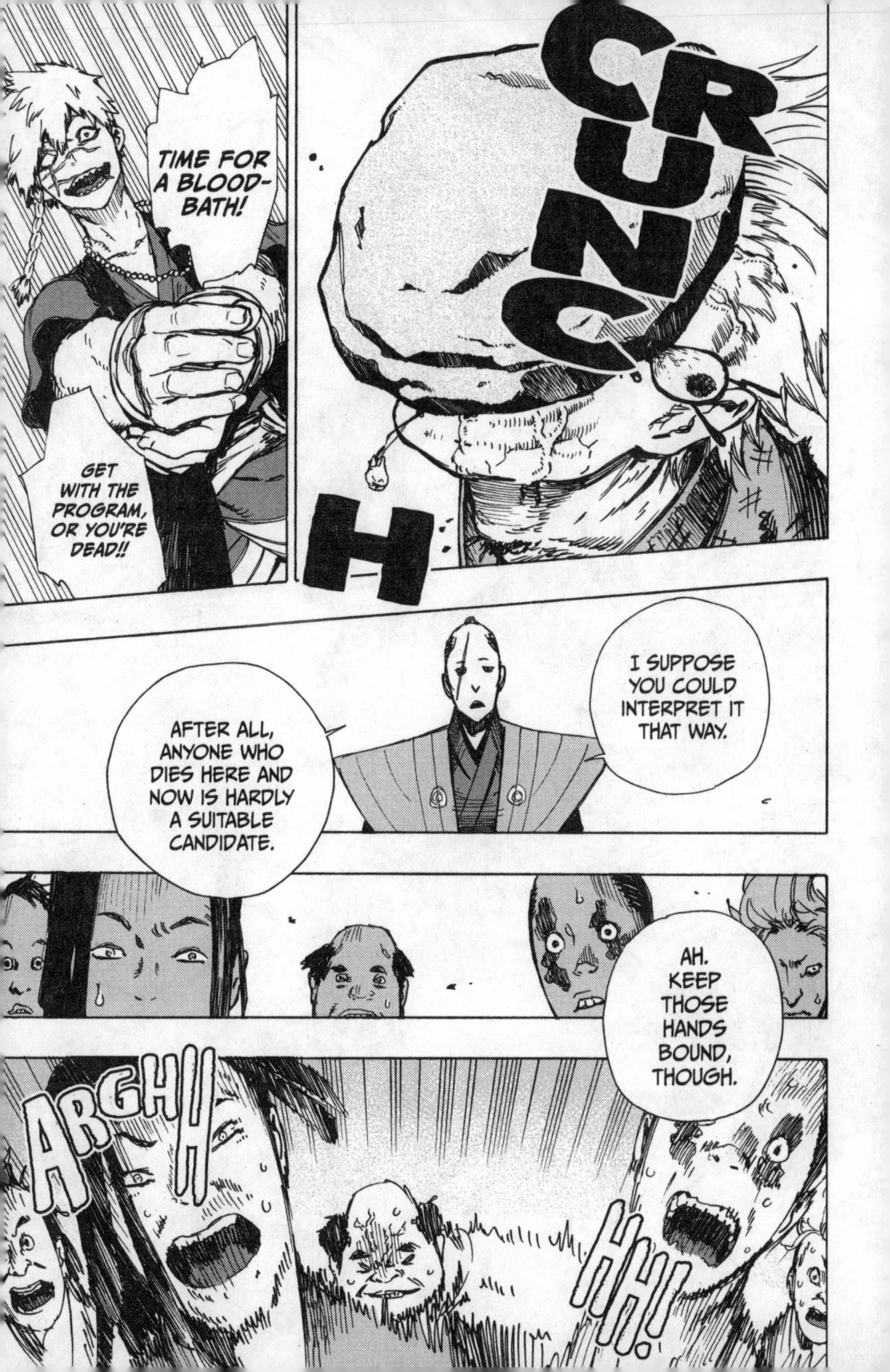
CRUNCH
TIME FOR A BLOOD-BATH!
GET WITH THE PROGRAM, OR YOU'RE DEAD!!
I SUPPOSE YOU COULD INTERPRET IT THAT WAY.
AFTER ALL, ANYONE WHO DIES HERE AND NOW IS HARDLY A SUITABLE CANDIDATE.
AH. KEEP THOSE HANDS BOUND, THOUGH.
ARGHH
HH!

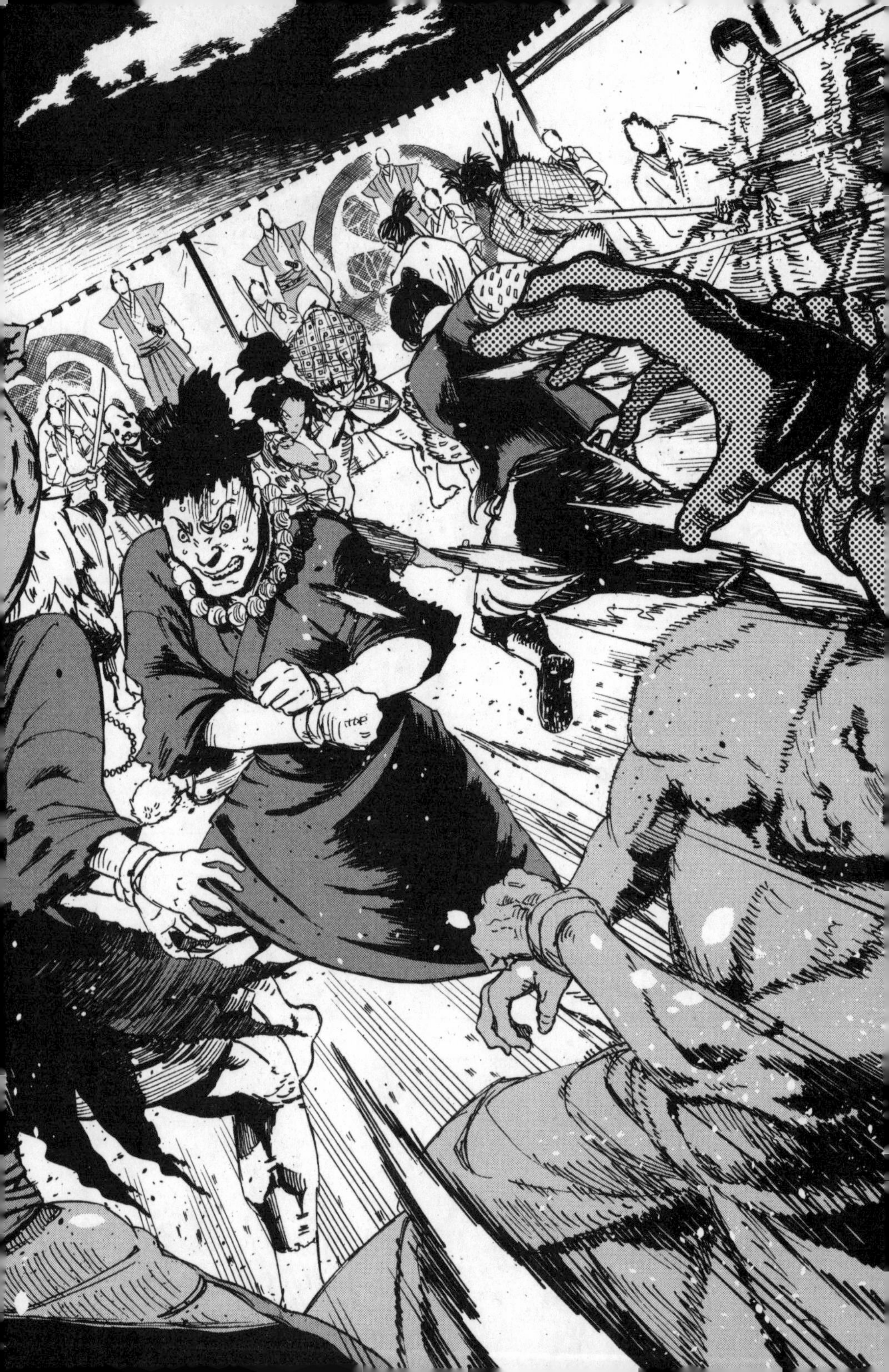

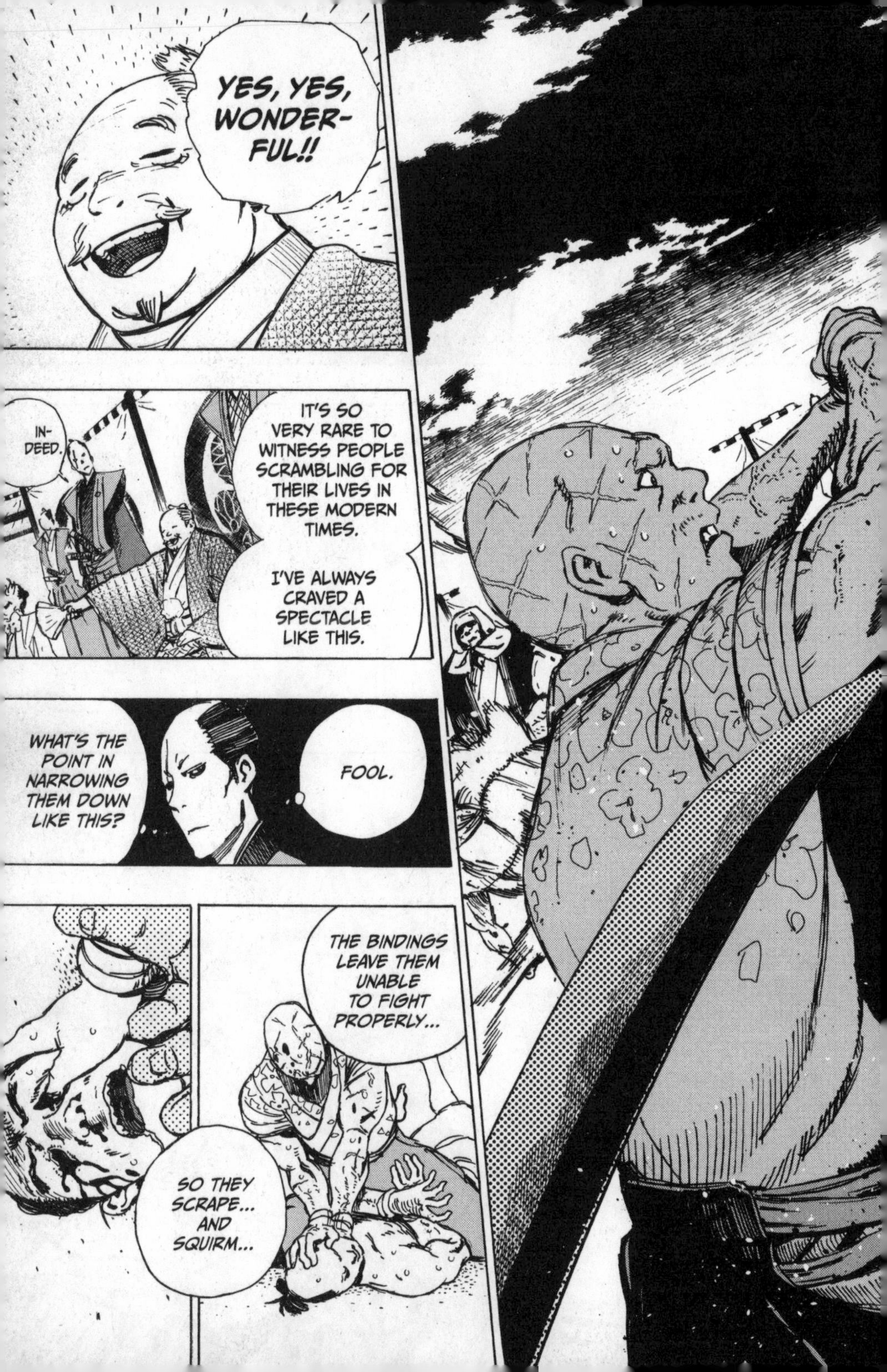
YES, YES, WONDERFUL!!
IT'S SO VERY RARE TO WITNESS PEOPLE SCRAMBLING FOR THEIR LIVES IN THESE MODERN TIMES.
I'VE ALWAYS CRAVED A SPECTACLE LIKE THIS.
INDEED.
FOOL.
WHAT'S THE POINT IN NARROWING THEM DOWN LIKE THIS?
THE BINDINGS LEAVE THEM UNABLE TO FIGHT PROPERLY...
SO THEY SCRAPE... AND SQUIRM...

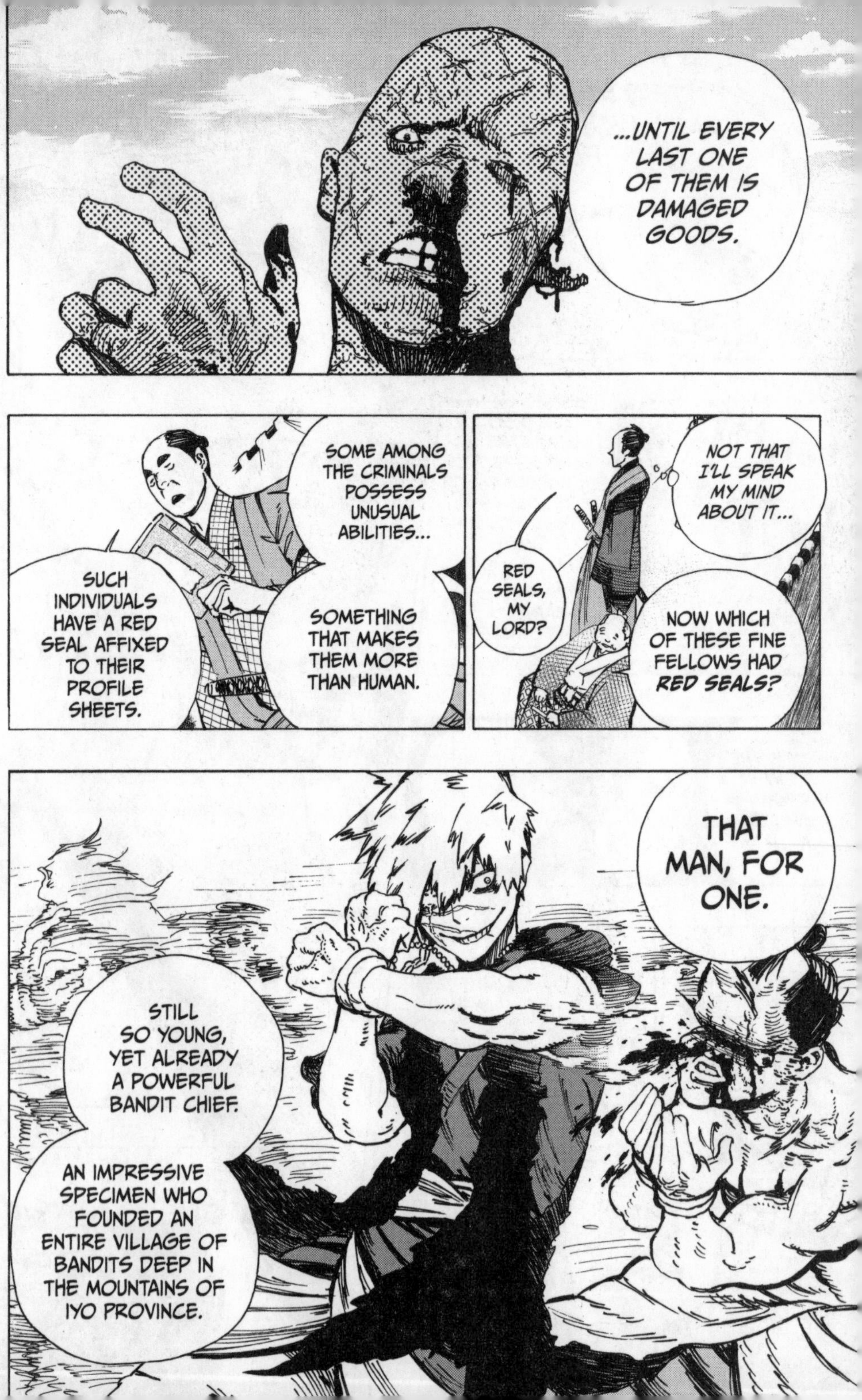
...UNTIL EVERY LAST ONE OF THEM IS DAMAGED GOODS.
NOT THAT I'LL SPEAK MY MIND ABOUT IT...
RED SEALS, MY LORD?
NOW WHICH OF THESE FINE FELLOWS HAD *RED SEALS?*
SOME AMONG THE CRIMINALS POSSESS UNUSUAL ABILITIES...
SOMETHING THAT MAKES THEM MORE THAN HUMAN.
SUCH INDIVIDUALS HAVE A RED SEAL AFFIXED TO THEIR PROFILE SHEETS.
THAT MAN, FOR ONE.
STILL SO YOUNG, YET ALREADY A POWERFUL BANDIT CHIEF.
AN IMPRESSIVE SPECIMEN WHO FOUNDED AN ENTIRE VILLAGE OF BANDITS DEEP IN THE MOUNTAINS OF IYO PROVINCE.

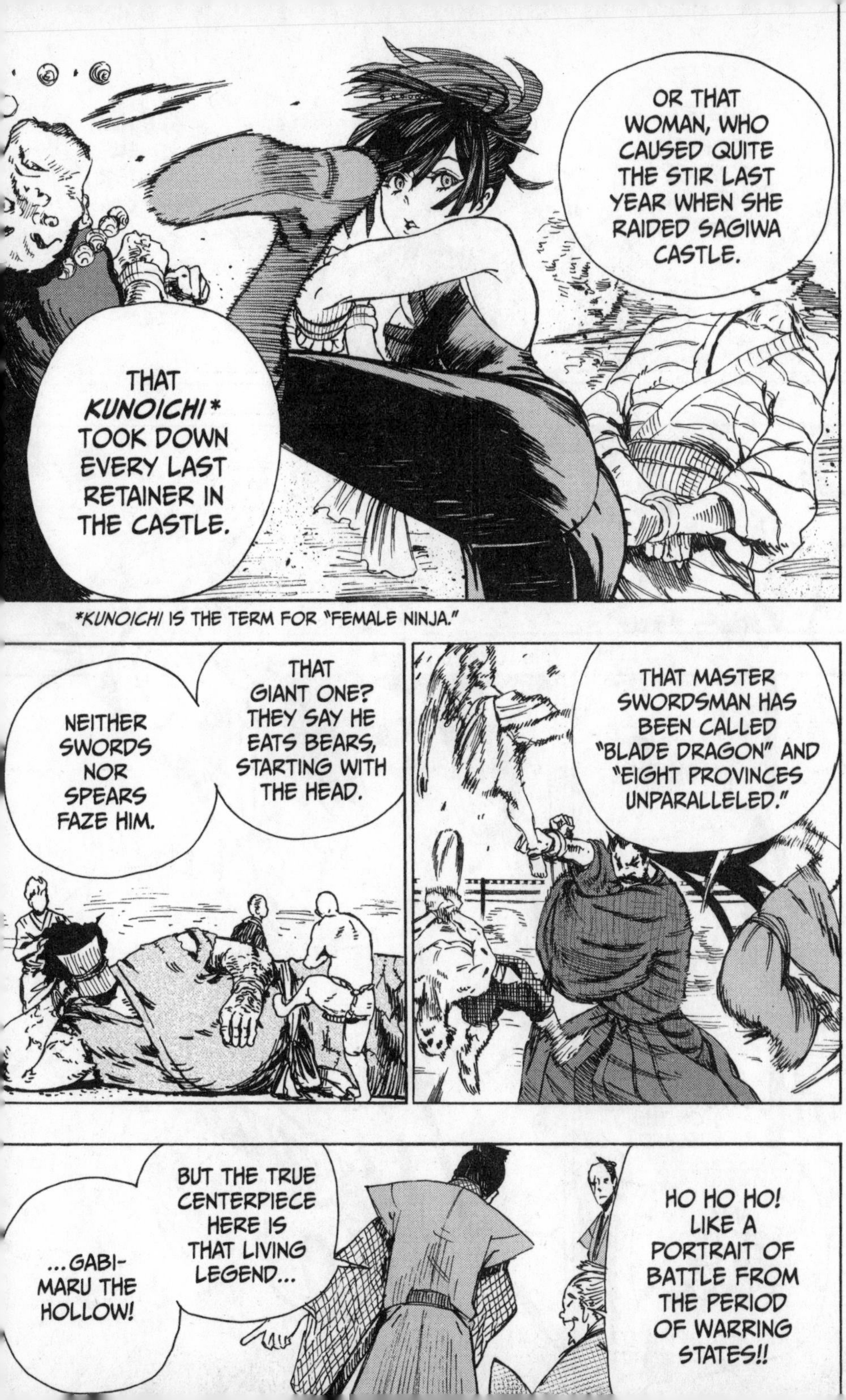
OR THAT WOMAN, WHO CAUSED QUITE THE STIR LAST YEAR WHEN SHE RAIDED SAGIWA CASTLE.
THAT *KUNOICHI** TOOK DOWN EVERY LAST RETAINER IN THE CASTLE.
THAT MASTER SWORDSMAN HAS BEEN CALLED "BLADE DRAGON" AND "EIGHT PROVINCES UNPARALLELED."
THAT GIANT ONE? THEY SAY HE EATS BEARS, STARTING WITH THE HEAD.
NEITHER SWORDS NOR SPEARS FAZE HIM.
HO HO HO! LIKE A PORTRAIT OF BATTLE FROM THE PERIOD OF WARRING STATES!!
BUT THE TRUE CENTERPIECE HERE IS THAT LIVING LEGEND...
...GABI-MARU THE HOLLOW!

**KUNOICHI* IS THE TERM FOR "FEMALE NINJA."

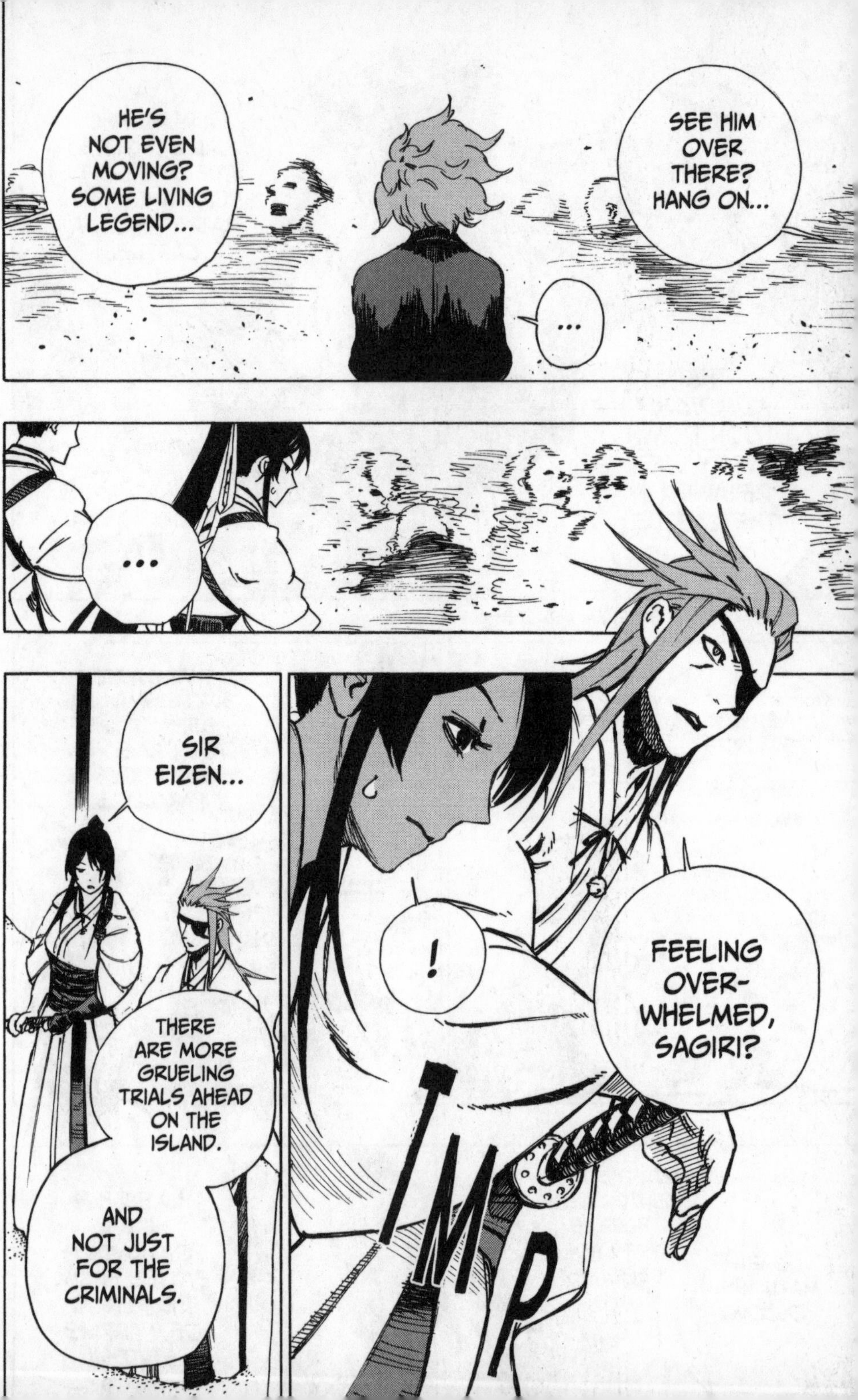
SEE HIM OVER THERE? HANG ON...
HE'S NOT EVEN MOVING? SOME LIVING LEGEND...
...
...
FEELING OVER-WHELMED, SAGIRI?
!
TMP
SIR EIZEN...
THERE ARE MORE GRUELING TRIALS AHEAD ON THE ISLAND.
AND NOT JUST FOR THE CRIMINALS.

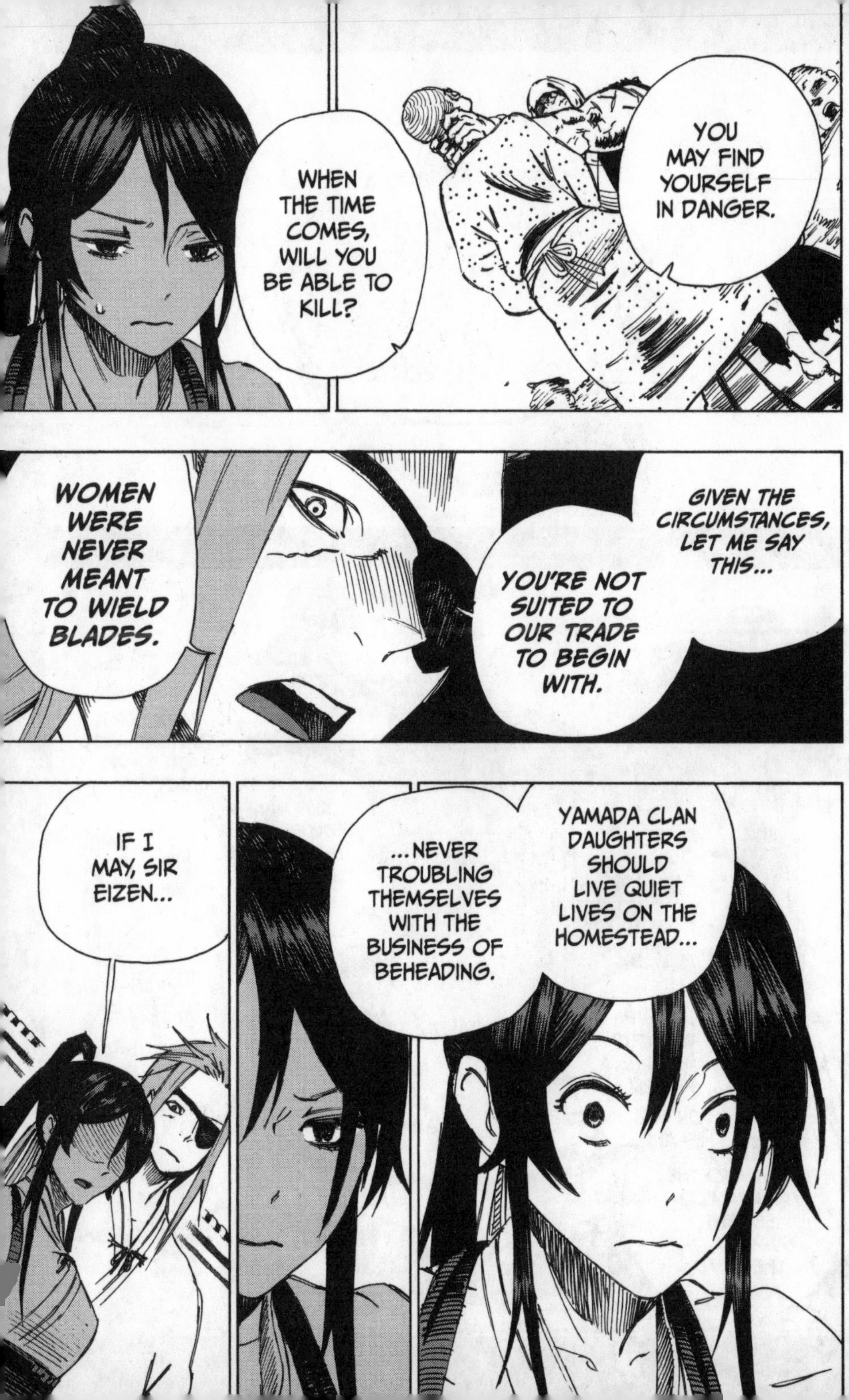
YOU MAY FIND YOURSELF IN DANGER.
WHEN THE TIME COMES, WILL YOU BE ABLE TO KILL?
GIVEN THE CIRCUMSTANCES, LET ME SAY THIS...
YOU'RE NOT SUITED TO OUR TRADE TO BEGIN WITH.
WOMEN WERE NEVER MEANT TO WIELD BLADES.
YAMADA CLAN DAUGHTERS SHOULD LIVE QUIET LIVES ON THE HOMESTEAD...
...NEVER TROUBLING THEMSELVES WITH THE BUSINESS OF BEHEADING.
IF I MAY, SIR EIZEN...

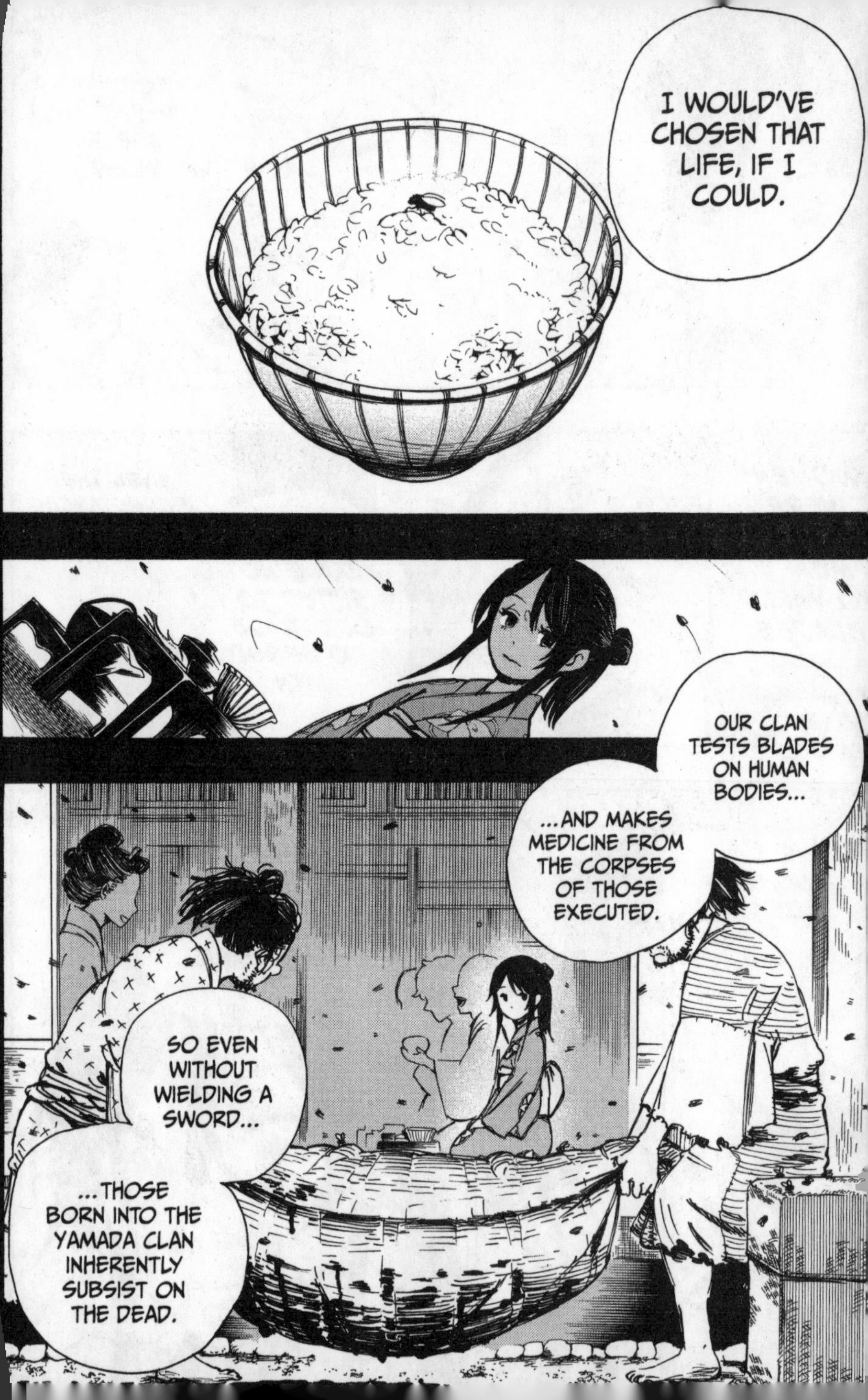
I WOULD'VE CHOSEN THAT LIFE, IF I COULD.
OUR CLAN TESTS BLADES ON HUMAN BODIES...
...AND MAKES MEDICINE FROM THE CORPSES OF THOSE EXECUTED.
SO EVEN WITHOUT WIELDING A SWORD...
...THOSE BORN INTO THE YAMADA CLAN INHERENTLY SUBSIST ON THE DEAD.

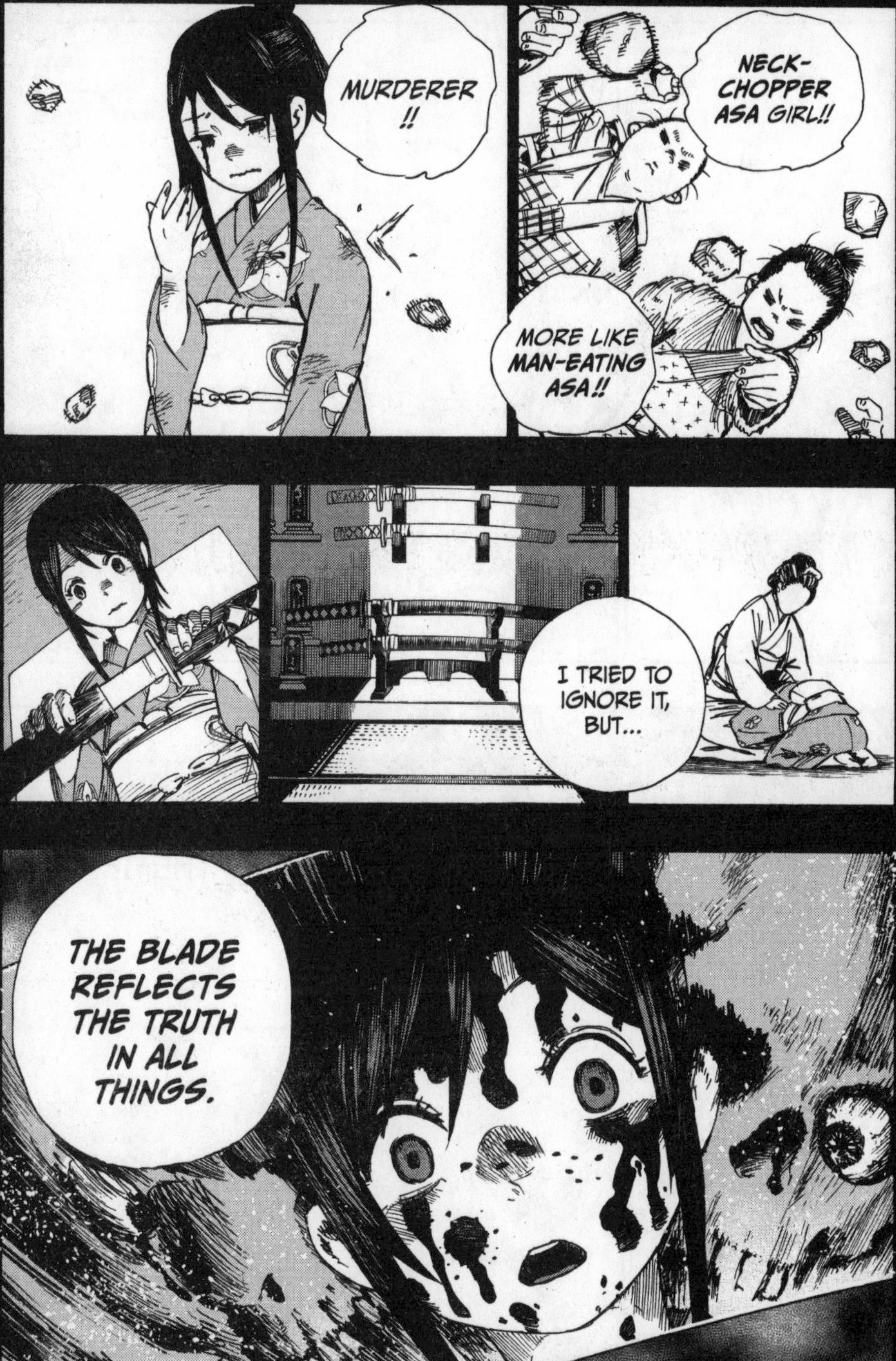
NECK-CHOPPER ASA GIRL!!
MORE LIKE MAN-EATING ASA!!
MURDERER !!
I TRIED TO IGNORE IT, BUT...
THE BLADE REFLECTS THE TRUTH IN ALL THINGS.

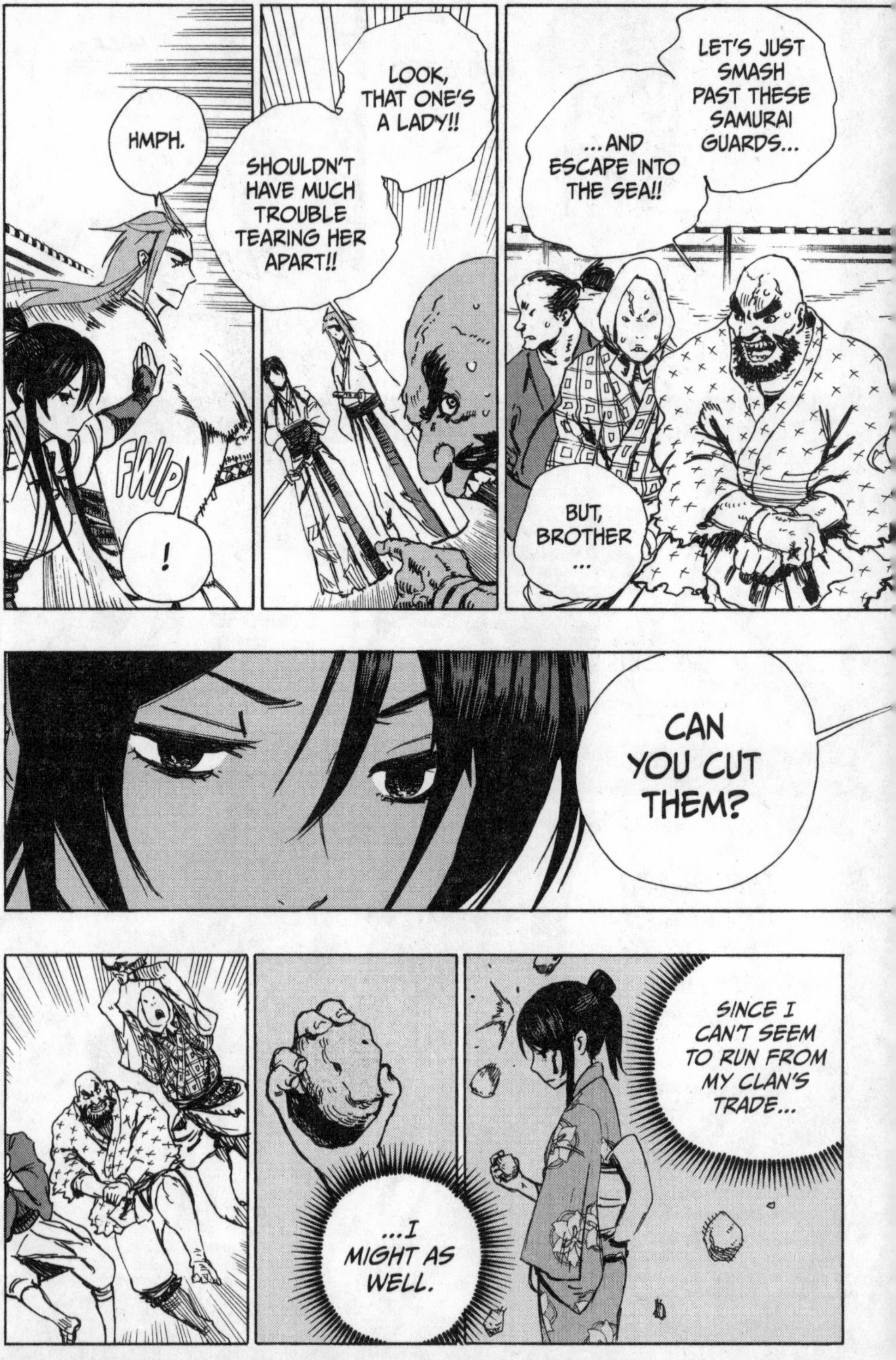
LET'S JUST SMASH PAST THESE SAMURAI GUARDS...
...AND ESCAPE INTO THE SEA!!
BUT, BROTHER ...
LOOK, THAT ONE'S A LADY!!
SHOULDN'T HAVE MUCH TROUBLE TEARING HER APART!!
HMPH.
FWIP
!
CAN YOU CUT THEM?
SINCE I CAN'T SEEM TO RUN FROM MY CLAN'S TRADE...
...I MIGHT AS WELL.

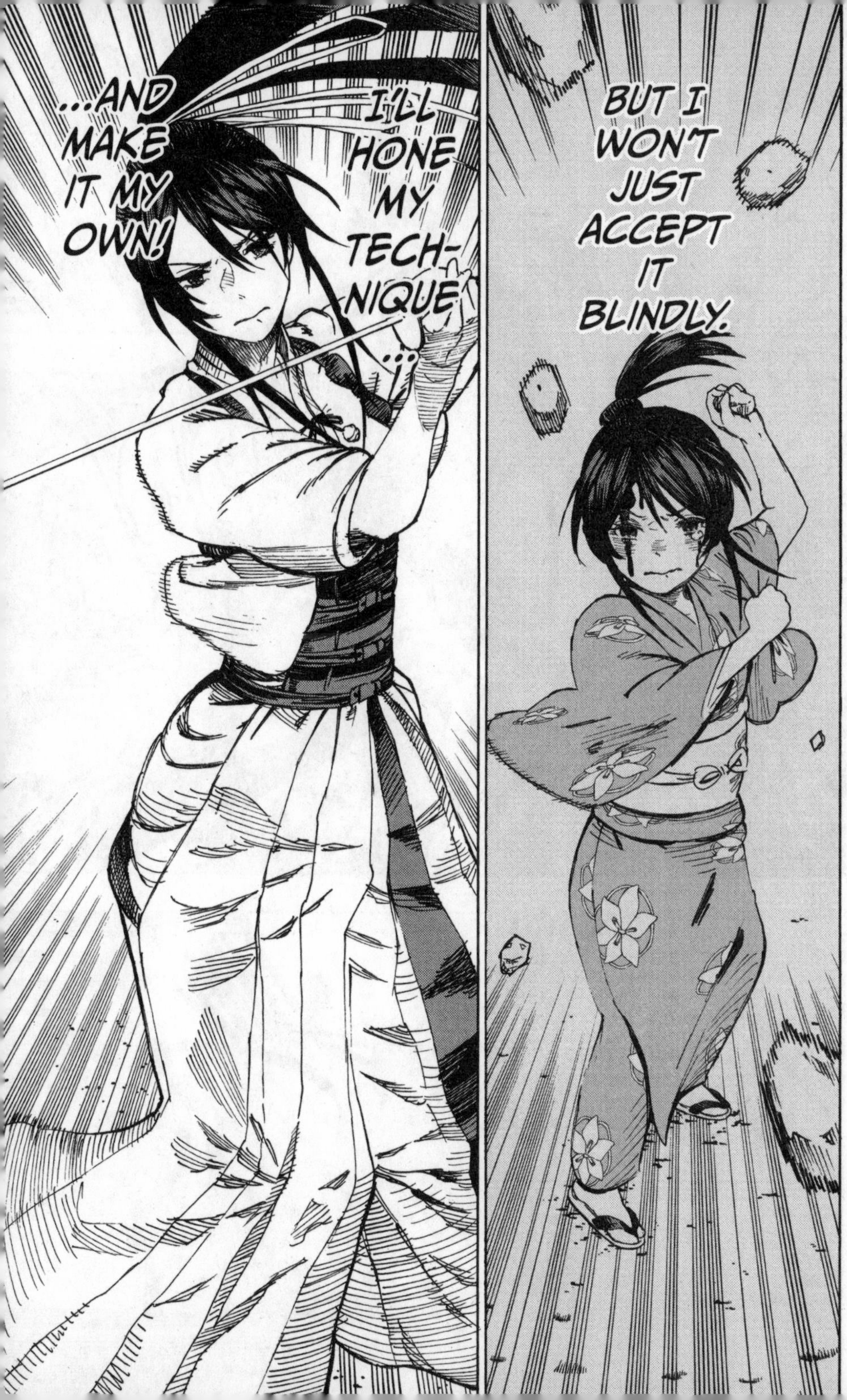
BUT I WON'T JUST ACCEPT IT BLINDLY.
I'LL HONE MY TECH-NIQUE...
...AND MAKE IT MY OWN!

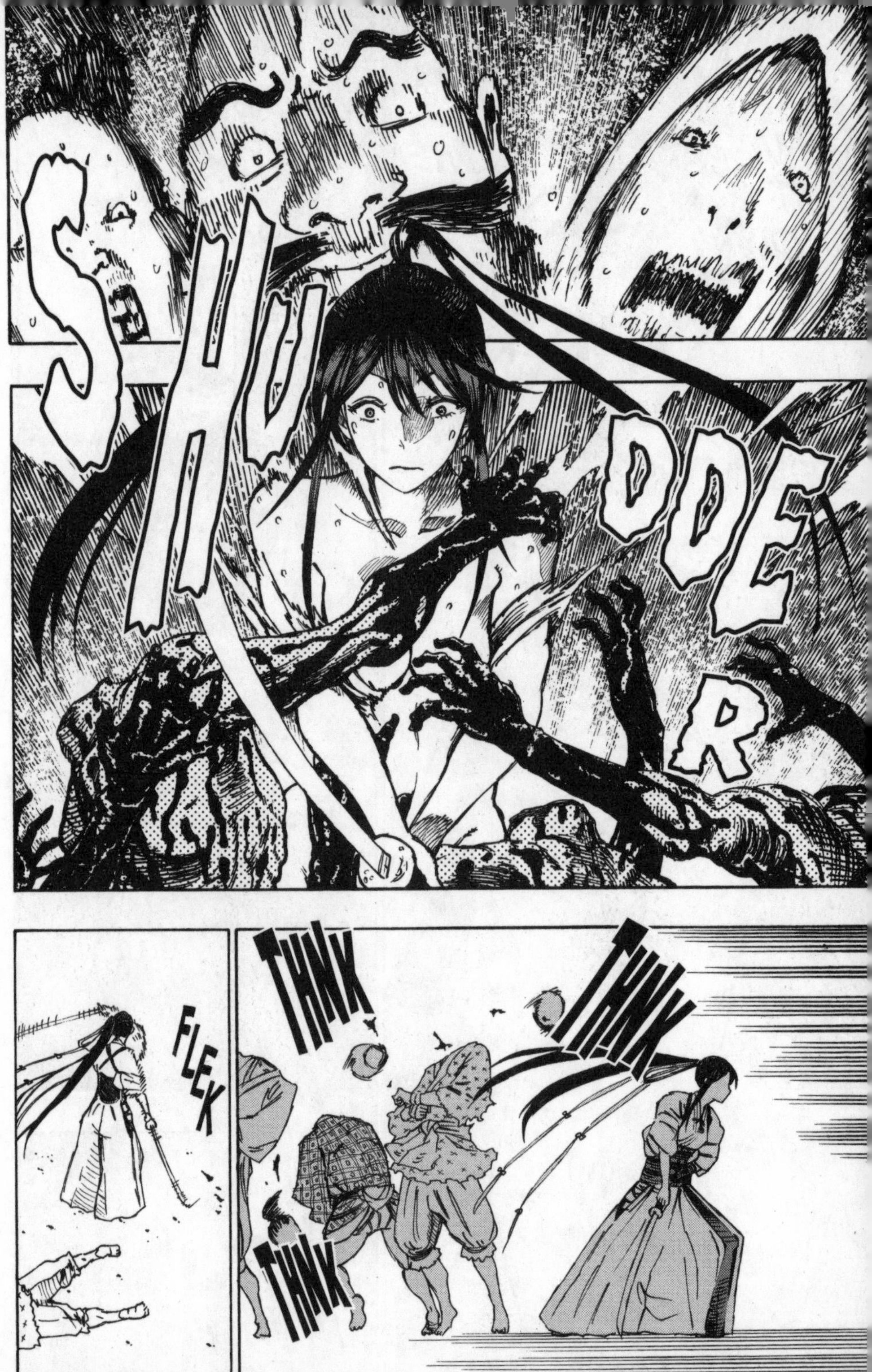
SHUDDER
THNK
THNK
THNK
FLEK

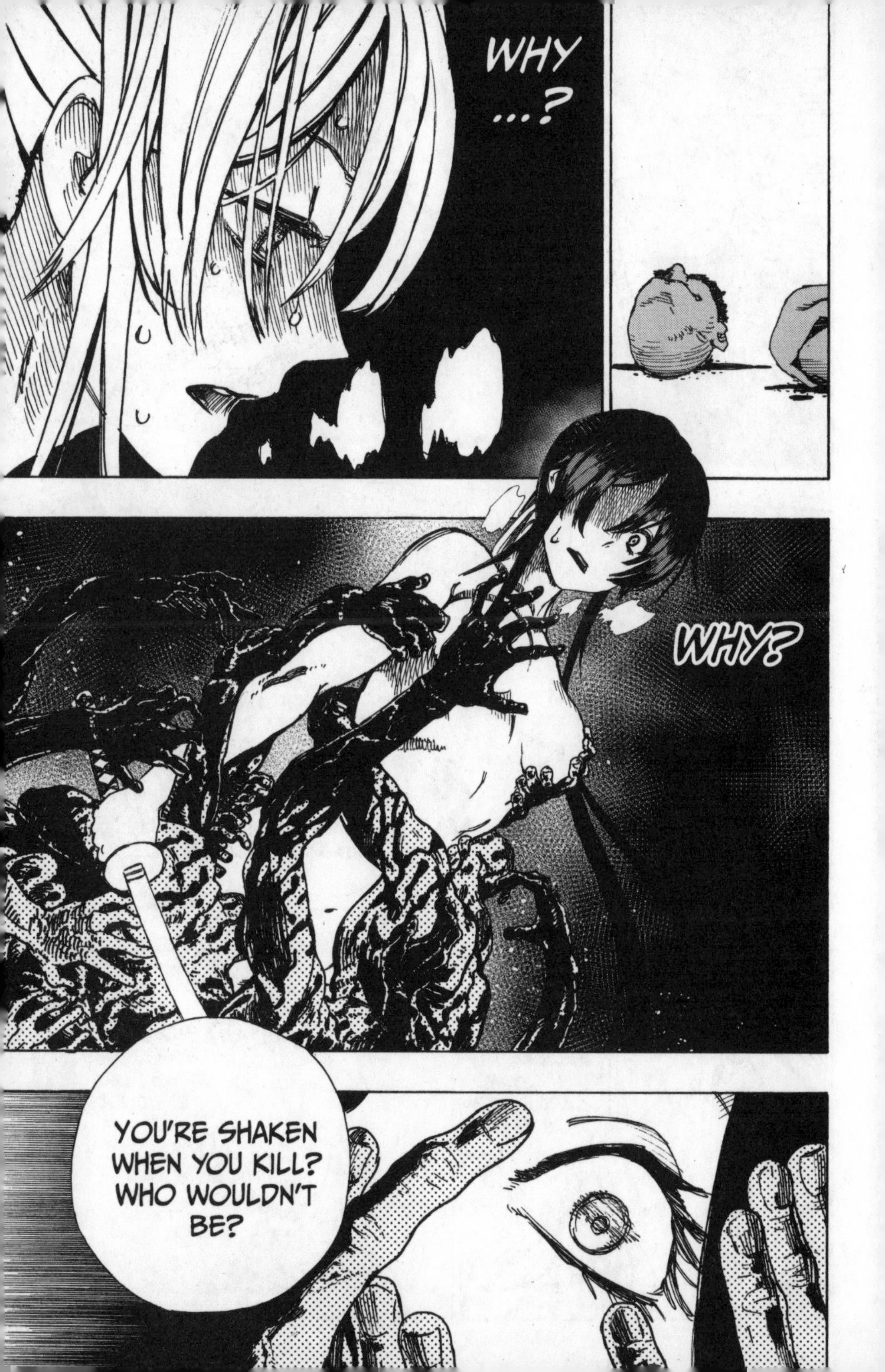
WHY ...?
WHY?
YOU'RE SHAKEN WHEN YOU KILL? WHO WOULDN'T BE?

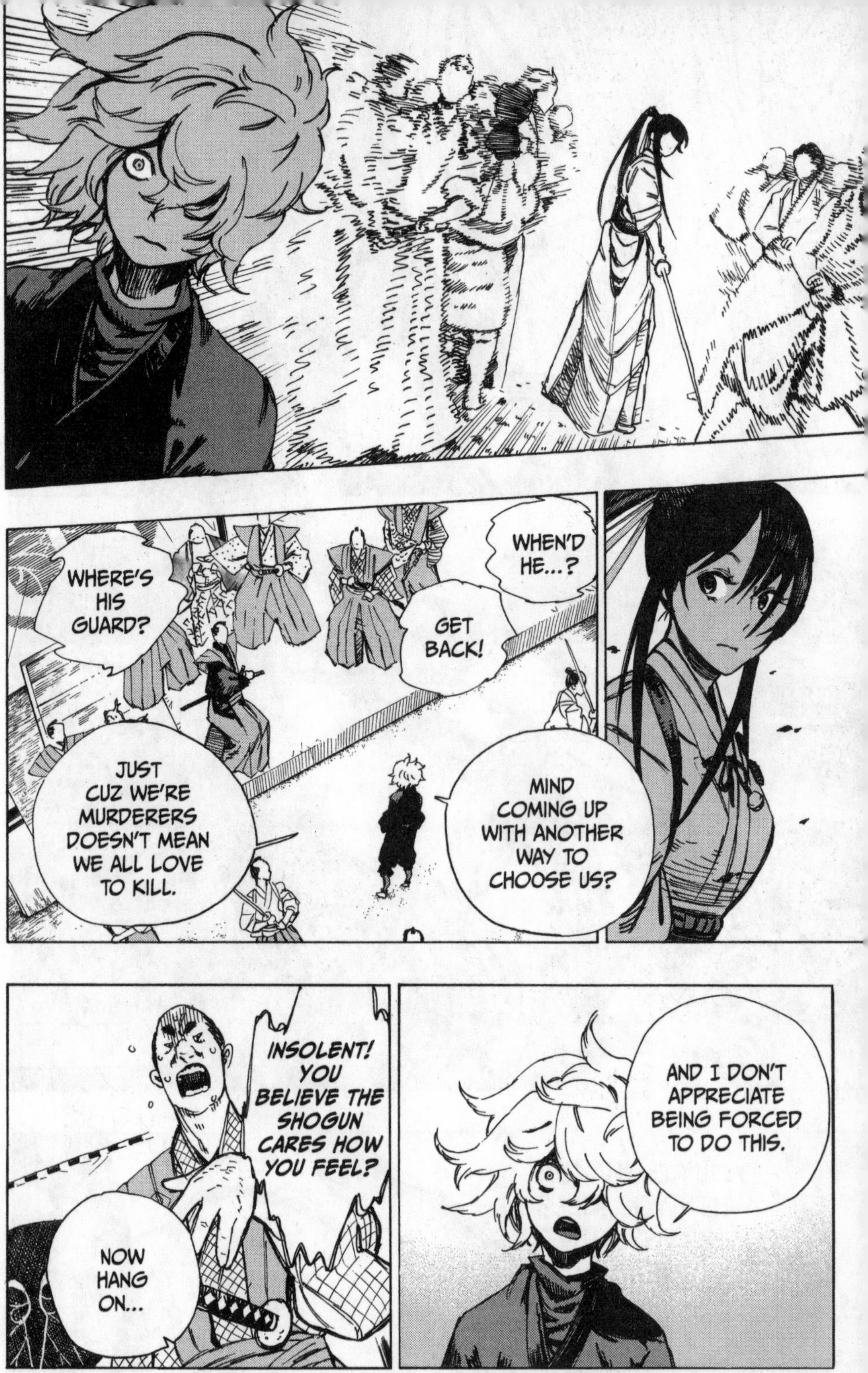
WHEN'D HE...?
GET BACK!
WHERE'S HIS GUARD?
MIND COMING UP WITH ANOTHER WAY TO CHOOSE US?
JUST CUZ WE'RE MURDERERS DOESN'T MEAN WE ALL LOVE TO KILL.
AND I DON'T APPRECIATE BEING FORCED TO DO THIS.
INSOLENT! YOU BELIEVE THE SHOGUN CARES HOW YOU FEEL?
NOW HANG ON...

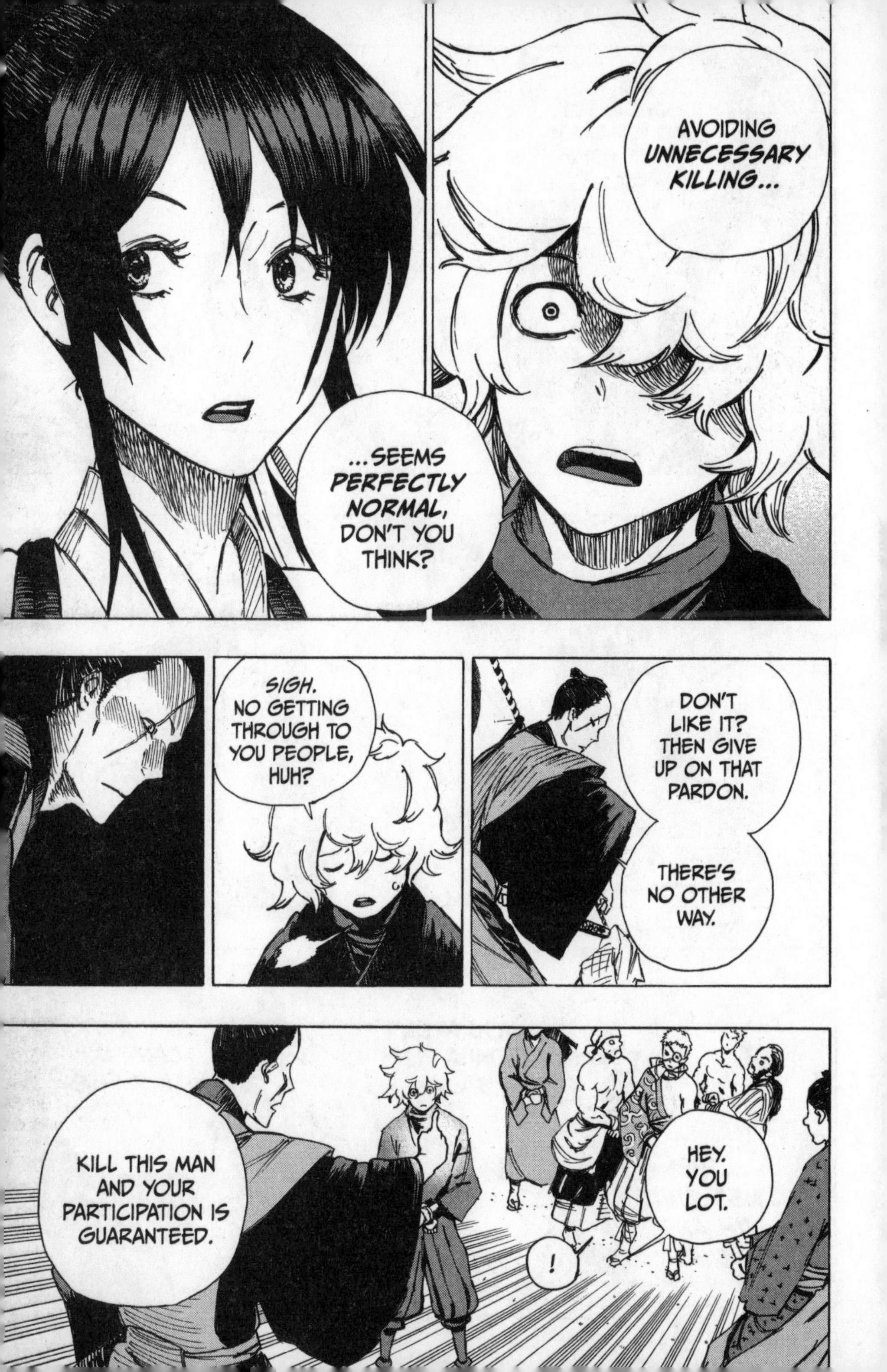
AVOIDING UNNECESSARY KILLING...
...SEEMS PERFECTLY NORMAL, DON'T YOU THINK?
DON'T LIKE IT? THEN GIVE UP ON THAT PARDON.
THERE'S NO OTHER WAY.
SIGH. NO GETTING THROUGH TO YOU PEOPLE, HUH?
HEY. YOU LOT.
KILL THIS MAN AND YOUR PARTICIPATION IS GUARANTEED.
!

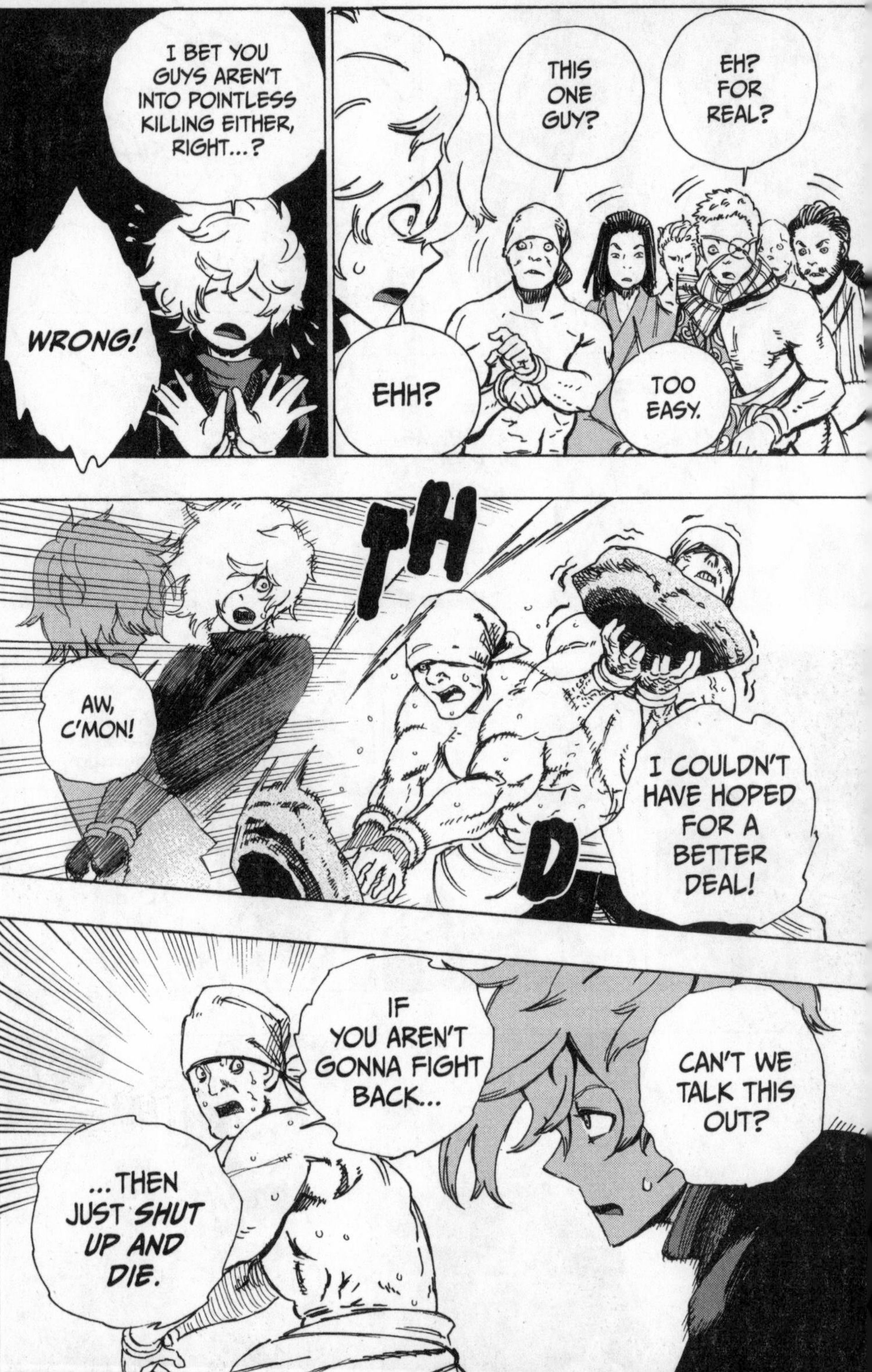
EH? FOR REAL?
THIS ONE GUY?
TOO EASY.
EHH?
I BET YOU GUYS AREN'T INTO POINTLESS KILLING EITHER, RIGHT...?
WRONG!
TH
I COULDN'T HAVE HOPED FOR A BETTER DEAL!
D
AW, C'MON!
CAN'T WE TALK THIS OUT?
IF YOU AREN'T GONNA FIGHT BACK...
...THEN JUST SHUT UP AND DIE.

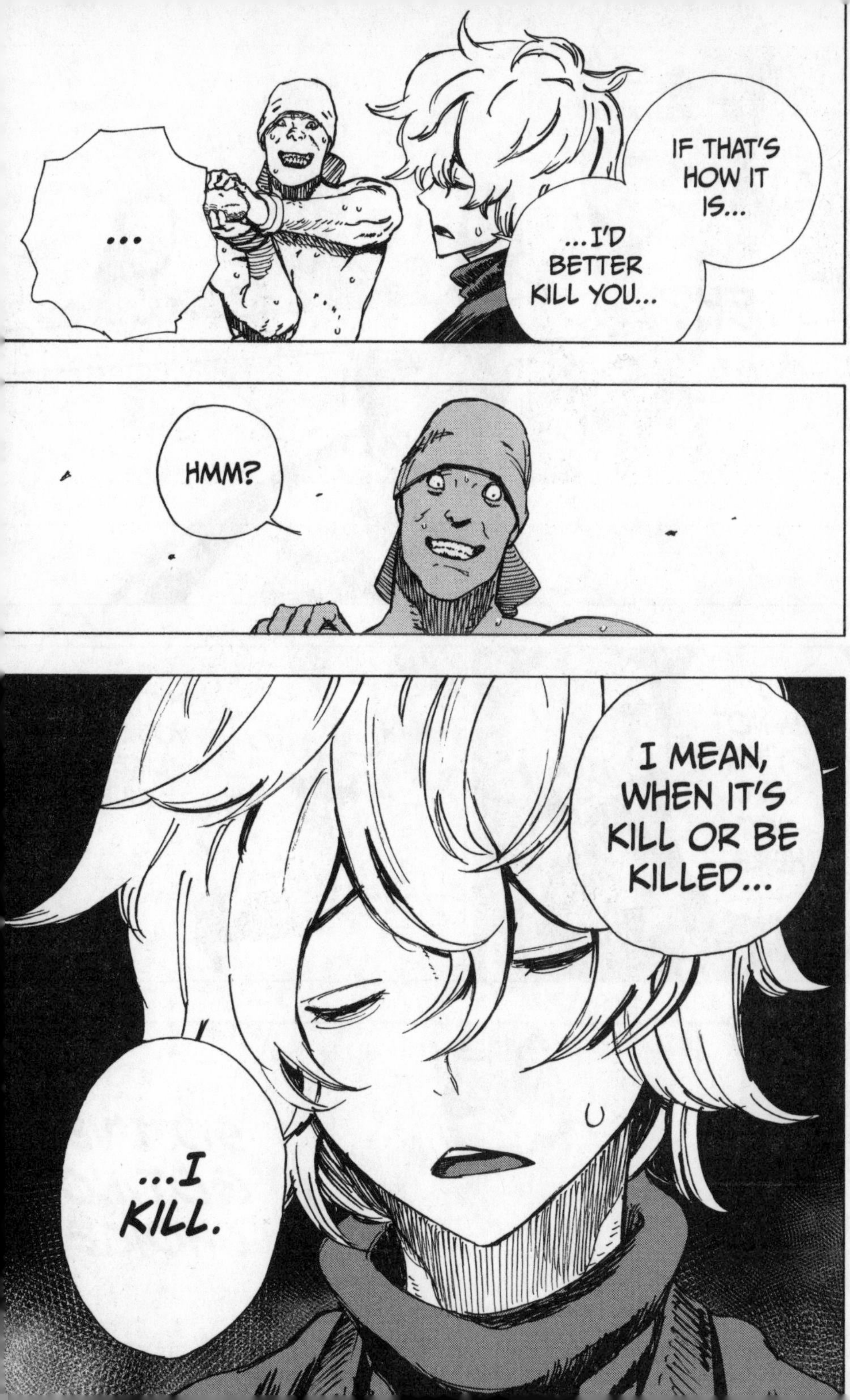
IF THAT'S HOW IT IS...
...I'D BETTER KILL YOU...
...
HMM?
I MEAN, WHEN IT'S KILL OR BE KILLED...
...I KILL.

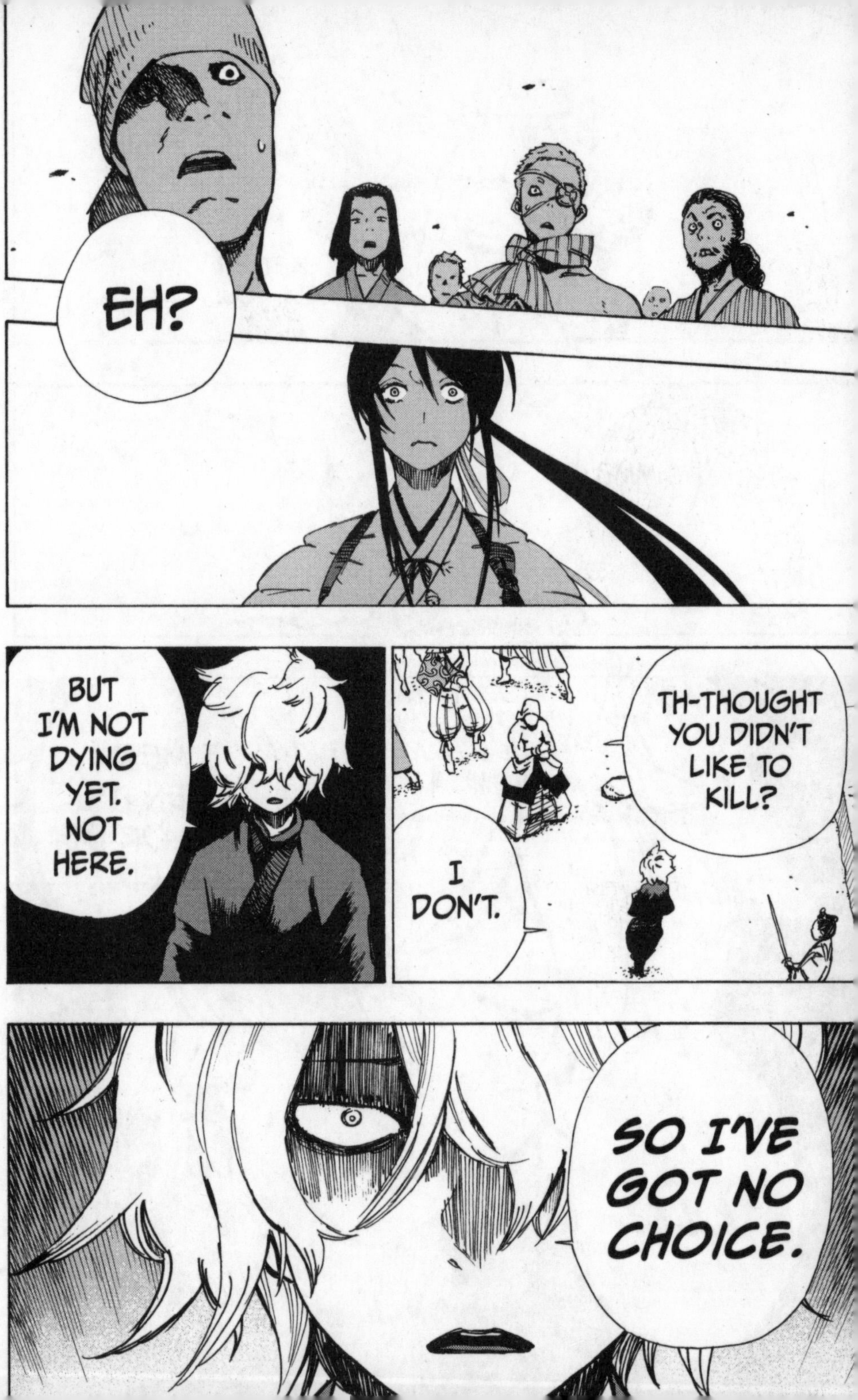
EH?
TH-THOUGHT YOU DIDN'T LIKE TO KILL?
I DON'T.
BUT I'M NOT DYING YET. NOT HERE.
SO I'VE GOT NO CHOICE.

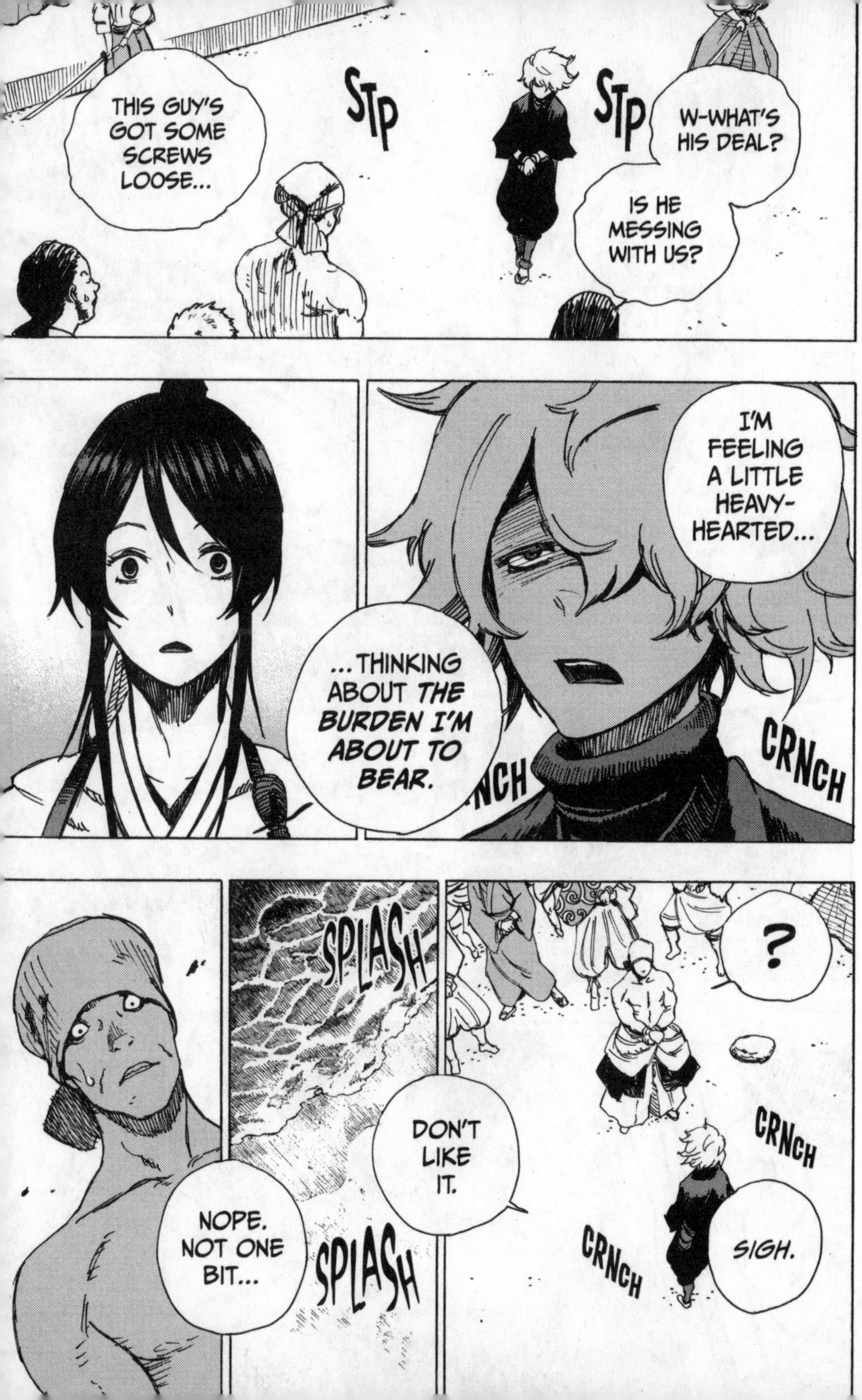
STP
W-WHAT'S HIS DEAL?
IS HE MESSING WITH US?
STP
THIS GUY'S GOT SOME SCREWS LOOSE...
I'M FEELING A LITTLE HEAVY-HEARTED...
...THINKING ABOUT THE BURDEN I'M ABOUT TO BEAR.
CRNCH
?
CRNCH
SIGH.
CRNCH
SPLASH
DON'T LIKE IT.
SPLASH
NOPE. NOT ONE BIT...

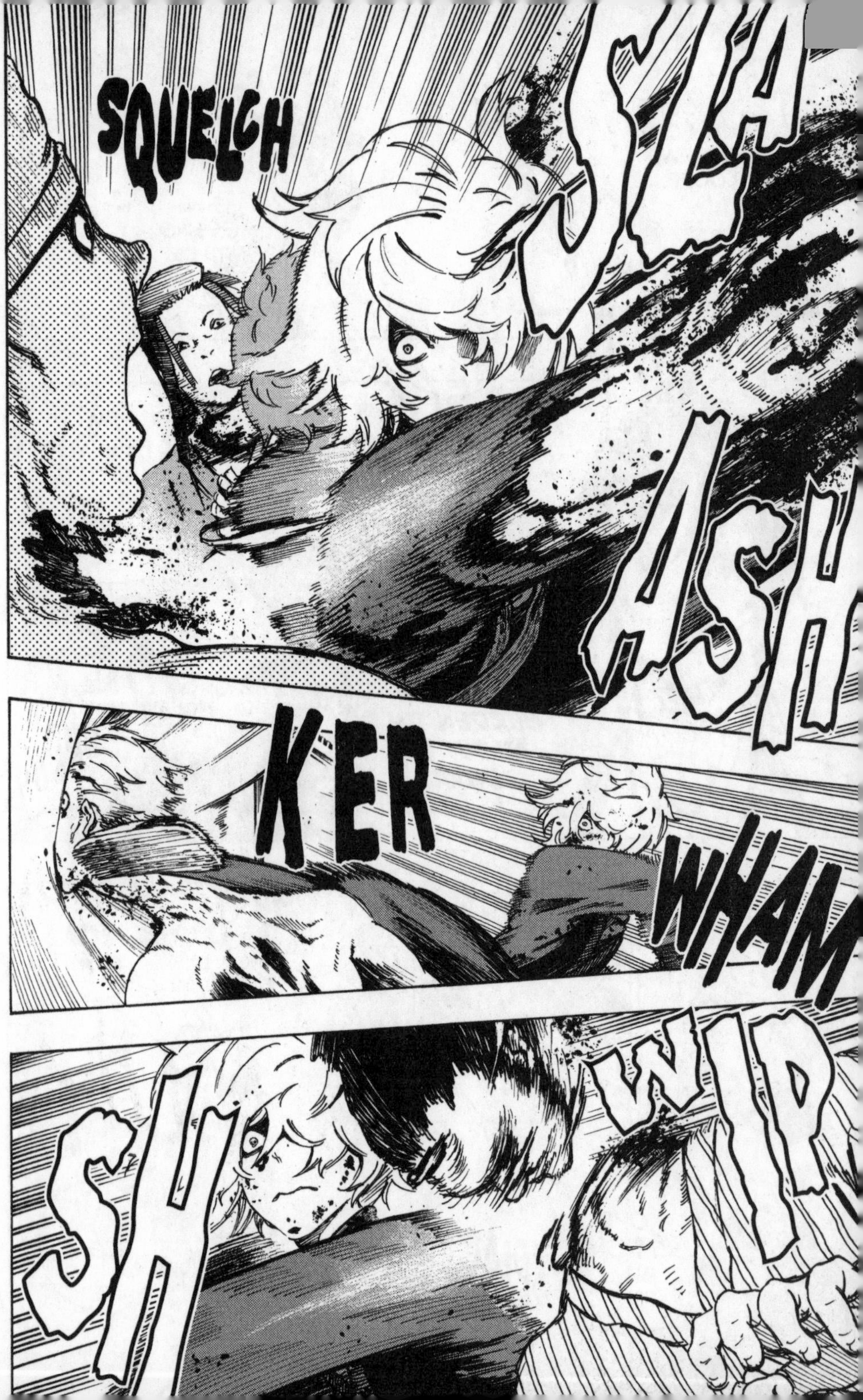
SLA
ASH
SQUELCH
WHAM
KER
WIP
SH

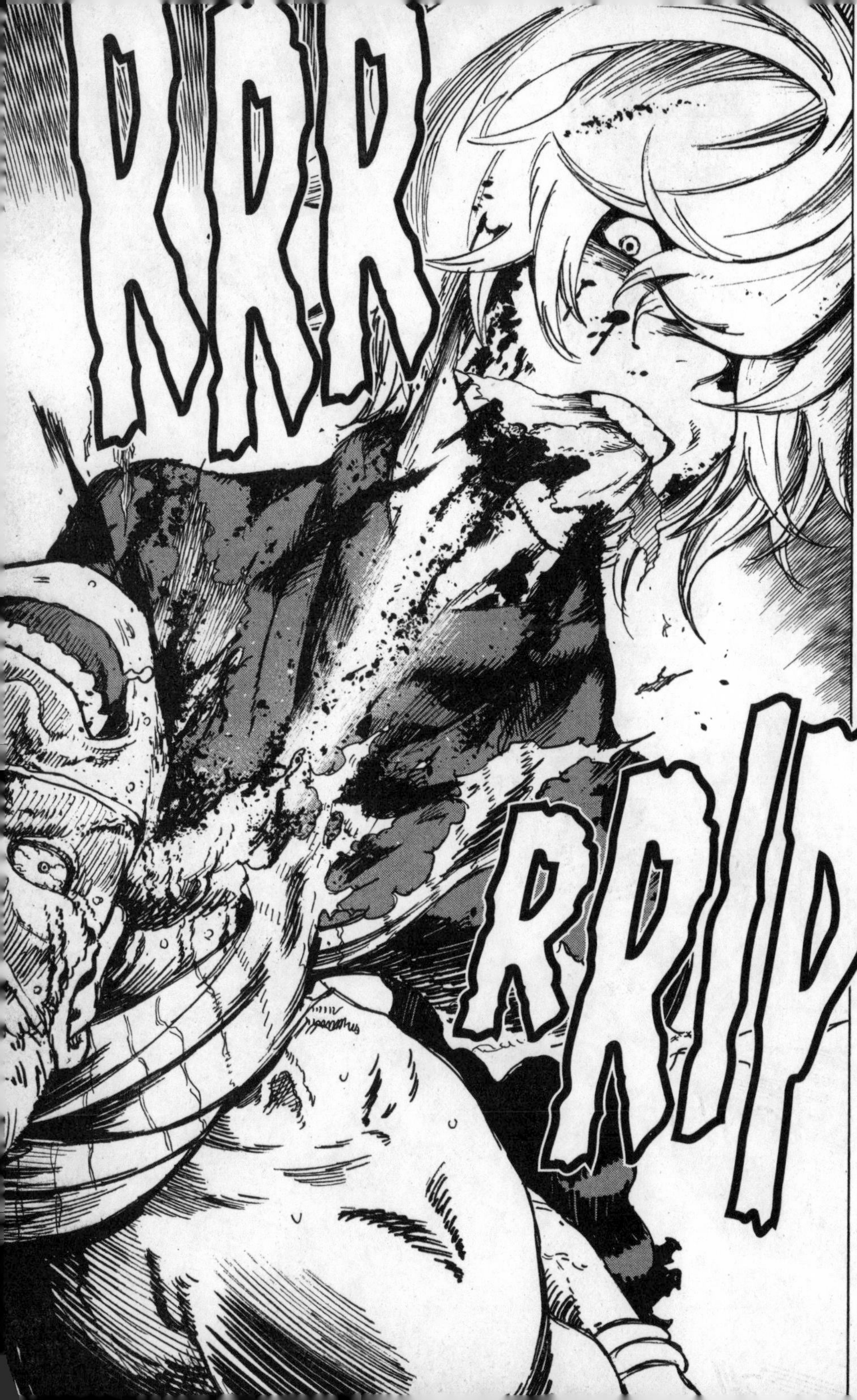
RRR
RRIP

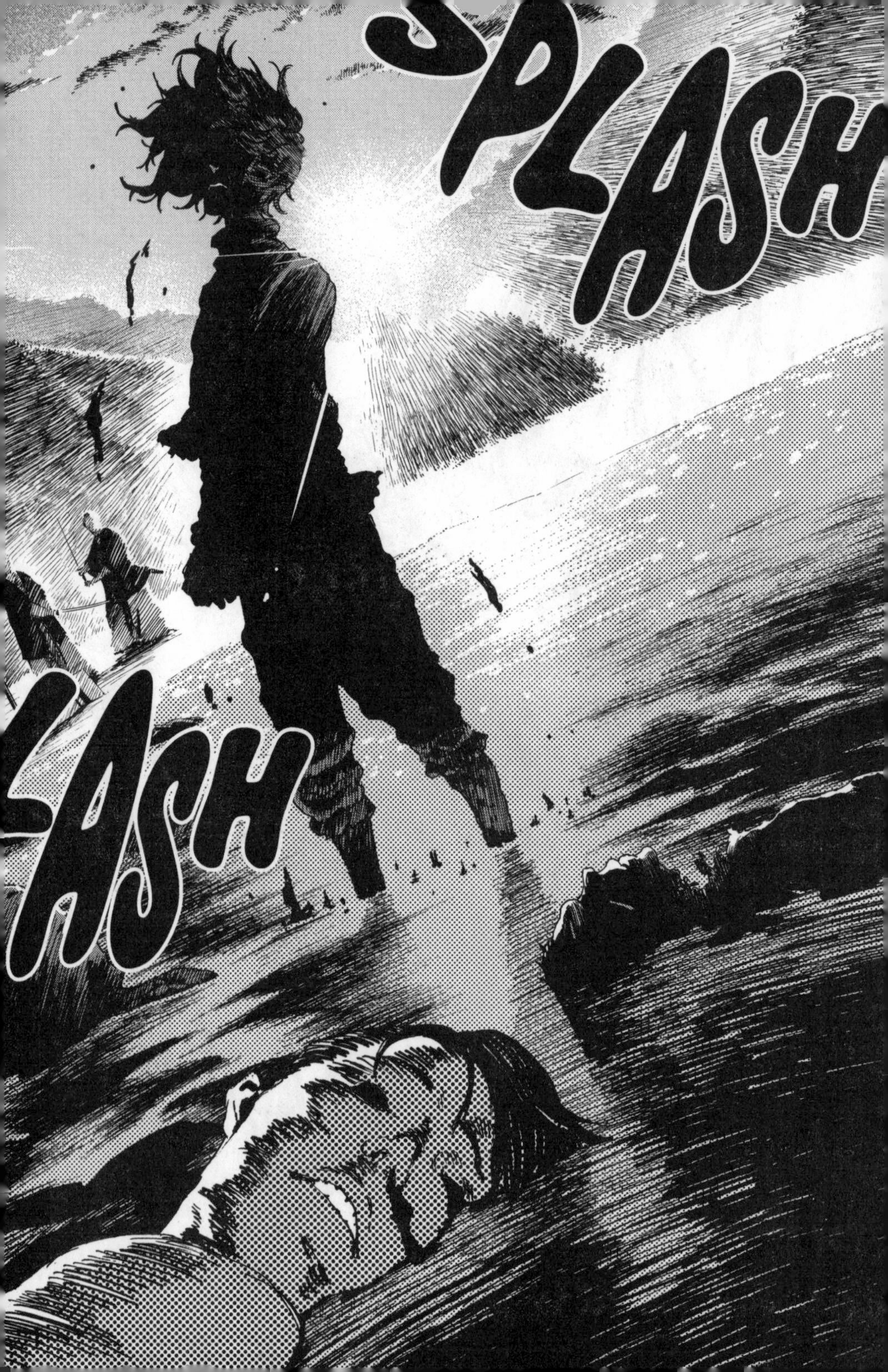
SPLASH
ASH

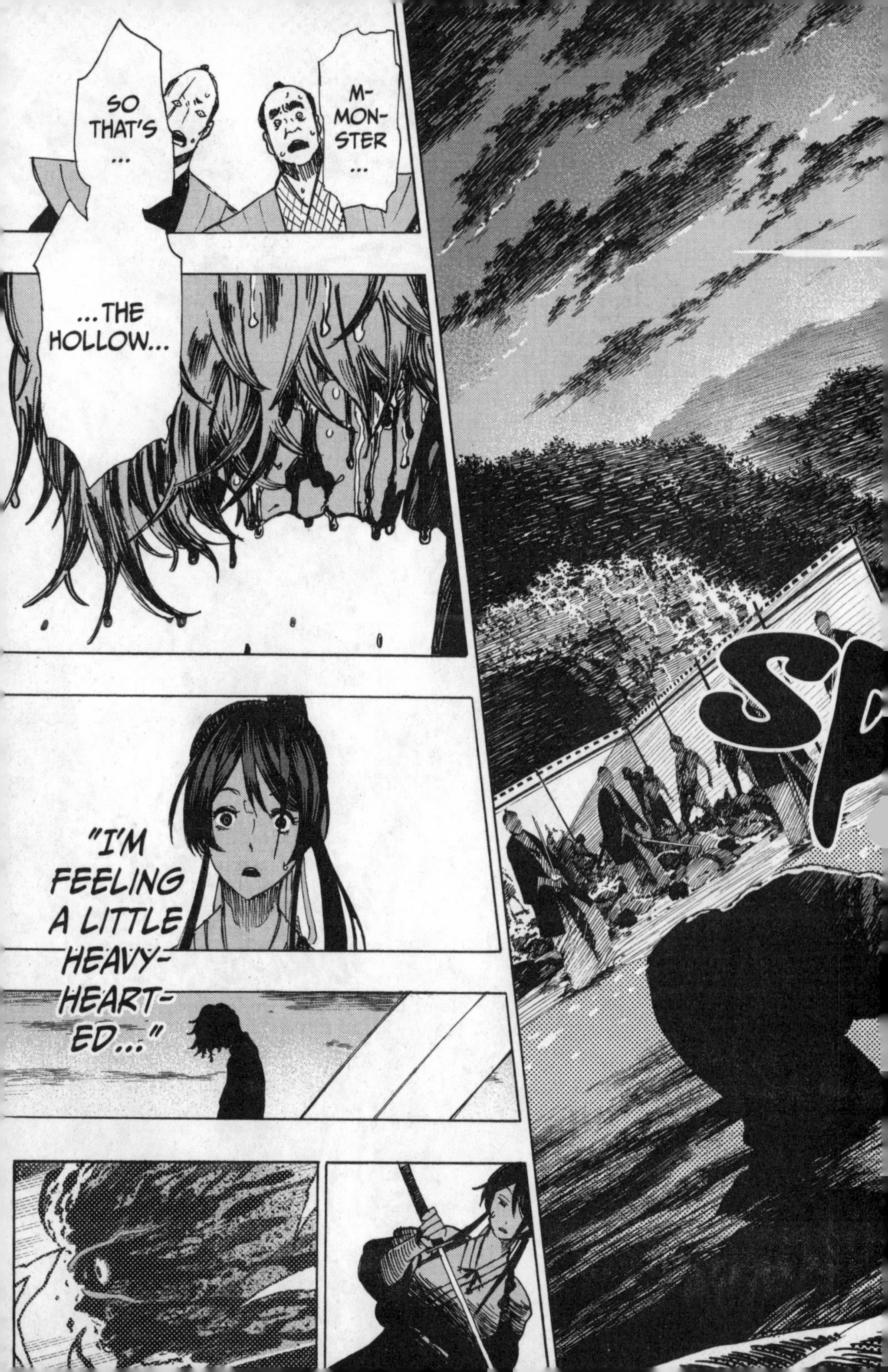
SP
M-MON-STER ...
SO THAT'S ...
... THE HOLLOW...
"I'M FEELING A LITTLE HEAVY-HEART-ED..."

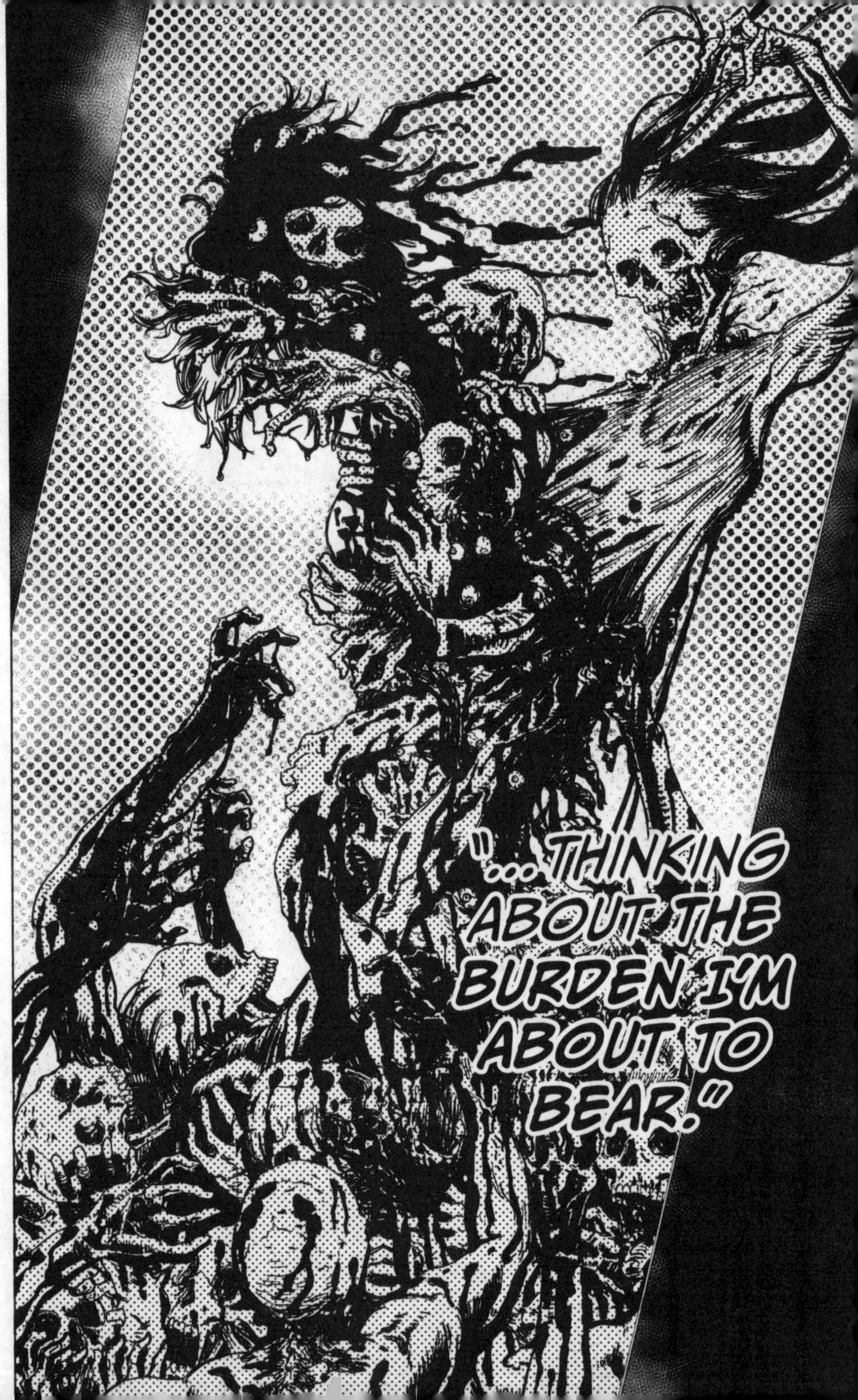
"...THINKING ABOUT THE BURDEN I'M ABOUT TO BEAR."

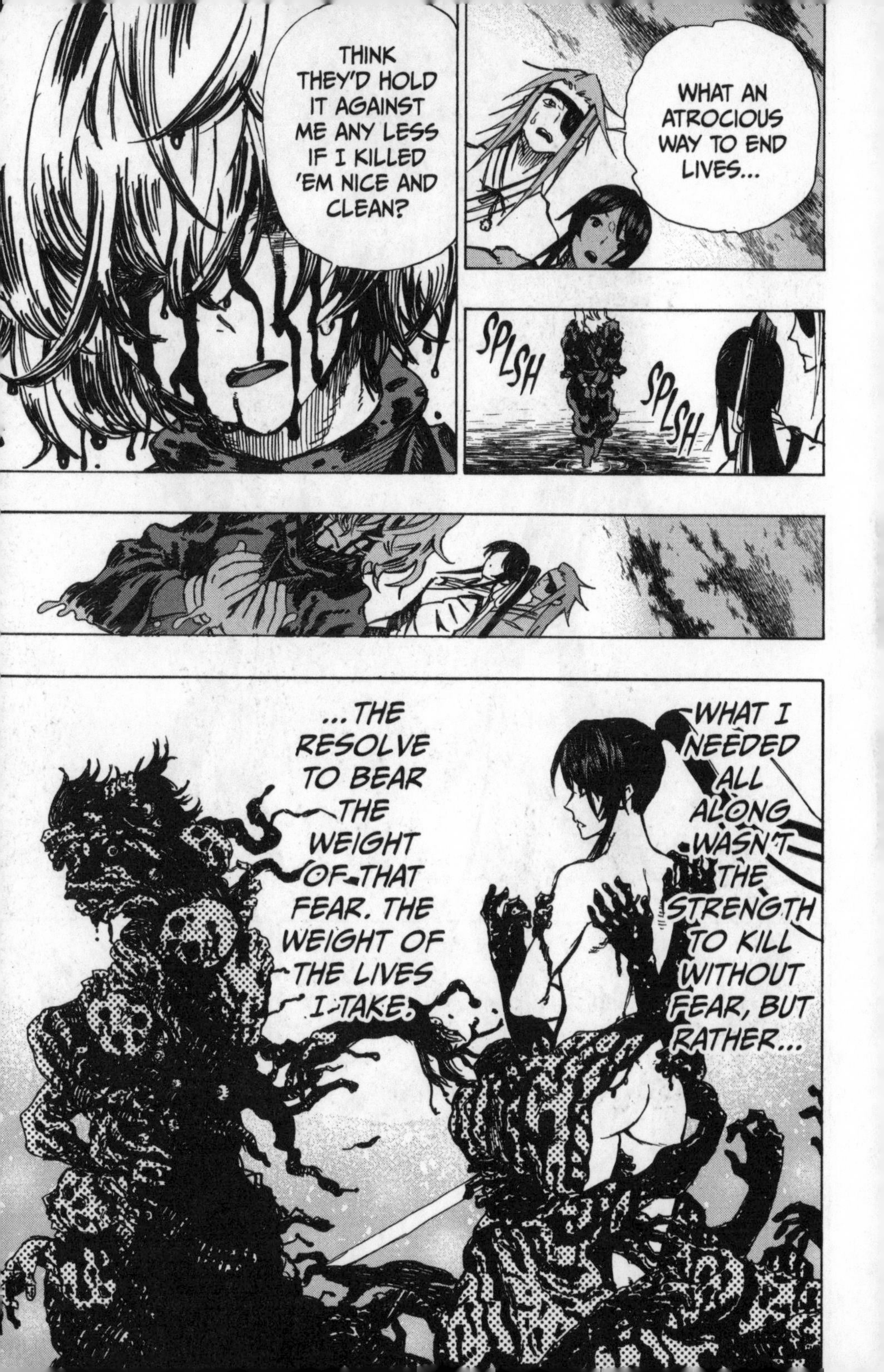
WHAT AN ATROCIOUS WAY TO END LIVES...
SPLSH
SPLSH
THINK THEY'D HOLD IT AGAINST ME ANY LESS IF I KILLED 'EM NICE AND CLEAN?
WHAT I NEEDED ALL ALONG WASN'T THE STRENGTH TO KILL WITHOUT FEAR, BUT RATHER...
...THE RESOLVE TO BEAR THE WEIGHT OF THAT FEAR. THE WEIGHT OF THE LIVES I TAKE.

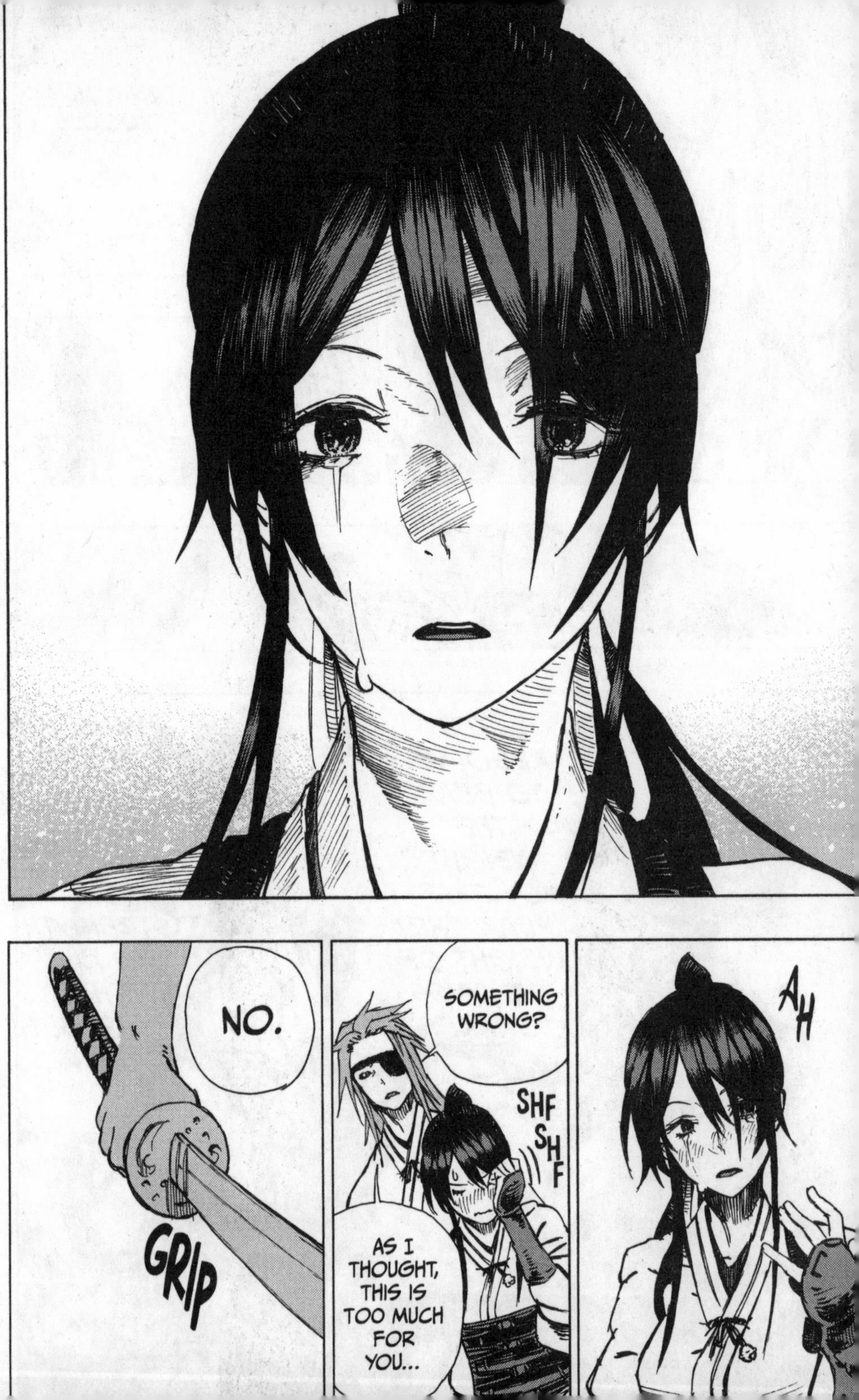
AH
SOMETHING WRONG?
SHF SHF
AS I THOUGHT, THIS IS TOO MUCH FOR YOU...
NO.
GRIP

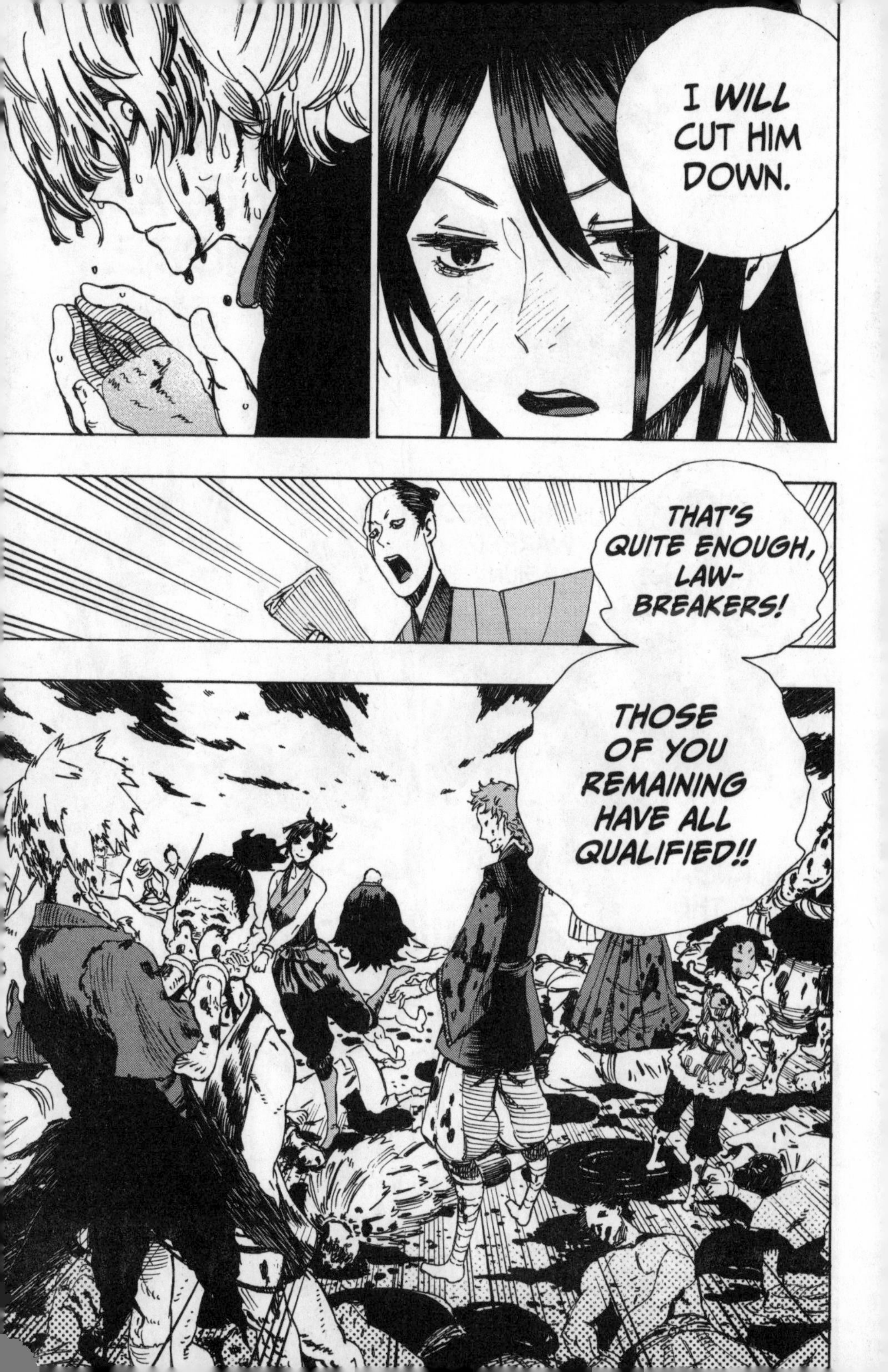
I WILL CUT HIM DOWN.
THAT'S QUITE ENOUGH, LAW-BREAKERS!
THOSE OF YOU REMAINING HAVE ALL QUALIFIED!!

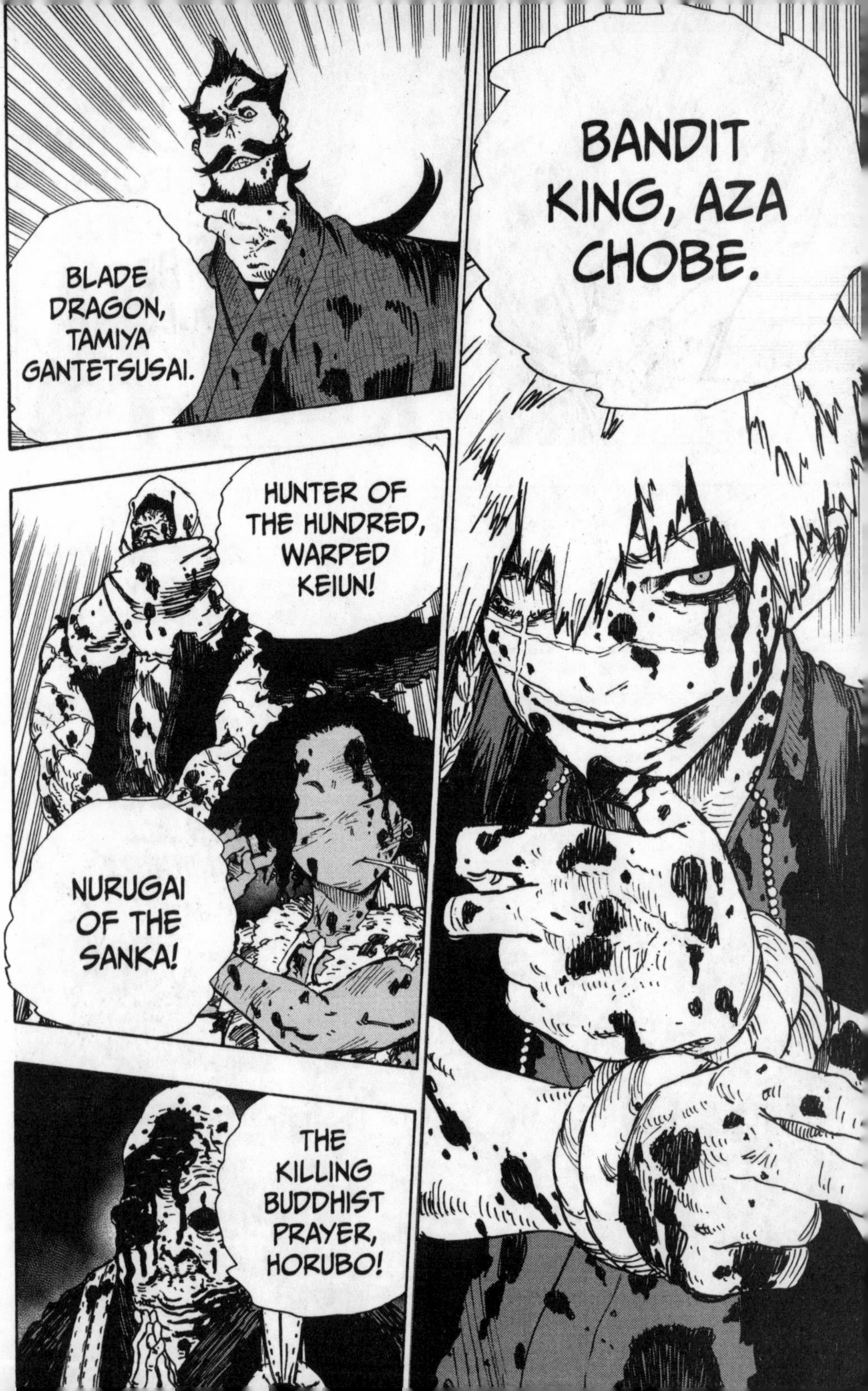
BANDIT KING, AZA CHOBE.
BLADE DRAGON, TAMIYA GANTETSUSAI.
HUNTER OF THE HUNDRED, WARPED KEIUN!
NURUGAI OF THE SANKA!
THE KILLING BUDDHIST PRAYER, HORUBO!

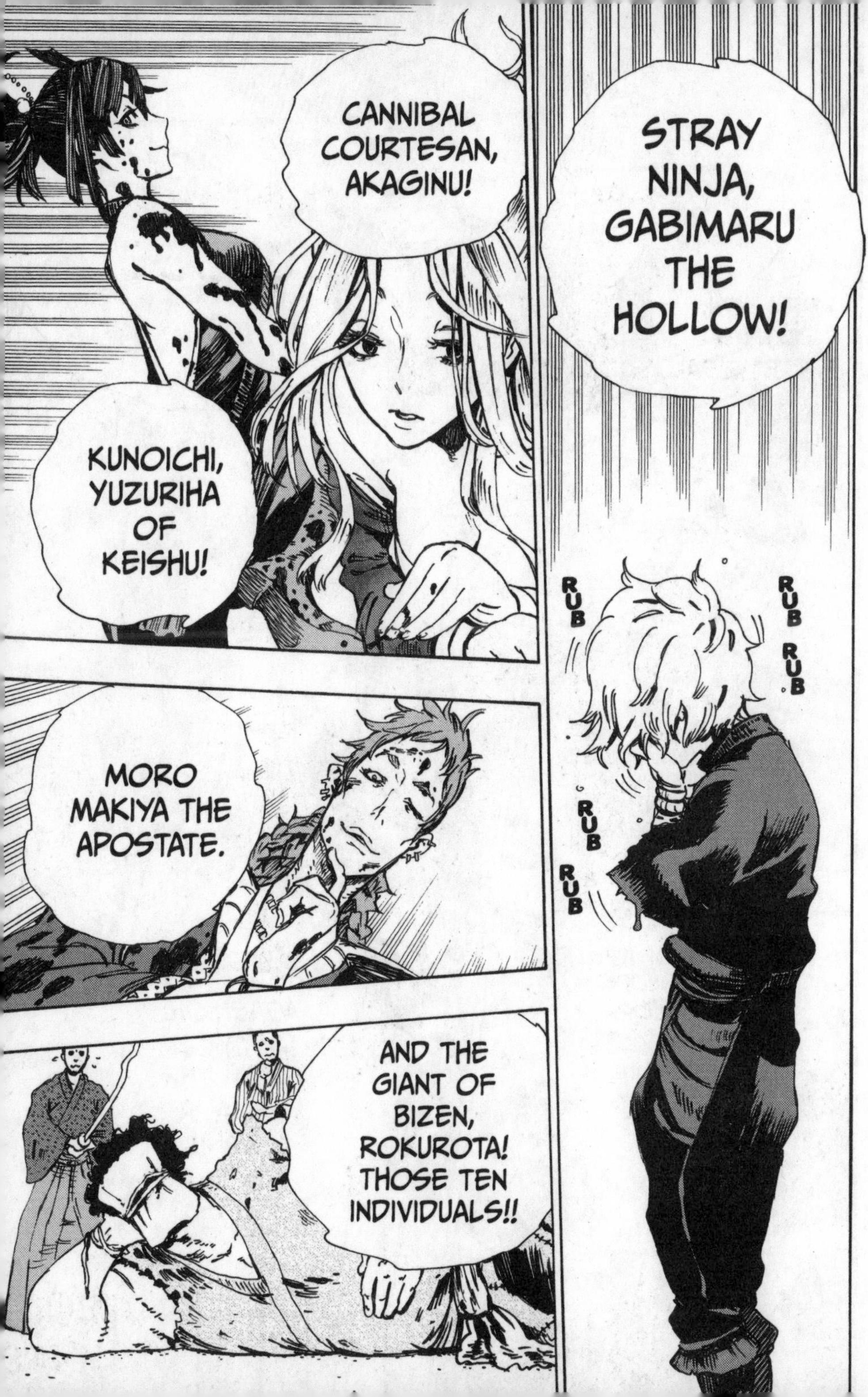
STRAY NINJA, GABIMARU THE HOLLOW!
RUB RUB RUB
RUB RUB RUB
CANNIBAL COURTESAN, AKAGINU!
KUNOICHI, YUZURIHA OF KEISHU!
MORO MAKIYA THE APOSTATE.
AND THE GIANT OF BIZEN, ROKUROTA! THOSE TEN INDIVIDUALS!!

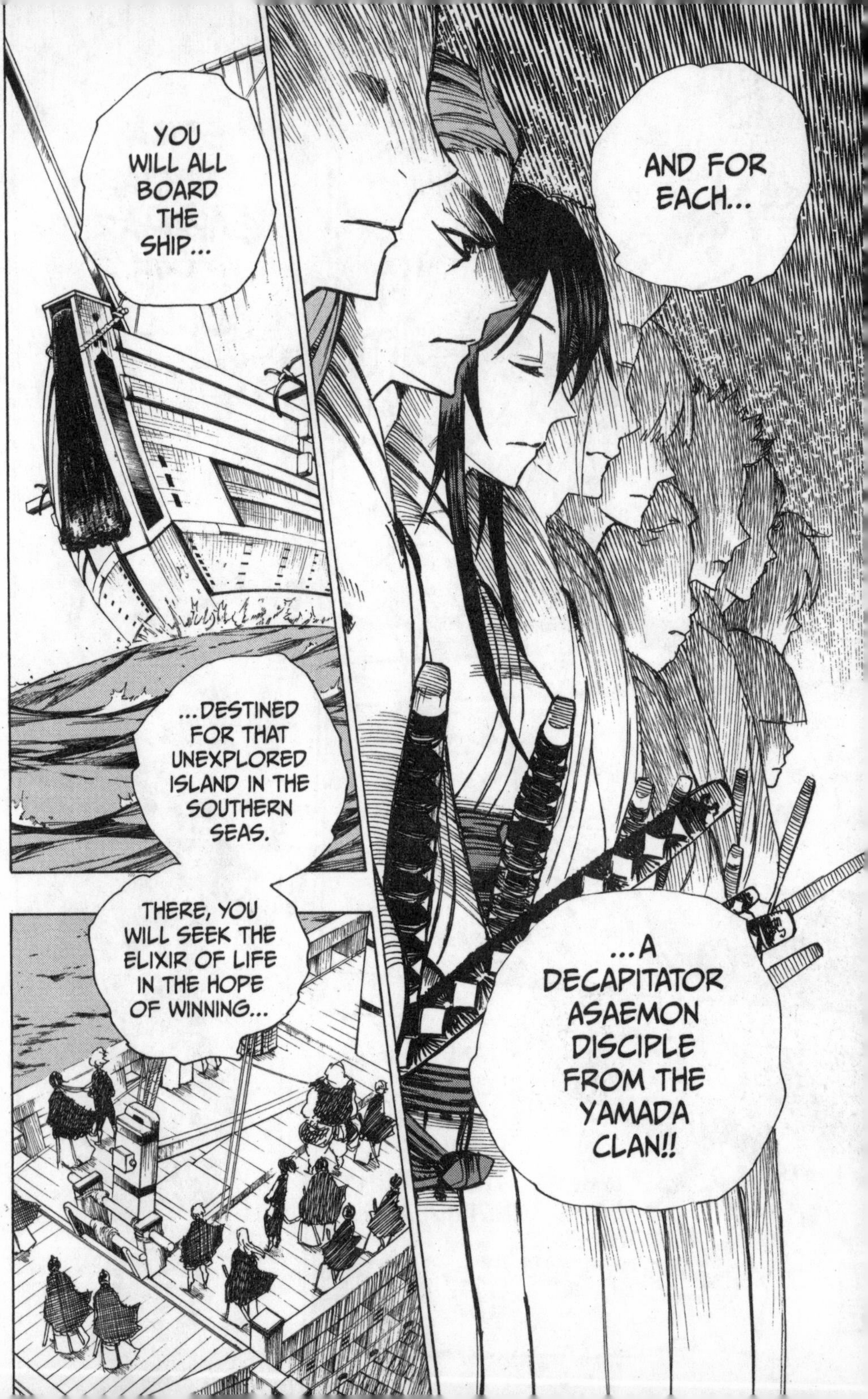
AND FOR EACH...
...A DECAPITATOR ASAEMON DISCIPLE FROM THE YAMADA CLAN!!
YOU WILL ALL BOARD THE SHIP...
...DESTINED FOR THAT UNEXPLORED ISLAND IN THE SOUTHERN SEAS.
THERE, YOU WILL SEEK THE ELIXIR OF LIFE IN THE HOPE OF WINNING...

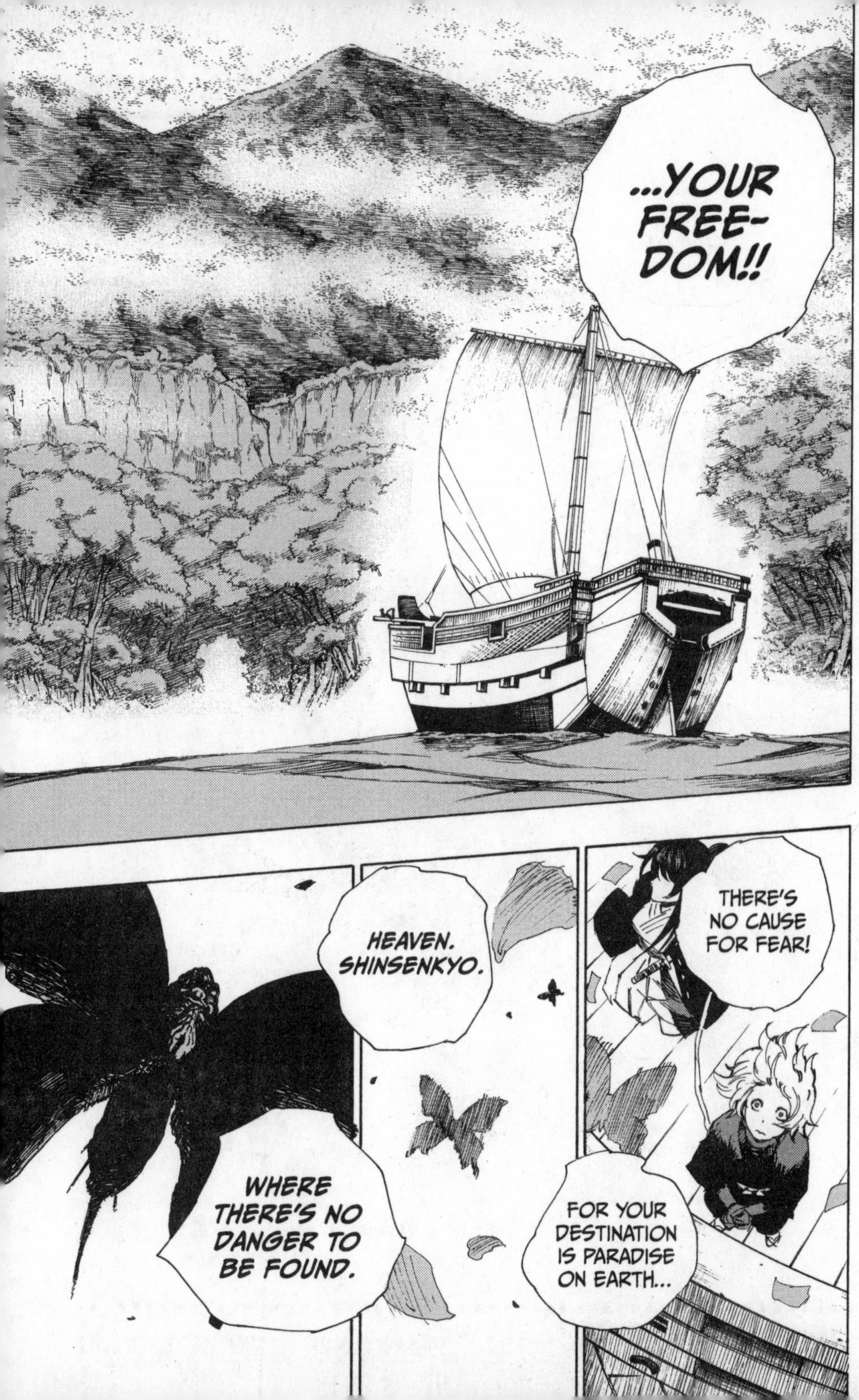
...YOUR FREE-DOM!!
THERE'S NO CAUSE FOR FEAR!
FOR YOUR DESTINATION IS PARADISE ON EARTH...
HEAVEN. SHINSENKYO.
WHERE THERE'S NO DANGER TO BE FOUND.

Hell's Paradise Fashion Review

Stray Shinobi, Formerly of Iwagakure

GABIMARU

Standard shinobi garb, combining a ***teppo-sode*** top with ***tattsuke-bakama*** style bottoms, cinched around the lower legs for easier movement. Terribly old-fashioned.

Sleeves widen at the cuffs (and are ripped and ragged).

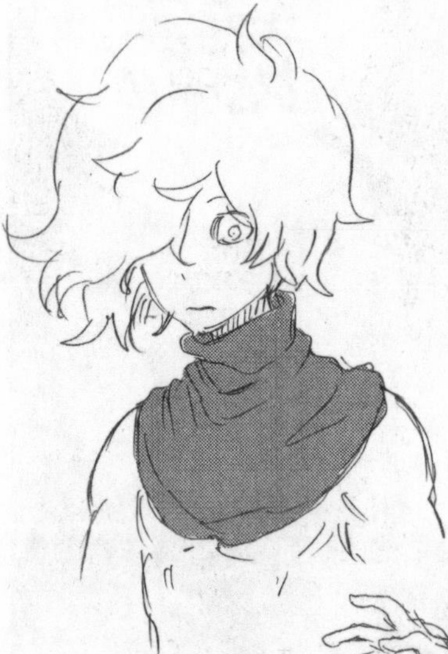

Shinobi ***tenugui*** kerchief covers neck down to chest. Made of special fibers that can stretch.

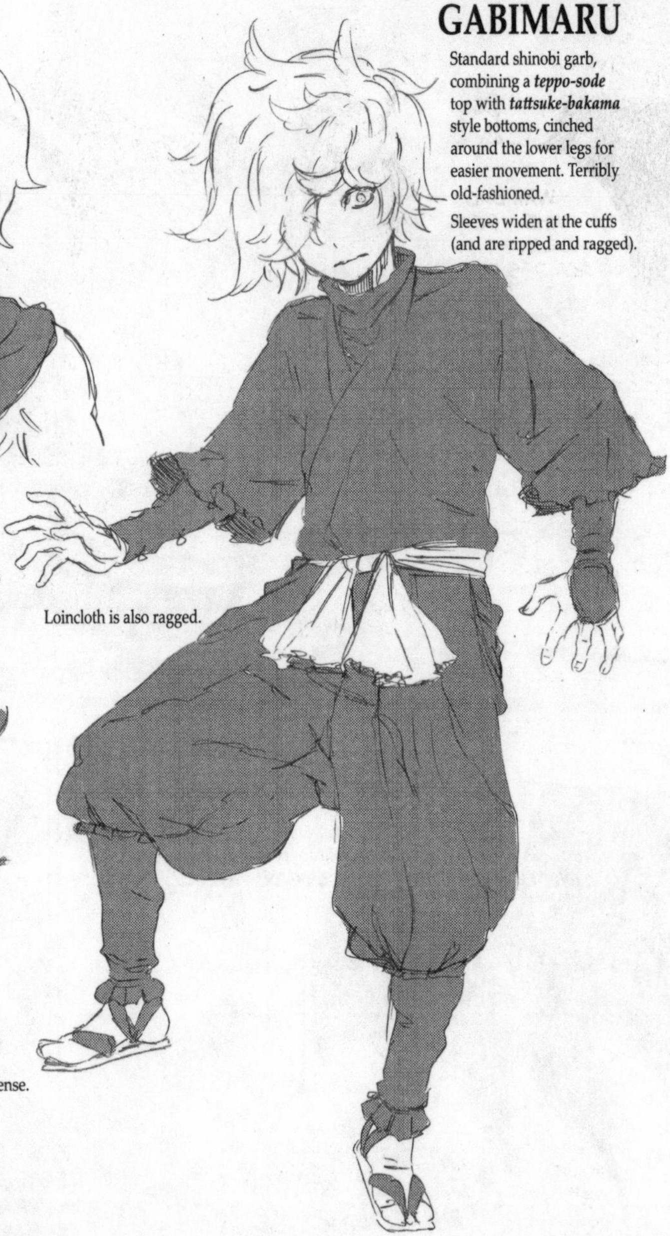

Loincloth is also ragged.

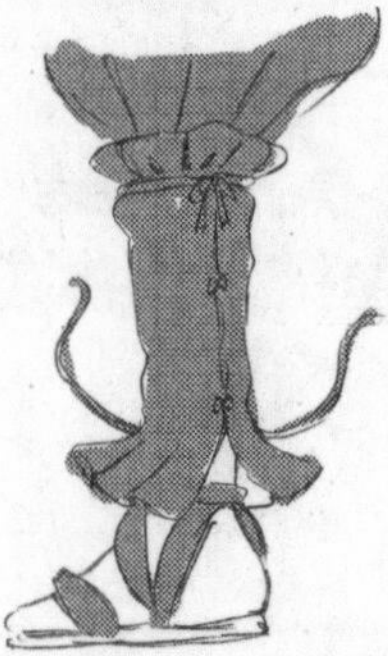

Kyahan gaiters layered over ***hakama*** legs, for additional defense.

EVALUATION ► PEASANT IS THE NEW BLACK ☆☆☆ SOMEONE TAKE THIS GUY SHOPPING FOR NEW DUDS!

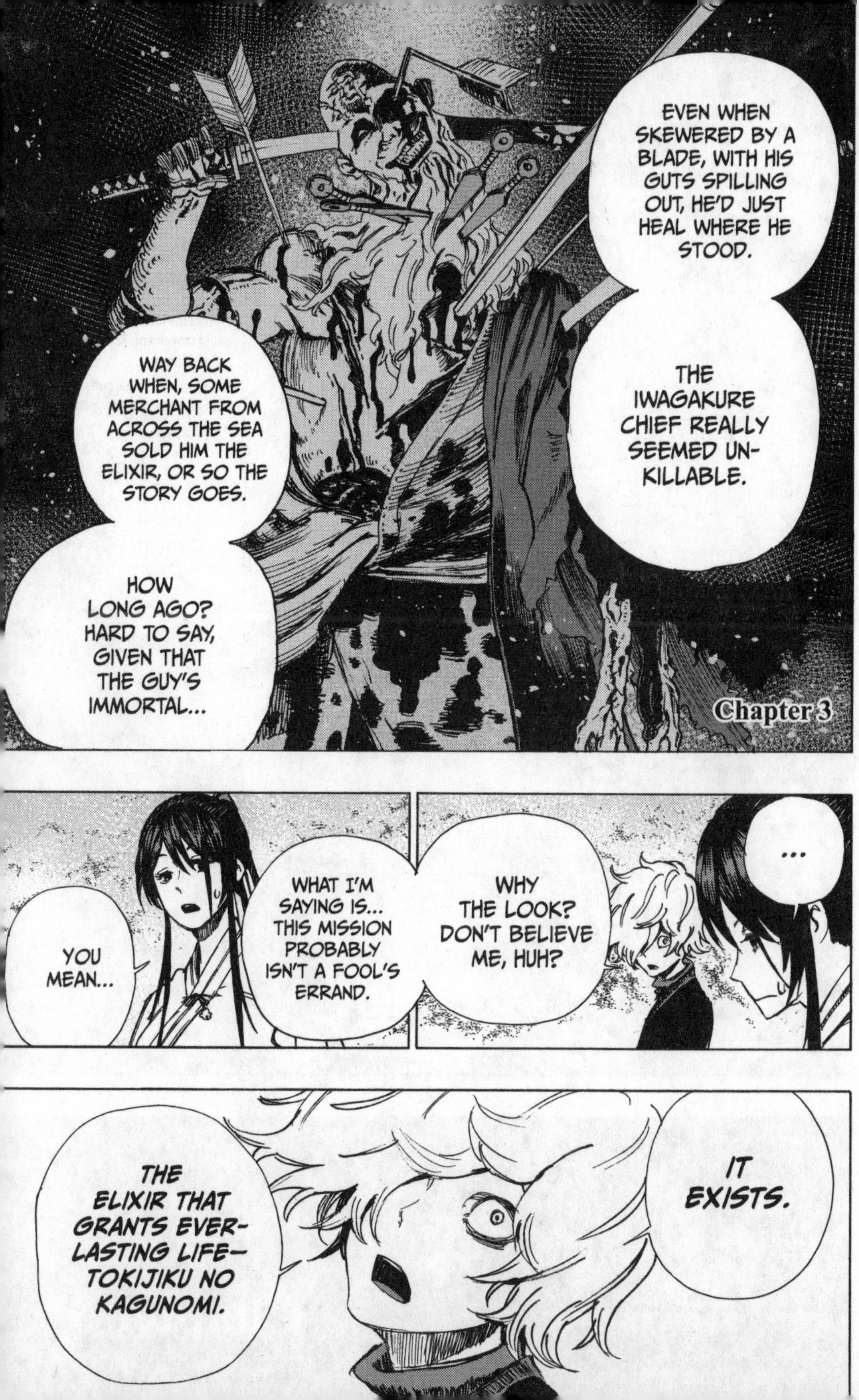
EVEN WHEN SKEWERED BY A BLADE, WITH HIS GUTS SPILLING OUT, HE'D JUST HEAL WHERE HE STOOD.
THE IWAGAKURE CHIEF REALLY SEEMED UN-KILLABLE.
WAY BACK WHEN, SOME MERCHANT FROM ACROSS THE SEA SOLD HIM THE ELIXIR, OR SO THE STORY GOES.
HOW LONG AGO? HARD TO SAY, GIVEN THAT THE GUY'S IMMORTAL...
Chapter 3
...
WHY THE LOOK? DON'T BELIEVE ME, HUH?
WHAT I'M SAYING IS... THIS MISSION PROBABLY ISN'T A FOOL'S ERRAND.
YOU MEAN...
IT EXISTS.
THE ELIXIR THAT GRANTS EVER-LASTING LIFE— TOKIJIKU NO KAGUNOMI.

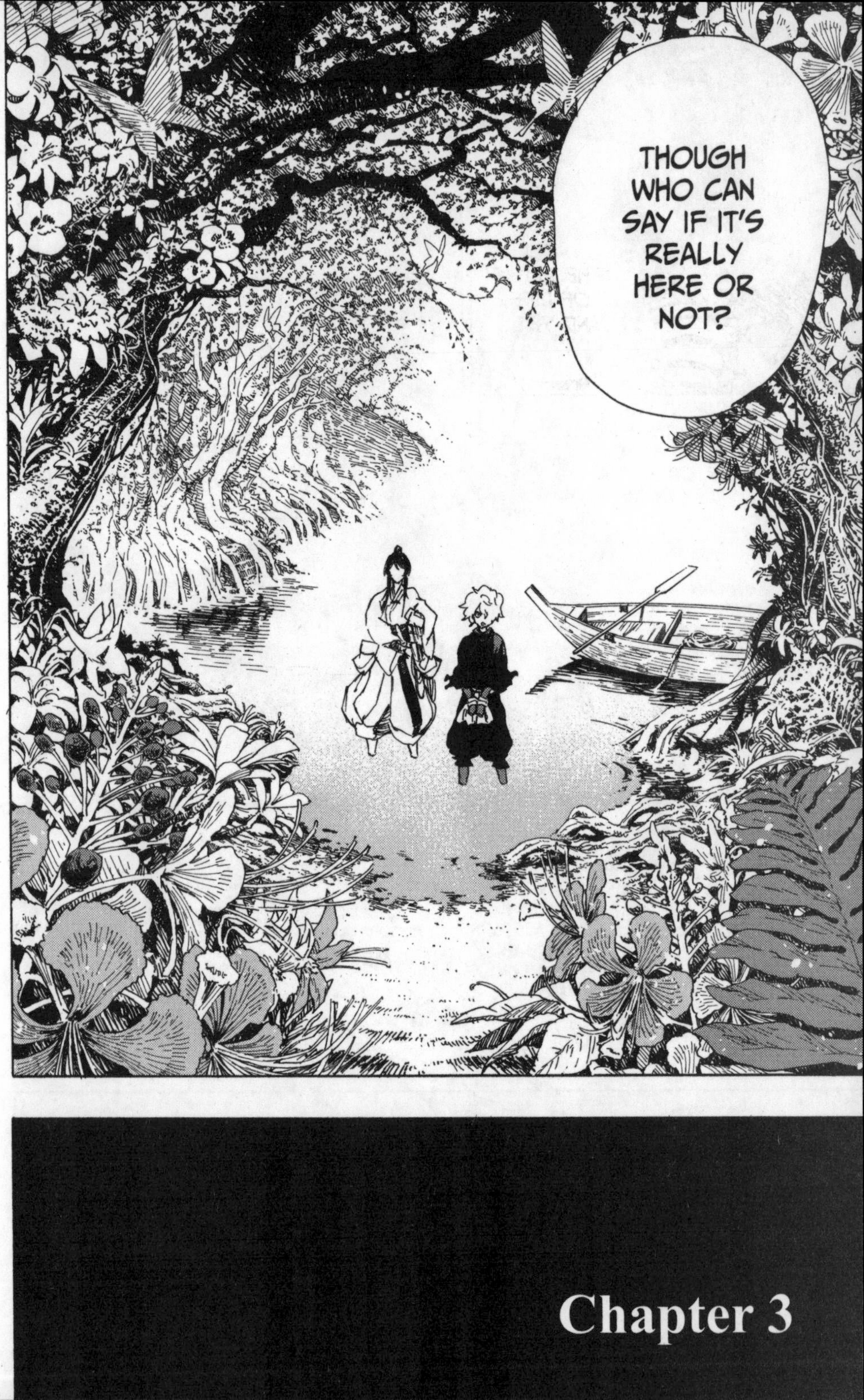
THOUGH WHO CAN SAY IF IT'S REALLY HERE OR NOT?

Chapter 3

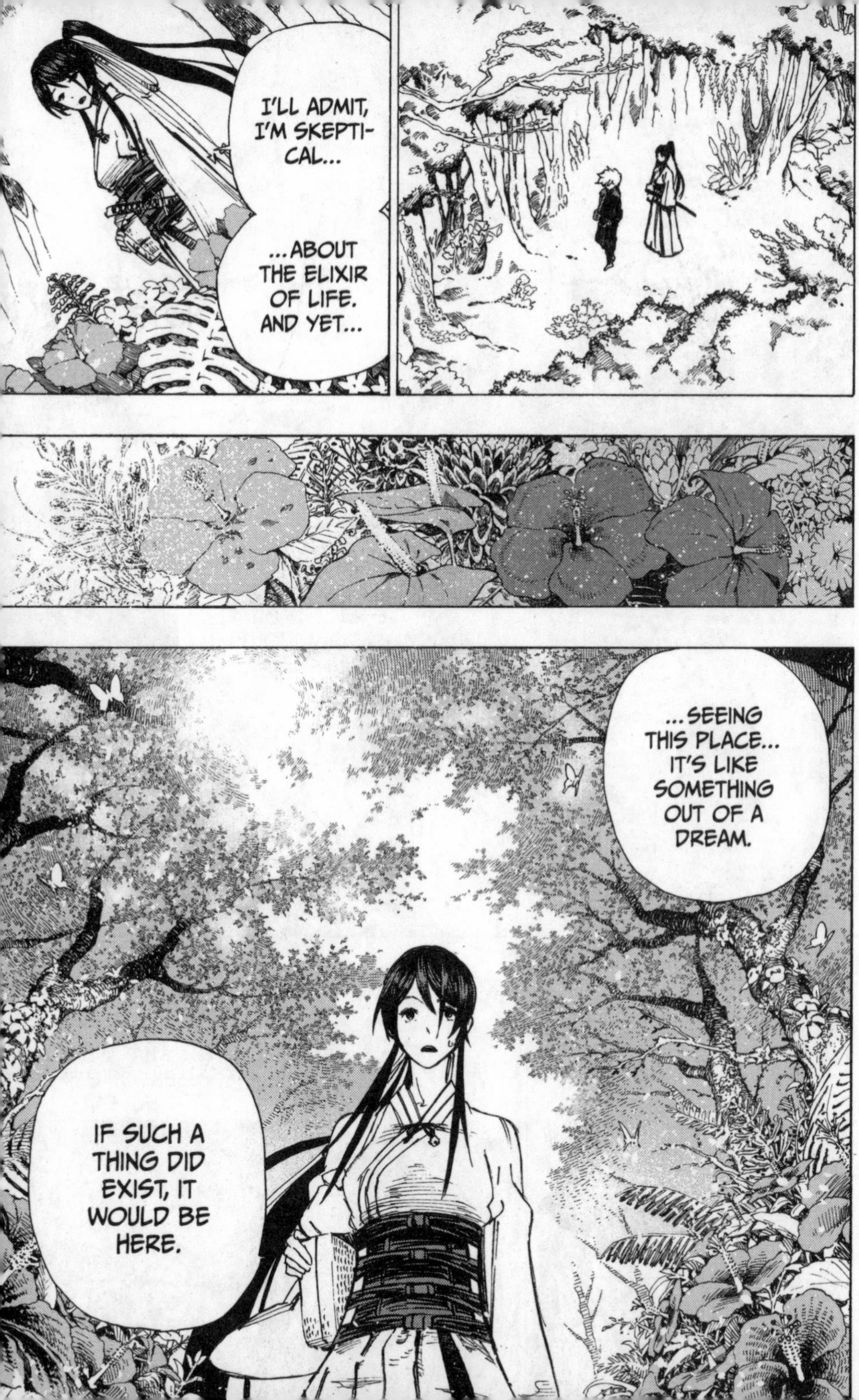
I'LL ADMIT, I'M SKEPTI-CAL...
...ABOUT THE ELIXIR OF LIFE. AND YET...
...SEEING THIS PLACE... IT'S LIKE SOMETHING OUT OF A DREAM.
IF SUCH A THING DID EXIST, IT WOULD BE HERE.

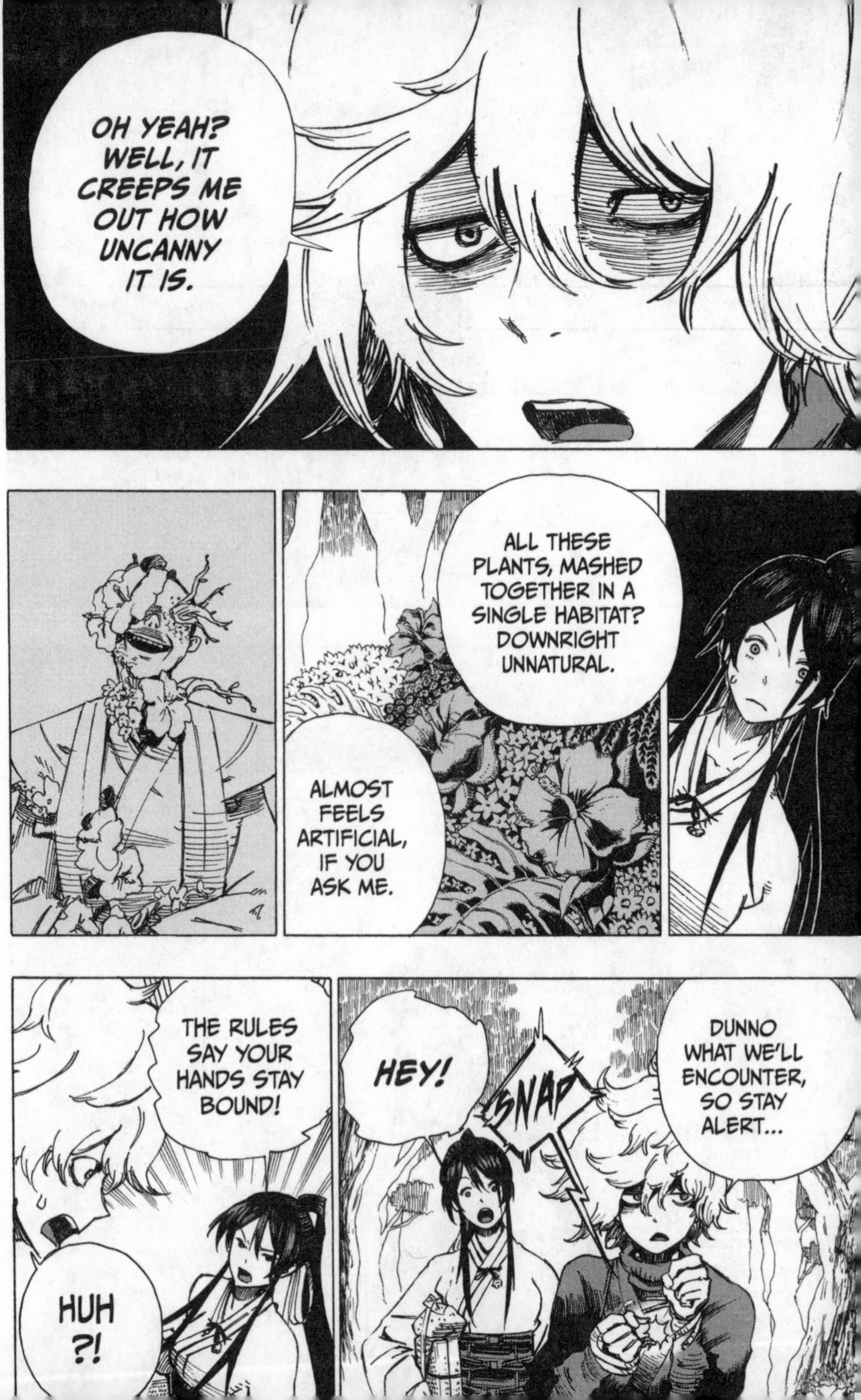
OH YEAH? WELL, IT CREEPS ME OUT HOW UNCANNY IT IS.
ALL THESE PLANTS, MASHED TOGETHER IN A SINGLE HABITAT? DOWNRIGHT UNNATURAL.
ALMOST FEELS ARTIFICIAL, IF YOU ASK ME.
DUNNO WHAT WE'LL ENCOUNTER, SO STAY ALERT...
SNAP
HEY!
THE RULES SAY YOUR HANDS STAY BOUND!
HUH ?!

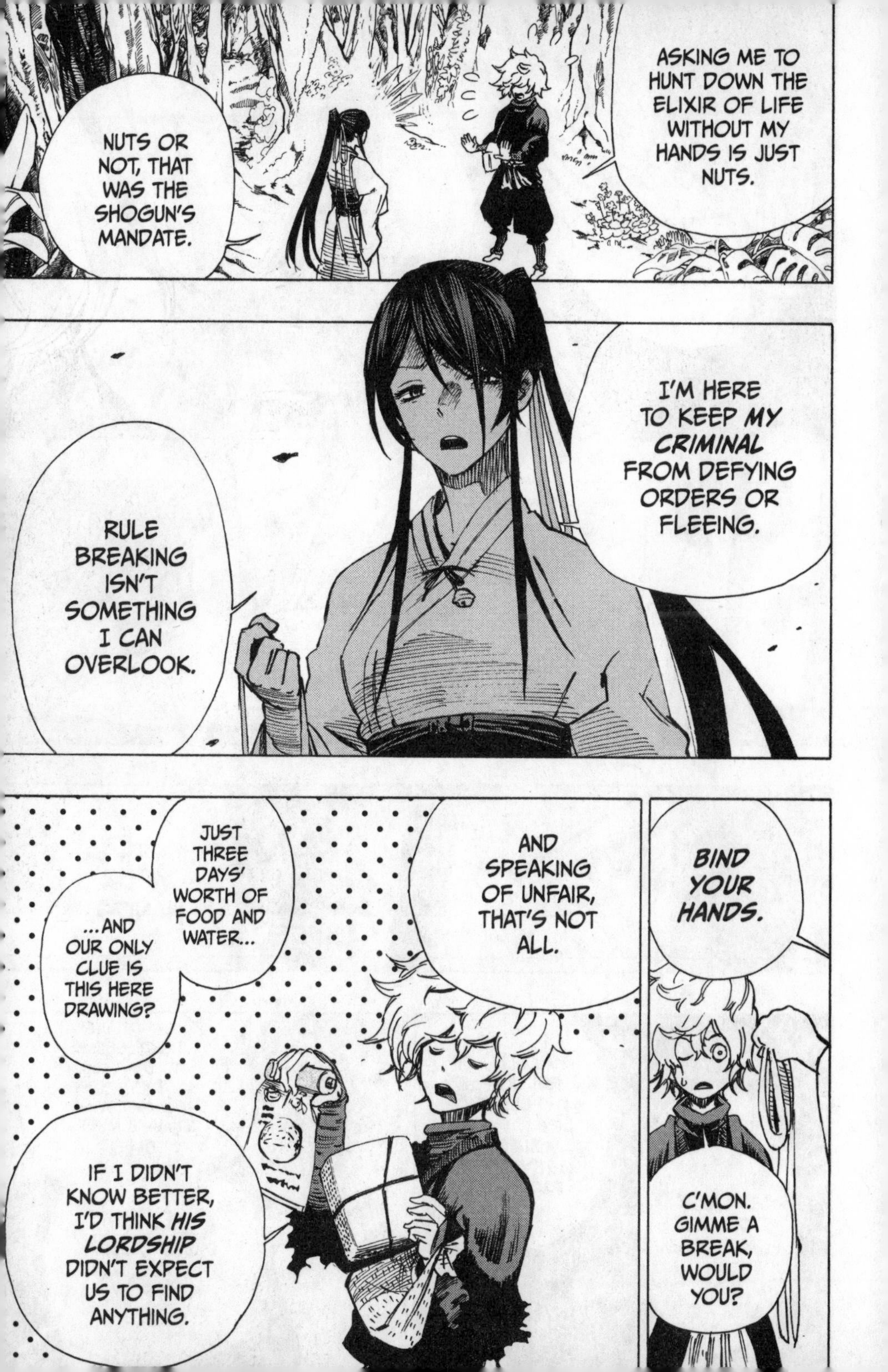
ASKING ME TO HUNT DOWN THE ELIXIR OF LIFE WITHOUT MY HANDS IS JUST NUTS.
NUTS OR NOT, THAT WAS THE SHOGUN'S MANDATE.
I'M HERE TO KEEP *MY CRIMINAL* FROM DEFYING ORDERS OR FLEEING.
RULE BREAKING ISN'T SOMETHING I CAN OVERLOOK.
BIND YOUR HANDS.
C'MON. GIMME A BREAK, WOULD YOU?
AND SPEAKING OF UNFAIR, THAT'S NOT ALL.
JUST THREE DAYS' WORTH OF FOOD AND WATER...
...AND OUR ONLY CLUE IS THIS HERE DRAWING?
IF I DIDN'T KNOW BETTER, I'D THINK *HIS LORDSHIP* DIDN'T EXPECT US TO FIND ANYTHING.

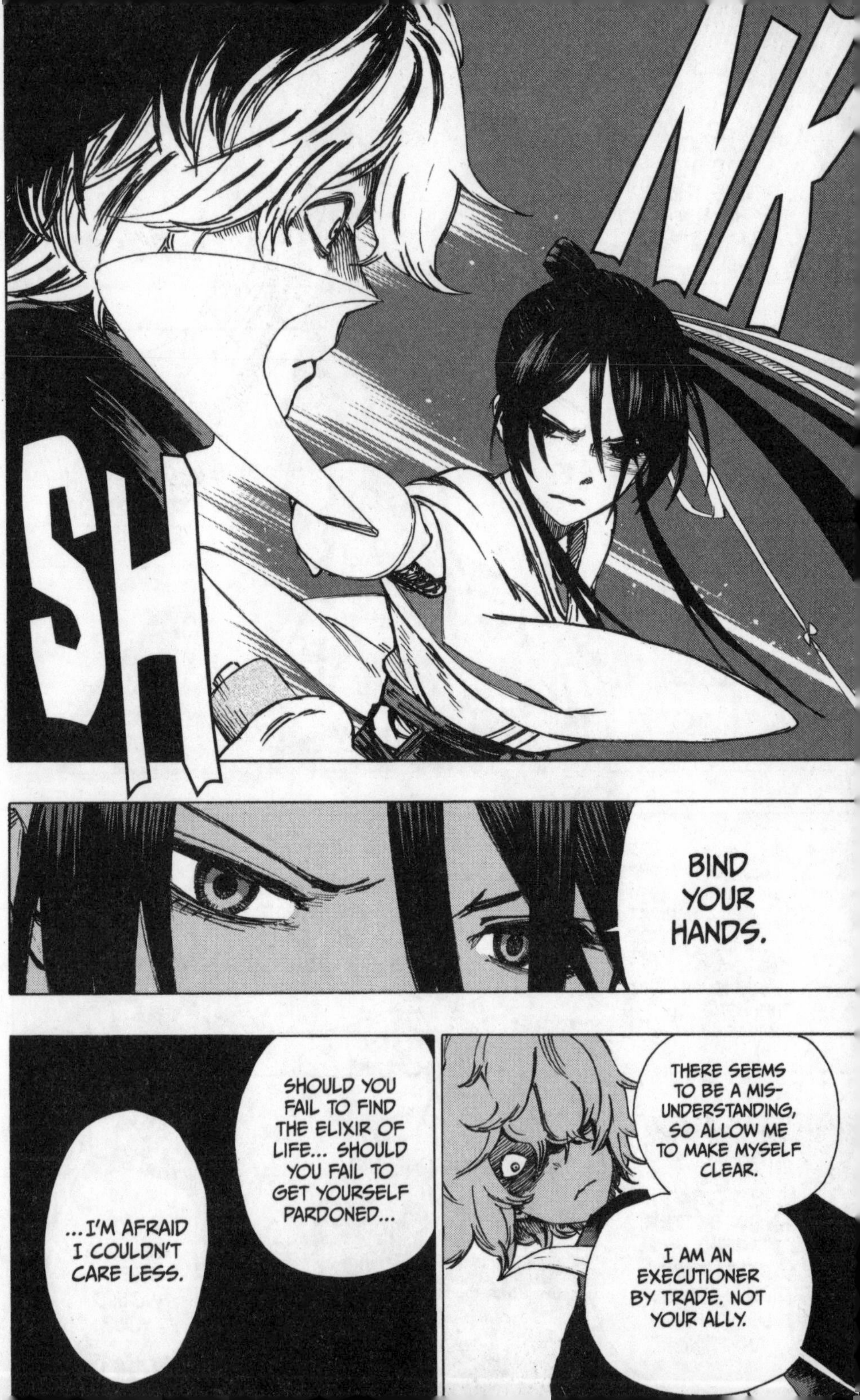
SH
NK
BIND YOUR HANDS.
THERE SEEMS TO BE A MIS-UNDERSTANDING, SO ALLOW ME TO MAKE MYSELF CLEAR.
I AM AN EXECUTIONER BY TRADE. NOT YOUR ALLY.
SHOULD YOU FAIL TO FIND THE ELIXIR OF LIFE... SHOULD YOU FAIL TO GET YOURSELF PARDONED...
...I'M AFRAID I COULDN'T CARE LESS.

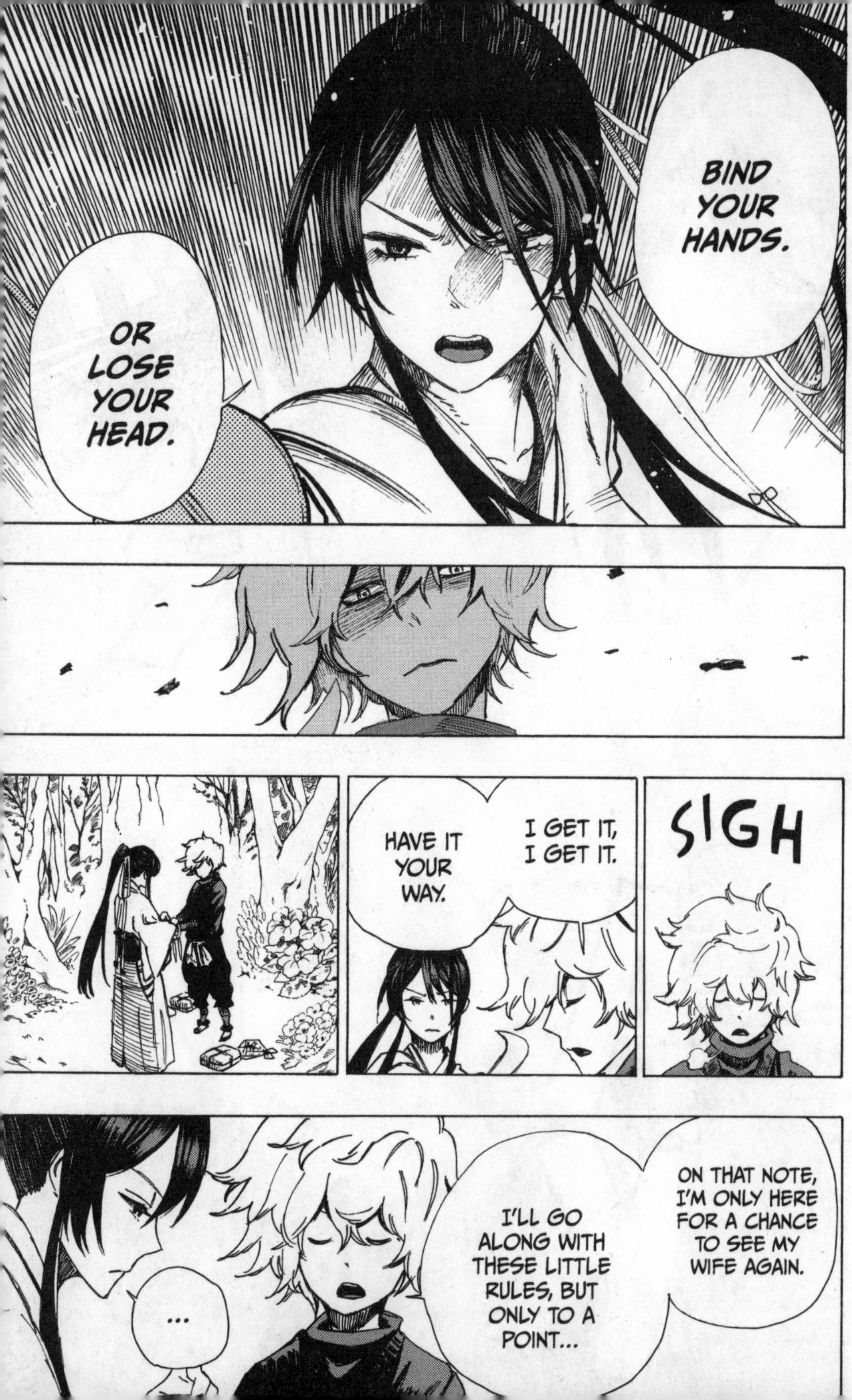
BIND YOUR HANDS.
OR LOSE YOUR HEAD.
SIGH
I GET IT, I GET IT.
HAVE IT YOUR WAY.
ON THAT NOTE, I'M ONLY HERE FOR A CHANCE TO SEE MY WIFE AGAIN.
I'LL GO ALONG WITH THESE LITTLE RULES, BUT ONLY TO A POINT...
...

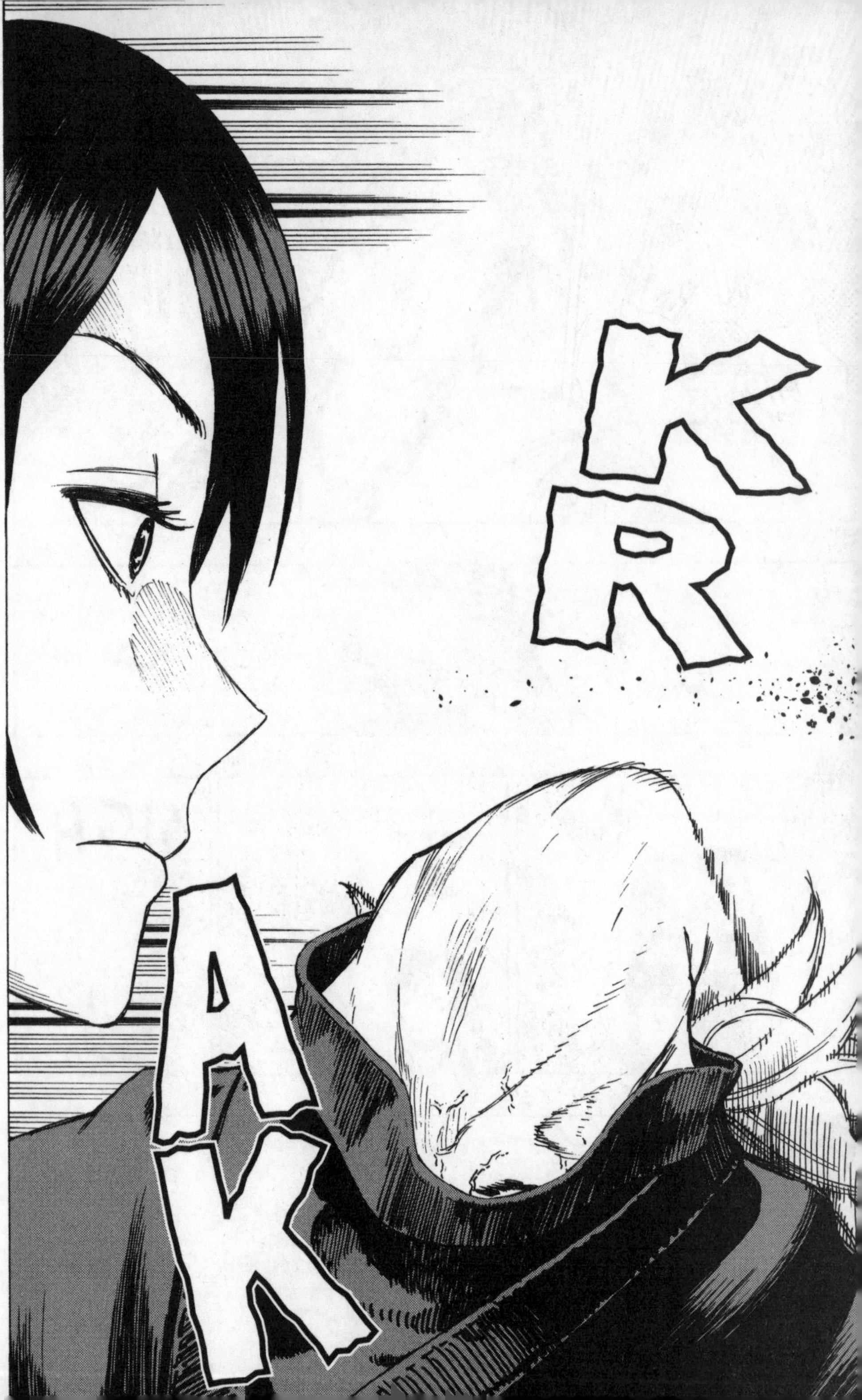
KR
AK

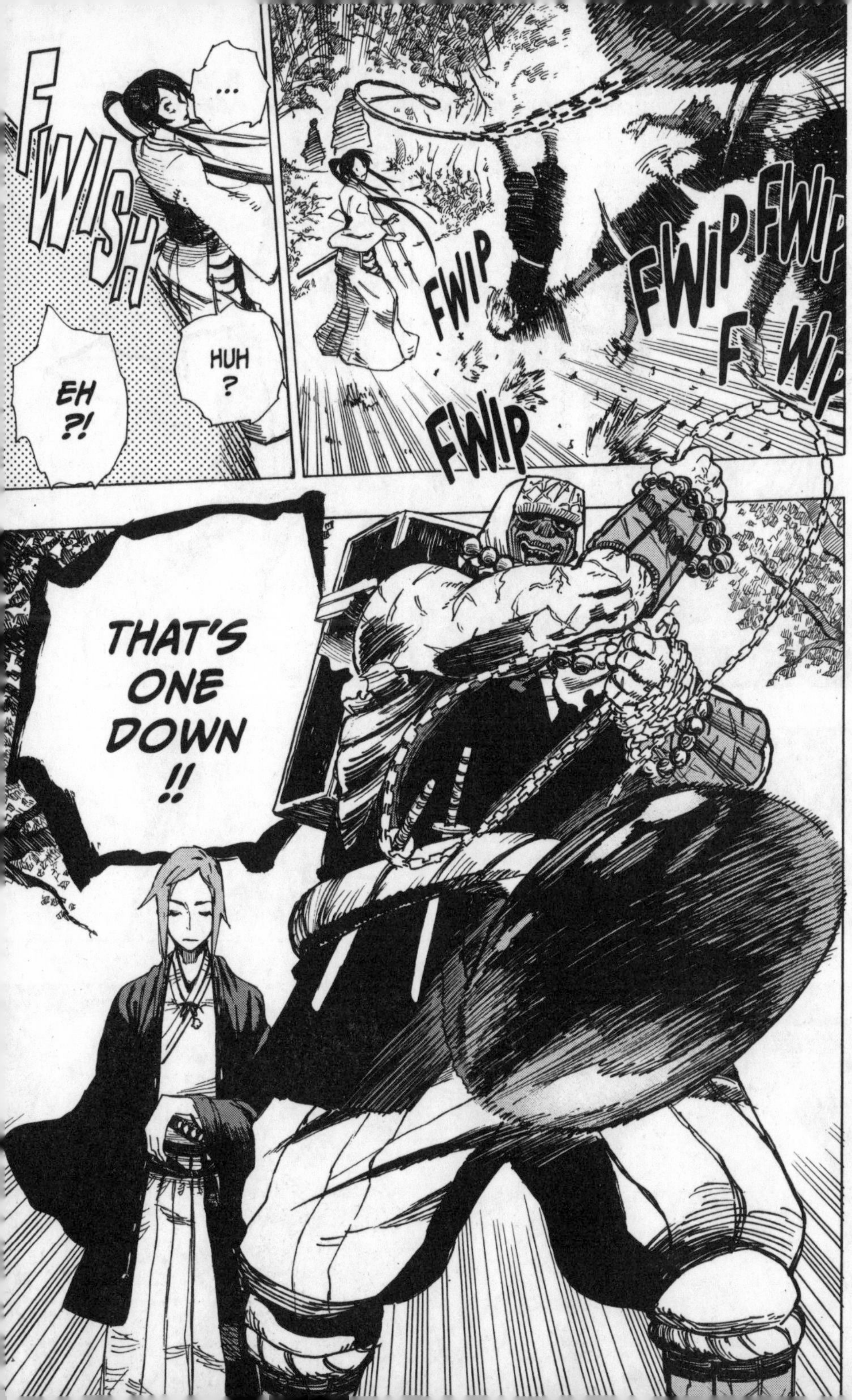
FWIP
FWIP
F WIP
FWIP
FWIP
FWIP
...
FWISH
HUH?
EH?!
THAT'S ONE DOWN!!

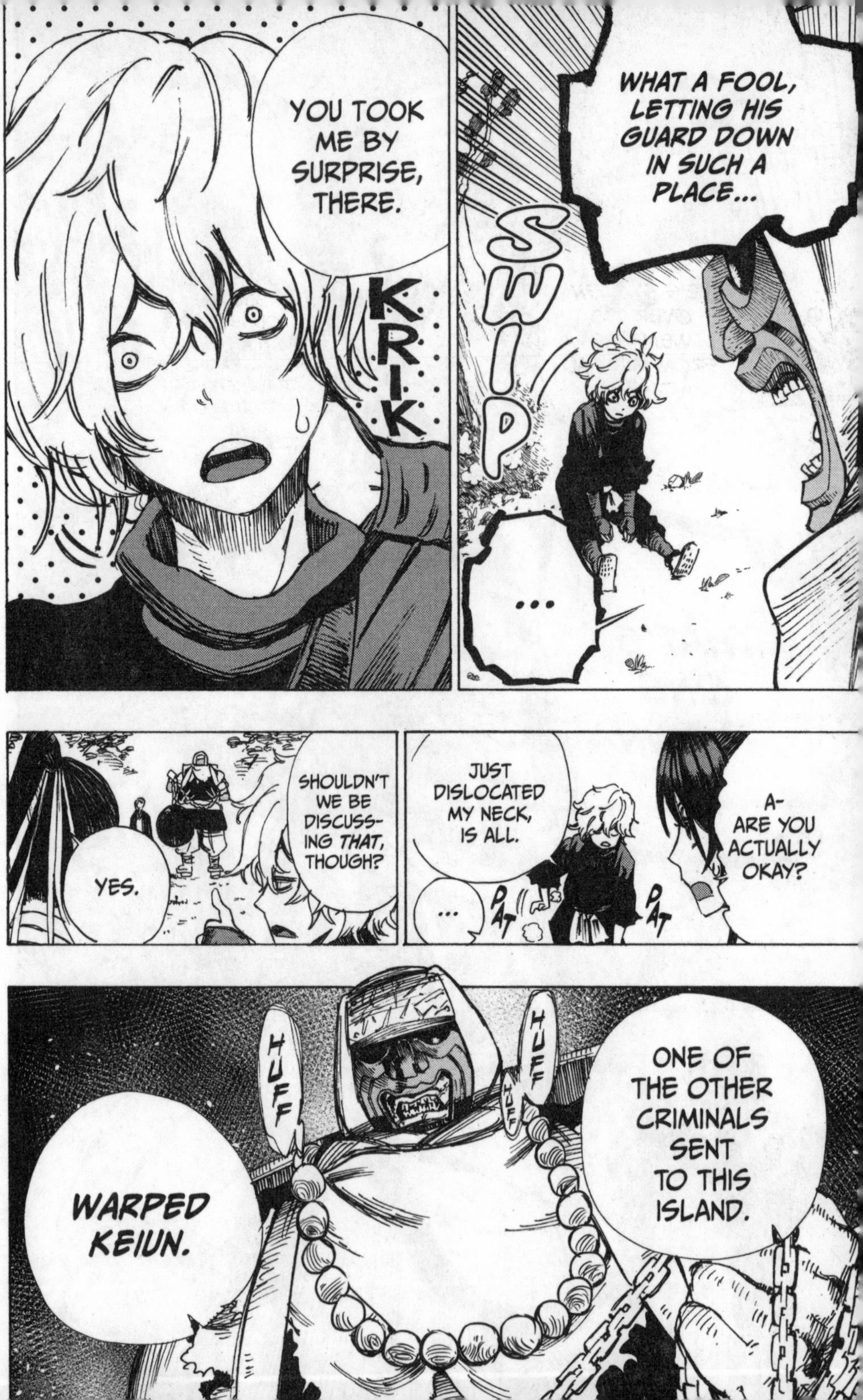
WHAT A FOOL, LETTING HIS GUARD DOWN IN SUCH A PLACE...
SWIP
...
KRIK
YOU TOOK ME BY SURPRISE, THERE.
A- ARE YOU ACTUALLY OKAY?
PAT
JUST DISLOCATED MY NECK, IS ALL.
...
PAT
SHOULDN'T WE BE DISCUSS-ING *THAT*, THOUGH?
YES.
ONE OF THE OTHER CRIMINALS SENT TO THIS ISLAND.
HUFF
HUFF
HUFF
WARPED KEIUN.

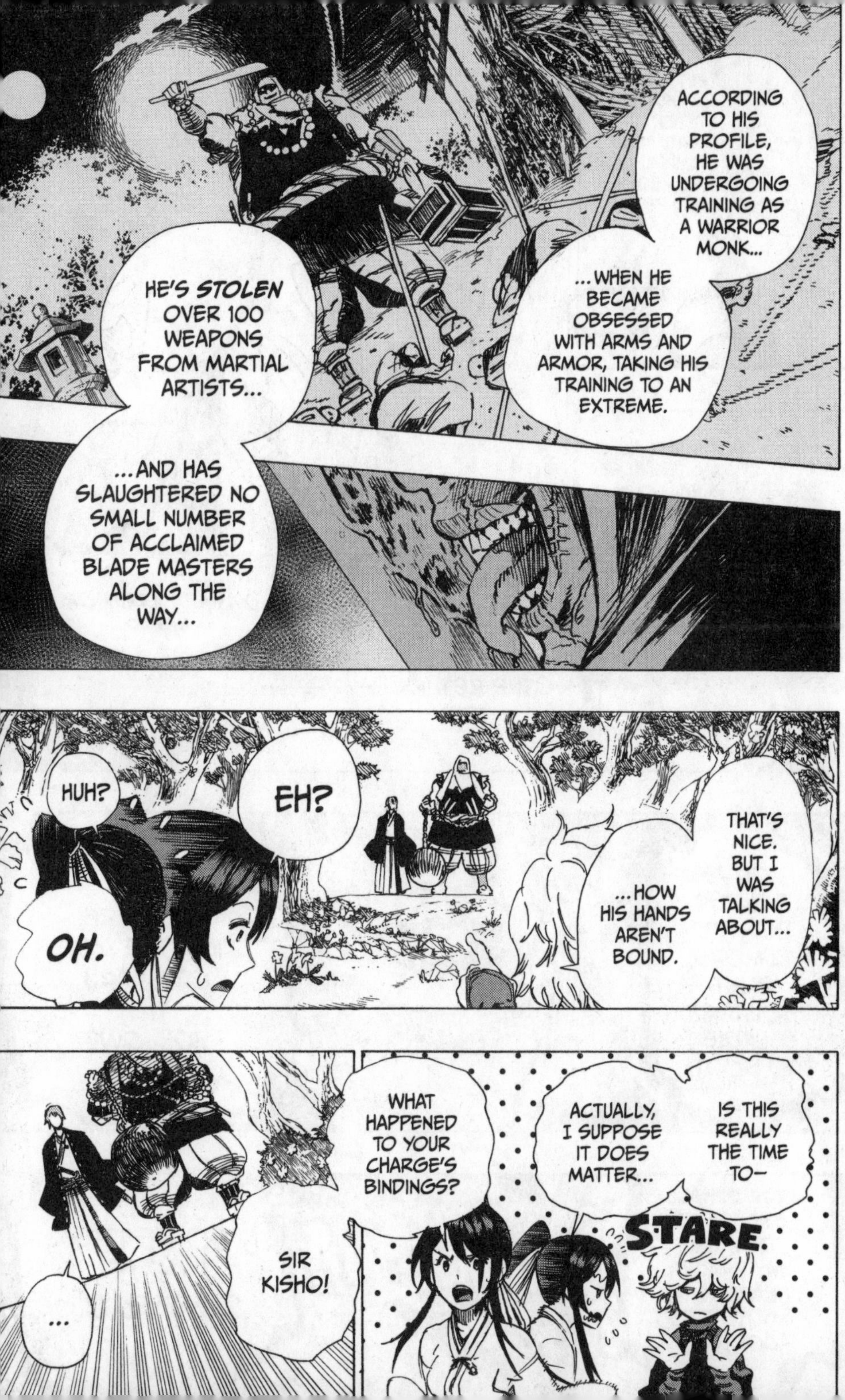
ACCORDING TO HIS PROFILE, HE WAS UNDERGOING TRAINING AS A WARRIOR MONK...
...WHEN HE BECAME OBSESSED WITH ARMS AND ARMOR, TAKING HIS TRAINING TO AN EXTREME.
HE'S *STOLEN* OVER 100 WEAPONS FROM MARTIAL ARTISTS...
...AND HAS SLAUGHTERED NO SMALL NUMBER OF ACCLAIMED BLADE MASTERS ALONG THE WAY...
THAT'S NICE. BUT I WAS TALKING ABOUT...
...HOW HIS HANDS AREN'T BOUND.
EH?
HUH?
OH.
IS THIS REALLY THE TIME TO—
ACTUALLY, I SUPPOSE IT DOES MATTER...
STARE
WHAT HAPPENED TO YOUR CHARGE'S BINDINGS?
SIR KISHO!
...

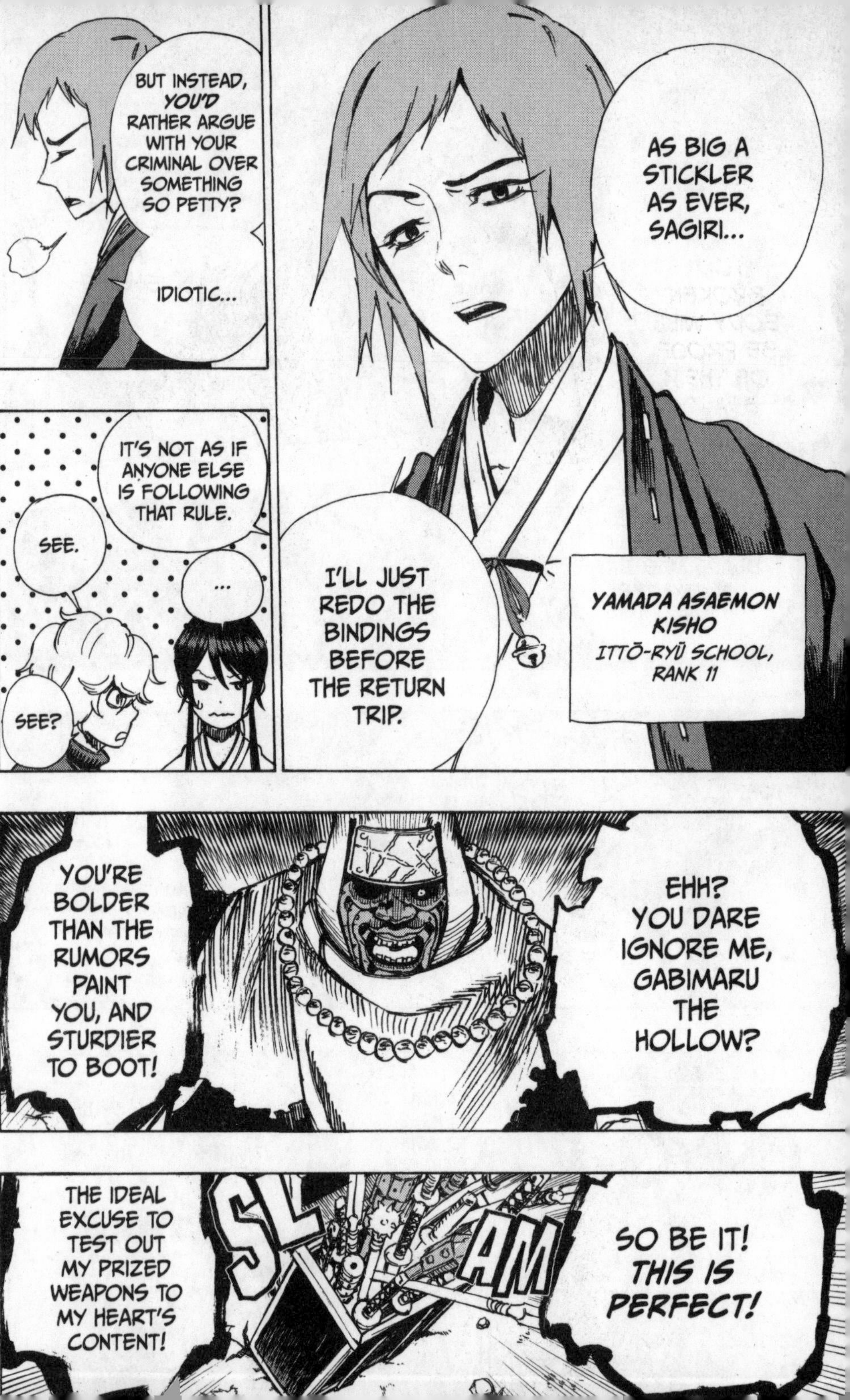
AS BIG A STICKLER AS EVER, SAGIRI...
YAMADA ASAEMON KISHO
ITTŌ-RYŪ SCHOOL, RANK 11
I'LL JUST REDO THE BINDINGS BEFORE THE RETURN TRIP.
BUT INSTEAD, *YOU'D* RATHER ARGUE WITH YOUR CRIMINAL OVER SOMETHING SO PETTY?
IDIOTIC...
IT'S NOT AS IF ANYONE ELSE IS FOLLOWING THAT RULE.
...
SEE.
SEE?
EHH? YOU DARE IGNORE ME, GABIMARU THE HOLLOW?
YOU'RE BOLDER THAN THE RUMORS PAINT YOU, AND STURDIER TO BOOT!
SO BE IT! *THIS IS PERFECT!*
SLAM
THE IDEAL EXCUSE TO TEST OUT MY PRIZED WEAPONS TO MY HEART'S CONTENT!

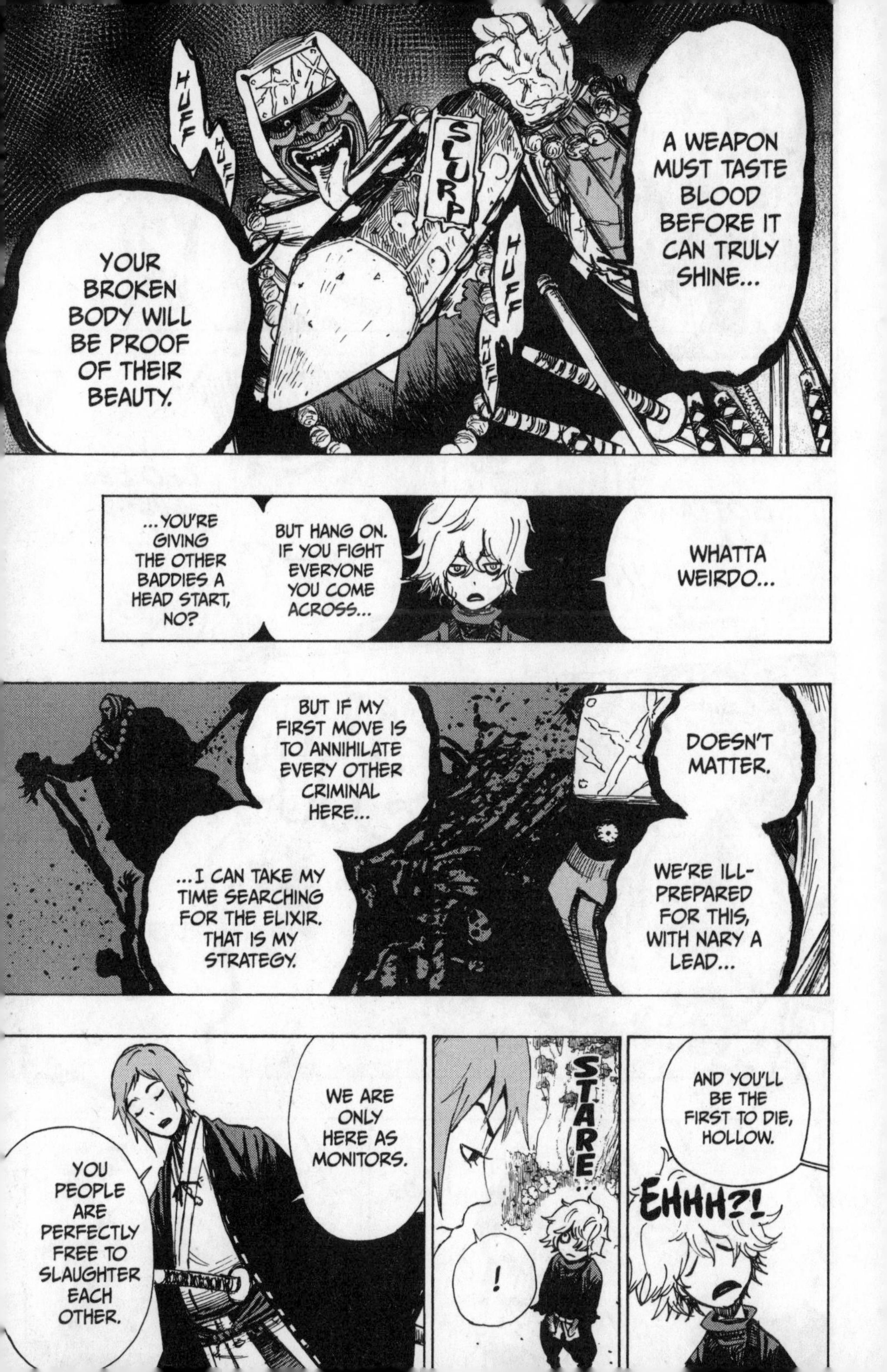
A WEAPON MUST TASTE BLOOD BEFORE IT CAN TRULY SHINE...
SLURP
HUFF
HUFF
HUFF
HUFF
HUFF
YOUR BROKEN BODY WILL BE PROOF OF THEIR BEAUTY.
WHATTA WEIRDO...
BUT HANG ON. IF YOU FIGHT EVERYONE YOU COME ACROSS...
...YOU'RE GIVING THE OTHER BADDIES A HEAD START, NO?
DOESN'T MATTER.
BUT IF MY FIRST MOVE IS TO ANNIHILATE EVERY OTHER CRIMINAL HERE...
WE'RE ILL-PREPARED FOR THIS, WITH NARY A LEAD...
...I CAN TAKE MY TIME SEARCHING FOR THE ELIXIR. THAT IS MY STRATEGY.
AND YOU'LL BE THE FIRST TO DIE, HOLLOW.
EHHH?!
STARE...
!
WE ARE ONLY HERE AS MONITORS.
YOU PEOPLE ARE PERFECTLY FREE TO SLAUGHTER EACH OTHER.

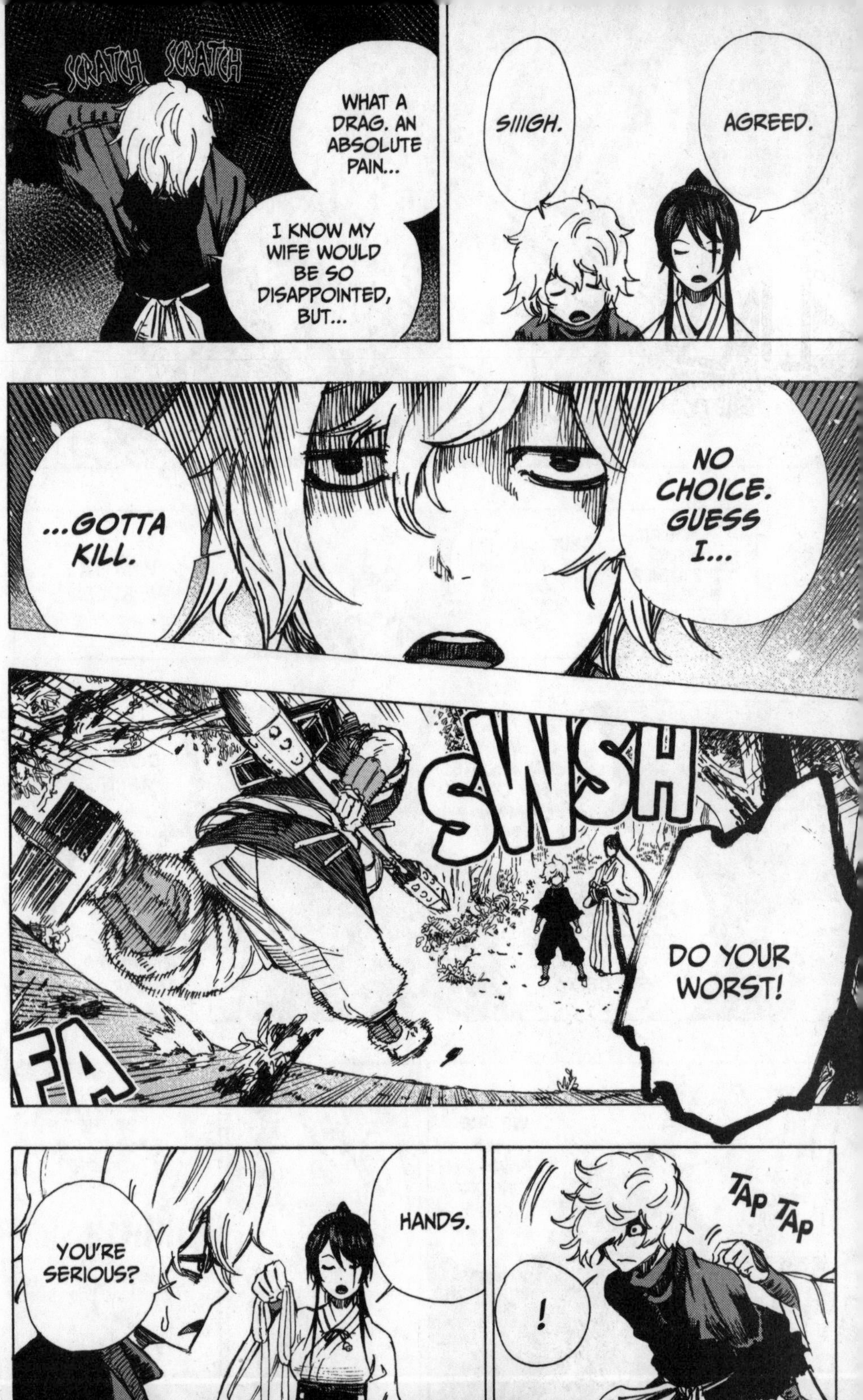
AGREED.
SIIIGH.
SCRATCH SCRATCH
WHAT A DRAG. AN ABSOLUTE PAIN...
I KNOW MY WIFE WOULD BE SO DISAPPOINTED, BUT...
NO CHOICE. GUESS I...
...GOTTA KILL.
SWSH
DO YOUR WORST!
FA
TAP TAP
!
HANDS.
YOU'RE SERIOUS?

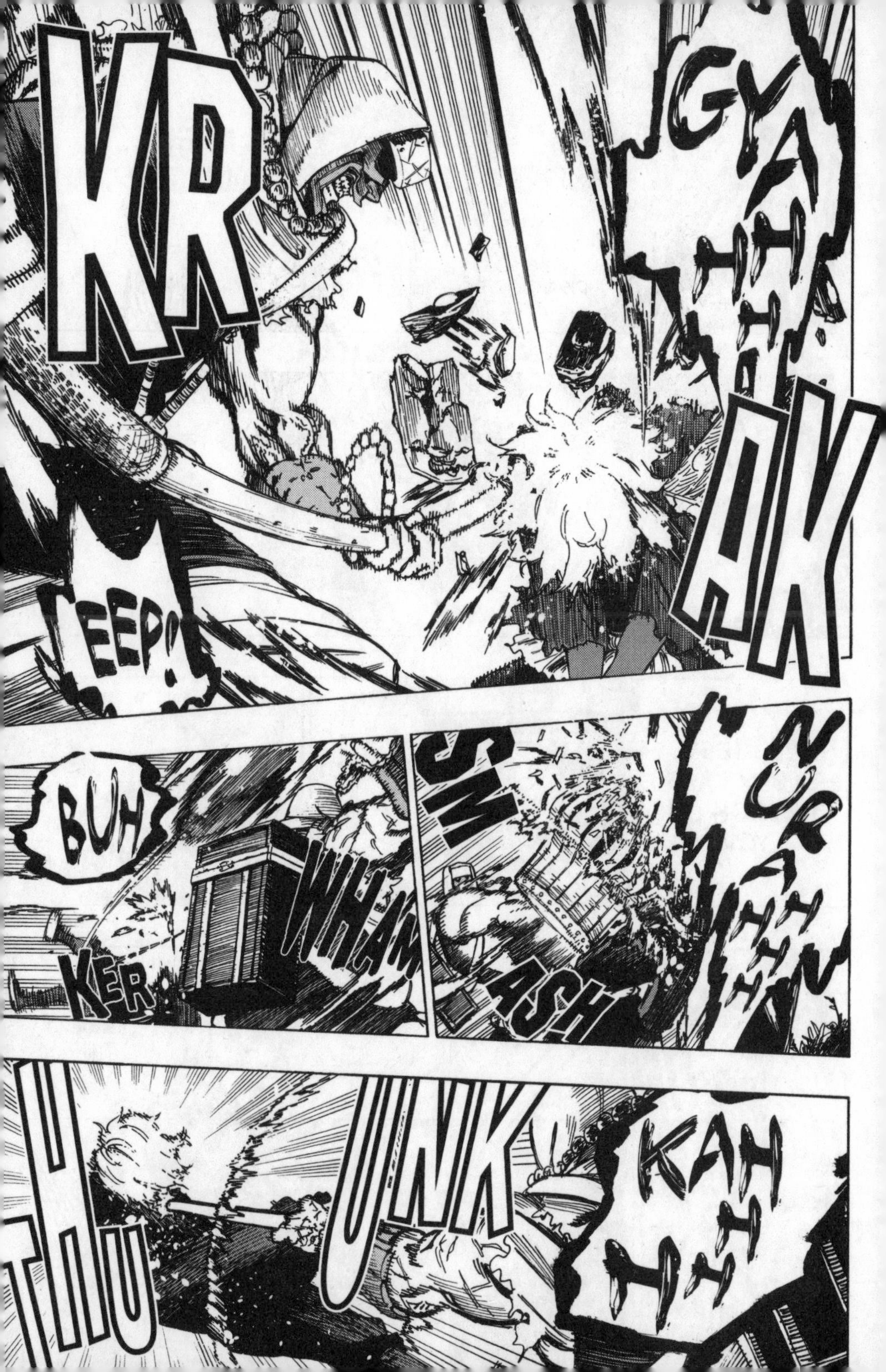
GYAHHHHH
KR
AK
EEP!!
NURAHHHHN
SM
ASH
BUH
KER
WHAM
KAHHHH
THU
NK

THERE. ALL TIED.

HUFF HUFF ...

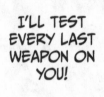

I'LL TEST EVERY LAST WEAPON ON YOU!

PERFECT ...

SHFF

WHAP

YOU REALLY THINK...

...I'VE GOT TIME FOR THAT?

TWIST

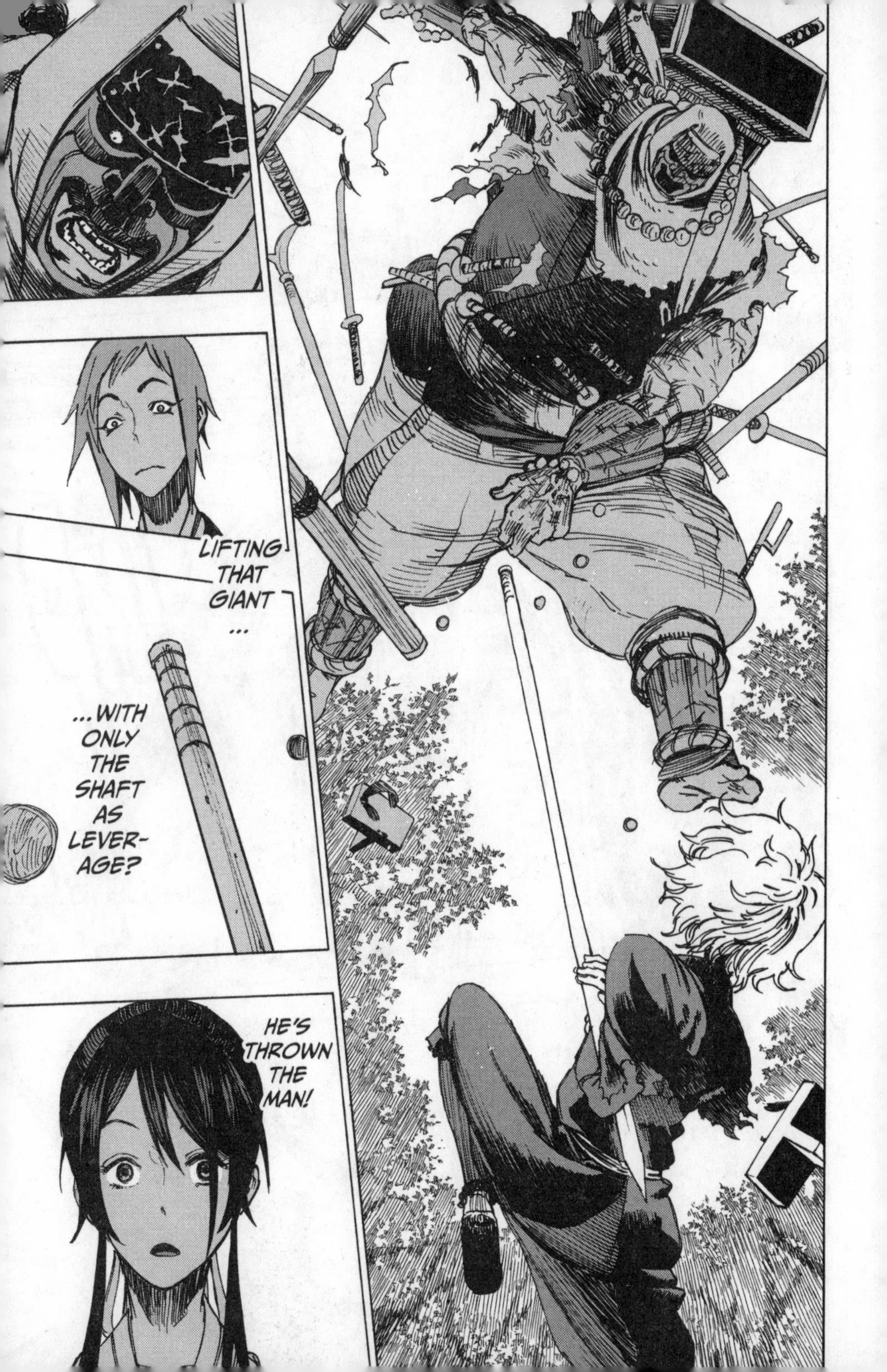
LIFTING THAT GIANT ...
...WITH ONLY THE SHAFT AS LEVER-AGE?
HE'S THROWN THE MAN!

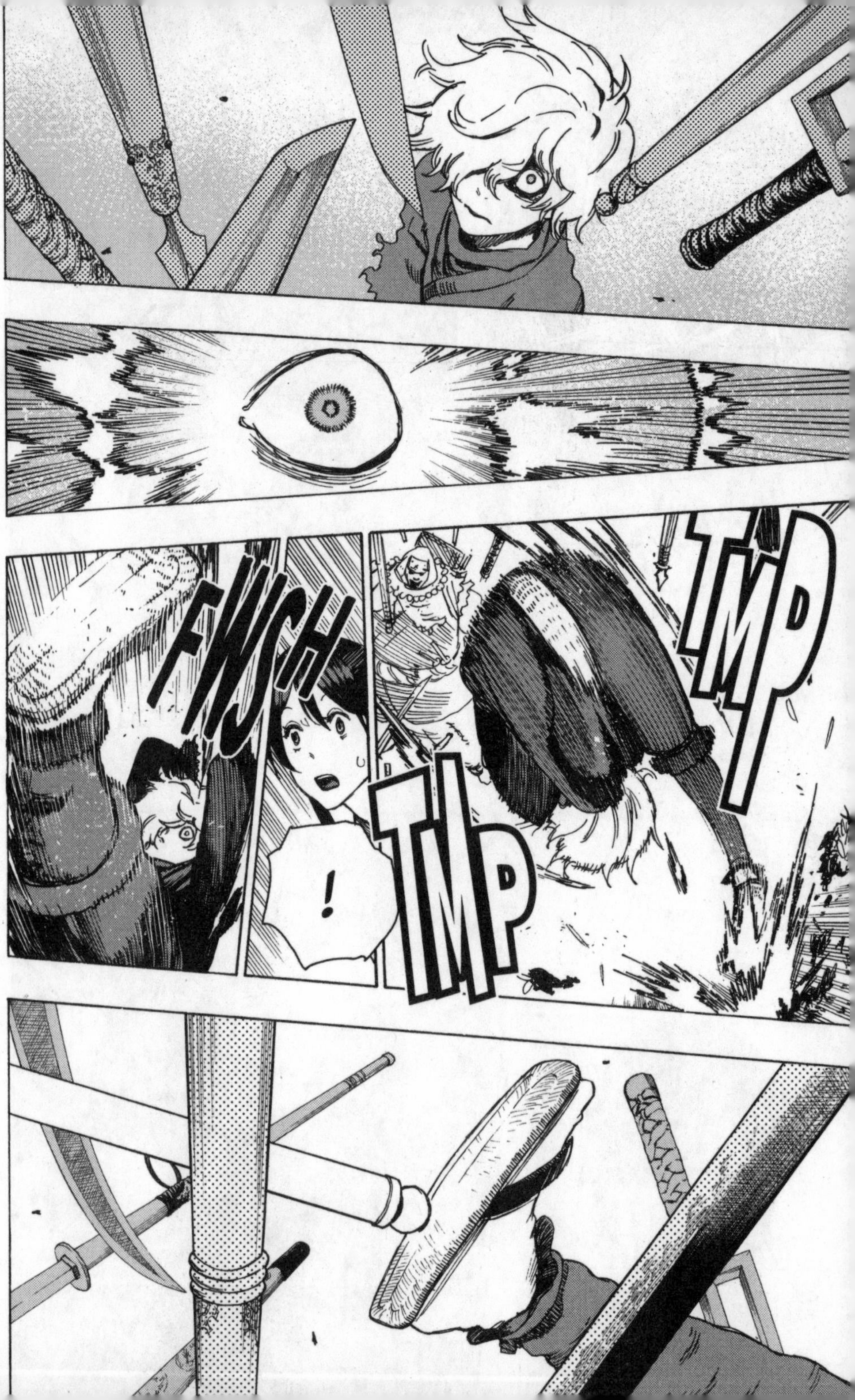
TMP
TMP
!
FWSCH

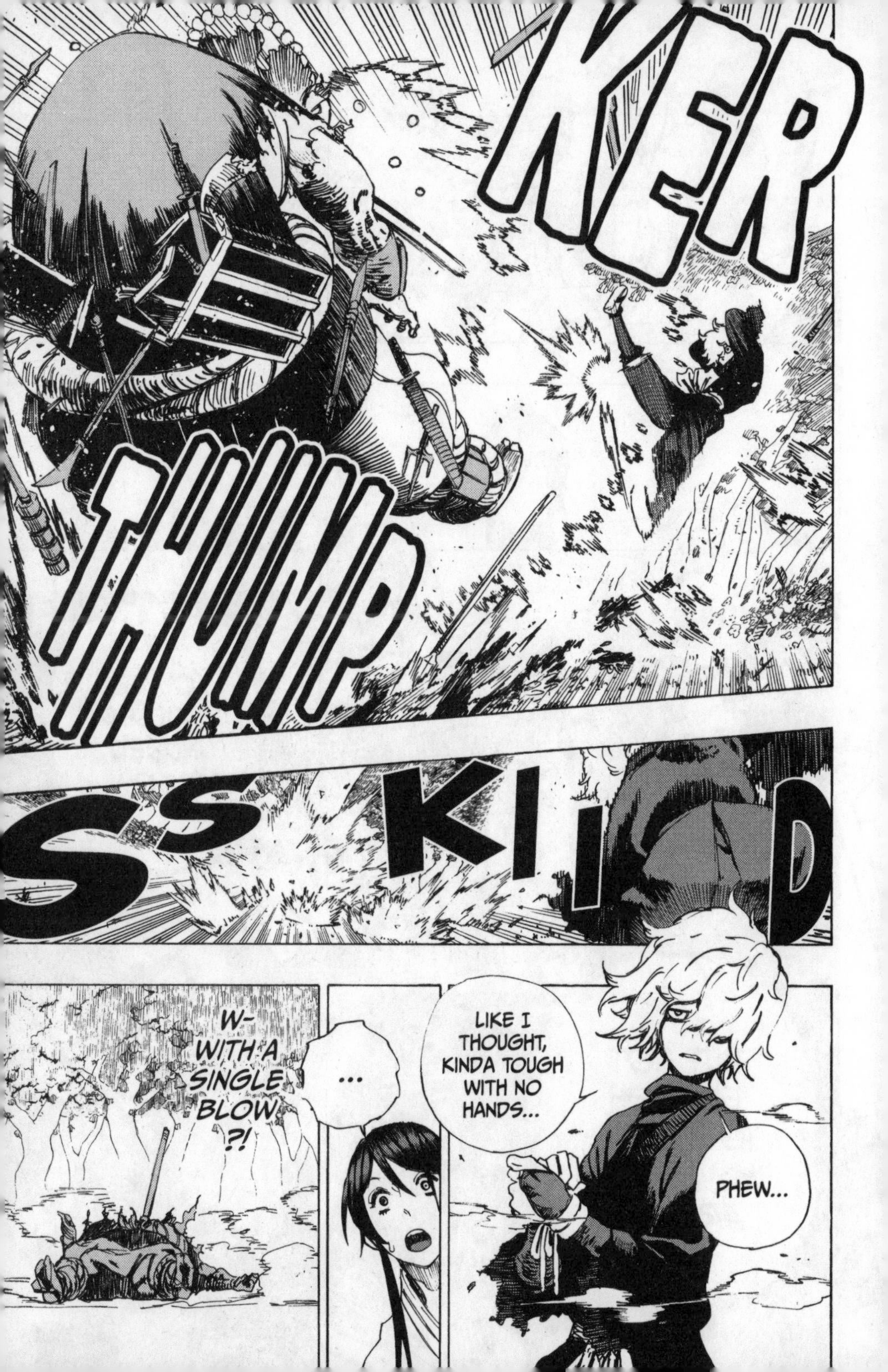
KER
THUMP
SSKID
LIKE I THOUGHT, KINDA TOUGH WITH NO HANDS...
PHEW...
...
W- WITH A SINGLE BLOW ?!

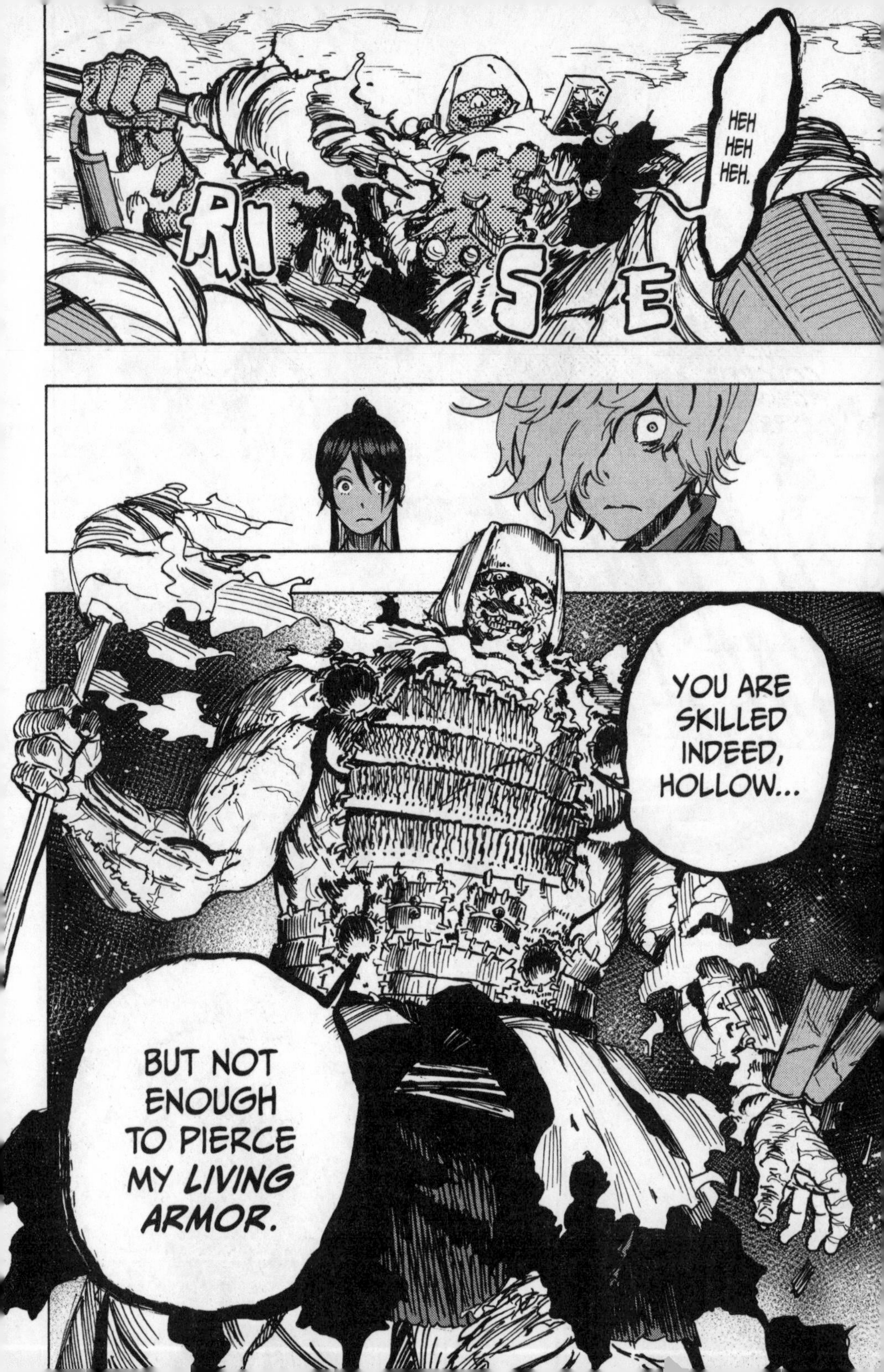
HEH HEH HEH.
RISE
YOU ARE SKILLED INDEED, HOLLOW...
BUT NOT ENOUGH TO PIERCE MY LIVING ARMOR.

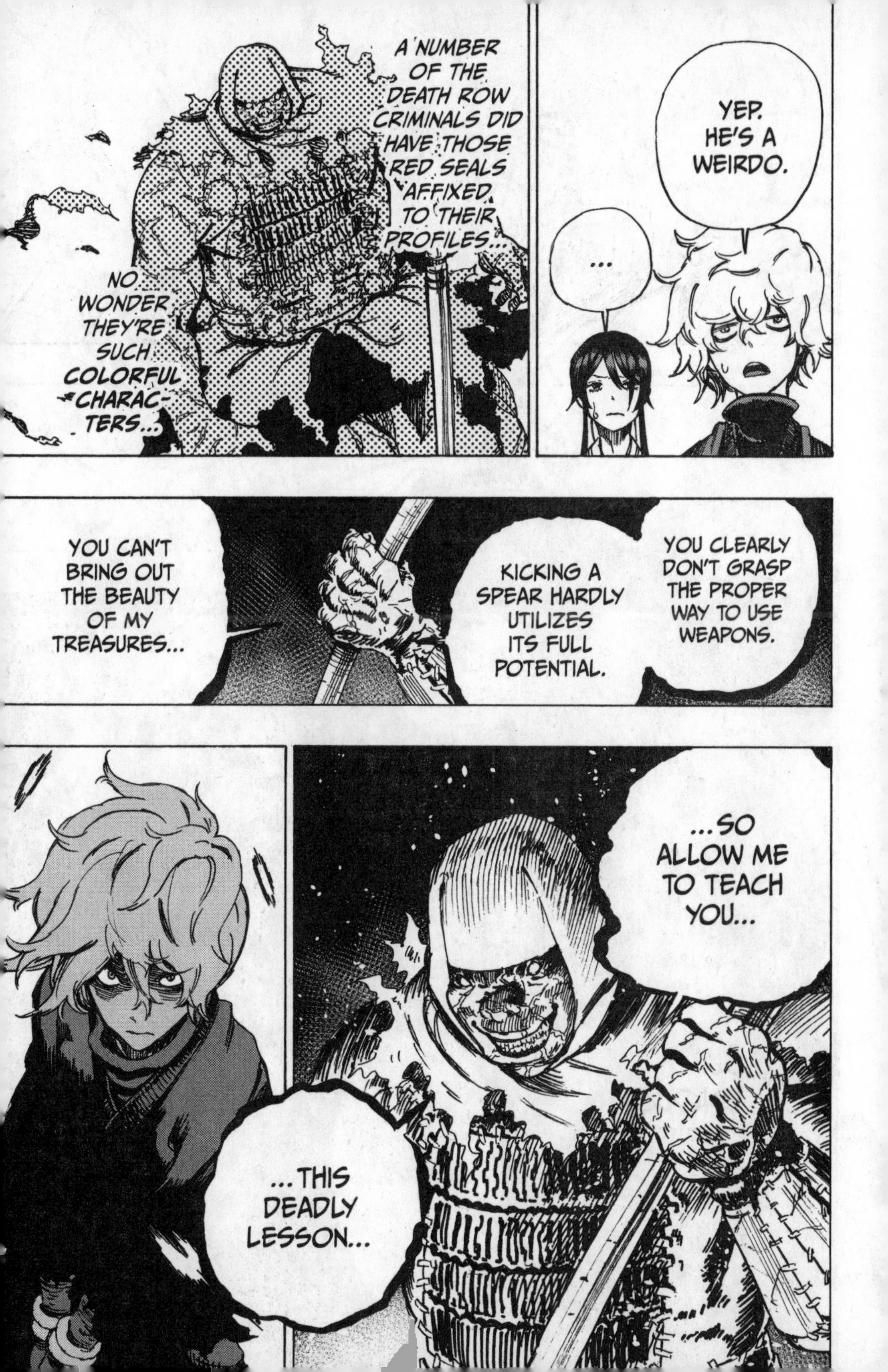
YEP. HE'S A WEIRDO.
...
A NUMBER OF THE DEATH ROW CRIMINALS DID HAVE THOSE RED SEALS AFFIXED TO THEIR PROFILES...
NO WONDER THEY'RE SUCH COLORFUL CHARAC-TERS...
YOU CLEARLY DON'T GRASP THE PROPER WAY TO USE WEAPONS.
KICKING A SPEAR HARDLY UTILIZES ITS FULL POTENTIAL.
YOU CAN'T BRING OUT THE BEAUTY OF MY TREASURES...
...SO ALLOW ME TO TEACH YOU...
...THIS DEADLY LESSON...

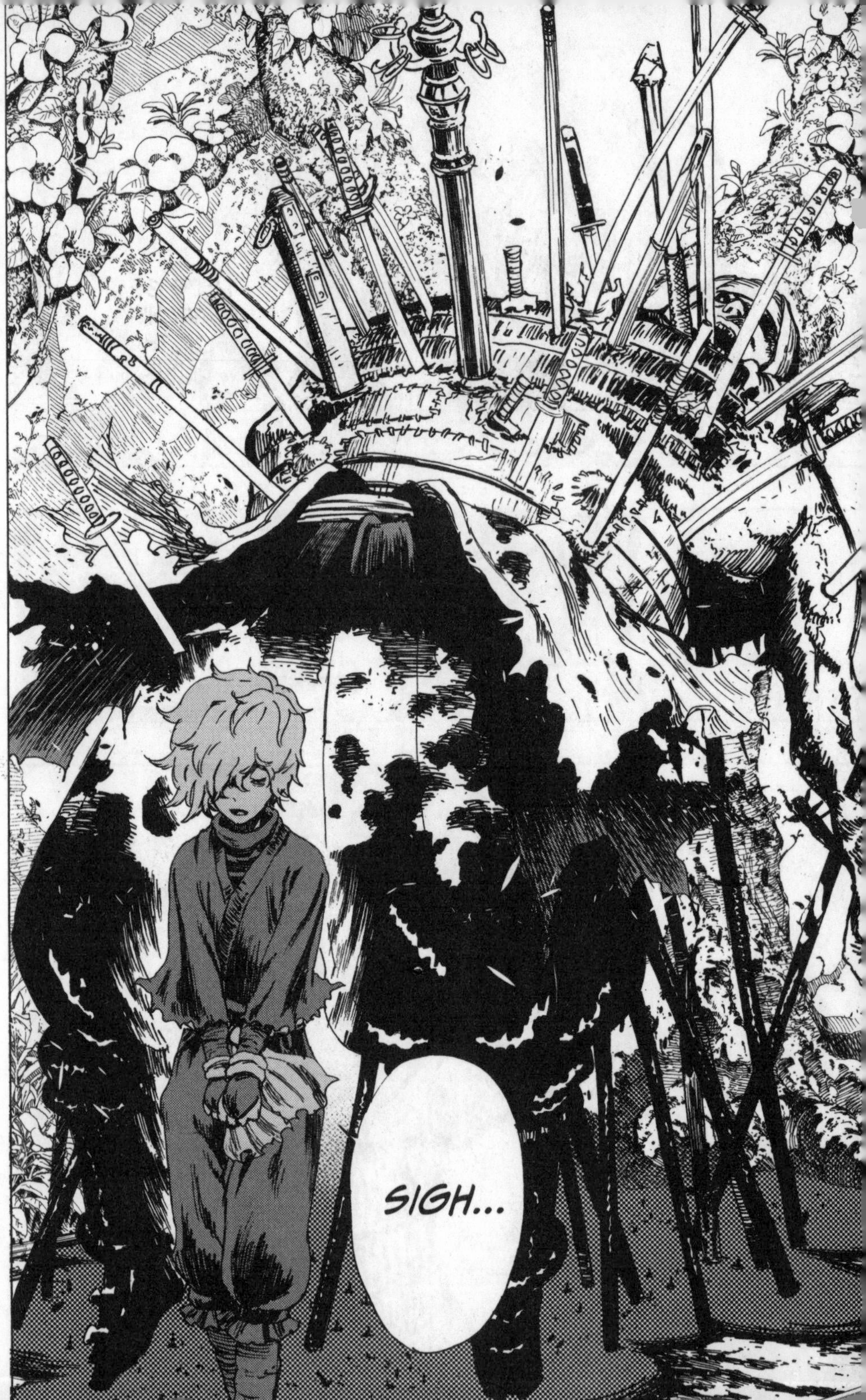
SIGH...

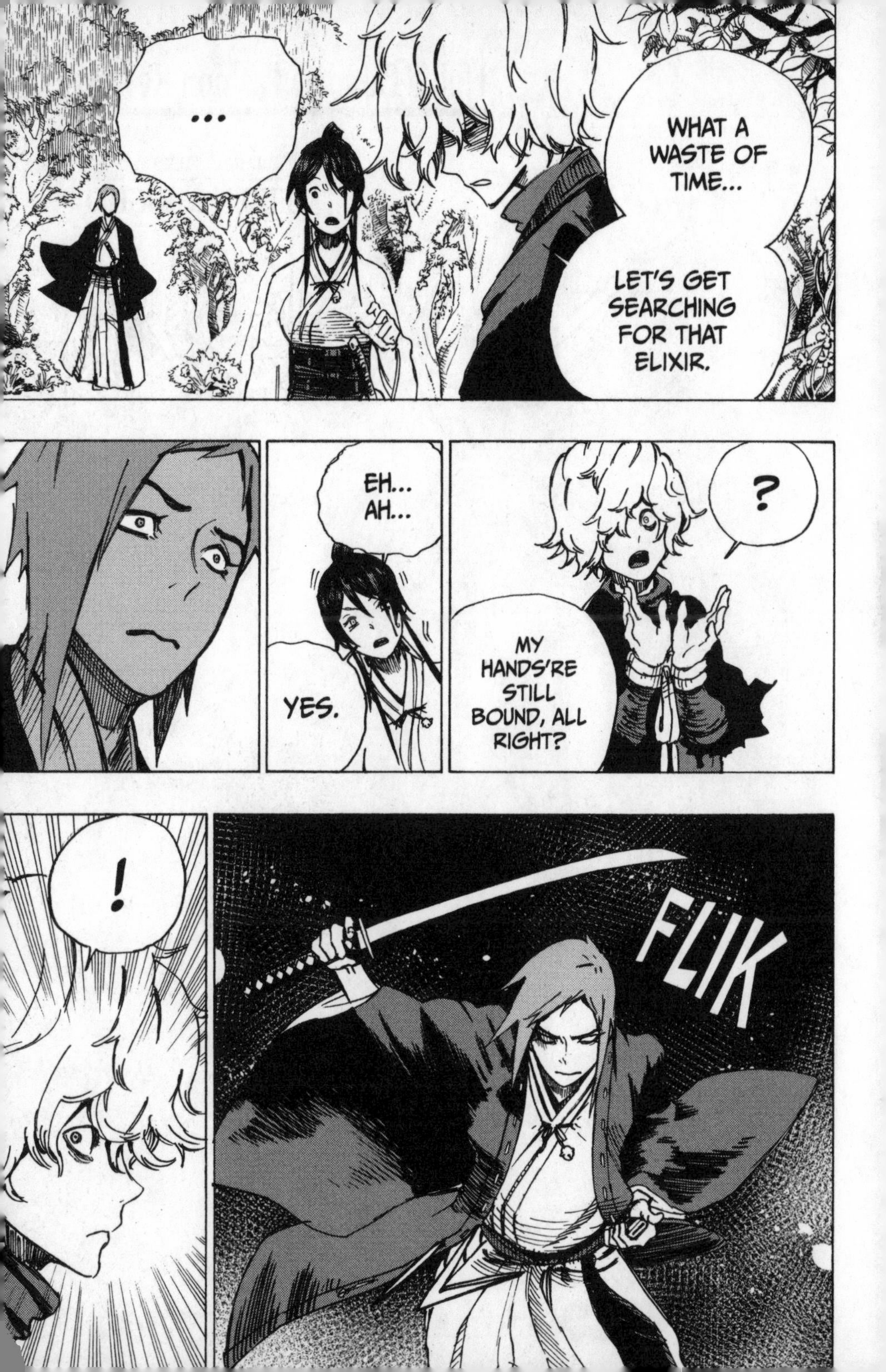
WHAT A WASTE OF TIME...
LET'S GET SEARCHING FOR THAT ELIXIR.
...
?
MY HANDS'RE STILL BOUND, ALL RIGHT?
EH... AH...
YES.
FLIK
!

Hell's Paradise Fashion Review

Yamada Asaemon

EIZEN & KISHO

Only the *haori* coat is black, with unique stitching.

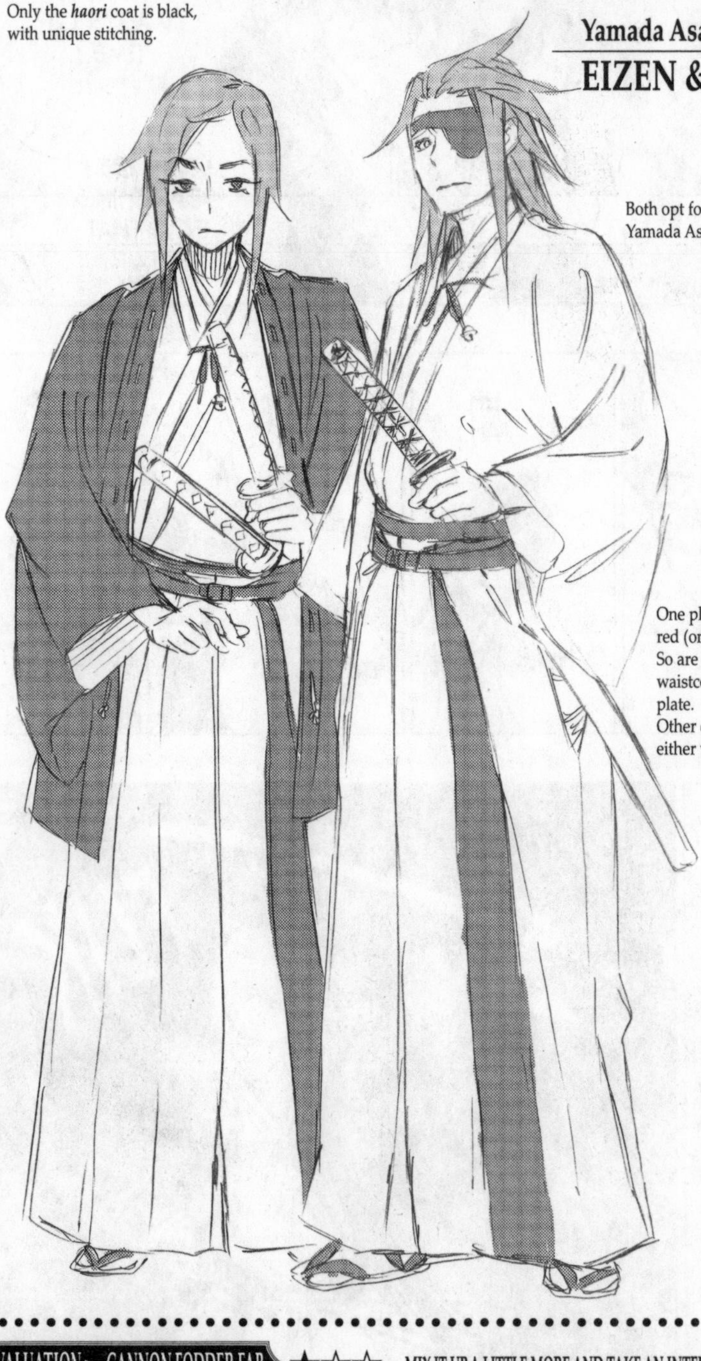

Both opt for the standard Yamada Asaemon garb.

One pleat of the *hakama* is red (on the left).
So are the *koshihimo* waistcord and *koshiita* plate.
Other components are also either white or red.

EVALUATION ► CANNON FODDER FAB ★☆☆ MIX IT UP A LITTLE MORE AND TAKE AN INTEREST IN FASHION, BOYS!

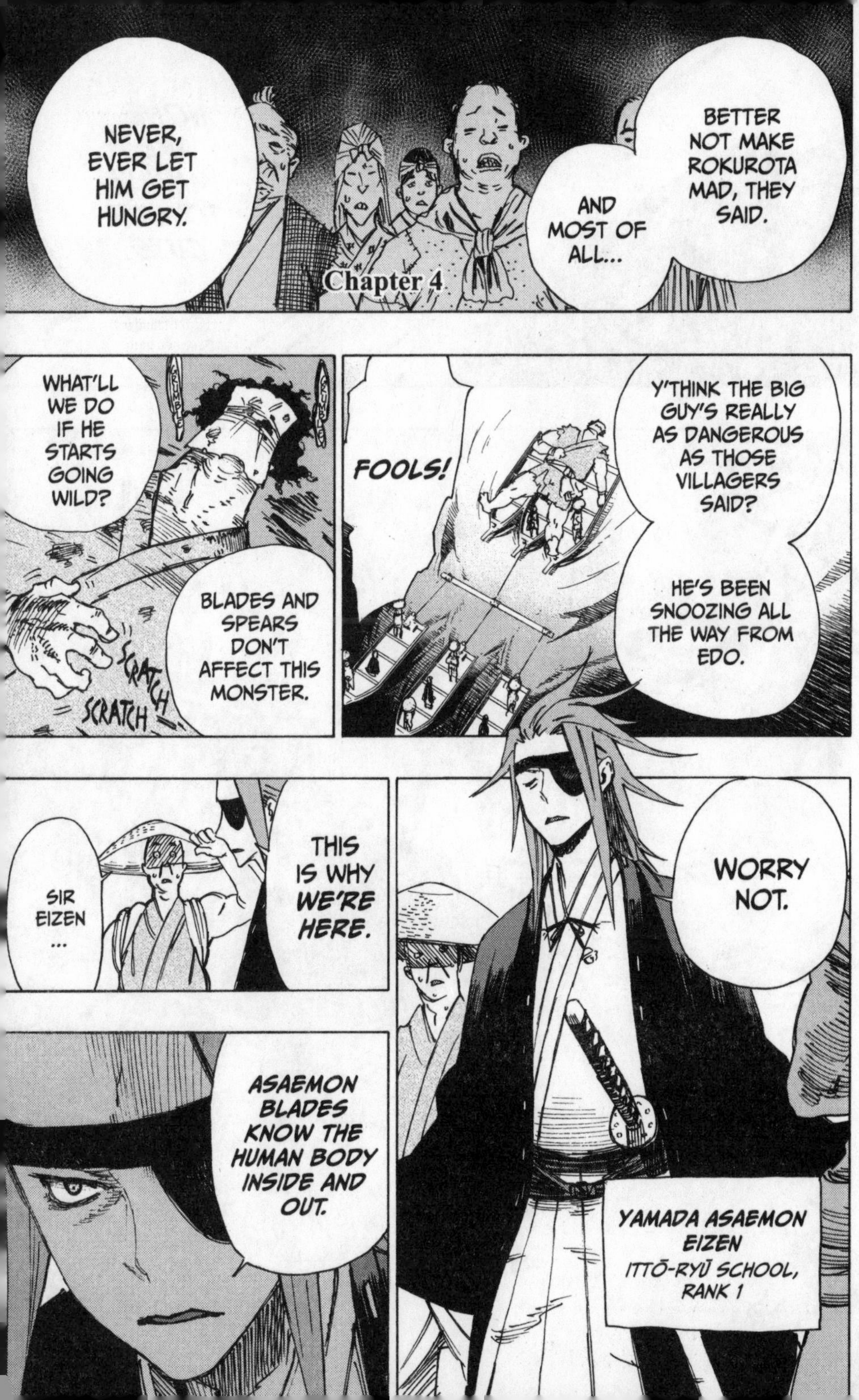
BETTER NOT MAKE ROKUROTA MAD, THEY SAID.
AND MOST OF ALL...
NEVER, EVER LET HIM GET HUNGRY.
Chapter 4
Y'THINK THE BIG GUY'S REALLY AS DANGEROUS AS THOSE VILLAGERS SAID?
HE'S BEEN SNOOZING ALL THE WAY FROM EDO.
FOOLS!
GRUMBLE
GRUMBLE
WHAT'LL WE DO IF HE STARTS GOING WILD?
BLADES AND SPEARS DON'T AFFECT THIS MONSTER.
SCRATCH
SCRATCH
WORRY NOT.
YAMADA ASAEMON EIZEN
ITTŌ-RYŪ SCHOOL, RANK 1
THIS IS WHY WE'RE HERE.
SIR EIZEN ...
ASAEMON BLADES KNOW THE HUMAN BODY INSIDE AND OUT.

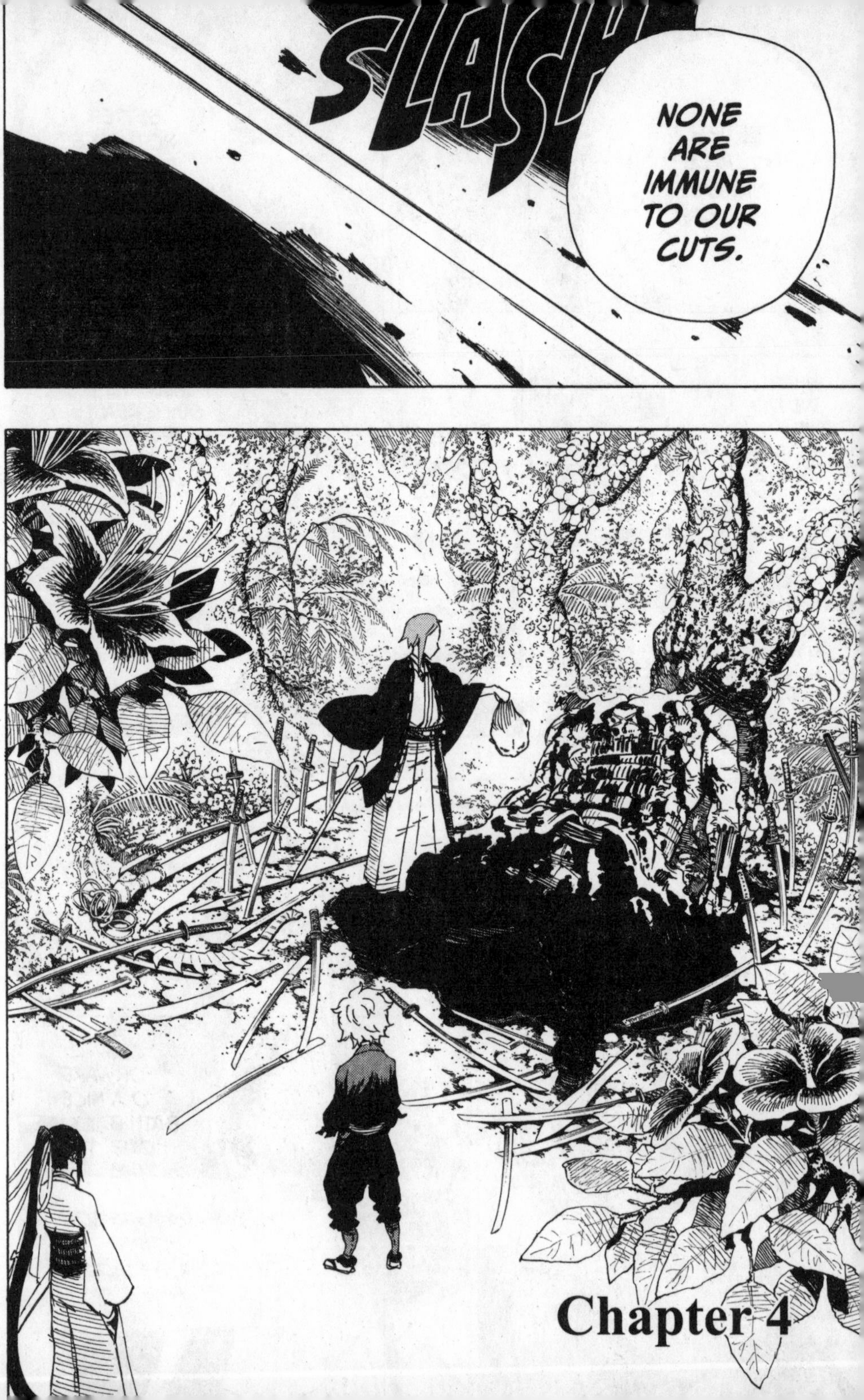
SLASH
NONE ARE IMMUNE TO OUR CUTS.
Chapter 4

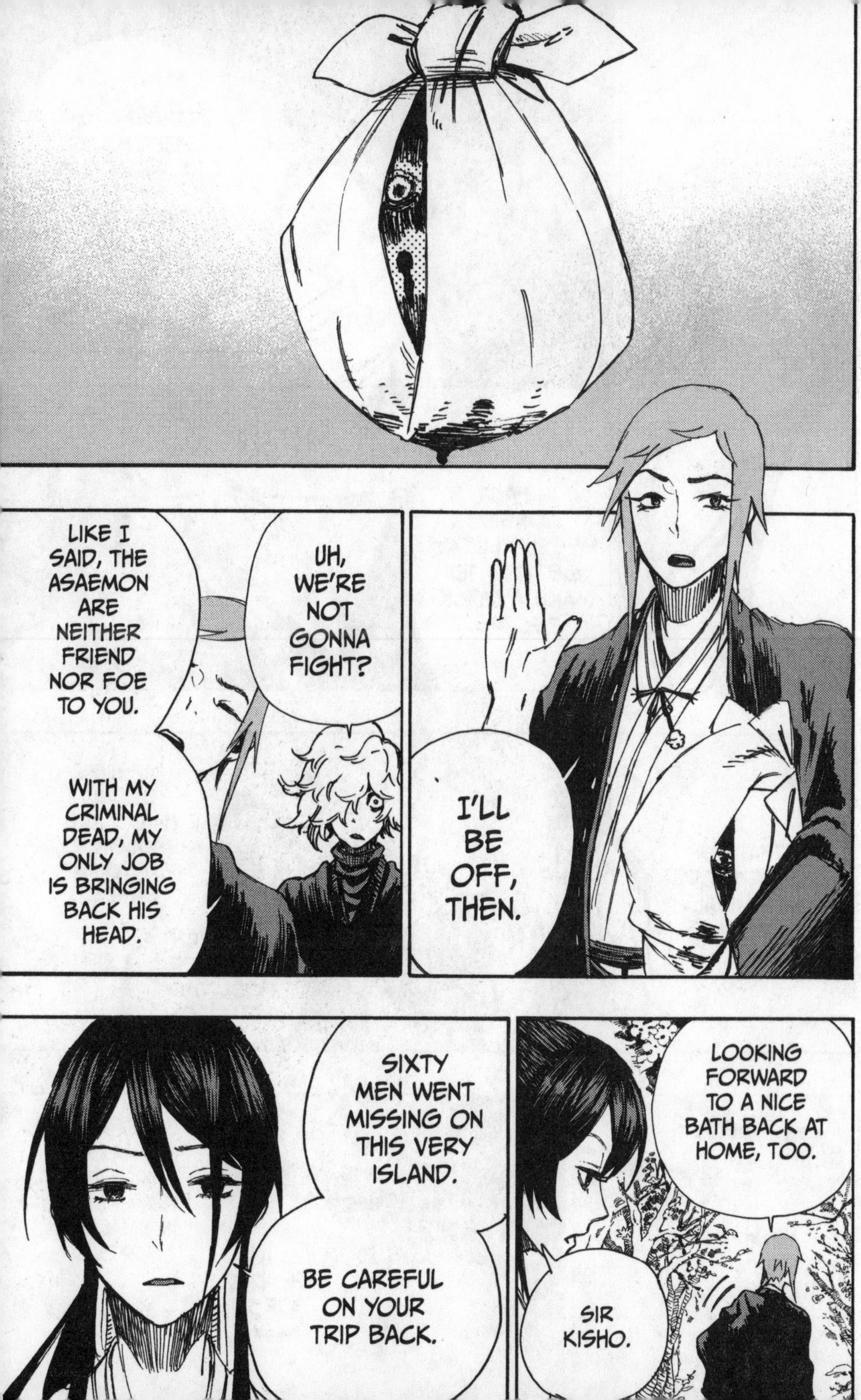
I'LL BE OFF, THEN.
UH, WE'RE NOT GONNA FIGHT?
LIKE I SAID, THE ASAEMON ARE NEITHER FRIEND NOR FOE TO YOU.
WITH MY CRIMINAL DEAD, MY ONLY JOB IS BRINGING BACK HIS HEAD.
LOOKING FORWARD TO A NICE BATH BACK AT HOME, TOO.
SIR KISHO.
SIXTY MEN WENT MISSING ON THIS VERY ISLAND.
BE CAREFUL ON YOUR TRIP BACK.

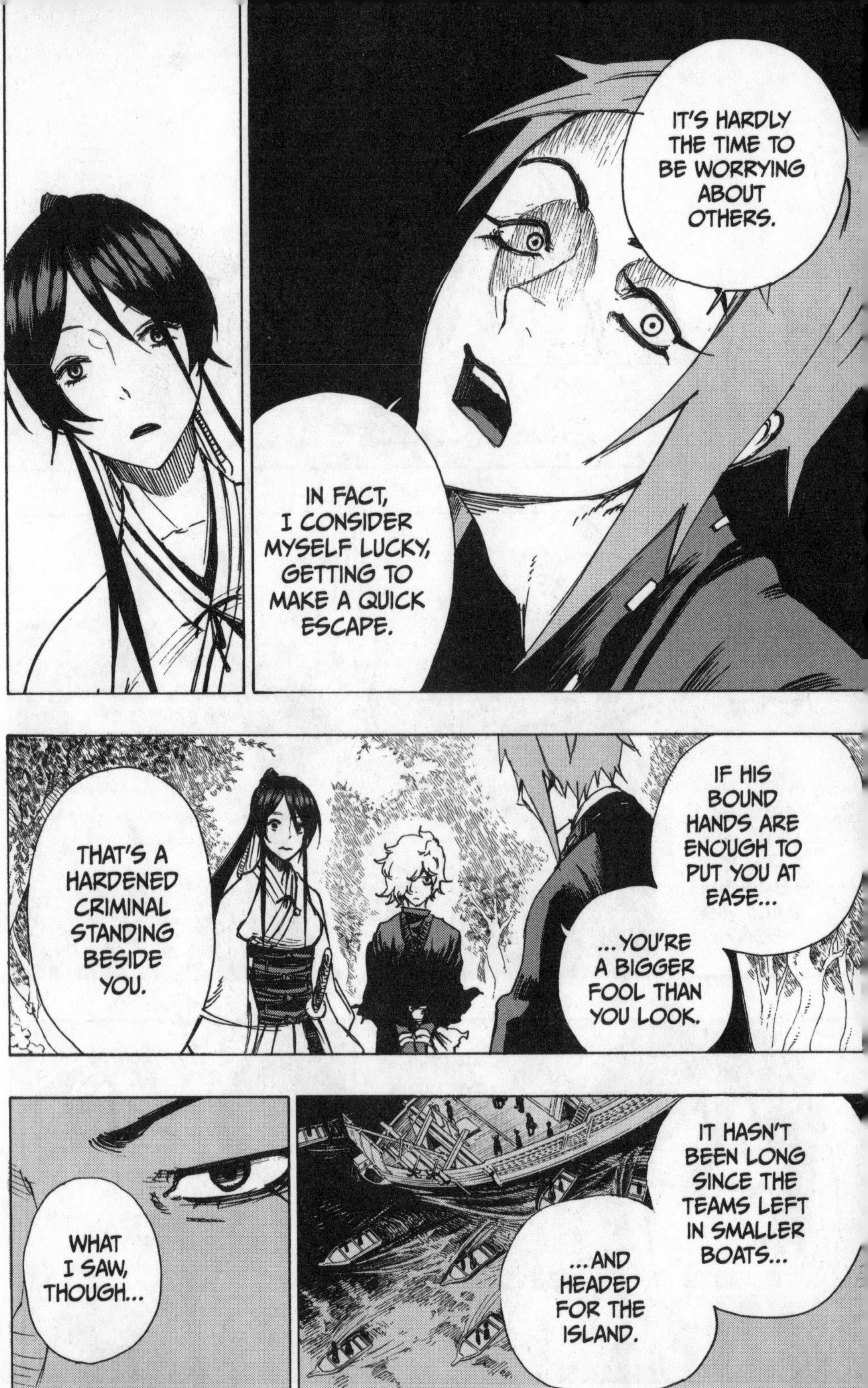
IT'S HARDLY THE TIME TO BE WORRYING ABOUT OTHERS.
IN FACT, I CONSIDER MYSELF LUCKY, GETTING TO MAKE A QUICK ESCAPE.
IF HIS BOUND HANDS ARE ENOUGH TO PUT YOU AT EASE...
...YOU'RE A BIGGER FOOL THAN YOU LOOK.
THAT'S A HARDENED CRIMINAL STANDING BESIDE YOU.
IT HASN'T BEEN LONG SINCE THE TEAMS LEFT IN SMALLER BOATS...
...AND HEADED FOR THE ISLAND.
WHAT I SAW, THOUGH...

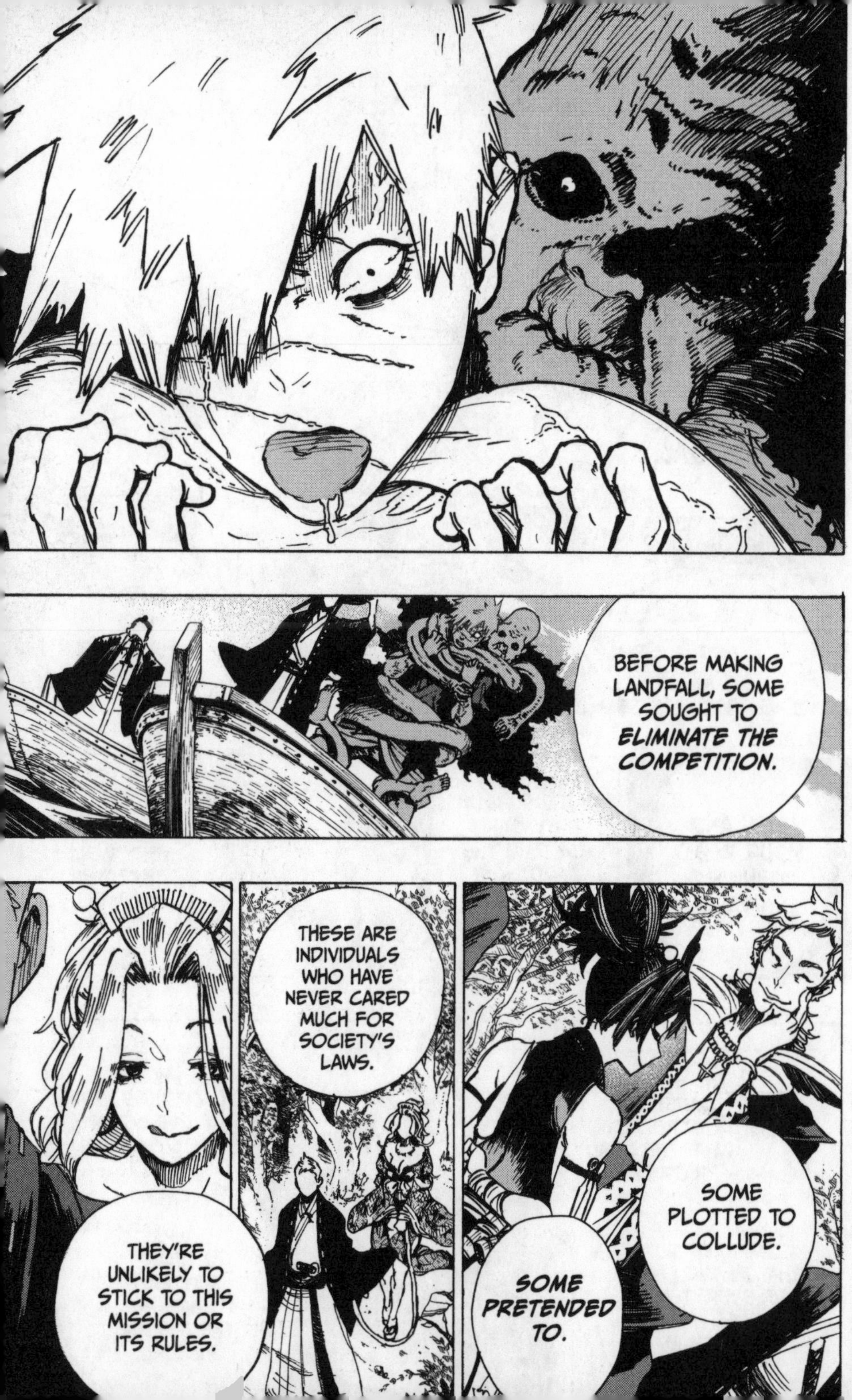
BEFORE MAKING LANDFALL, SOME SOUGHT TO *ELIMINATE THE COMPETITION.*
SOME PLOTTED TO COLLUDE.
SOME PRETENDED TO.
THESE ARE INDIVIDUALS WHO HAVE NEVER CARED MUCH FOR SOCIETY'S LAWS.
THEY'RE UNLIKELY TO STICK TO THIS MISSION OR ITS RULES.

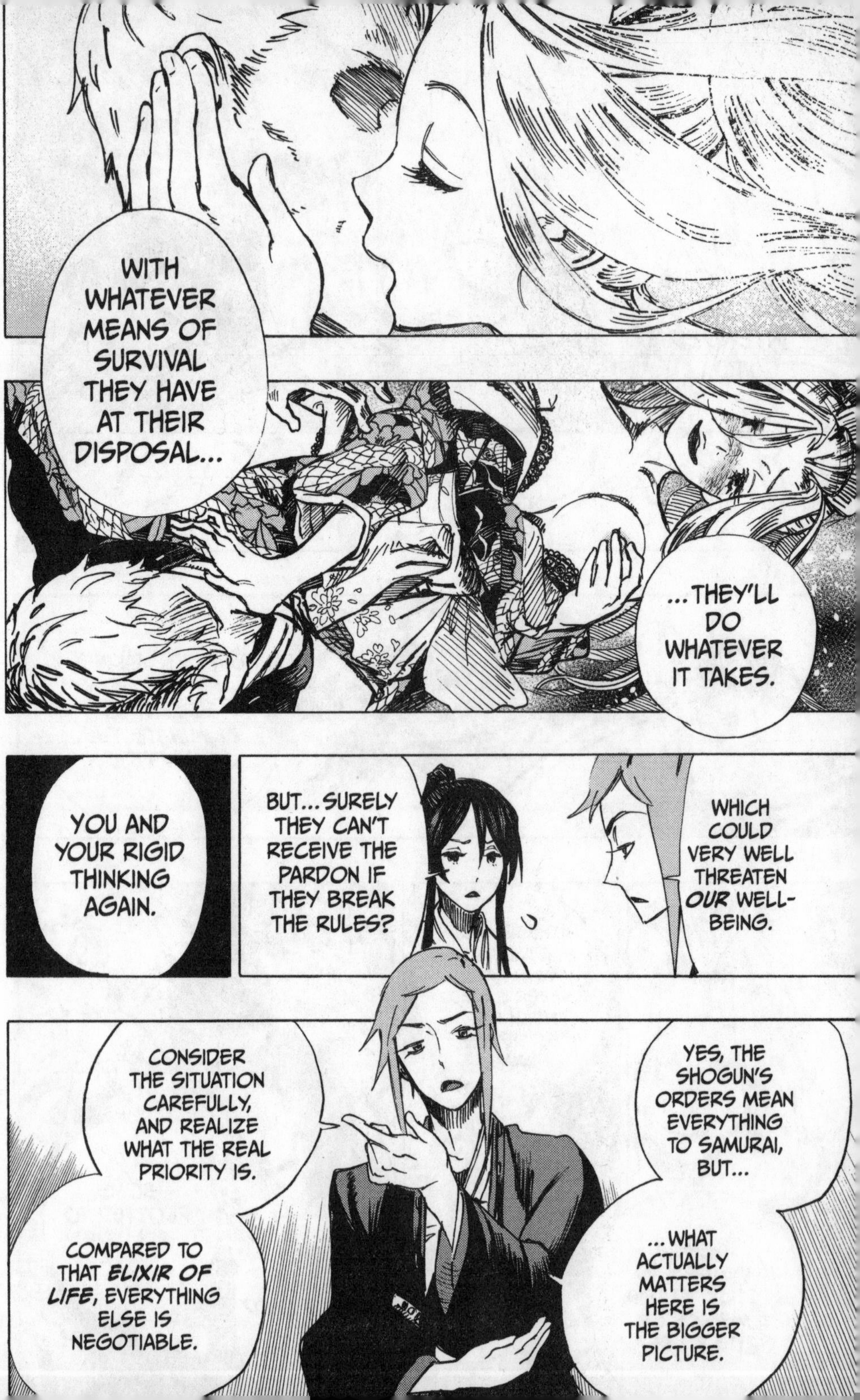
WITH WHATEVER MEANS OF SURVIVAL THEY HAVE AT THEIR DISPOSAL...
...THEY'LL DO WHATEVER IT TAKES.
WHICH COULD VERY WELL THREATEN *OUR* WELL-BEING.
BUT...SURELY THEY CAN'T RECEIVE THE PARDON IF THEY BREAK THE RULES?
YOU AND YOUR RIGID THINKING AGAIN.
YES, THE SHOGUN'S ORDERS MEAN EVERYTHING TO SAMURAI, BUT...
...WHAT ACTUALLY MATTERS HERE IS THE BIGGER PICTURE.
CONSIDER THE SITUATION CAREFULLY, AND REALIZE WHAT THE REAL PRIORITY IS.
COMPARED TO THAT *ELIXIR OF LIFE*, EVERYTHING ELSE IS NEGOTIABLE.

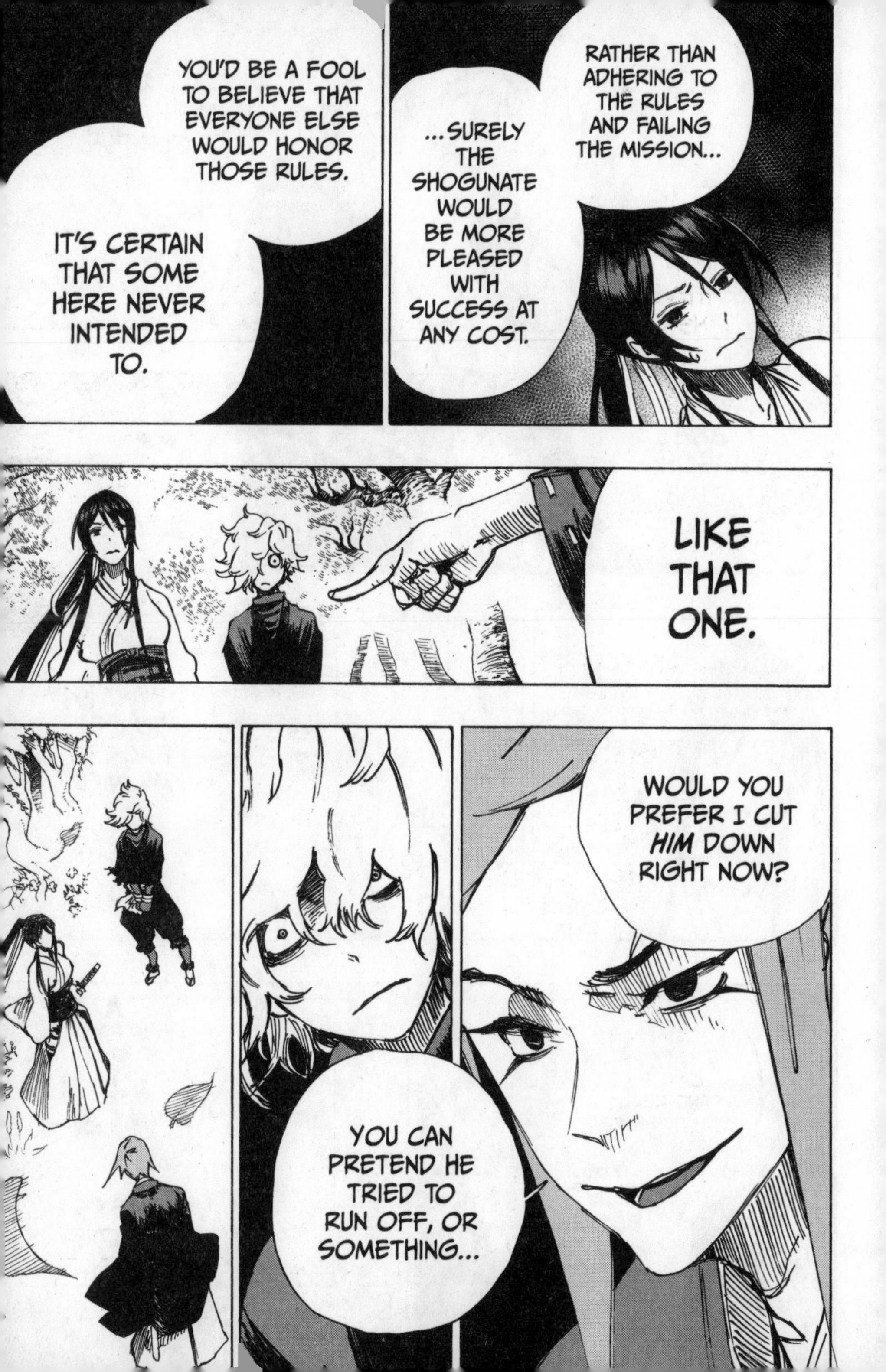
RATHER THAN ADHERING TO THE RULES AND FAILING THE MISSION...
...SURELY THE SHOGUNATE WOULD BE MORE PLEASED WITH SUCCESS AT ANY COST.
YOU'D BE A FOOL TO BELIEVE THAT EVERYONE ELSE WOULD HONOR THOSE RULES.
IT'S CERTAIN THAT SOME HERE NEVER INTENDED TO.
LIKE THAT ONE.
WOULD YOU PREFER I CUT *HIM* DOWN RIGHT NOW?
YOU CAN PRETEND HE TRIED TO RUN OFF, OR SOMETHING...

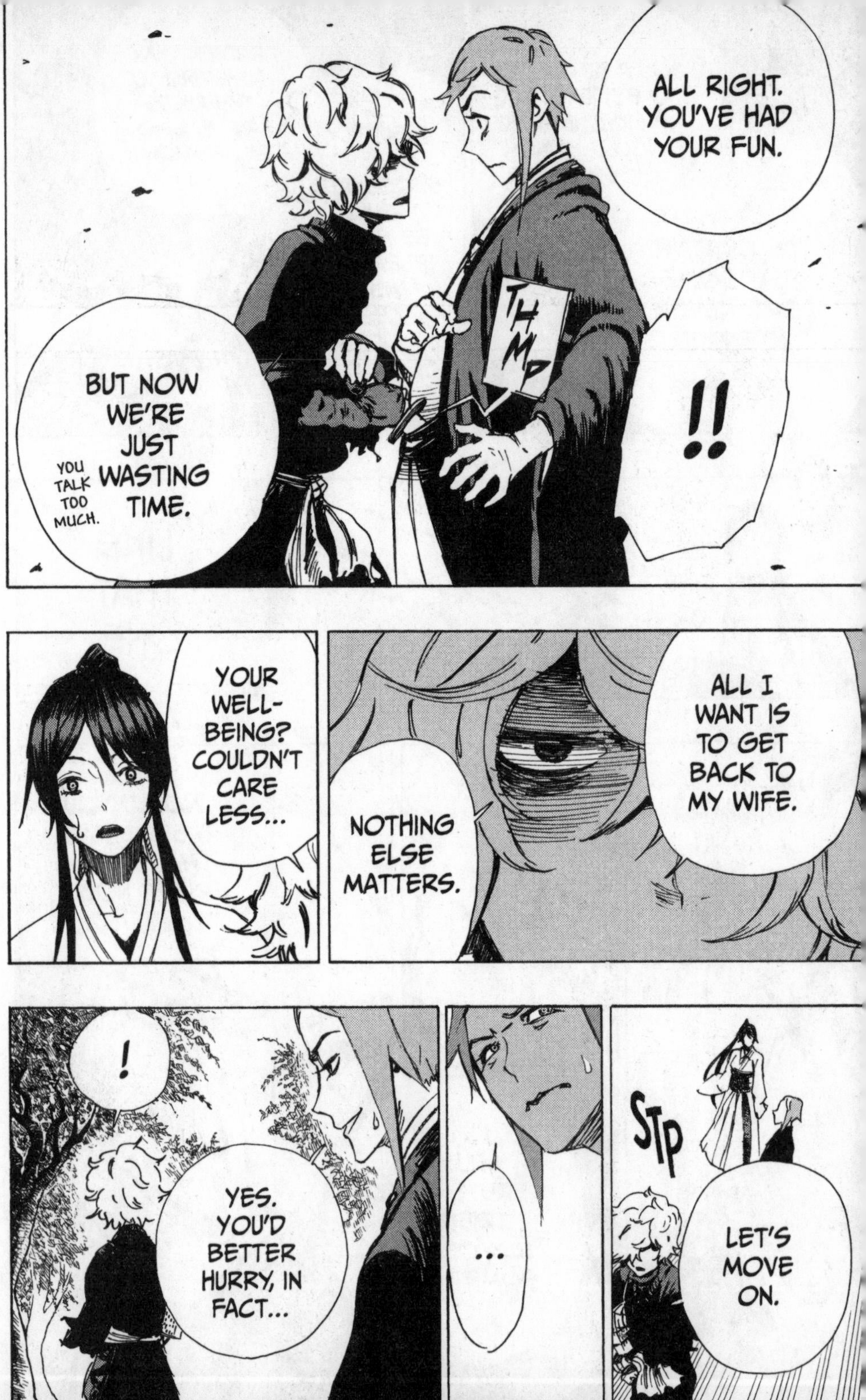
ALL RIGHT. YOU'VE HAD YOUR FUN.
THMP
!!
BUT NOW WE'RE JUST WASTING TIME.
YOU TALK TOO MUCH.
ALL I WANT IS TO GET BACK TO MY WIFE.
NOTHING ELSE MATTERS.
YOUR WELL-BEING? COULDN'T CARE LESS...
STP
LET'S MOVE ON.
...
!
YES. YOU'D BETTER HURRY, IN FACT...

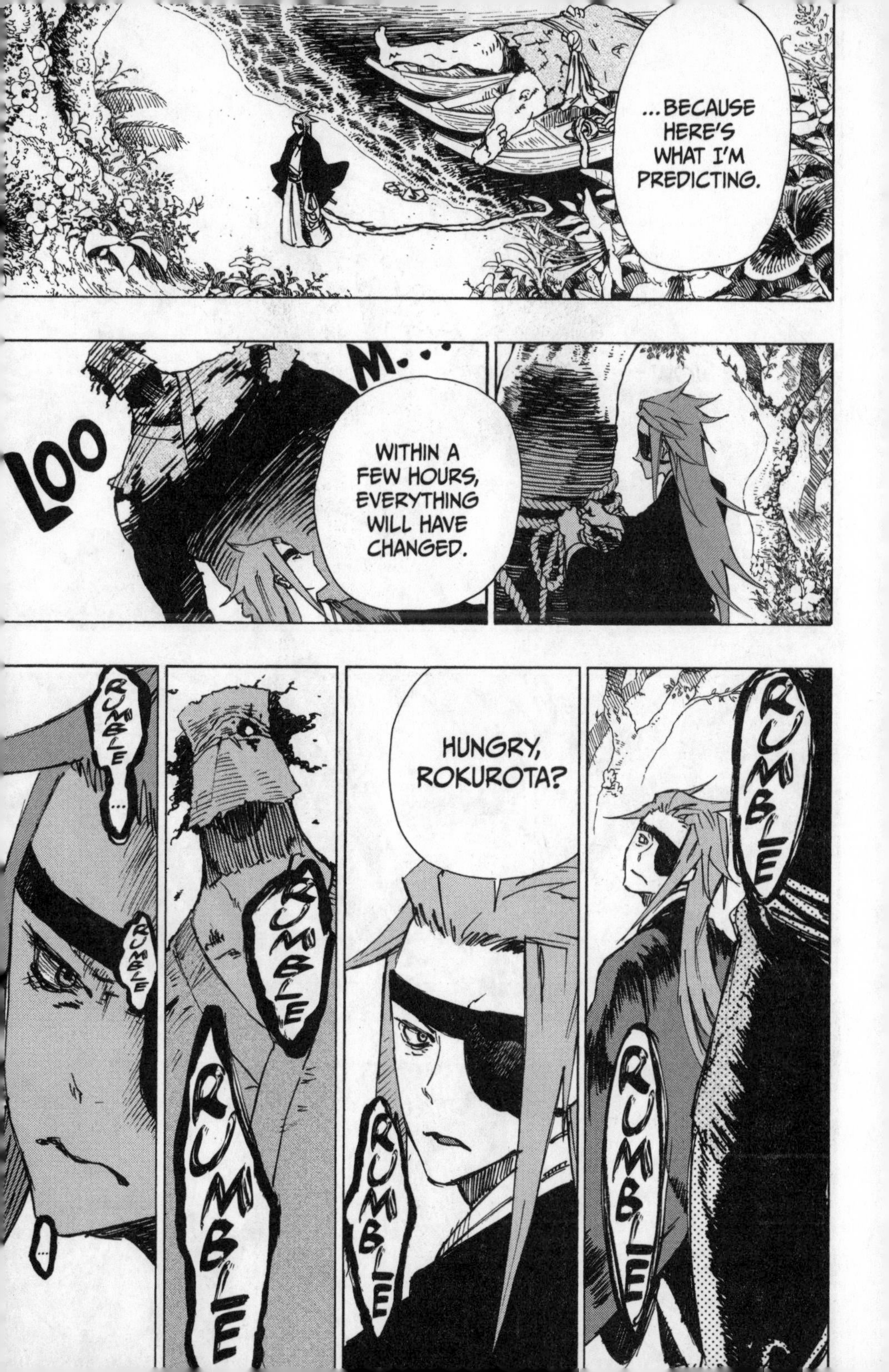
...BECAUSE HERE'S WHAT I'M PREDICTING.
WITHIN A FEW HOURS, EVERYTHING WILL HAVE CHANGED.
LOOM...
RUMBLE
RUMBLE
HUNGRY, ROKUROTA?
RUMBLE
RUMBLE
RUMBLE
RUMBLE...
RUMBLE
...

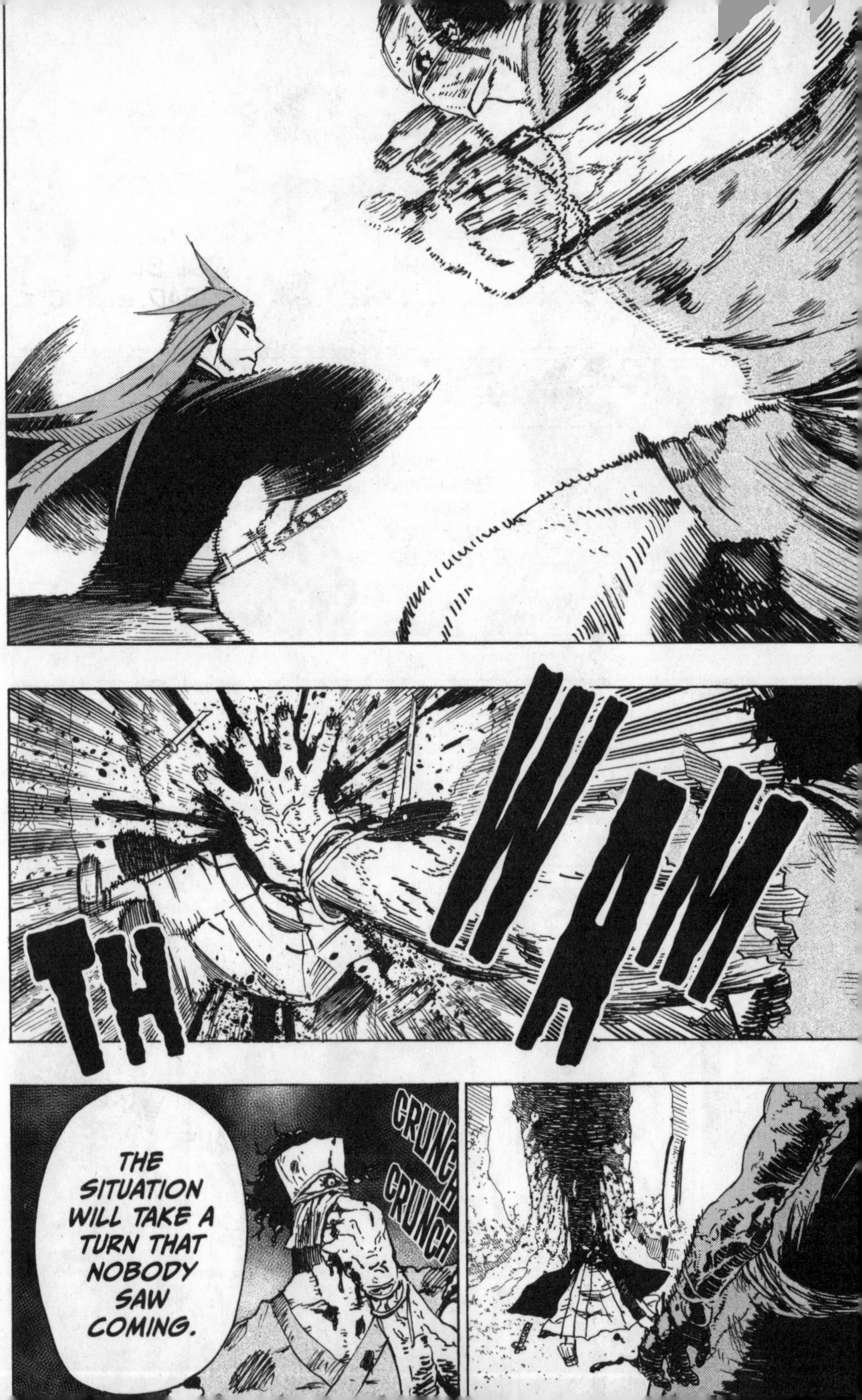
THWAM
CRUNCH CRUNCH
THE SITUATION WILL TAKE A TURN THAT NOBODY SAW COMING.

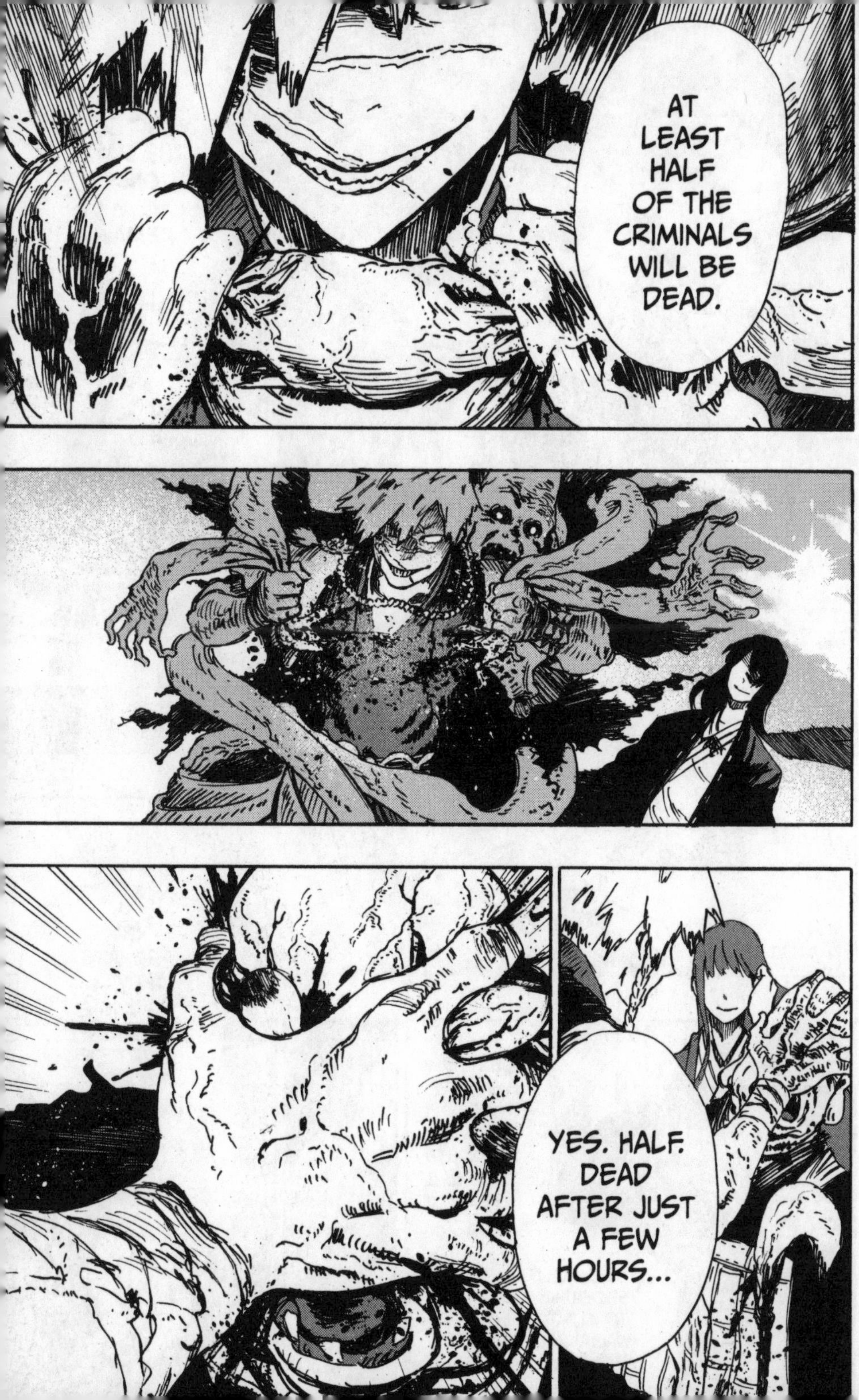
AT LEAST HALF OF THE CRIMINALS WILL BE DEAD.
YES. HALF. DEAD AFTER JUST A FEW HOURS...

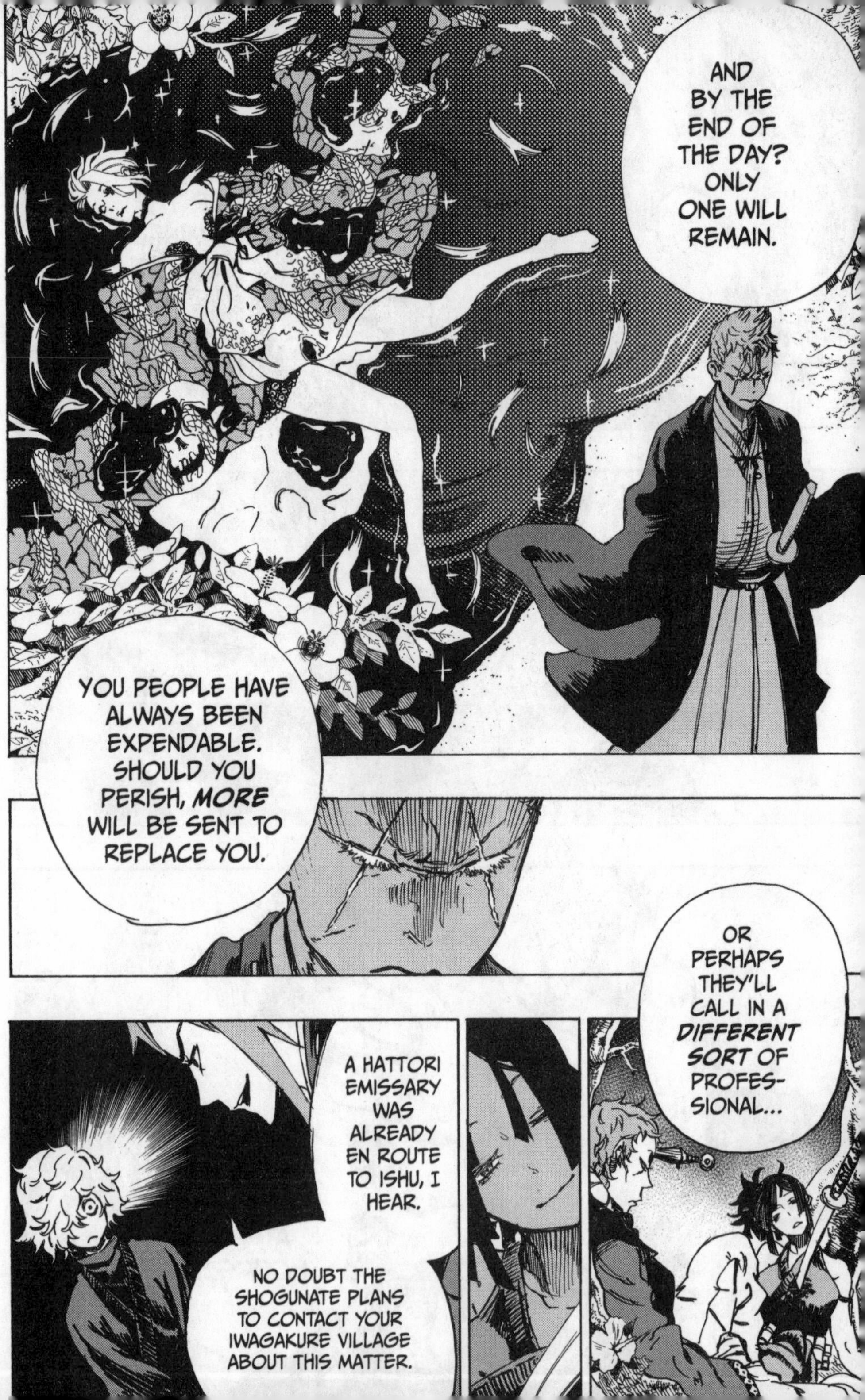
AND BY THE END OF THE DAY? ONLY ONE WILL REMAIN.
YOU PEOPLE HAVE ALWAYS BEEN EXPENDABLE. SHOULD YOU PERISH, *MORE* WILL BE SENT TO REPLACE YOU.
OR PERHAPS THEY'LL CALL IN A *DIFFERENT SORT* OF PROFES- SIONAL...
A HATTORI EMISSARY WAS ALREADY EN ROUTE TO ISHU, I HEAR.
NO DOUBT THE SHOGUNATE PLANS TO CONTACT YOUR IWAGAKURE VILLAGE ABOUT THIS MATTER.

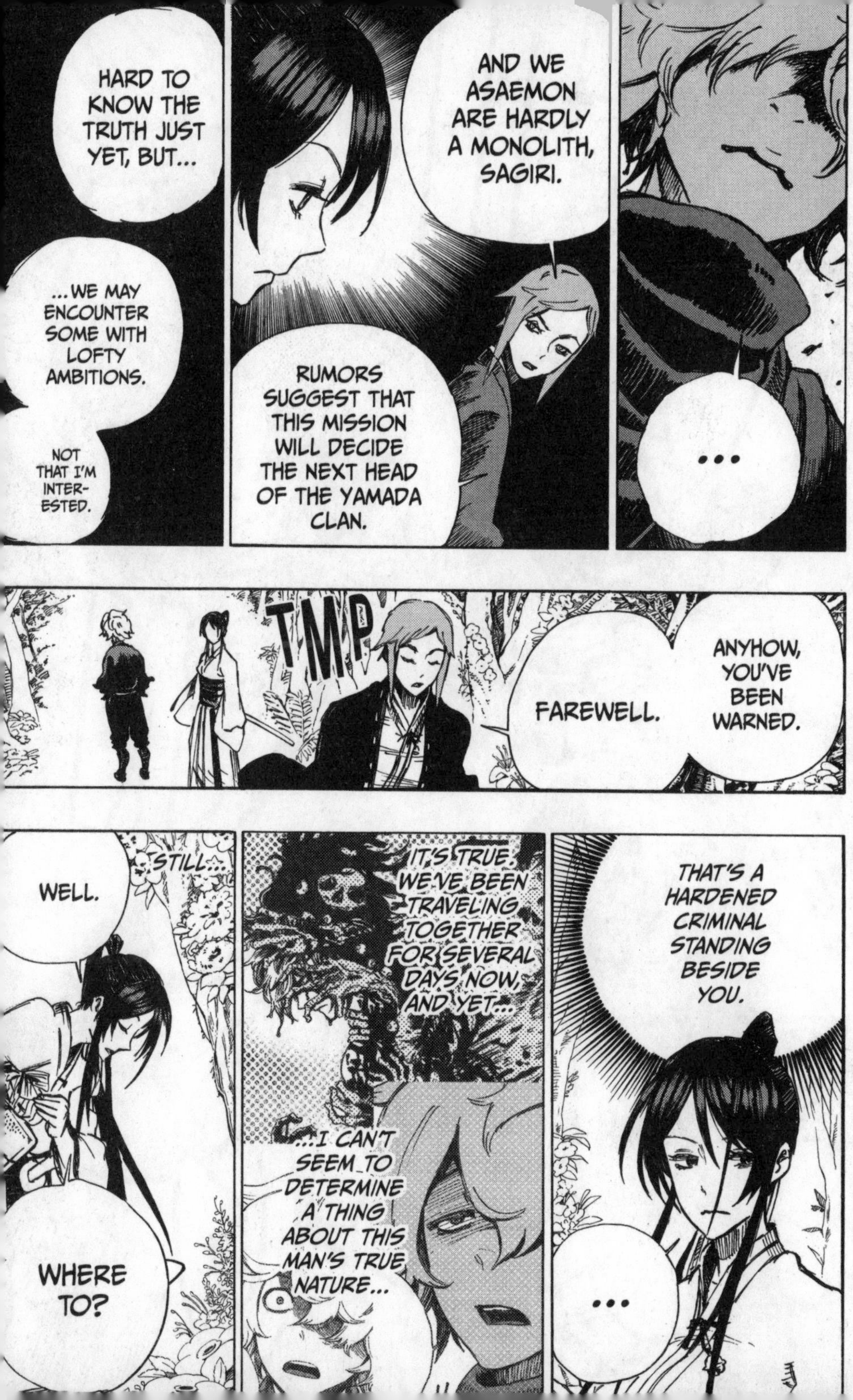
...
AND WE ASAEMON ARE HARDLY A MONOLITH, SAGIRI.
RUMORS SUGGEST THAT THIS MISSION WILL DECIDE THE NEXT HEAD OF THE YAMADA CLAN.
HARD TO KNOW THE TRUTH JUST YET, BUT...
...WE MAY ENCOUNTER SOME WITH LOFTY AMBITIONS.
NOT THAT I'M INTER-ESTED.
ANYHOW, YOU'VE BEEN WARNED.
FAREWELL.
TMP
THAT'S A HARDENED CRIMINAL STANDING BESIDE YOU.
...
IT'S TRUE. WE'VE BEEN TRAVELING TOGETHER FOR SEVERAL DAYS NOW, AND YET...
...I CAN'T SEEM TO DETERMINE A THING ABOUT THIS MAN'S TRUE NATURE...
STILL...
WELL.
WHERE TO?

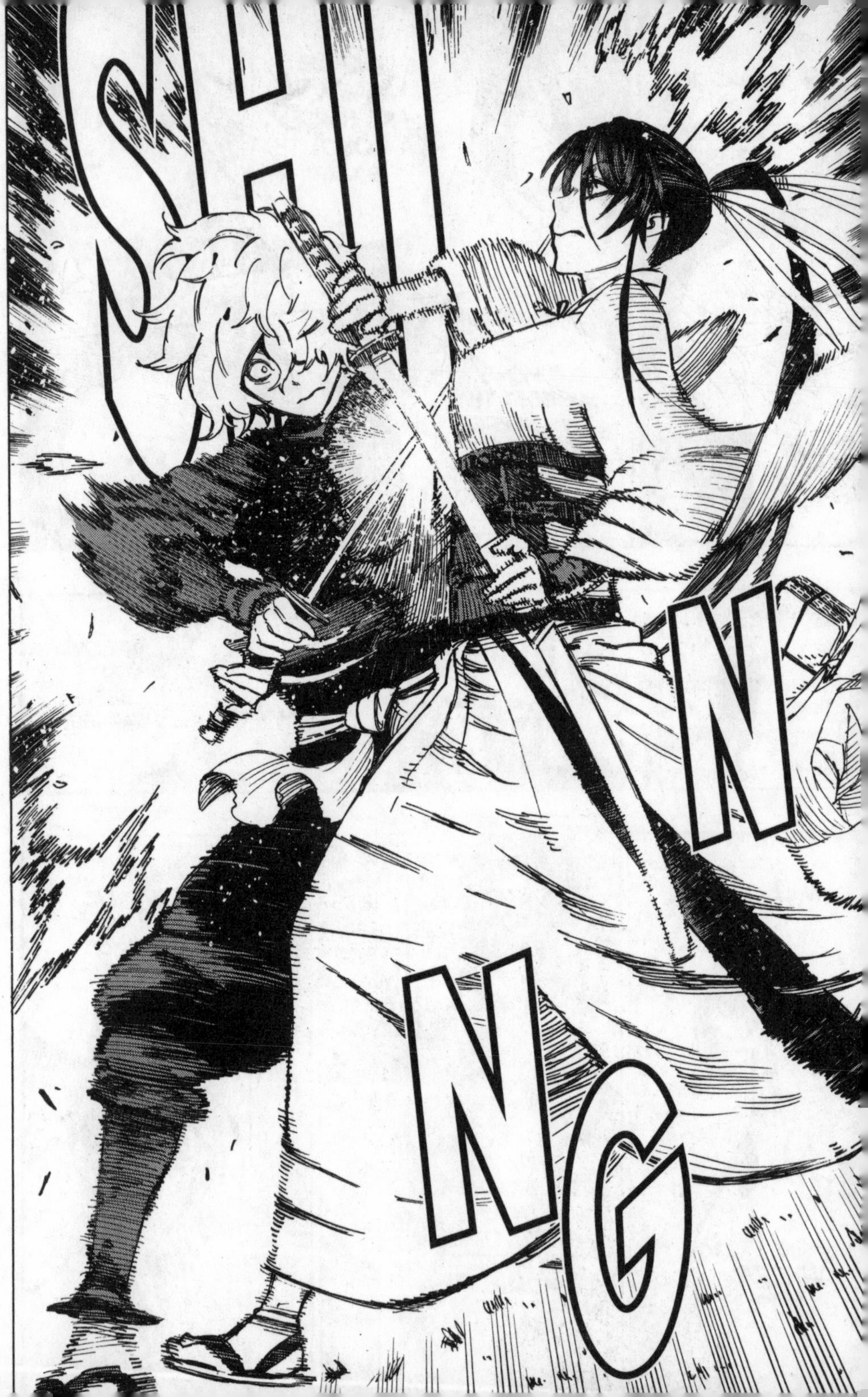
SHIINNG

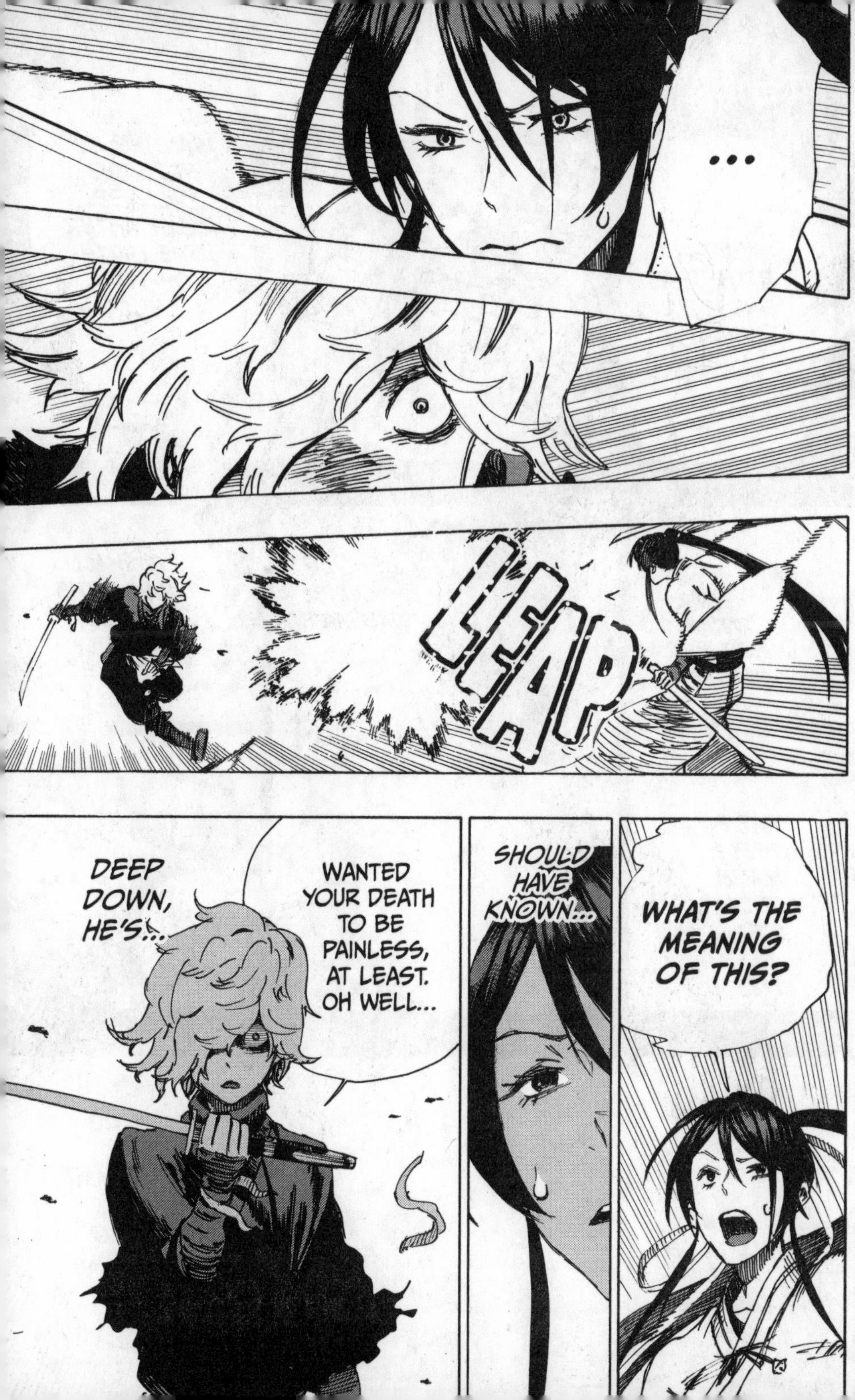
...
LEAP
WHAT'S THE MEANING OF THIS?
SHOULD HAVE KNOWN...
WANTED YOUR DEATH TO BE PAINLESS, AT LEAST. OH WELL...
DEEP DOWN, HE'S...

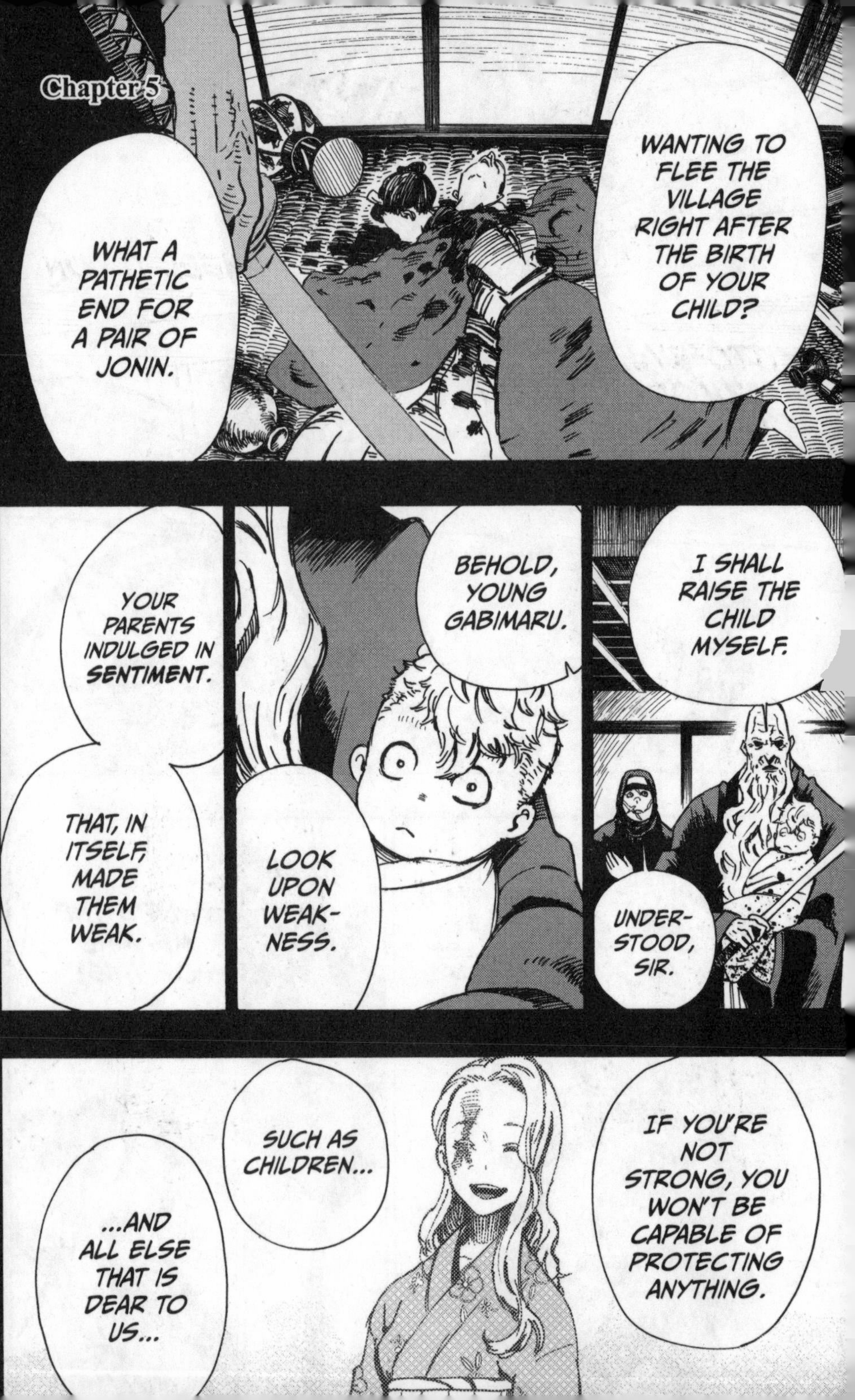
Chapter 5
WANTING TO FLEE THE VILLAGE RIGHT AFTER THE BIRTH OF YOUR CHILD?
WHAT A PATHETIC END FOR A PAIR OF JONIN.
I SHALL RAISE THE CHILD MYSELF.
UNDER-STOOD, SIR.
BEHOLD, YOUNG GABIMARU.
LOOK UPON WEAK-NESS.
YOUR PARENTS INDULGED IN SENTIMENT.
THAT, IN ITSELF, MADE THEM WEAK.
IF YOU'RE NOT STRONG, YOU WON'T BE CAPABLE OF PROTECTING ANYTHING.
SUCH AS CHILDREN...
...AND ALL ELSE THAT IS DEAR TO US...

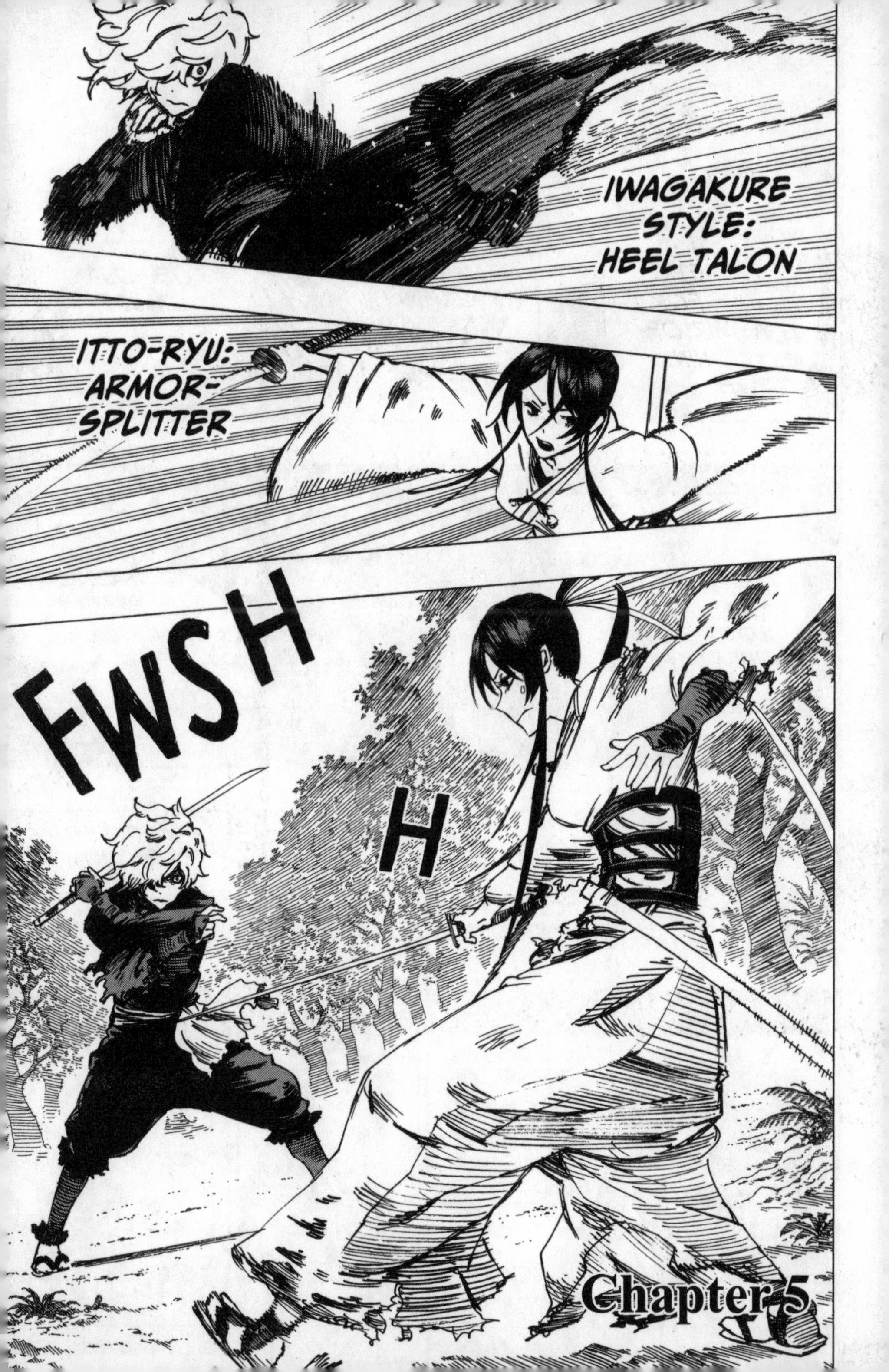
IWAGAKURE STYLE: HEEL TALON
ITTO-RYU: ARMOR-SPLITTER
FWSH
H
Chapter 5

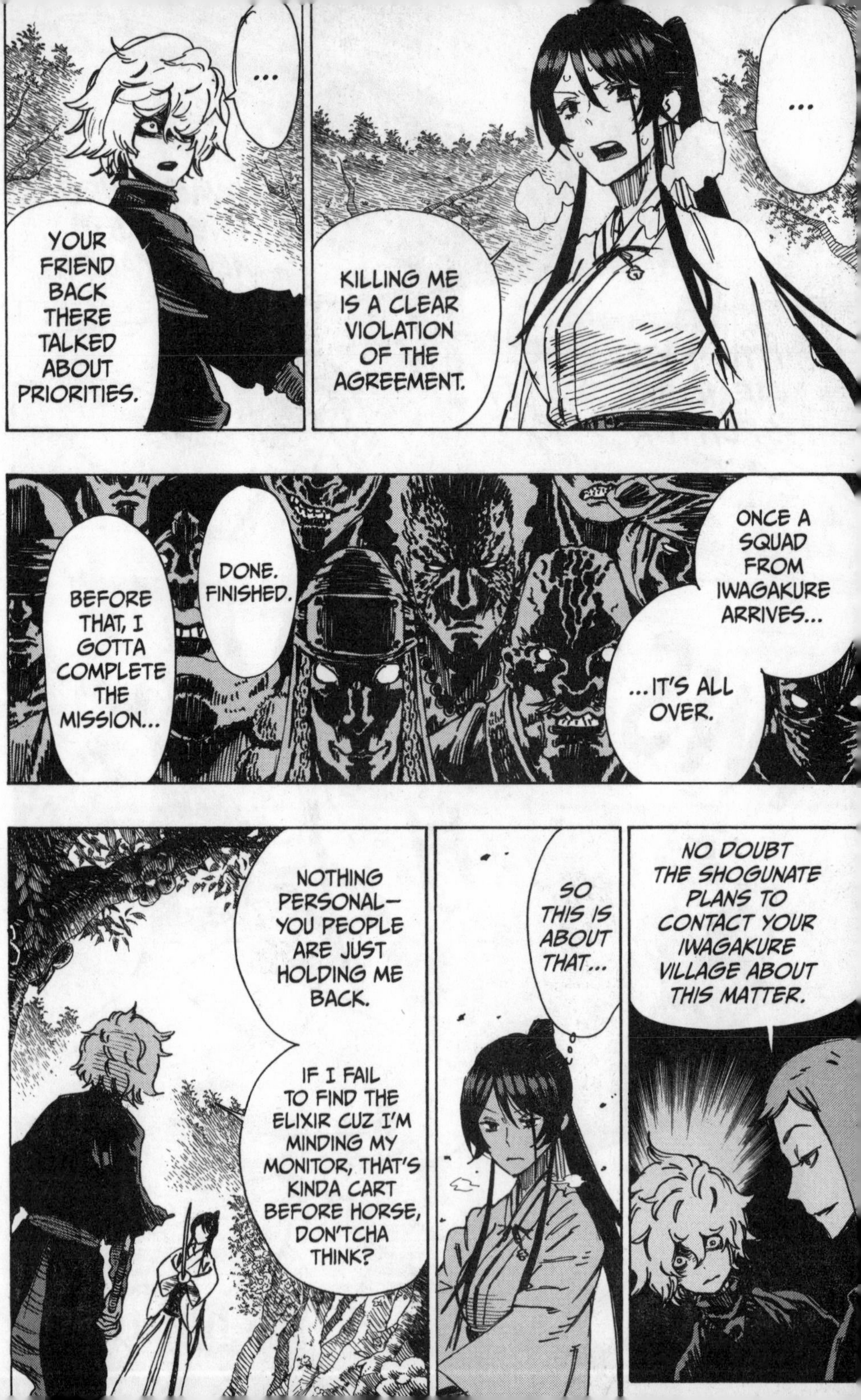
...
KILLING ME IS A CLEAR VIOLATION OF THE AGREEMENT.
...
YOUR FRIEND BACK THERE TALKED ABOUT PRIORITIES.
ONCE A SQUAD FROM IWAGAKURE ARRIVES...
...IT'S ALL OVER.
DONE. FINISHED.
BEFORE THAT, I GOTTA COMPLETE THE MISSION...
NO DOUBT THE SHOGUNATE PLANS TO CONTACT YOUR IWAGAKURE VILLAGE ABOUT THIS MATTER.
SO THIS IS ABOUT THAT...
NOTHING PERSONAL—YOU PEOPLE ARE JUST HOLDING ME BACK.
IF I FAIL TO FIND THE ELIXIR CUZ I'M MINDING MY MONITOR, THAT'S KINDA CART BEFORE HORSE, DON'TCHA THINK?

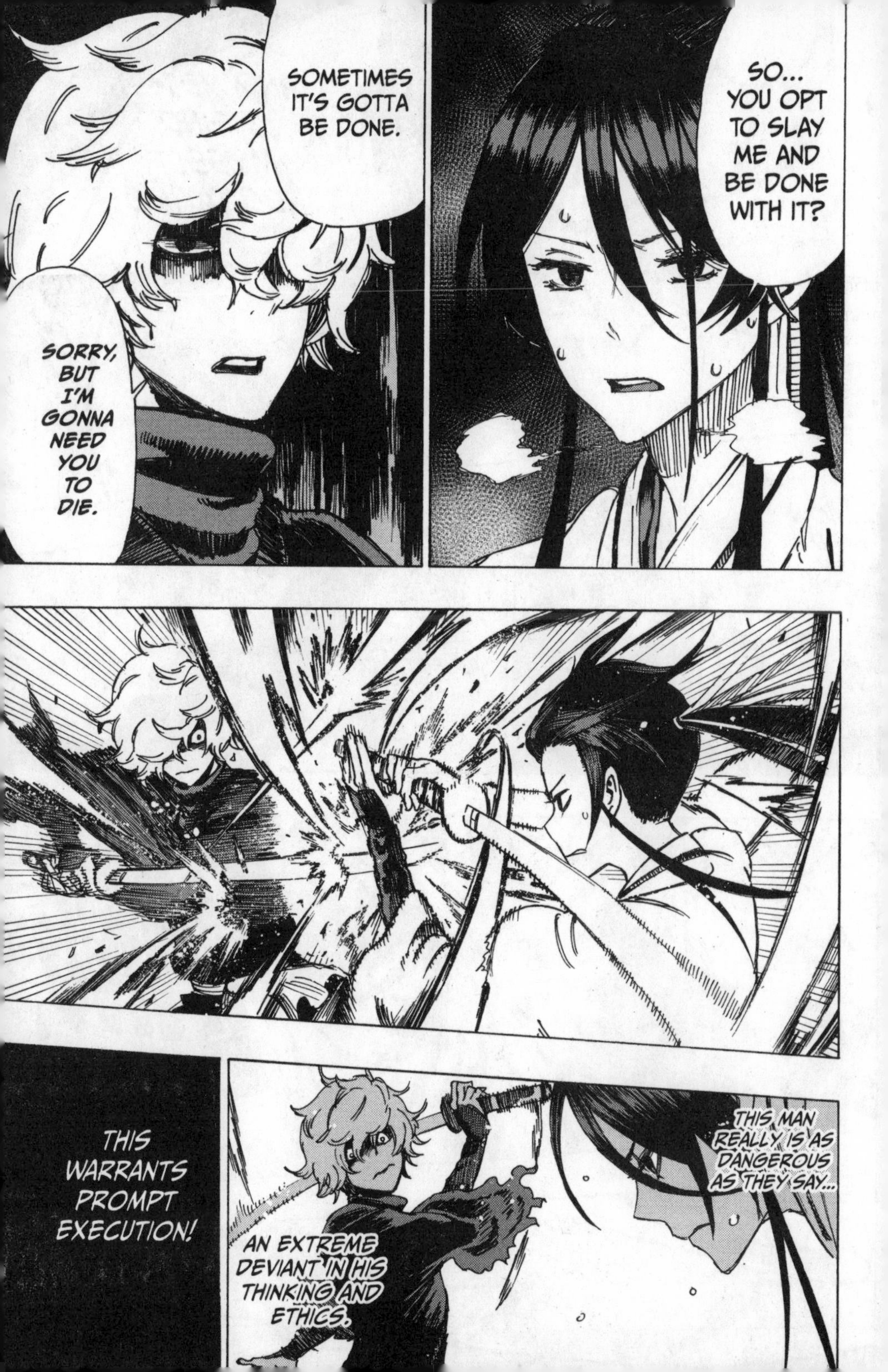
SO... YOU OPT TO SLAY ME AND BE DONE WITH IT?
SOMETIMES IT'S GOTTA BE DONE.
SORRY, BUT I'M GONNA NEED YOU TO DIE.
THIS MAN REALLY IS AS DANGEROUS AS THEY SAY...
AN EXTREME DEVIANT IN HIS THINKING AND ETHICS.
THIS WARRANTS PROMPT EXECUTION!

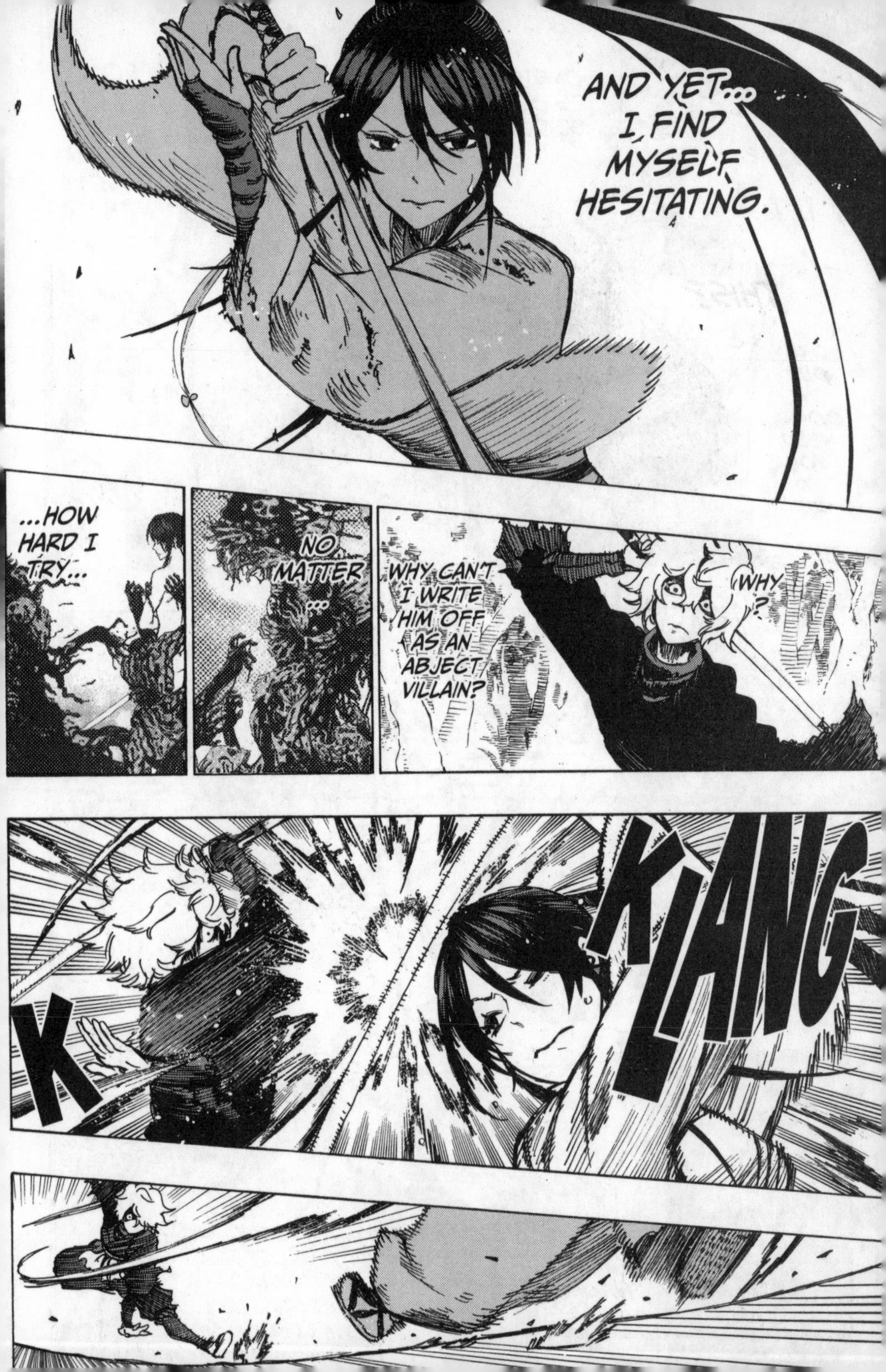
AND YET... I FIND MYSELF HESITATING.
WHY?
WHY CAN'T I WRITE HIM OFF AS AN ABJECT VILLAIN?
NO MATTER...
...HOW HARD I TRY...
KANG
K

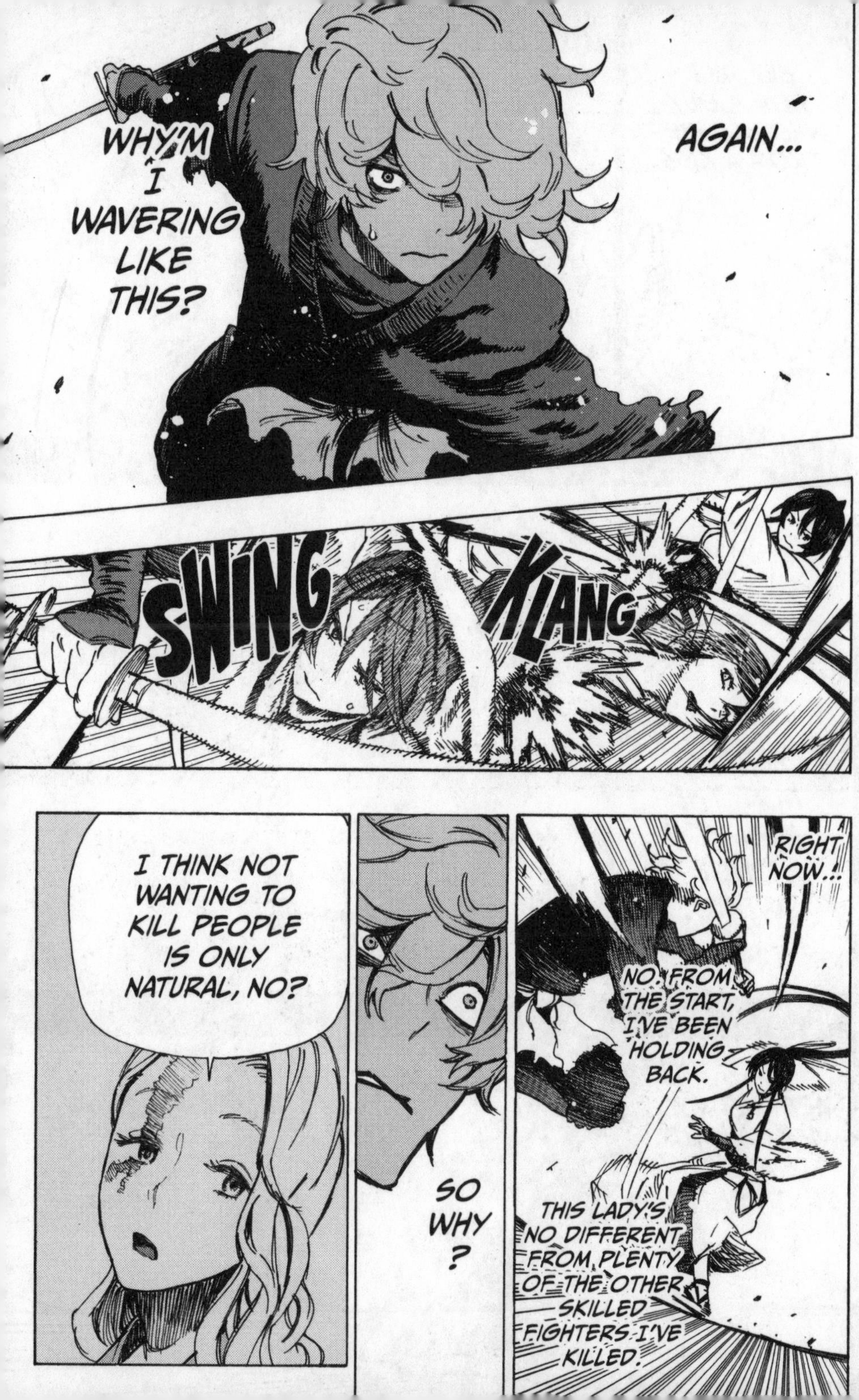
AGAIN...
WHY'M I WAVERING LIKE THIS?
KLANG
SWING
RIGHT NOW...
NO, FROM THE START, I'VE BEEN HOLDING BACK.
THIS LADY'S NO DIFFERENT FROM PLENTY OF THE OTHER SKILLED FIGHTERS I'VE KILLED.
SO WHY?
I THINK NOT WANTING TO KILL PEOPLE IS ONLY NATURAL, NO?

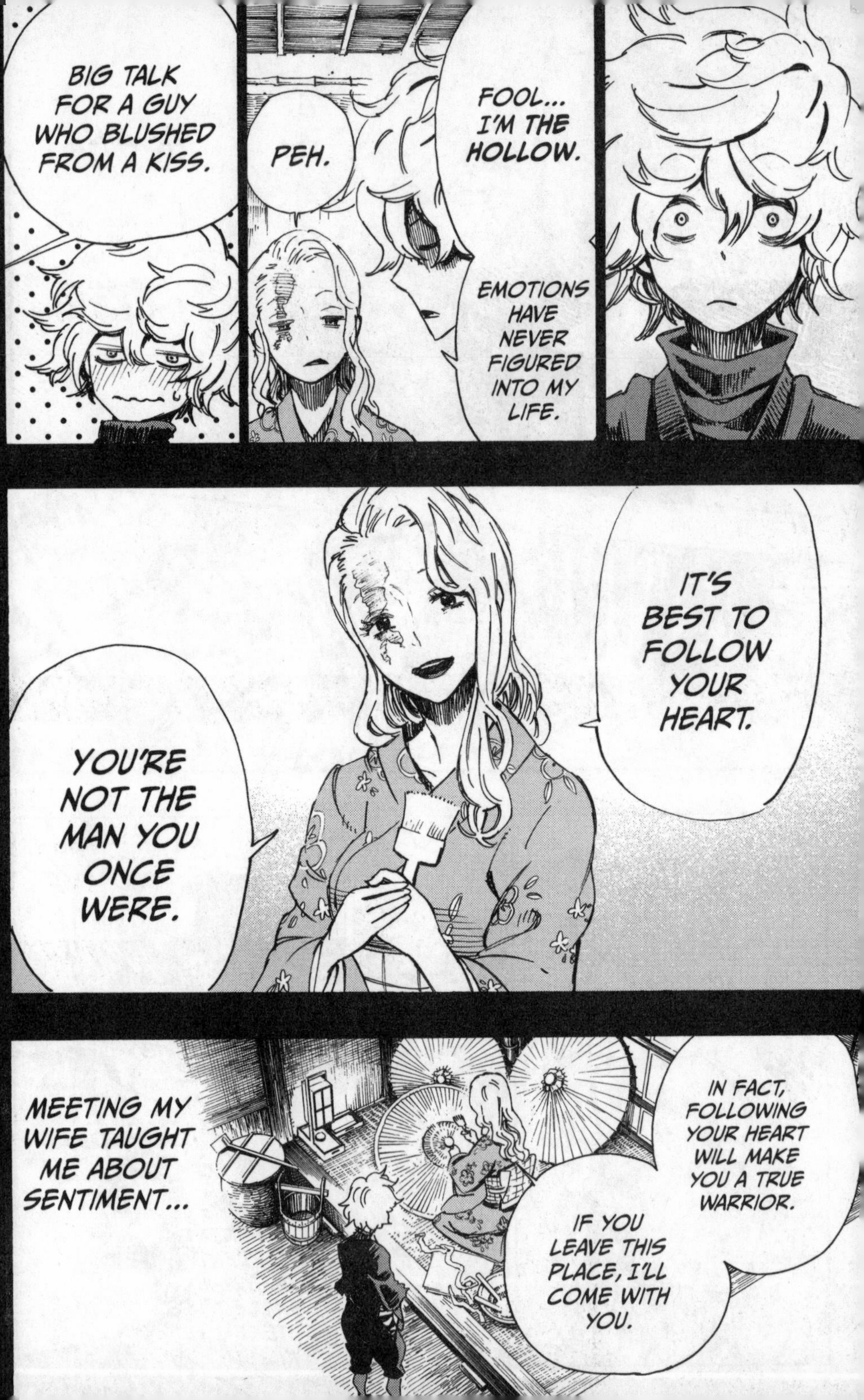
FOOL... I'M THE HOLLOW.
PEH.
EMOTIONS HAVE NEVER FIGURED INTO MY LIFE.
BIG TALK FOR A GUY WHO BLUSHED FROM A KISS.
IT'S BEST TO FOLLOW YOUR HEART.
YOU'RE NOT THE MAN YOU ONCE WERE.
IN FACT, FOLLOWING YOUR HEART WILL MAKE YOU A TRUE WARRIOR.
IF YOU LEAVE THIS PLACE, I'LL COME WITH YOU.
MEETING MY WIFE TAUGHT ME ABOUT SENTIMENT...

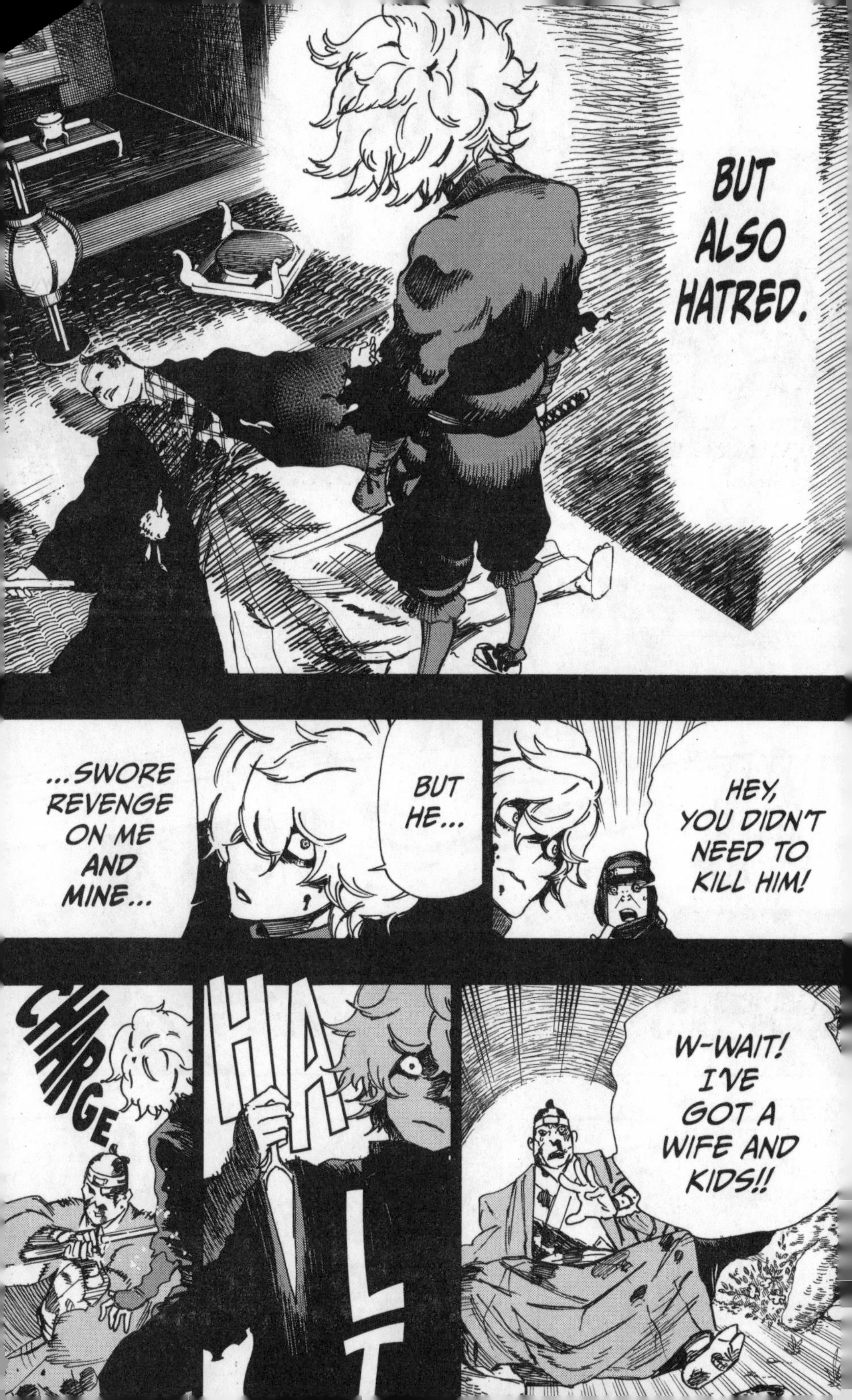
BUT ALSO HATRED.
HEY, YOU DIDN'T NEED TO KILL HIM!
BUT HE...
...SWORE REVENGE ON ME AND MINE...
W-WAIT! I'VE GOT A WIFE AND KIDS!!
HALT
CHARGE

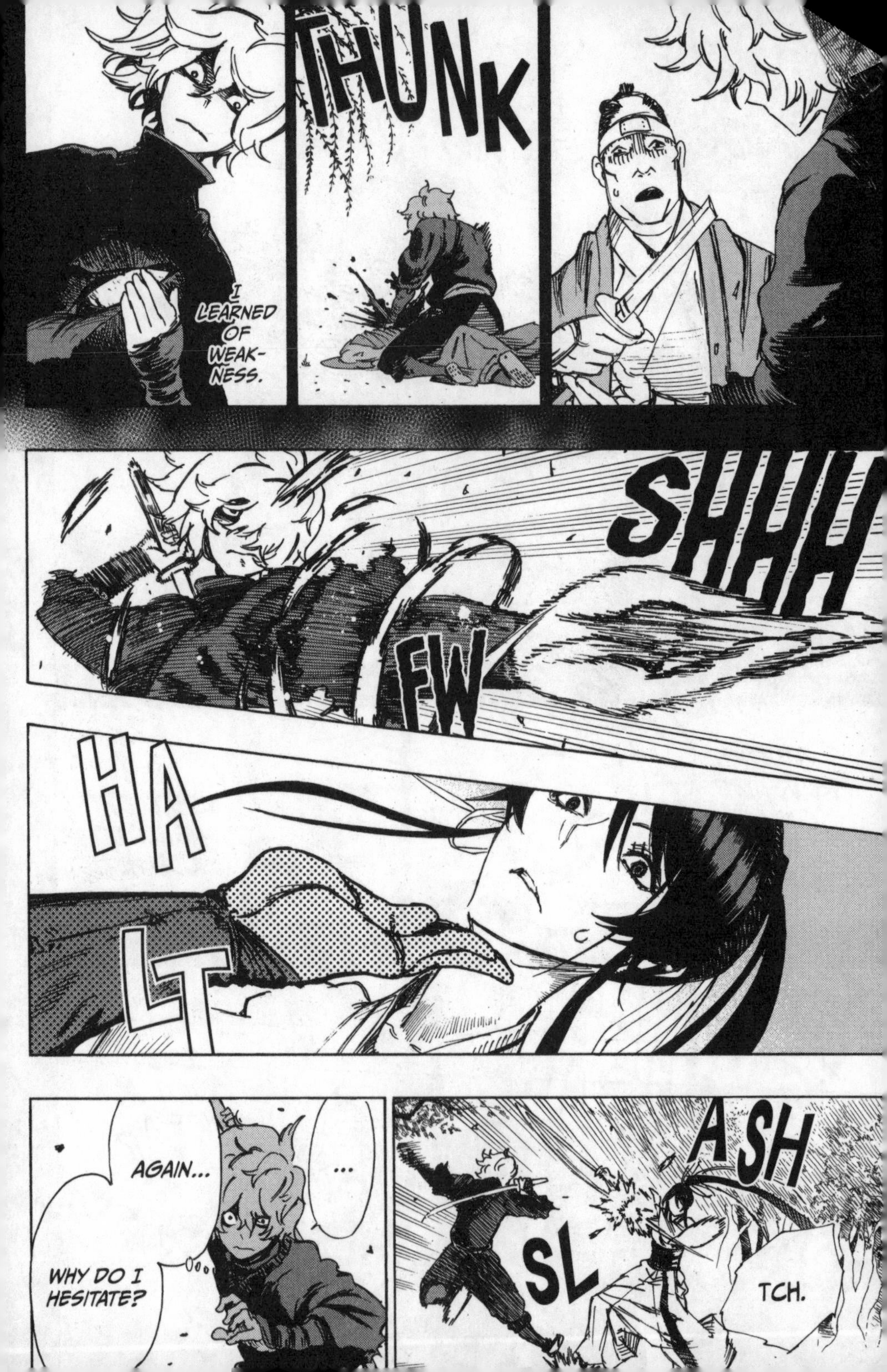
THUNK
I LEARNED OF WEAK-NESS.
SHHH
FW
HA
LT
ASH
SL
TCH.
...
AGAIN...
WHY DO I HESITATE?

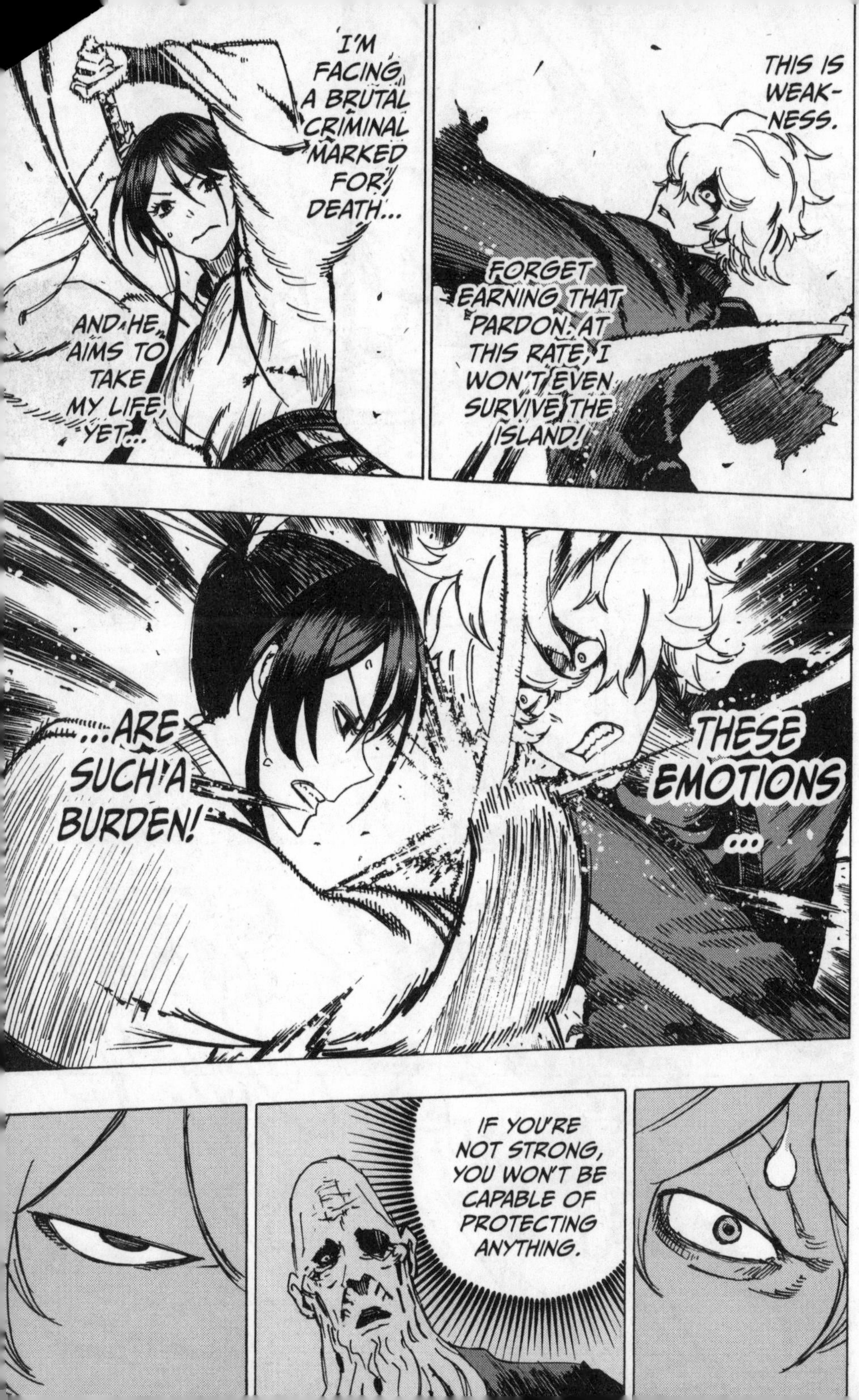
THIS IS WEAK-NESS.
FORGET EARNING THAT PARDON. AT THIS RATE, I WON'T EVEN SURVIVE THE ISLAND!
I'M FACING A BRUTAL CRIMINAL MARKED FOR DEATH...
AND HE AIMS TO TAKE MY LIFE, YET...
THESE EMOTIONS...
...ARE SUCH A BURDEN!
IF YOU'RE NOT STRONG, YOU WON'T BE CAPABLE OF PROTECTING ANYTHING.

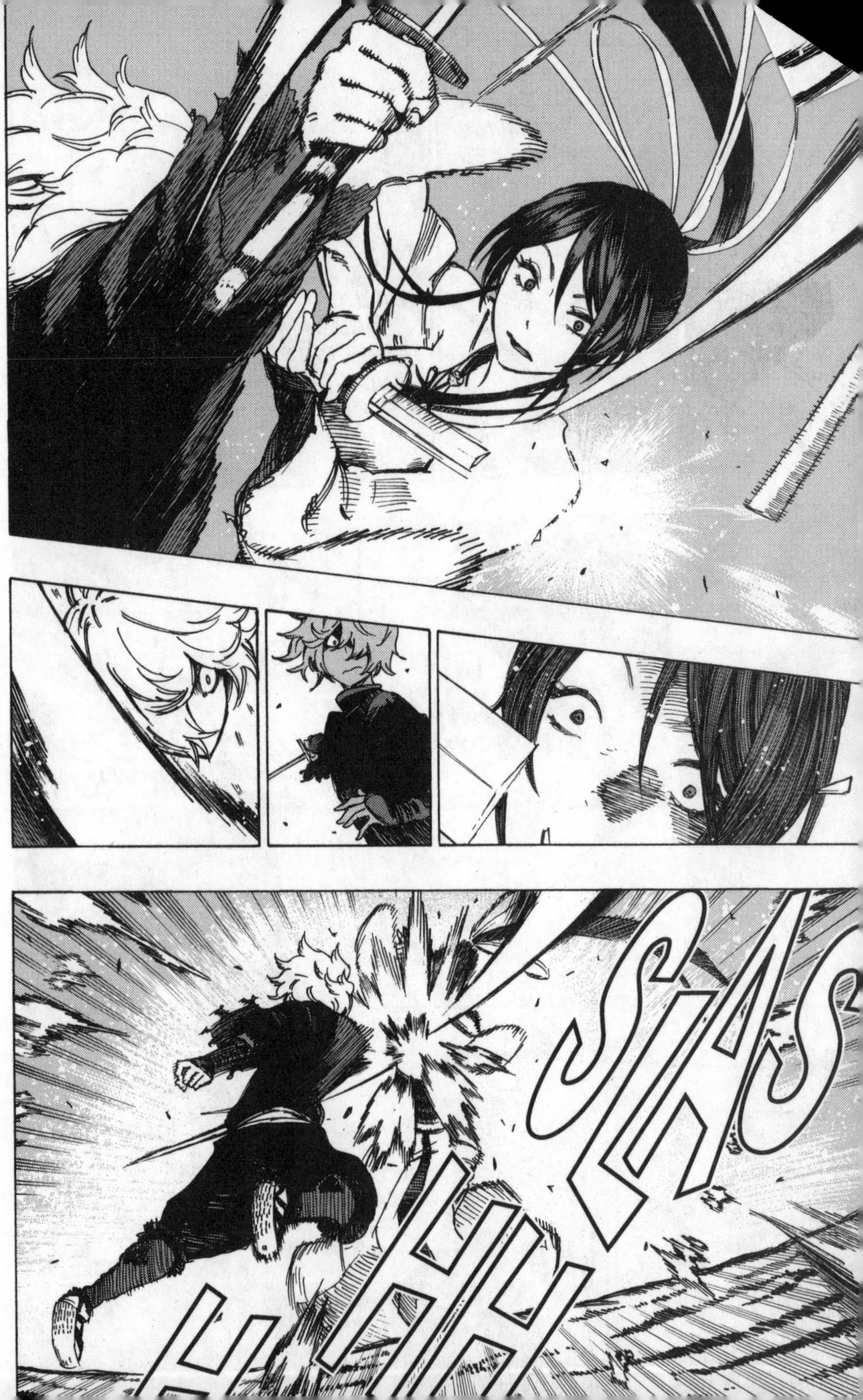
SHASHHHH

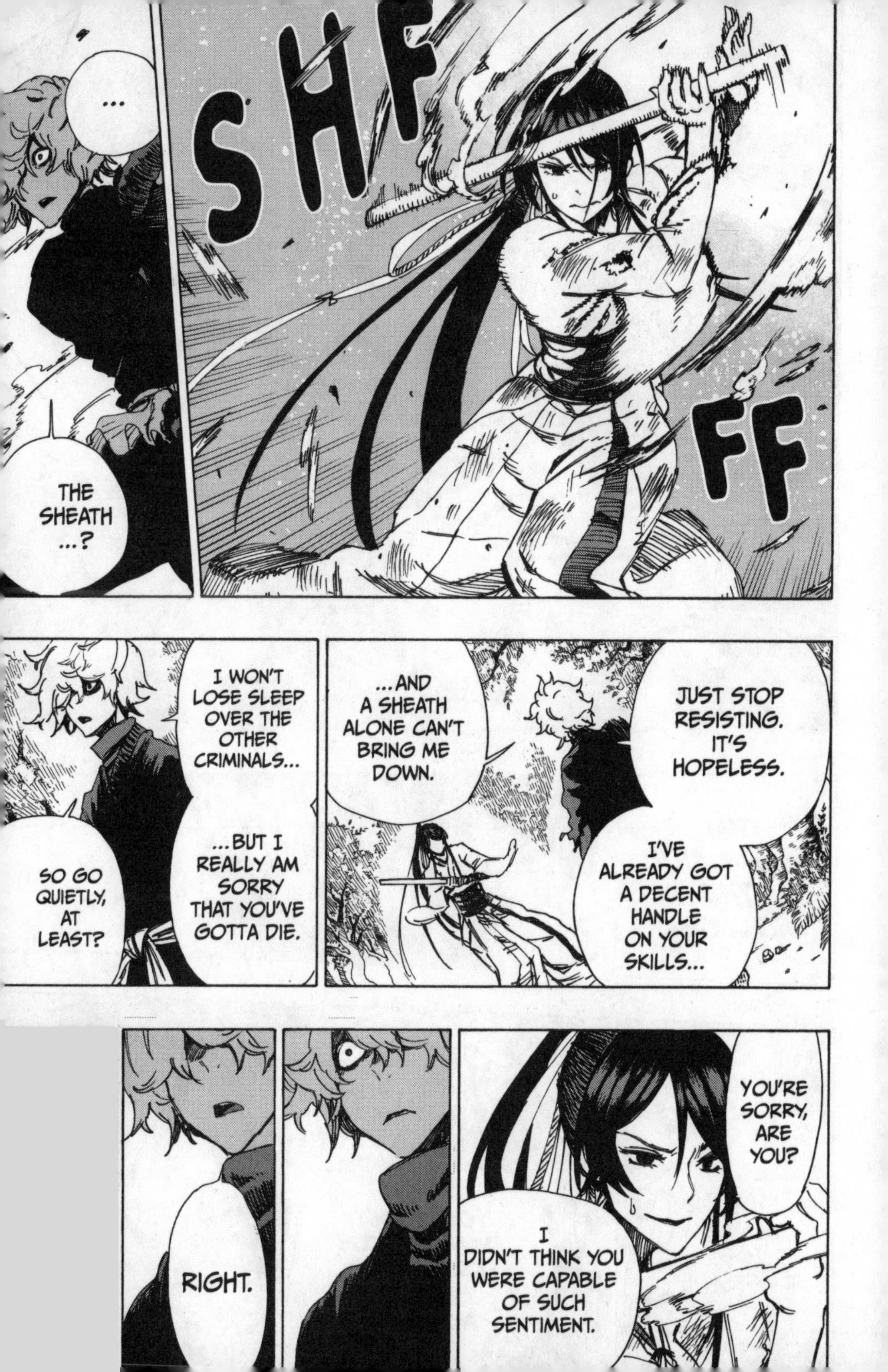
SHFFF
...
THE SHEATH ...?
JUST STOP RESISTING. IT'S HOPELESS.
I'VE ALREADY GOT A DECENT HANDLE ON YOUR SKILLS...
...AND A SHEATH ALONE CAN'T BRING ME DOWN.
I WON'T LOSE SLEEP OVER THE OTHER CRIMINALS...
...BUT I REALLY AM SORRY THAT YOU'VE GOTTA DIE.
SO GO QUIETLY, AT LEAST?
YOU'RE SORRY, ARE YOU?
I DIDN'T THINK YOU WERE CAPABLE OF SUCH SENTIMENT.
RIGHT.

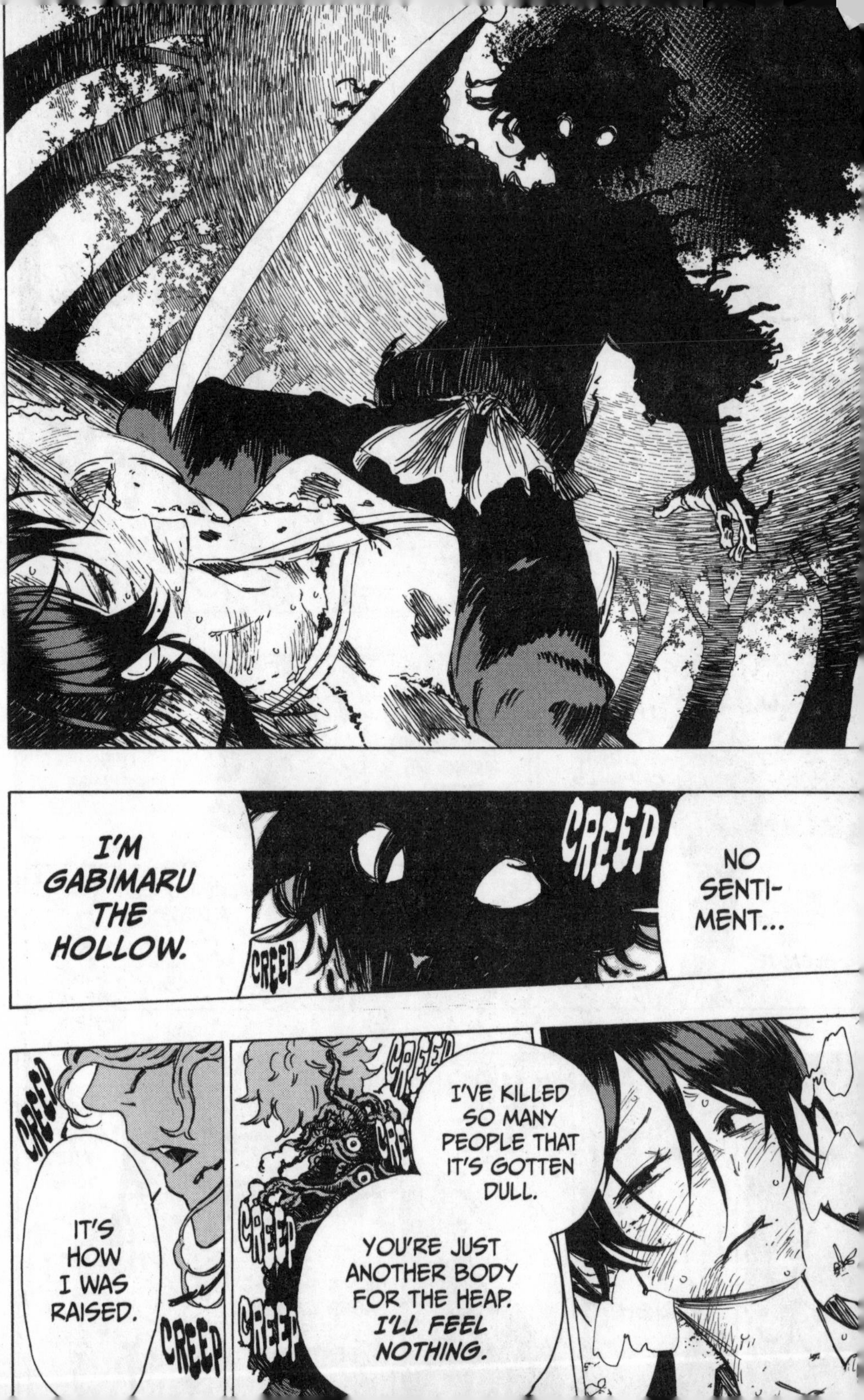
NO SENTI-MENT...
CREEP
CREEP
I'M GABIMARU THE HOLLOW.
I'VE KILLED SO MANY PEOPLE THAT IT'S GOTTEN DULL.
YOU'RE JUST ANOTHER BODY FOR THE HEAP. *I'LL FEEL NOTHING.*
CREEP
CREEP
CREEP
CREEP
CREEP
CREEP
IT'S HOW I WAS RAISED.
CREEP

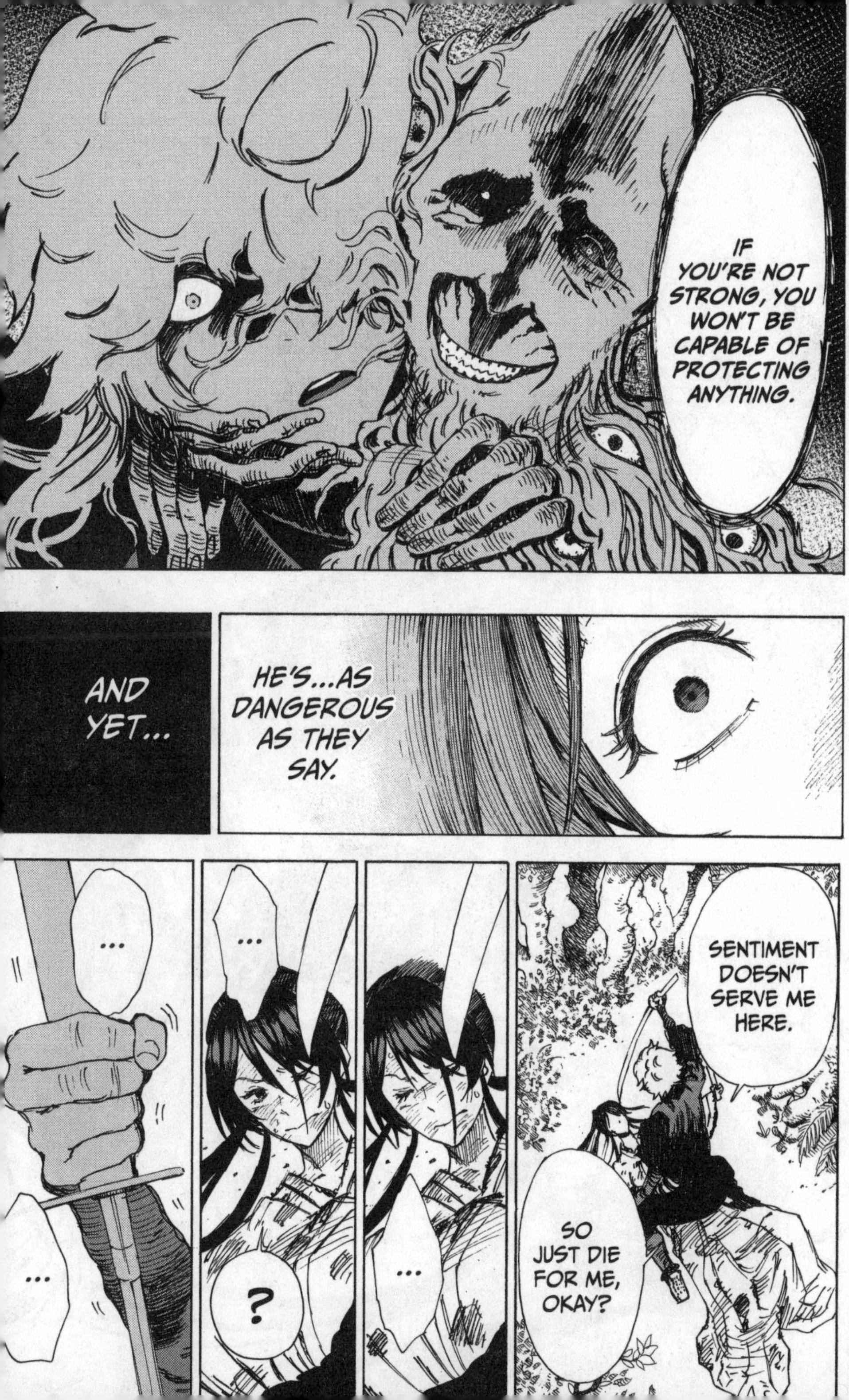
IF YOU'RE NOT STRONG, YOU WON'T BE CAPABLE OF PROTECTING ANYTHING.
HE'S...AS DANGEROUS AS THEY SAY.
AND YET...
SENTIMENT DOESN'T SERVE ME HERE.
SO JUST DIE FOR ME, OKAY?
...
...
...
?
...
...

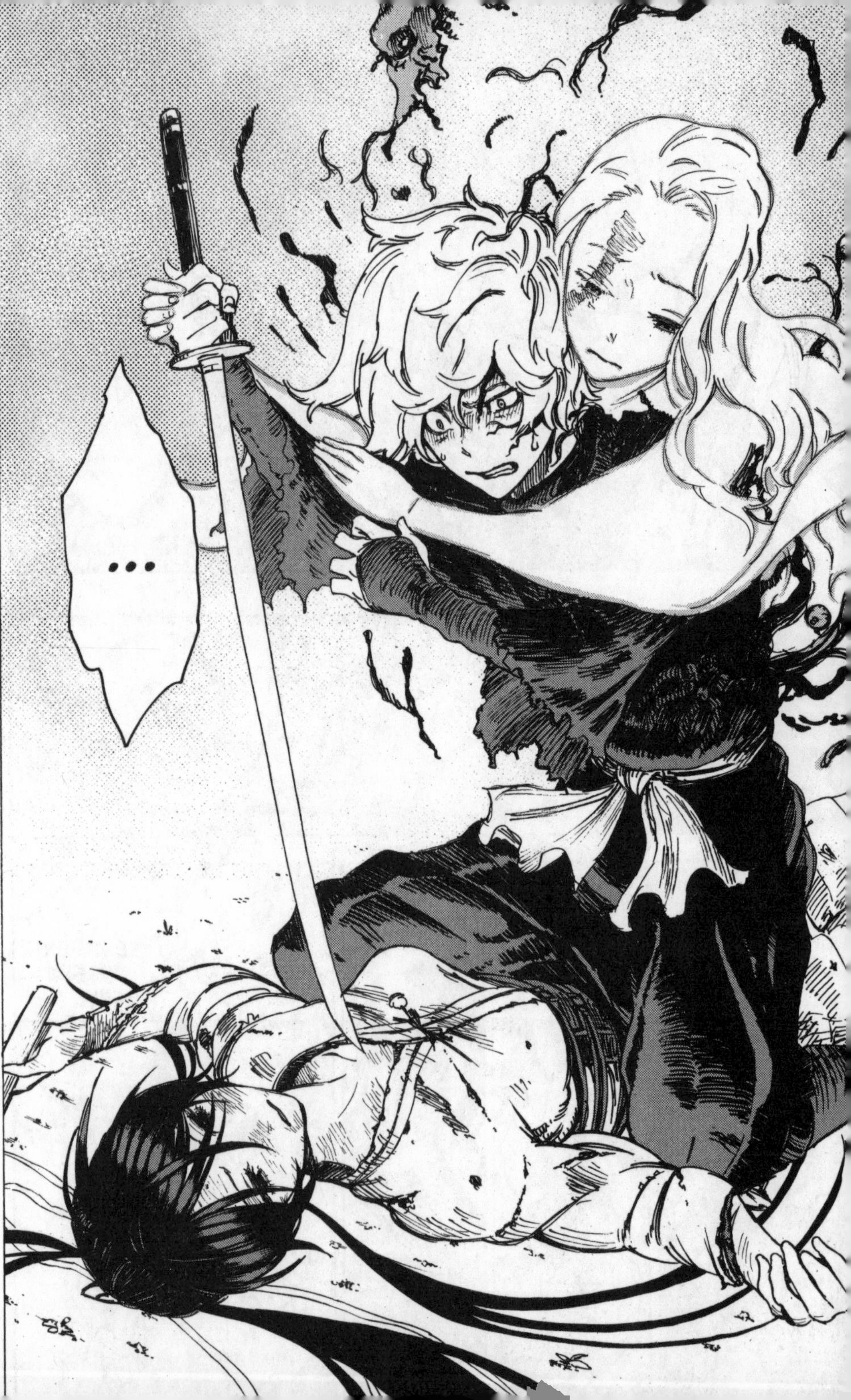
...

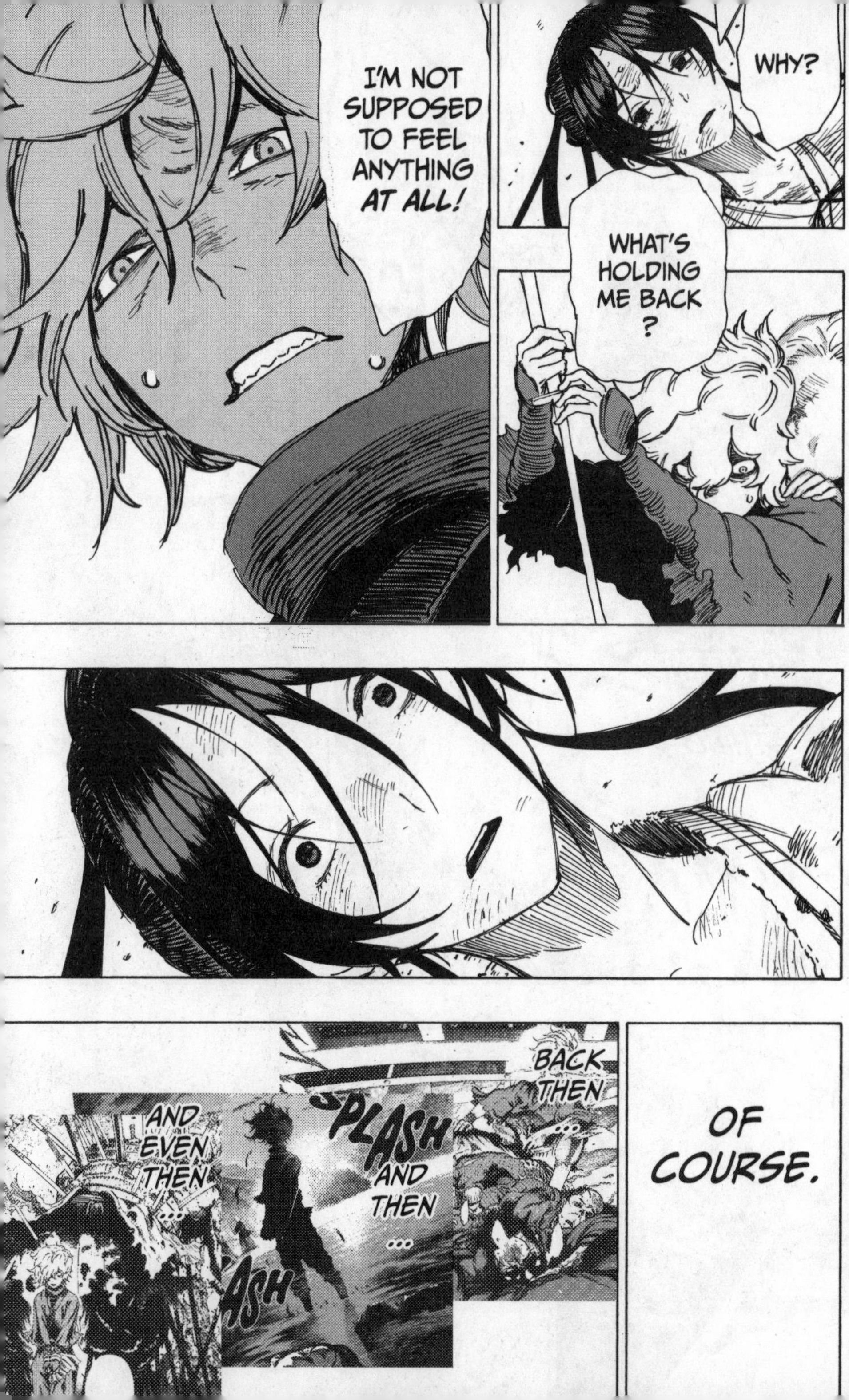

WHY?
WHAT'S HOLDING ME BACK?
I'M NOT SUPPOSED TO FEEL ANYTHING AT ALL!
OF COURSE.
BACK THEN ...
SPLASH
AND THEN ...
AND EVEN THEN ...

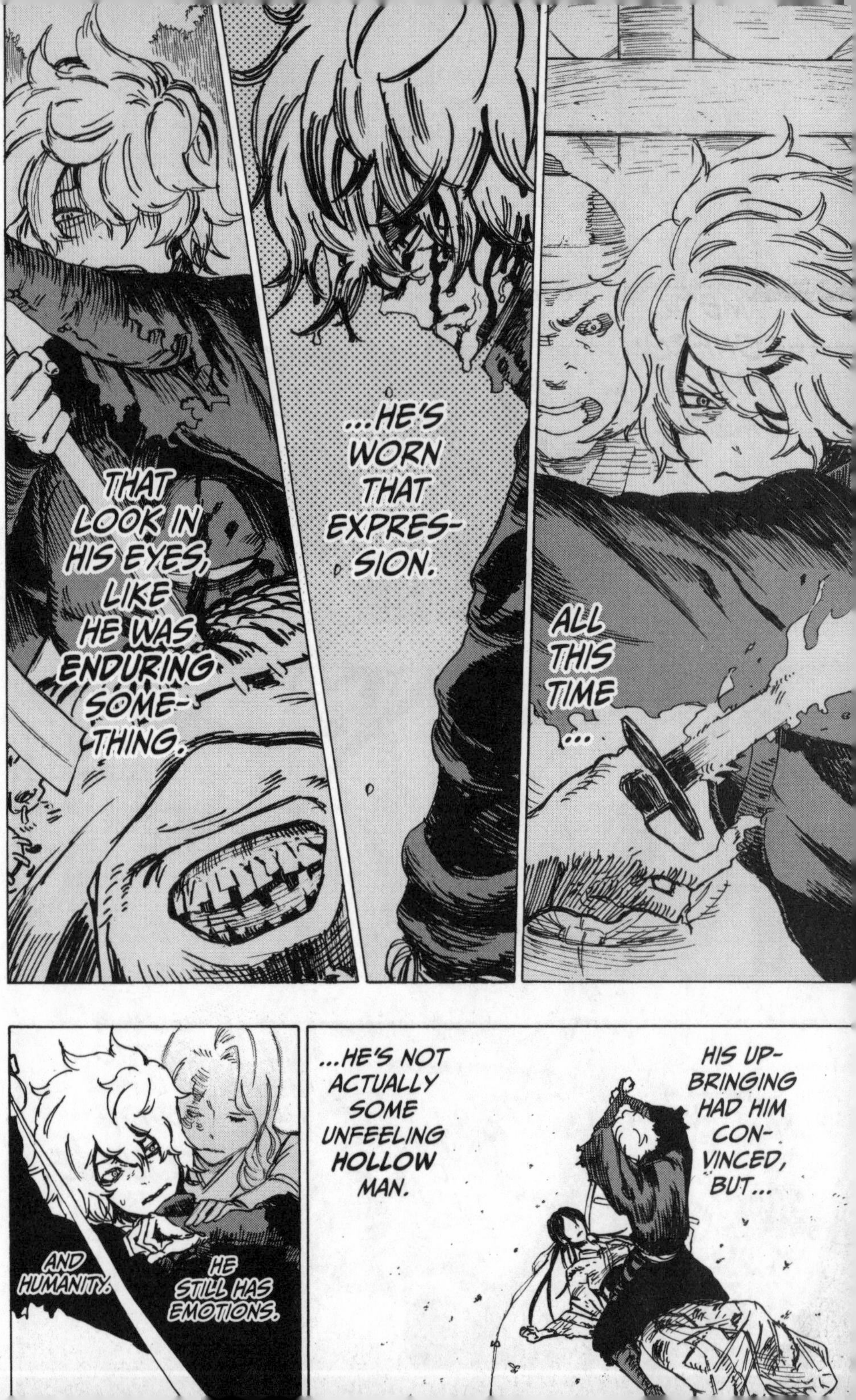
ALL THIS TIME ...
...HE'S WORN THAT EXPRES-SION.
THAT LOOK IN HIS EYES, LIKE HE WAS ENDURING SOME-THING.
HIS UP-BRINGING HAD HIM CON-VINCED, BUT...
...HE'S NOT ACTUALLY SOME UNFEELING HOLLOW MAN.
HE STILL HAS EMOTIONS.
AND HUMANITY.

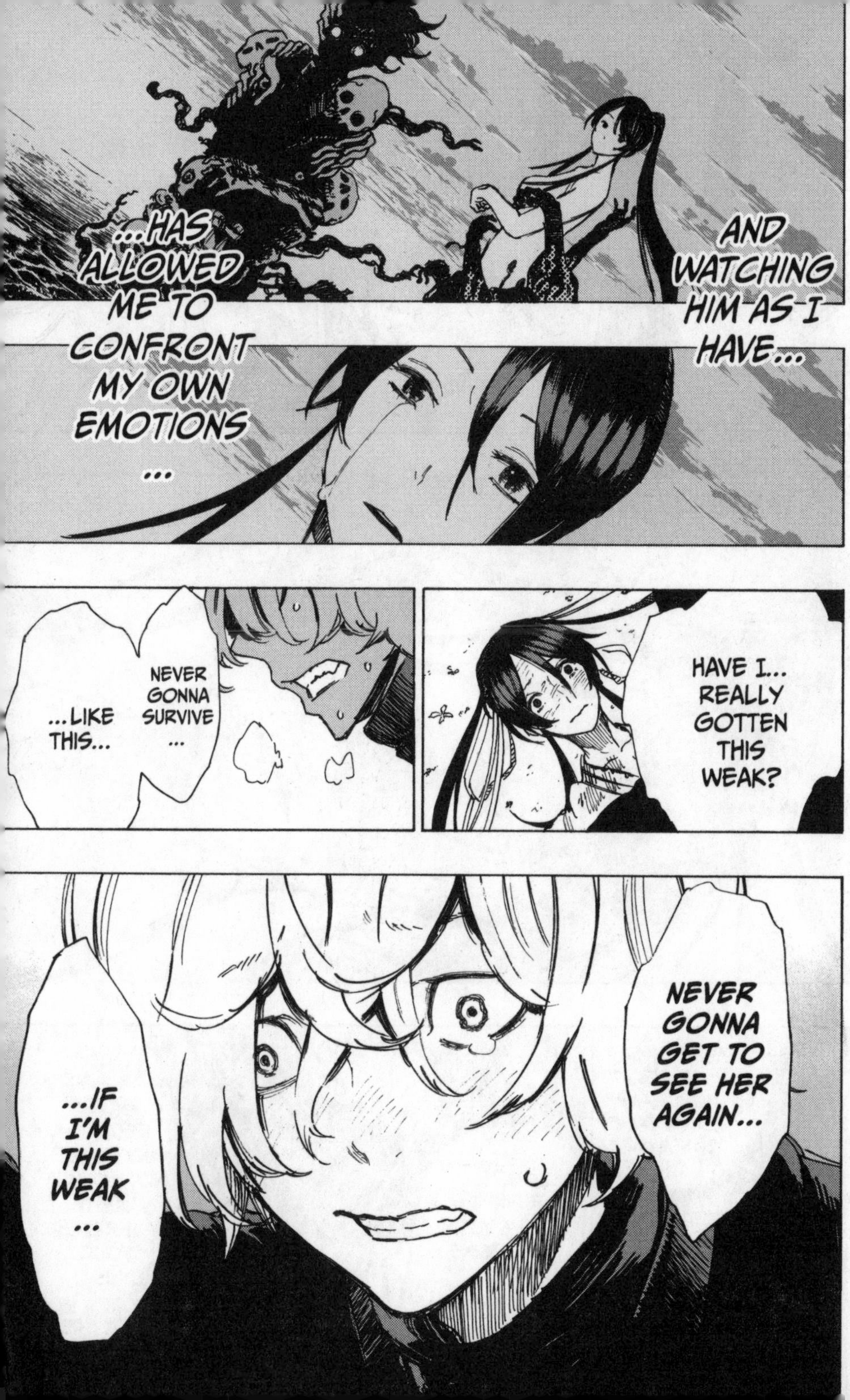
AND WATCHING HIM AS I HAVE...
...HAS ALLOWED ME TO CONFRONT MY OWN EMOTIONS ...
HAVE I... REALLY GOTTEN THIS WEAK?
NEVER GONNA SURVIVE ...
...LIKE THIS...
NEVER GONNA GET TO SEE HER AGAIN...
...IF I'M THIS WEAK ...

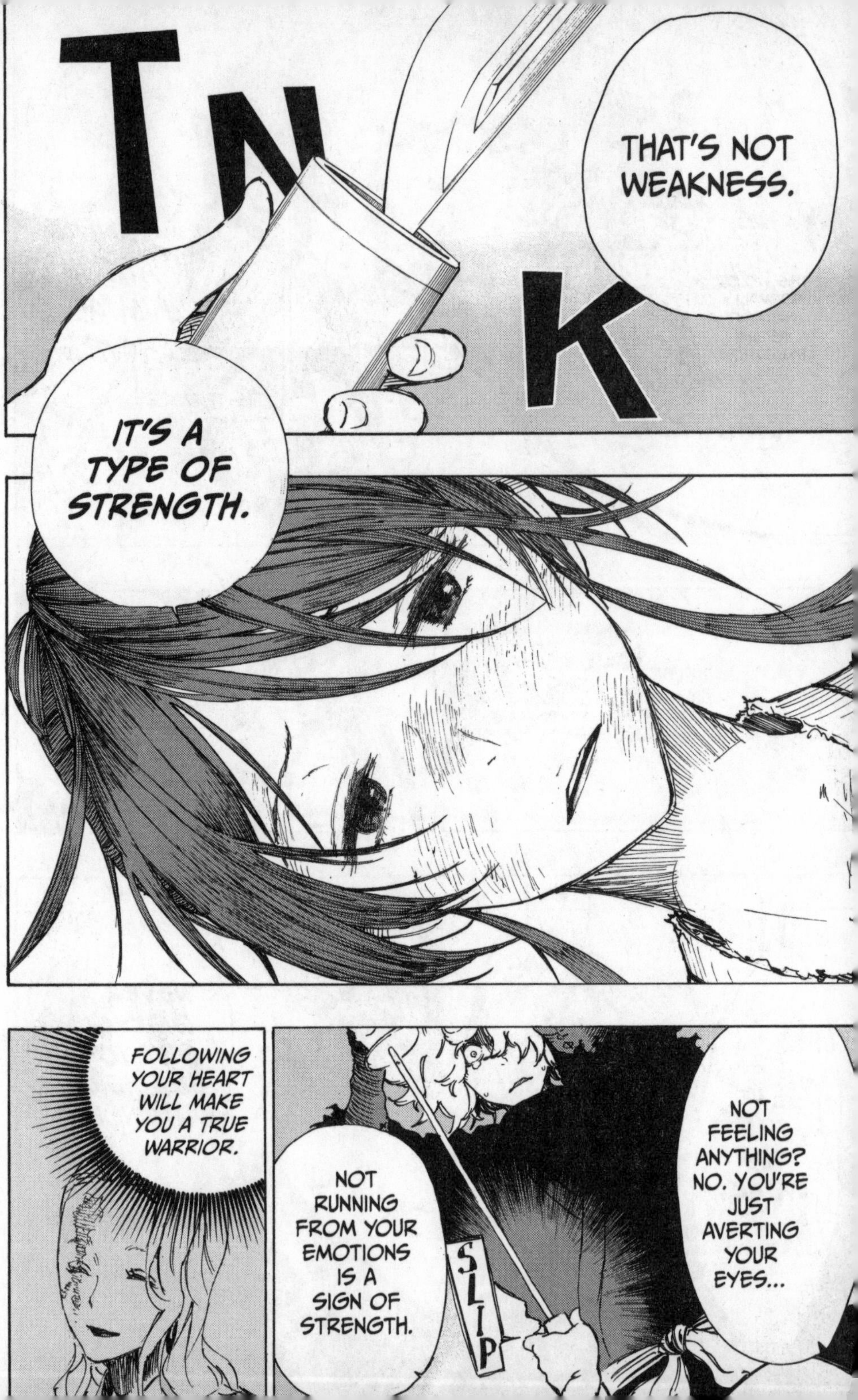
THAT'S NOT WEAKNESS.
TNK
IT'S A TYPE OF STRENGTH.
NOT FEELING ANYTHING? NO. YOU'RE JUST AVERTING YOUR EYES...
NOT RUNNING FROM YOUR EMOTIONS IS A SIGN OF STRENGTH.
SLIP
FOLLOWING YOUR HEART WILL MAKE YOU A TRUE WARRIOR.

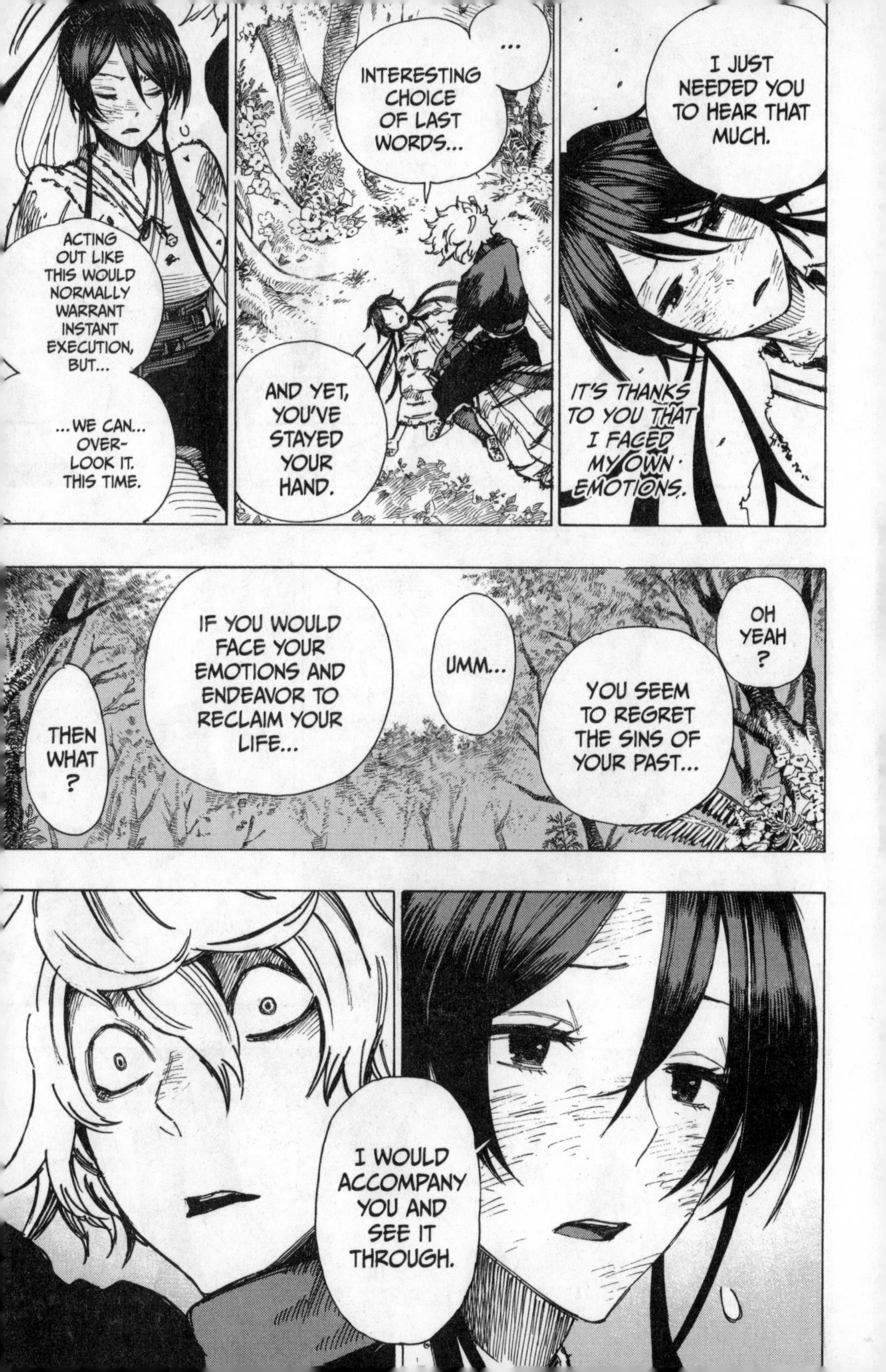
I JUST NEEDED YOU TO HEAR THAT MUCH.
IT'S THANKS TO YOU THAT I FACED MY OWN EMOTIONS.
...
INTERESTING CHOICE OF LAST WORDS...
AND YET, YOU'VE STAYED YOUR HAND.
ACTING OUT LIKE THIS WOULD NORMALLY WARRANT INSTANT EXECUTION, BUT...
...WE CAN... OVER-LOOK IT. THIS TIME.
OH YEAH?
YOU SEEM TO REGRET THE SINS OF YOUR PAST...
UMM...
IF YOU WOULD FACE YOUR EMOTIONS AND ENDEAVOR TO RECLAIM YOUR LIFE...
THEN WHAT?
I WOULD ACCOMPANY YOU AND SEE IT THROUGH.

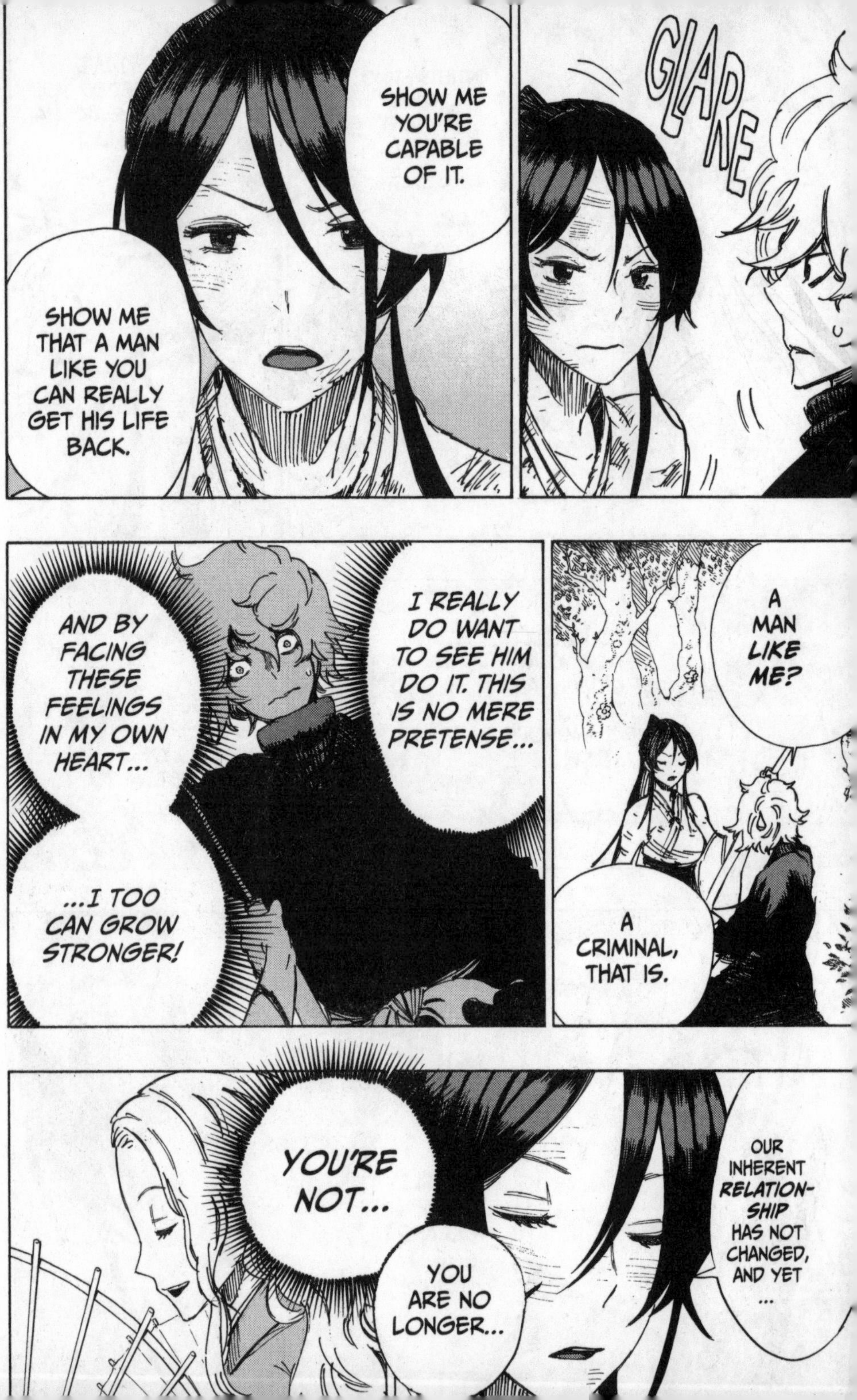
GLARE
SHOW ME YOU'RE CAPABLE OF IT.
SHOW ME THAT A MAN LIKE YOU CAN REALLY GET HIS LIFE BACK.
A MAN LIKE ME?
A CRIMINAL, THAT IS.
I REALLY DO WANT TO SEE HIM DO IT. THIS IS NO MERE PRETENSE...
AND BY FACING THESE FEELINGS IN MY OWN HEART...
...I TOO CAN GROW STRONGER!
OUR INHERENT RELATION-SHIP HAS NOT CHANGED, AND YET ...
YOU'RE NOT...
YOU ARE NO LONGER...

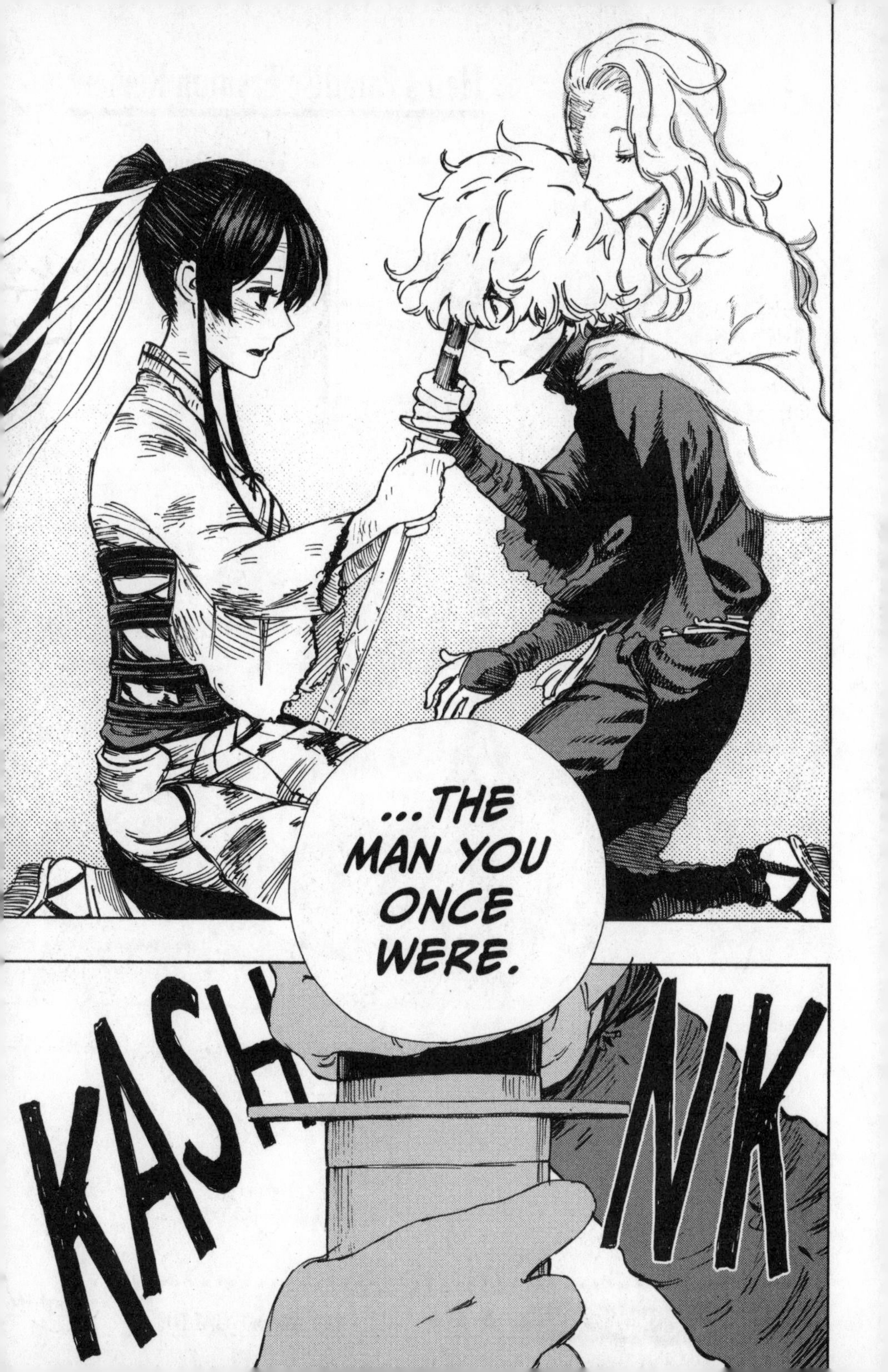
...THE MAN YOU ONCE WERE.
KASHNK

Hell's Paradise Fashion Review

Cannibal Courtesan
AKAGINU

Striking designs of *obi, uchikake* robe and *juban* singlet are all ahead of the times.

Skull, serpent and peony motif.

Unique *takageta* clogs.

Juban singlet resembles a Western brassiere.

EVALUATION ► FASHION GODDESS ★★★ ALL VERY AVANT-GARDE!

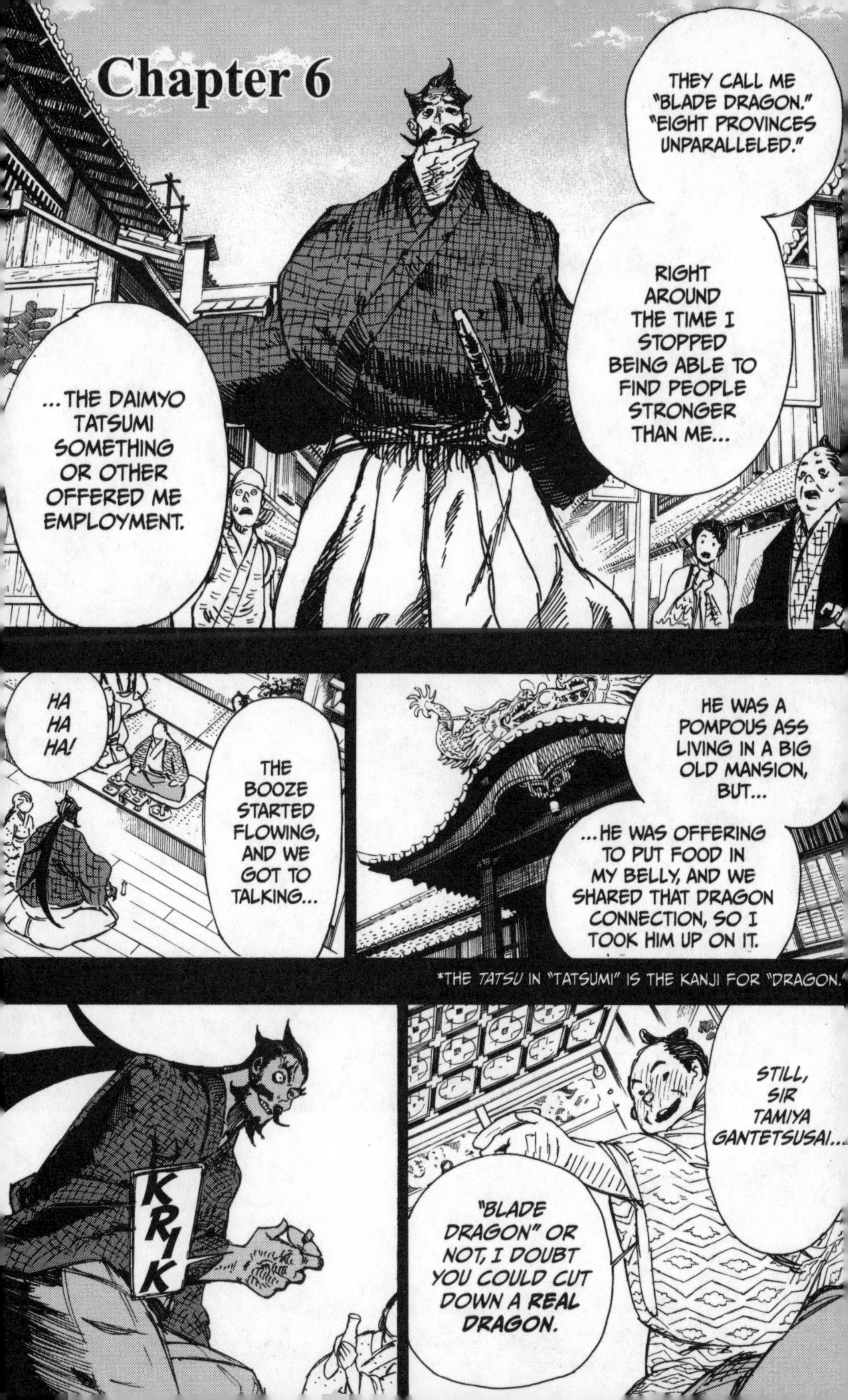
Chapter 6
THEY CALL ME "BLADE DRAGON." "EIGHT PROVINCES UNPARALLELED."
RIGHT AROUND THE TIME I STOPPED BEING ABLE TO FIND PEOPLE STRONGER THAN ME...
...THE DAIMYO TATSUMI SOMETHING OR OTHER OFFERED ME EMPLOYMENT.
HE WAS A POMPOUS ASS LIVING IN A BIG OLD MANSION, BUT...
...HE WAS OFFERING TO PUT FOOD IN MY BELLY, AND WE SHARED THAT DRAGON CONNECTION, SO I TOOK HIM UP ON IT.
THE BOOZE STARTED FLOWING, AND WE GOT TO TALKING...
HA HA HA!
*THE TATSU IN "TATSUMI" IS THE KANJI FOR "DRAGON."
STILL, SIR TAMIYA GANTETSUSAI...
"BLADE DRAGON" OR NOT, I DOUBT YOU COULD CUT DOWN A REAL DRAGON.
KRIK

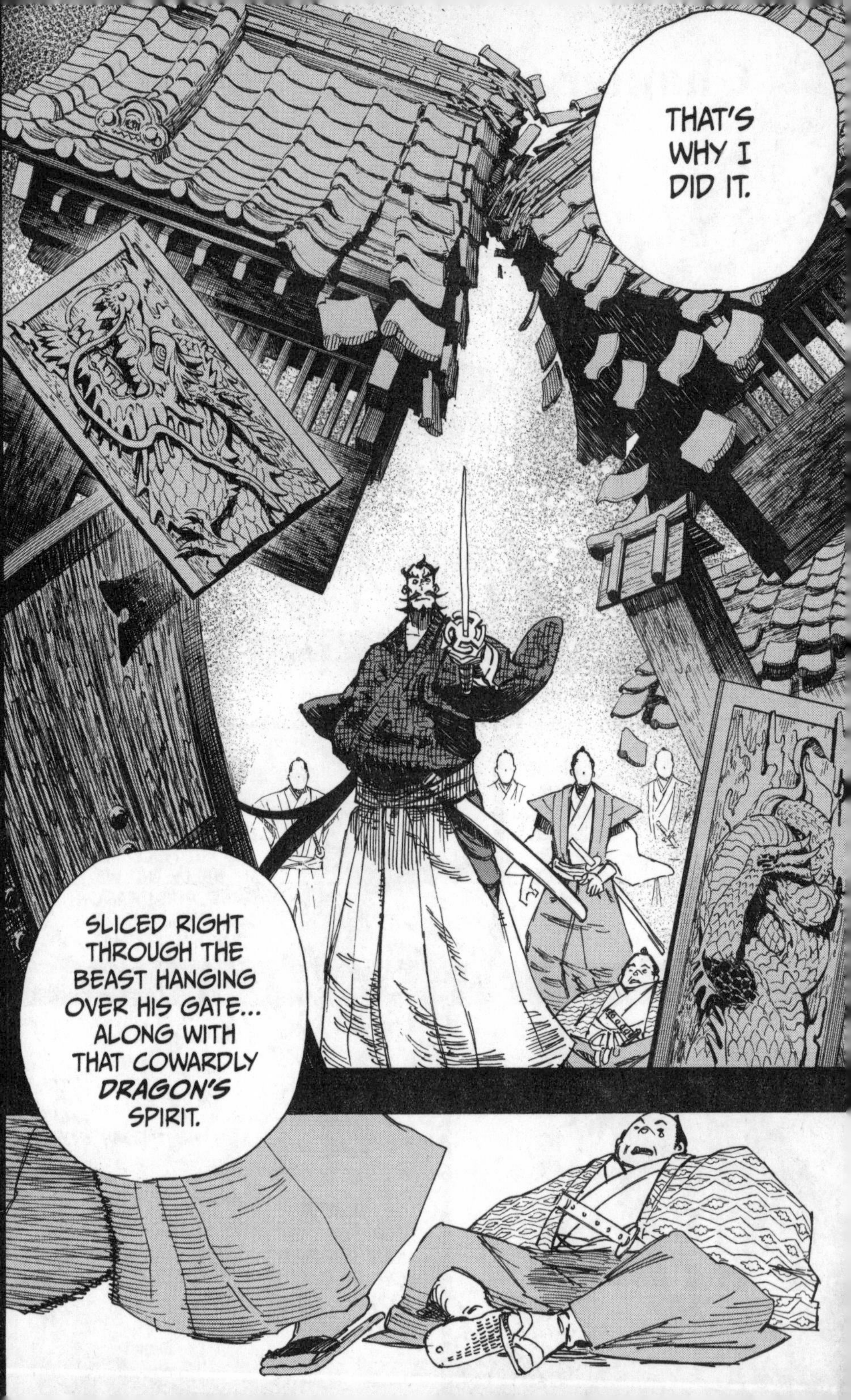
THAT'S WHY I DID IT.
SLICED RIGHT THROUGH THE BEAST HANGING OVER HIS GATE... ALONG WITH THAT COWARDLY *DRAGON'S* SPIRIT.

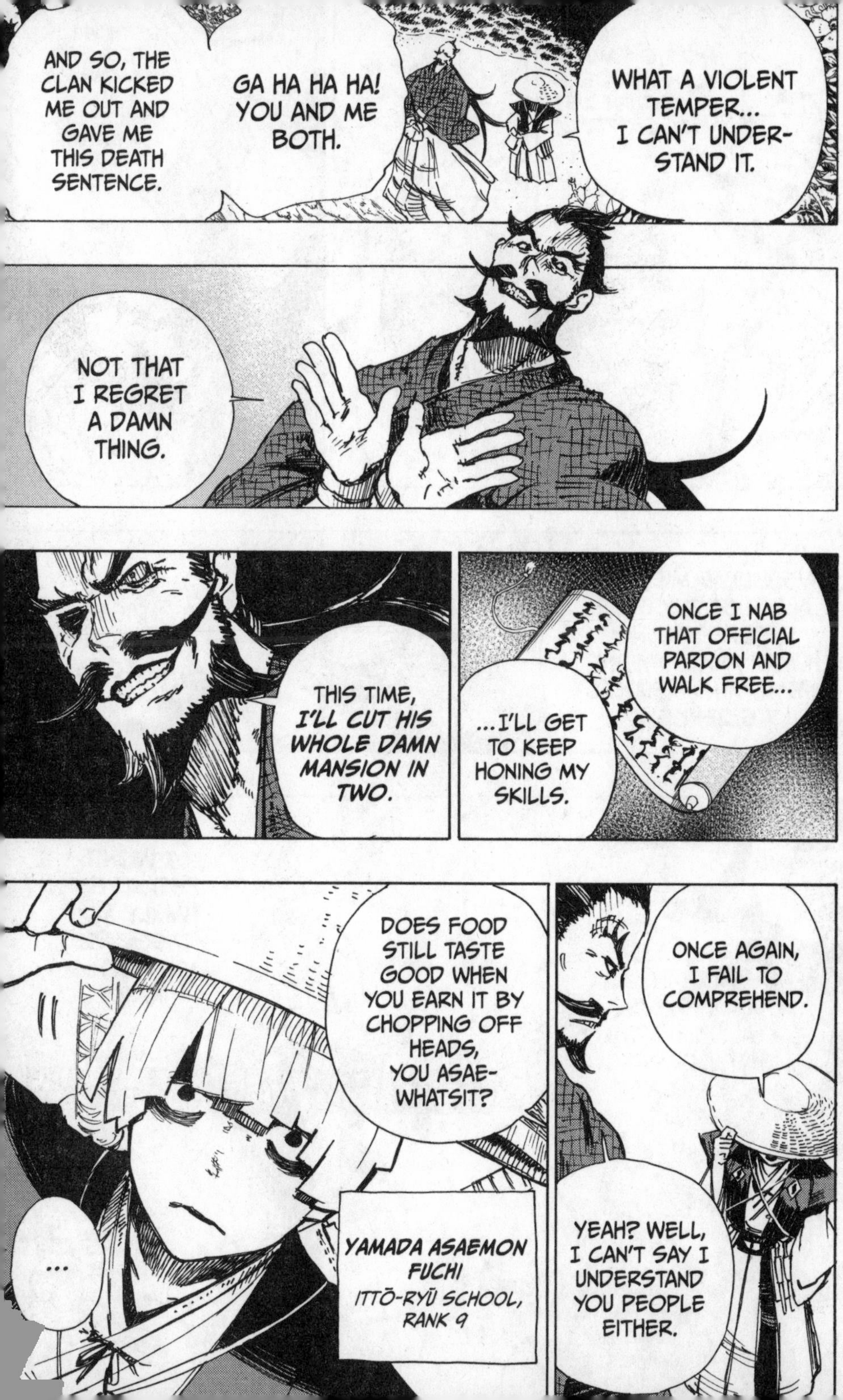
WHAT A VIOLENT TEMPER... I CAN'T UNDERSTAND IT.
GA HA HA HA! YOU AND ME BOTH.
AND SO, THE CLAN KICKED ME OUT AND GAVE ME THIS DEATH SENTENCE.
NOT THAT I REGRET A DAMN THING.
ONCE I NAB THAT OFFICIAL PARDON AND WALK FREE...
...I'LL GET TO KEEP HONING MY SKILLS.
THIS TIME, *I'LL CUT HIS WHOLE DAMN MANSION IN TWO.*
ONCE AGAIN, I FAIL TO COMPREHEND.
YEAH? WELL, I CAN'T SAY I UNDERSTAND YOU PEOPLE EITHER.
DOES FOOD STILL TASTE GOOD WHEN YOU EARN IT BY CHOPPING OFF HEADS, YOU ASAE-WHATSIT?
YAMADA ASAEMON FUCHI
ITTŌ-RYŪ SCHOOL, RANK 9
...

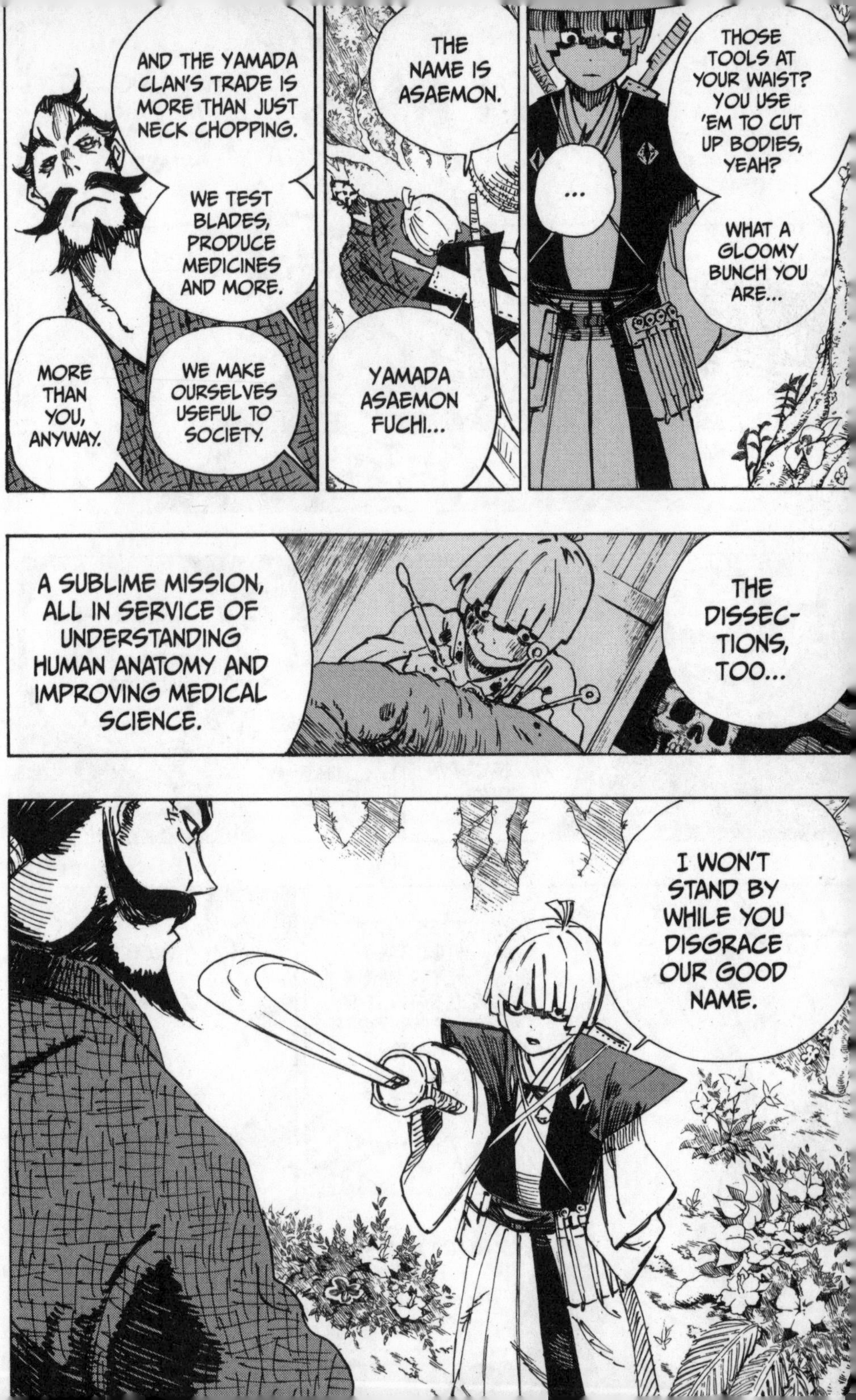
THOSE TOOLS AT YOUR WAIST? YOU USE 'EM TO CUT UP BODIES, YEAH?
...
WHAT A GLOOMY BUNCH YOU ARE...
THE NAME IS ASAEMON.
YAMADA ASAEMON FUCHI...
AND THE YAMADA CLAN'S TRADE IS MORE THAN JUST NECK CHOPPING.
WE TEST BLADES, PRODUCE MEDICINES AND MORE.
WE MAKE OURSELVES USEFUL TO SOCIETY.
MORE THAN YOU, ANYWAY.
THE DISSEC-TIONS, TOO...
A SUBLIME MISSION, ALL IN SERVICE OF UNDERSTANDING HUMAN ANATOMY AND IMPROVING MEDICAL SCIENCE.
I WON'T STAND BY WHILE YOU DISGRACE OUR GOOD NAME.

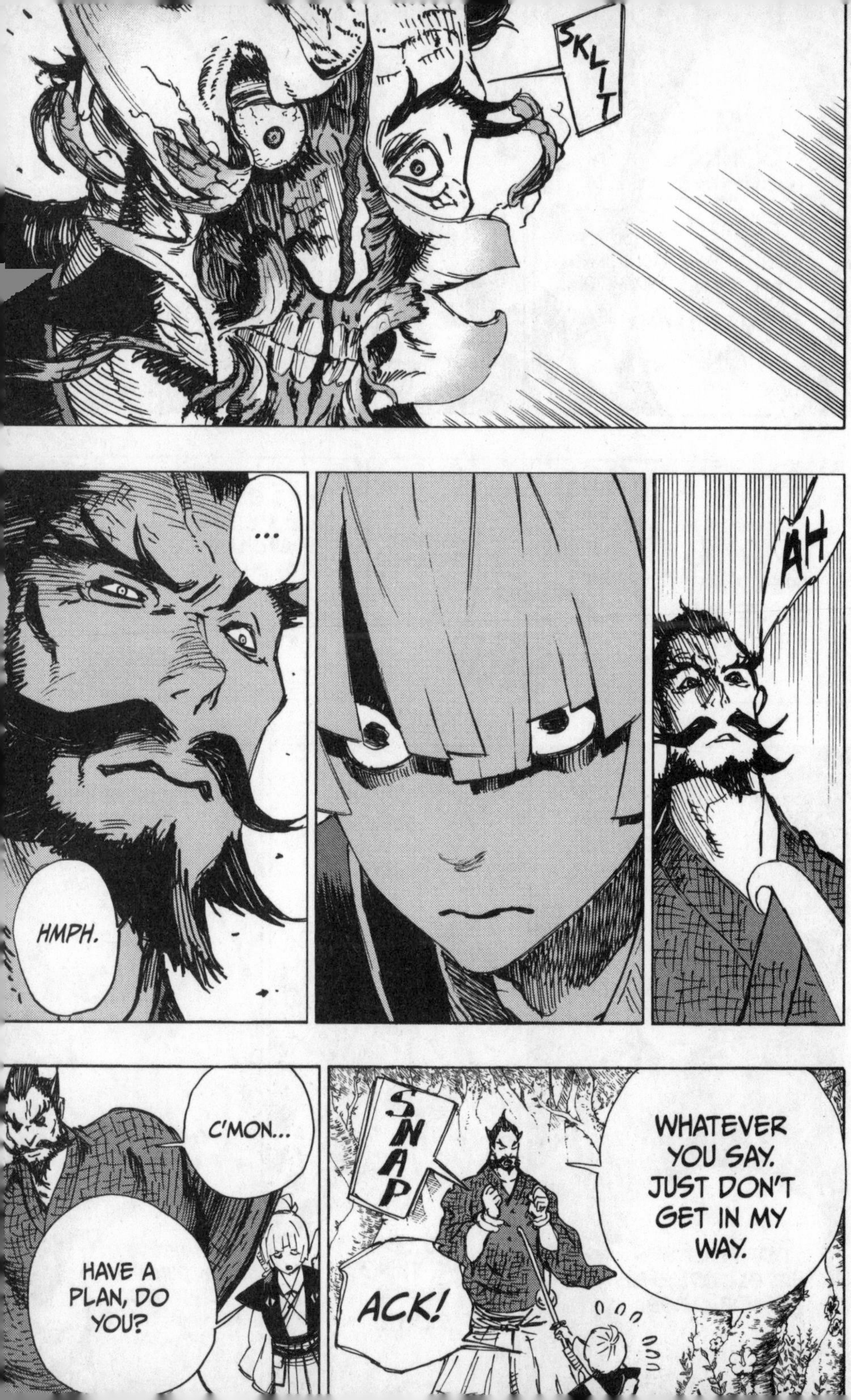
SKLIT
AH
...
HMPH.
WHATEVER YOU SAY. JUST DON'T GET IN MY WAY.
SNAP
ACK!
C'MON...
HAVE A PLAN, DO YOU?

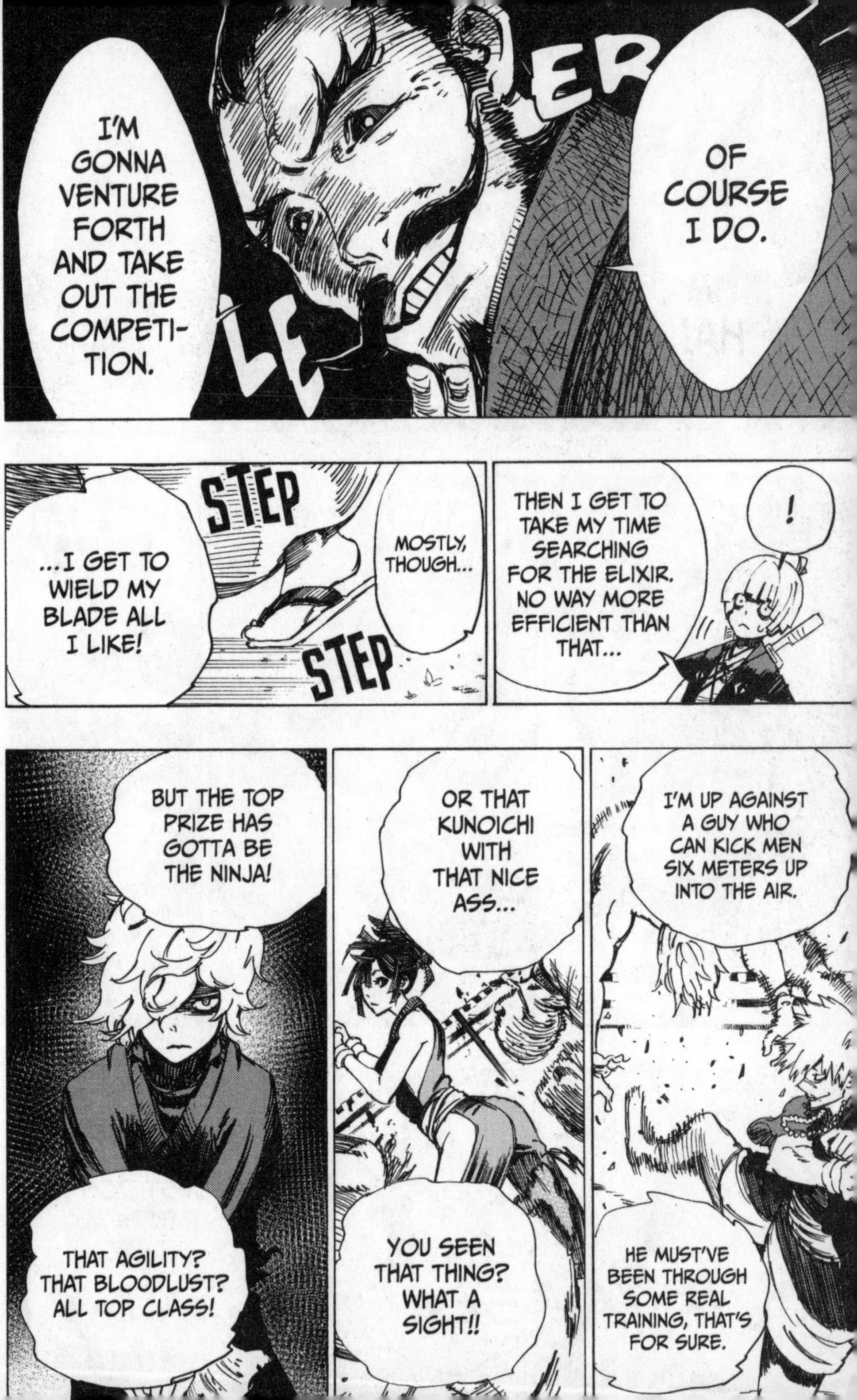
OF COURSE I DO.
I'M GONNA VENTURE FORTH AND TAKE OUT THE COMPETITION.
!
THEN I GET TO TAKE MY TIME SEARCHING FOR THE ELIXIR. NO WAY MORE EFFICIENT THAN THAT...
MOSTLY, THOUGH...
STEP
STEP
...I GET TO WIELD MY BLADE ALL I LIKE!
I'M UP AGAINST A GUY WHO CAN KICK MEN SIX METERS UP INTO THE AIR.
HE MUST'VE BEEN THROUGH SOME REAL TRAINING, THAT'S FOR SURE.
OR THAT KUNOICHI WITH THAT NICE ASS...
YOU SEEN THAT THING? WHAT A SIGHT!!
BUT THE TOP PRIZE HAS GOTTA BE THE NINJA!
THAT AGILITY? THAT BLOODLUST? ALL TOP CLASS!

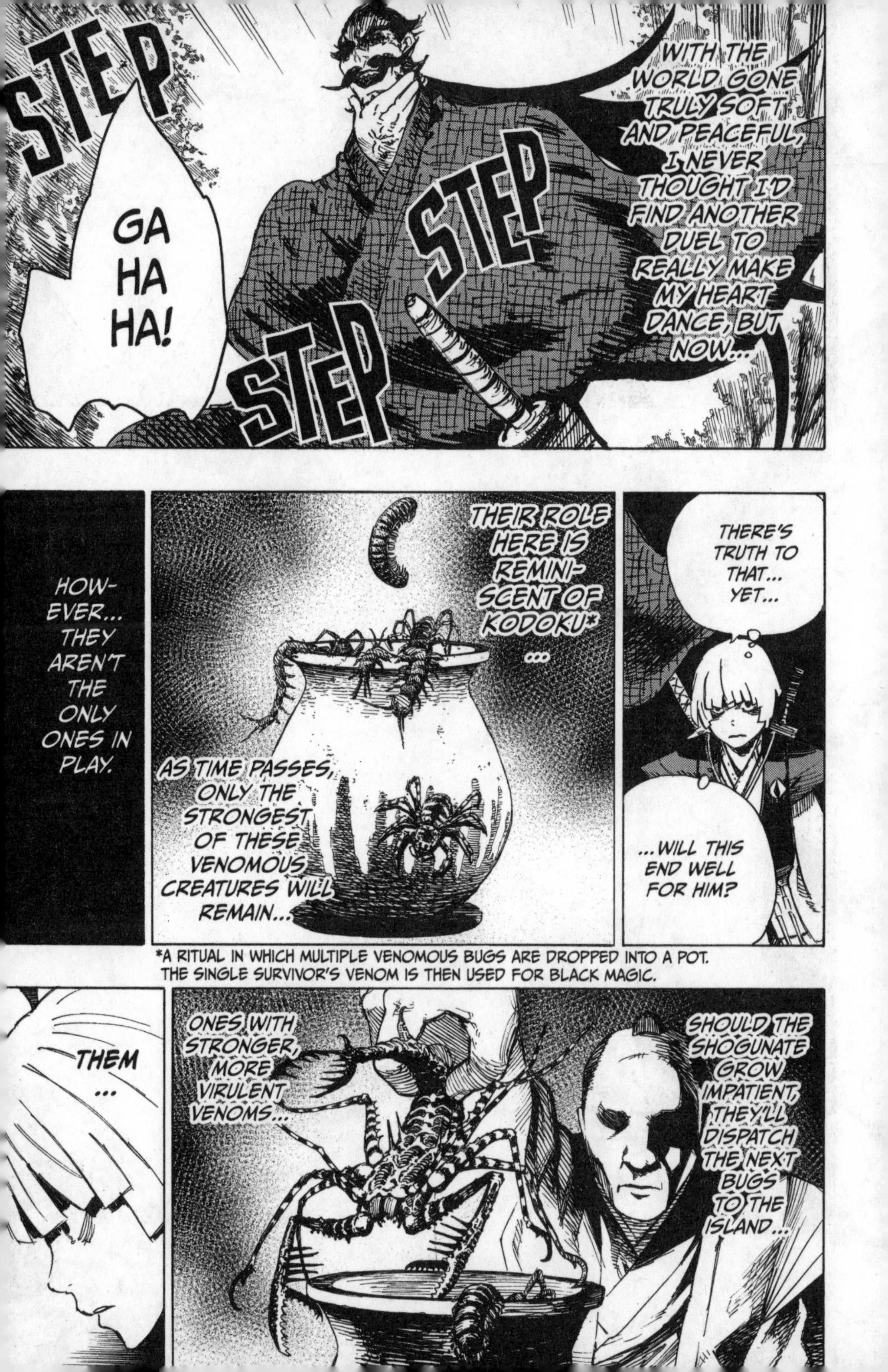
WITH THE WORLD GONE TRULY SOFT AND PEACEFUL, I NEVER THOUGHT I'D FIND ANOTHER DUEL TO REALLY MAKE MY HEART DANCE, BUT NOW...
STEP
STEP
STEP
GA HA HA!
THERE'S TRUTH TO THAT... YET...
...WILL THIS END WELL FOR HIM?
THEIR ROLE HERE IS REMINI-SCENT OF KODOKU*...
AS TIME PASSES, ONLY THE STRONGEST OF THESE VENOMOUS CREATURES WILL REMAIN...
HOW-EVER... THEY AREN'T THE ONLY ONES IN PLAY.
SHOULD THE SHOGUNATE GROW IMPATIENT, THEY'LL DISPATCH THE NEXT BUGS TO THE ISLAND...
ONES WITH STRONGER, MORE VIRULENT VENOMS...
THEM...

*A RITUAL IN WHICH MULTIPLE VENOMOUS BUGS ARE DROPPED INTO A POT. THE SINGLE SURVIVOR'S VENOM IS THEN USED FOR BLACK MAGIC.

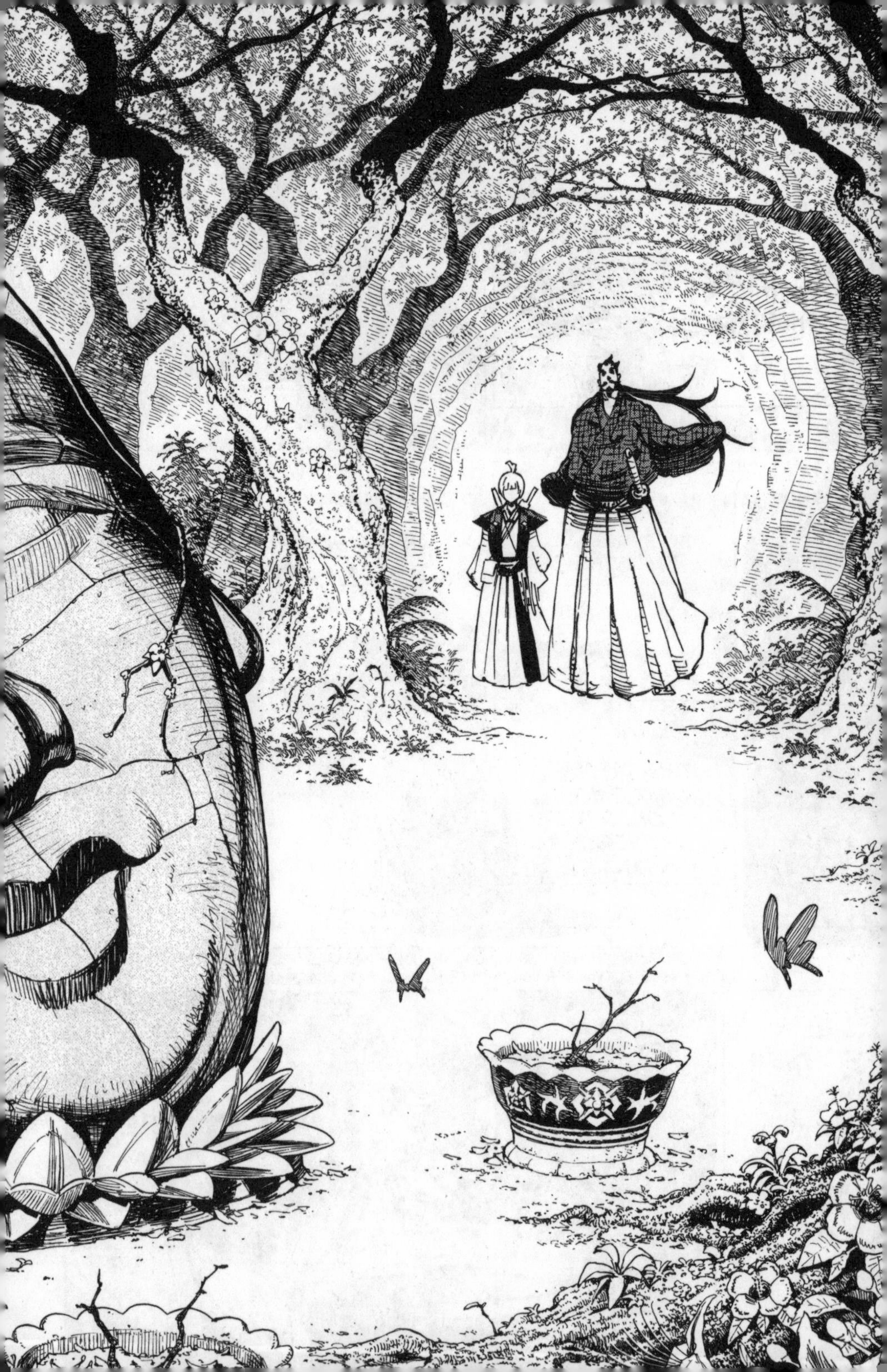

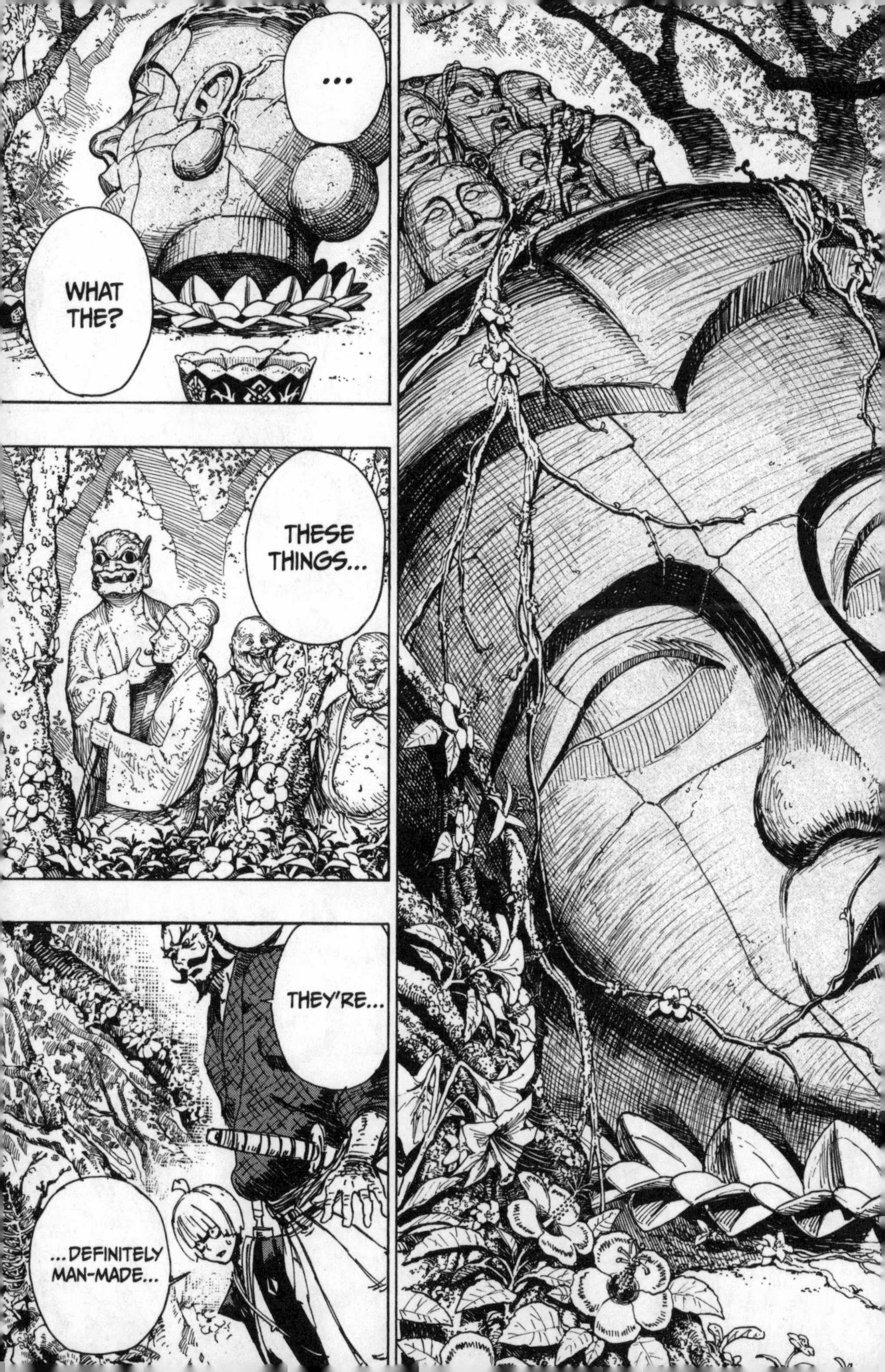
...
WHAT THE?
THESE THINGS...
THEY'RE...
...DEFINITELY MAN-MADE...

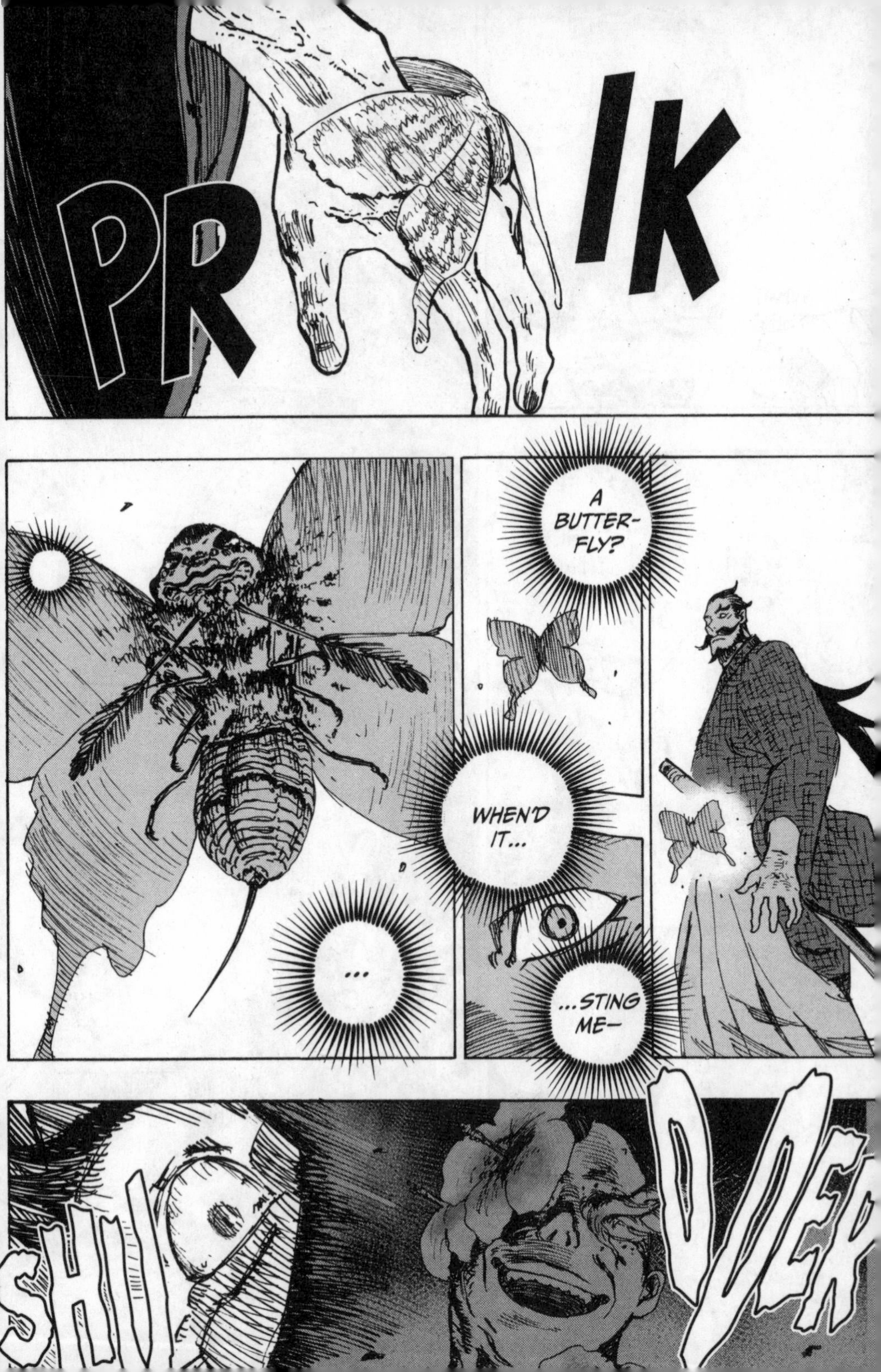
PR
IK
A BUTTER-FLY?
WHEN'D IT...
...STING ME—
...
SHI
VER

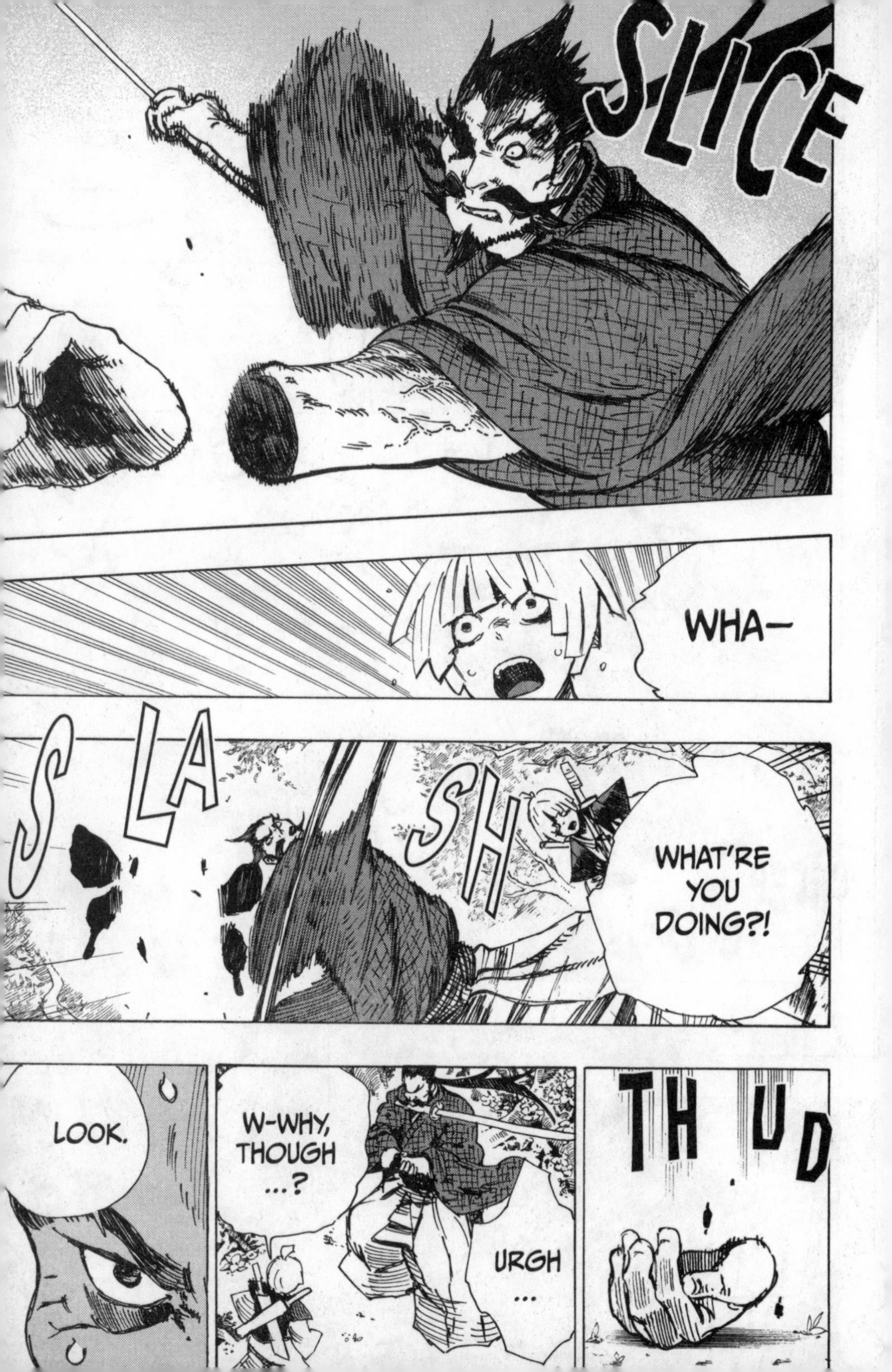
SLICE
WHA-
SLASH
WHAT'RE YOU DOING?!
THUD
W-WHY, THOUGH ...?
URGH ...
LOOK.

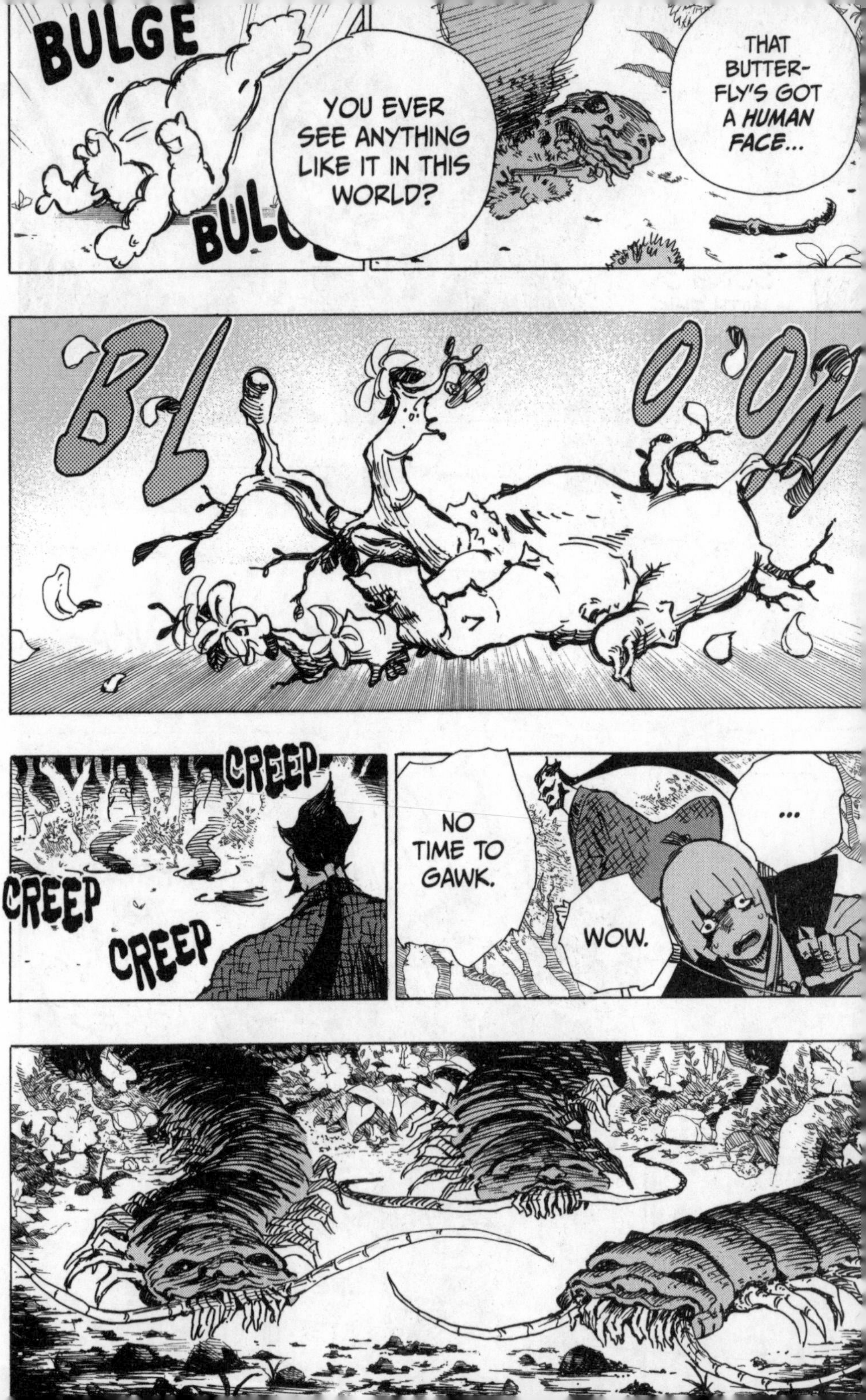
THAT BUTTER-FLY'S GOT A HUMAN FACE...
YOU EVER SEE ANYTHING LIKE IT IN THIS WORLD?
BULGE
BLOOM
...
NO TIME TO GAWK.
WOW.
CREEP
CREEP
CREEP

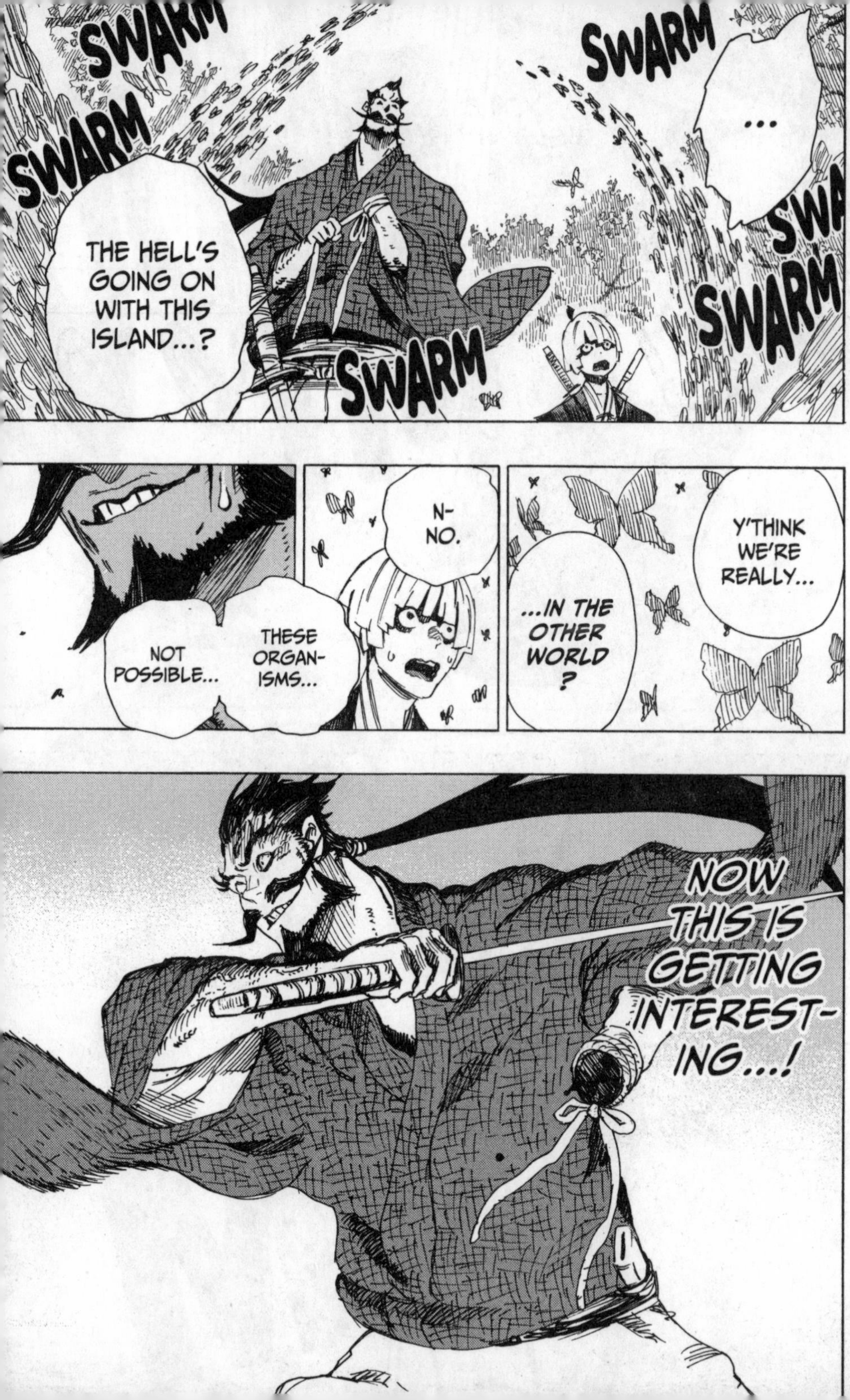
SWARM
...
SWA
SWARM
SWARM
SWARM
THE HELL'S GOING ON WITH THIS ISLAND...?
SWARM
Y'THINK WE'RE REALLY...
...IN THE OTHER WORLD?
N- NO.
THESE ORGAN-ISMS...
NOT POSSIBLE...
NOW THIS IS GETTING INTEREST-ING...!

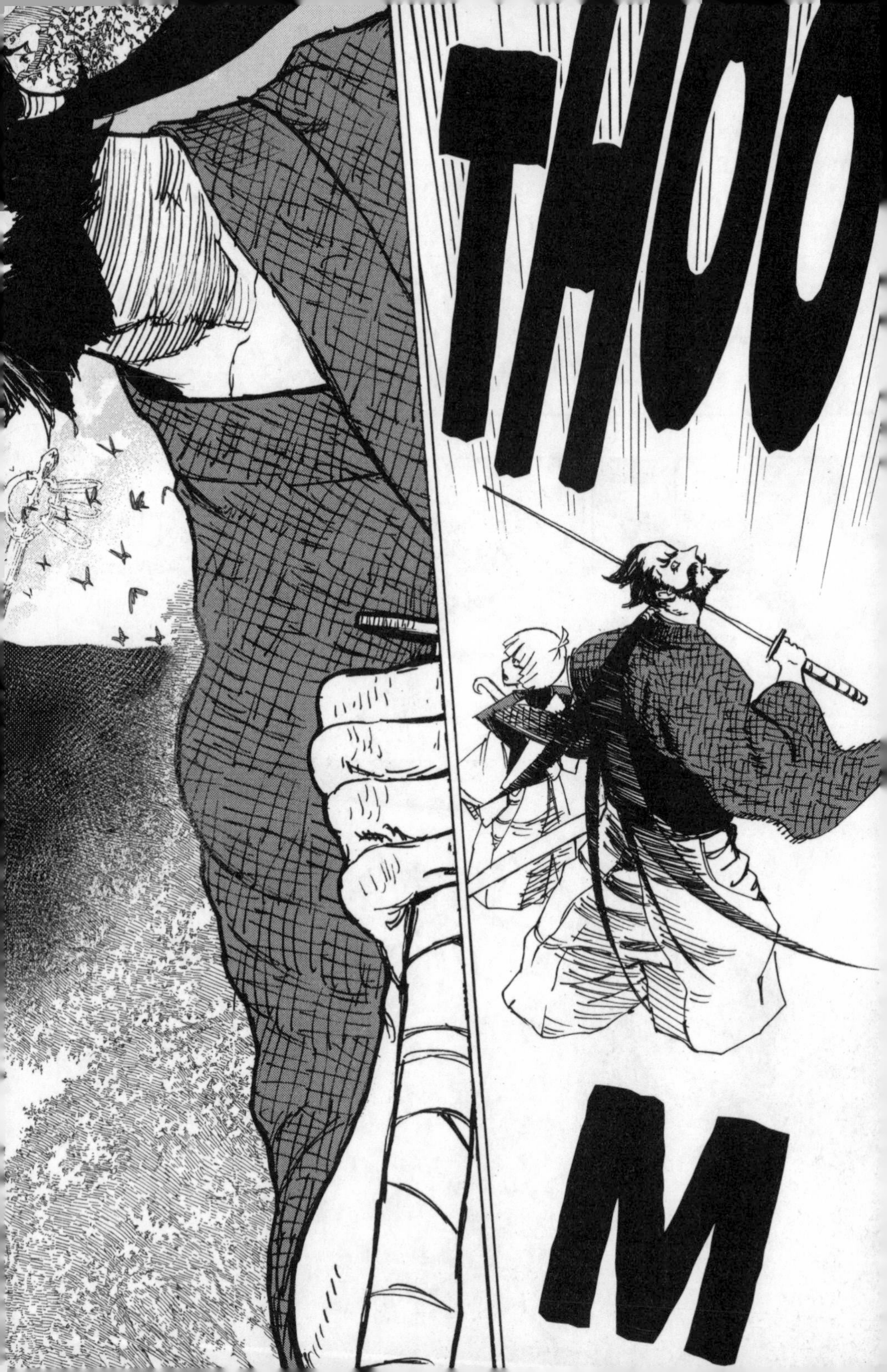
THOOM

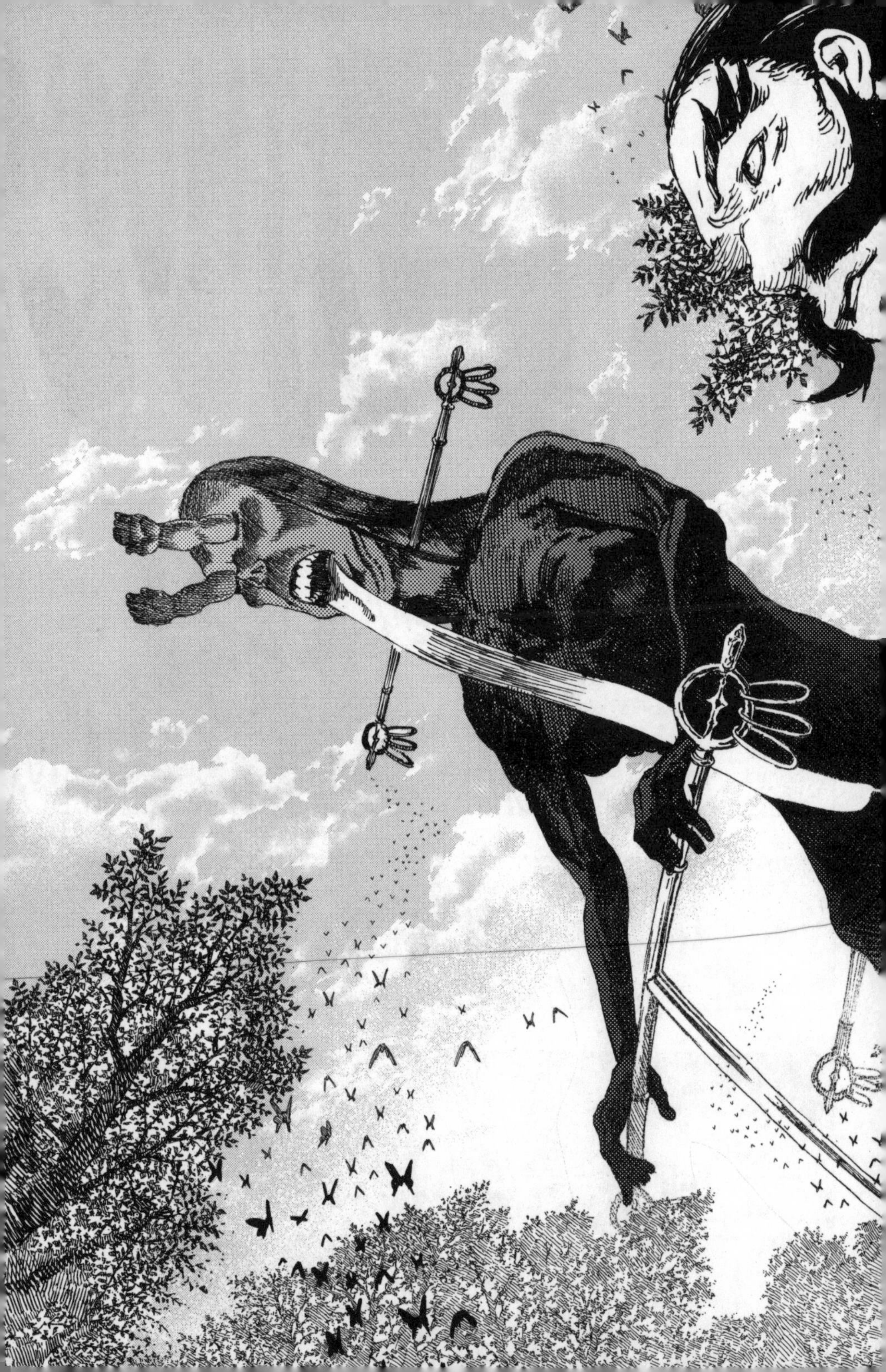

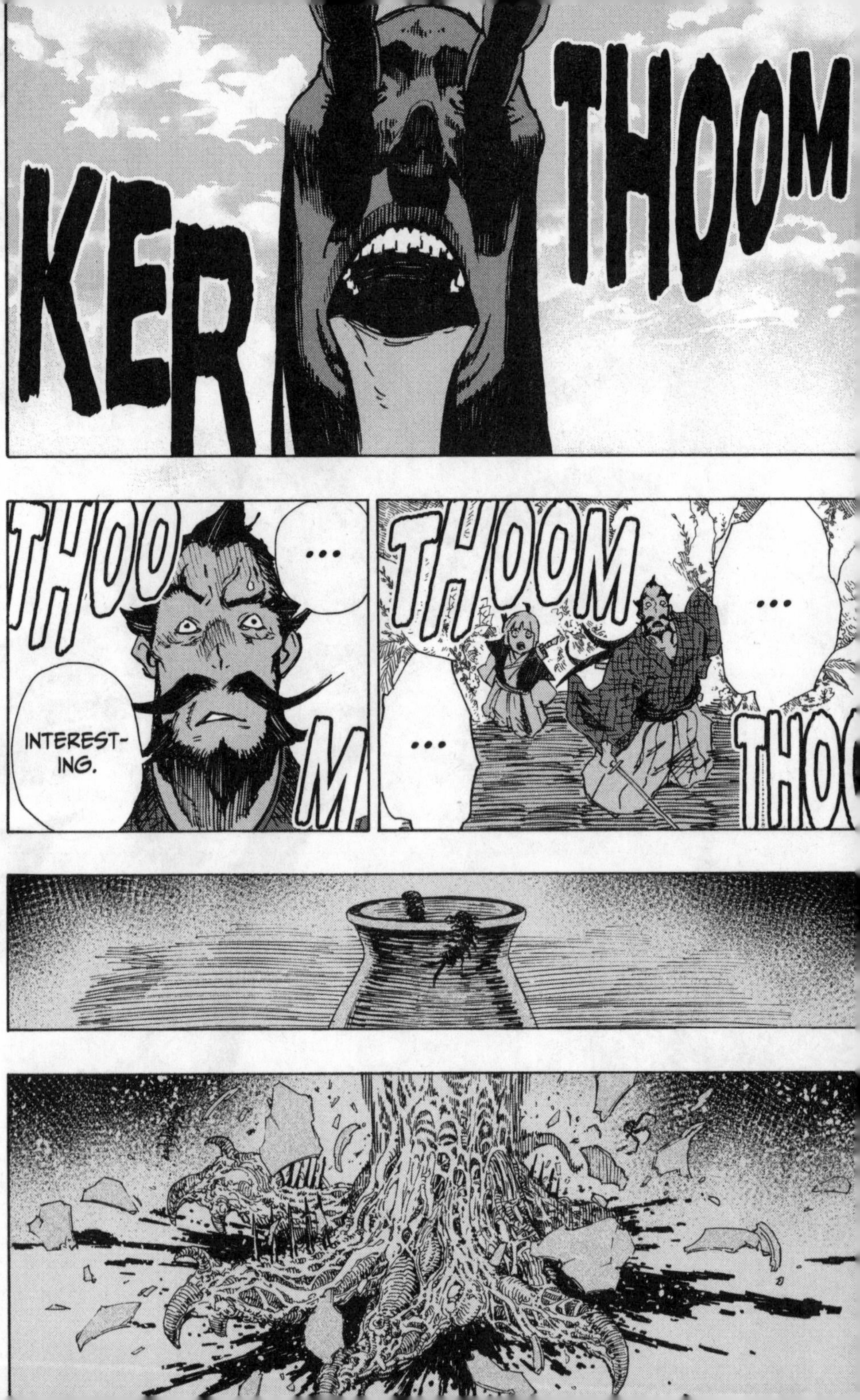
KER THOOM
...
THOOM
THOO
...
...
THOOM
INTEREST-ING.

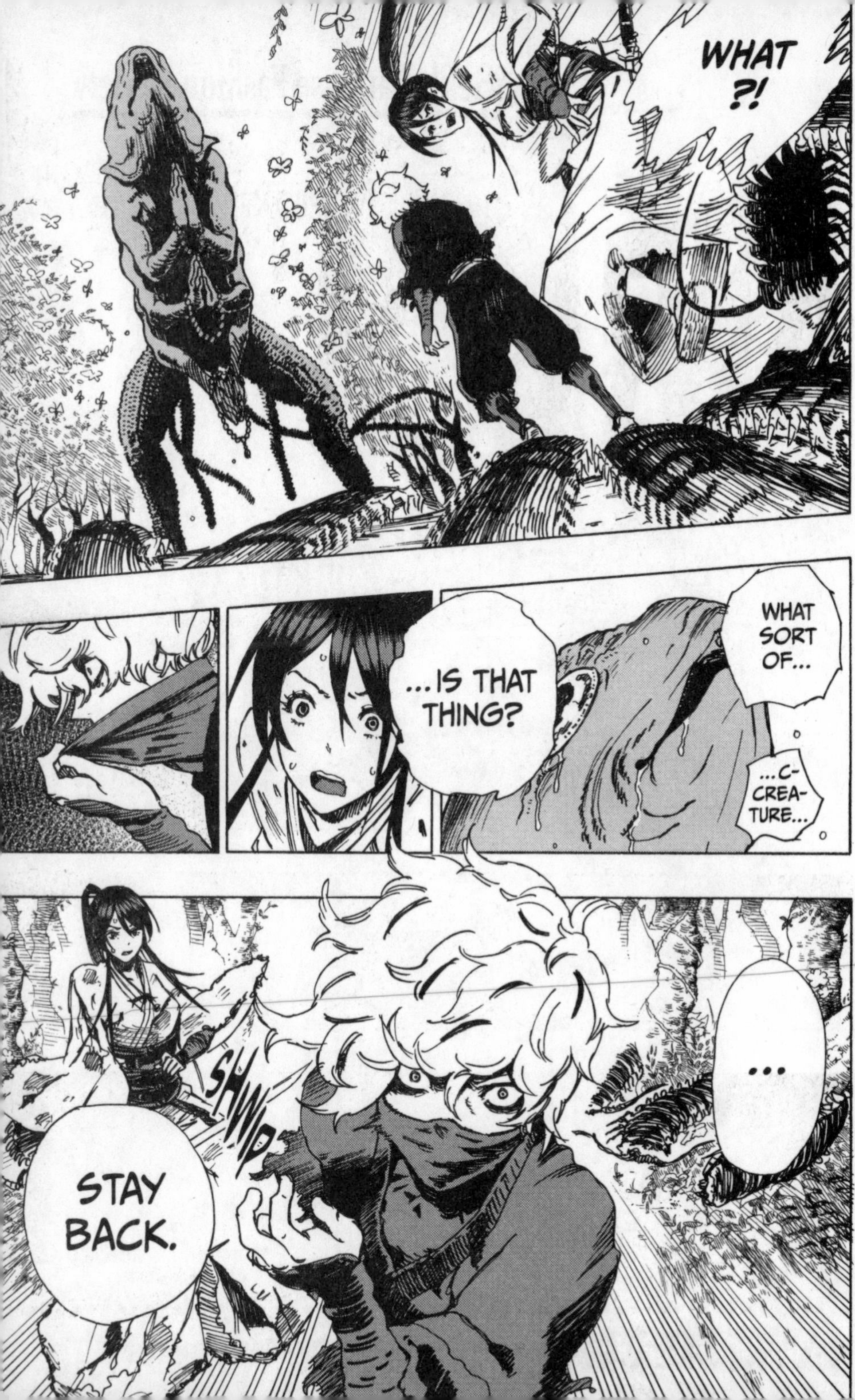
WHAT ?!
WHAT SORT OF...
...C-CREATURE...
...IS THAT THING?
...
SHWIP
STAY BACK.

Hell's Paradise Fashion Review

Hunter of the Hundred

WARPED KEIUN (Living Armor)

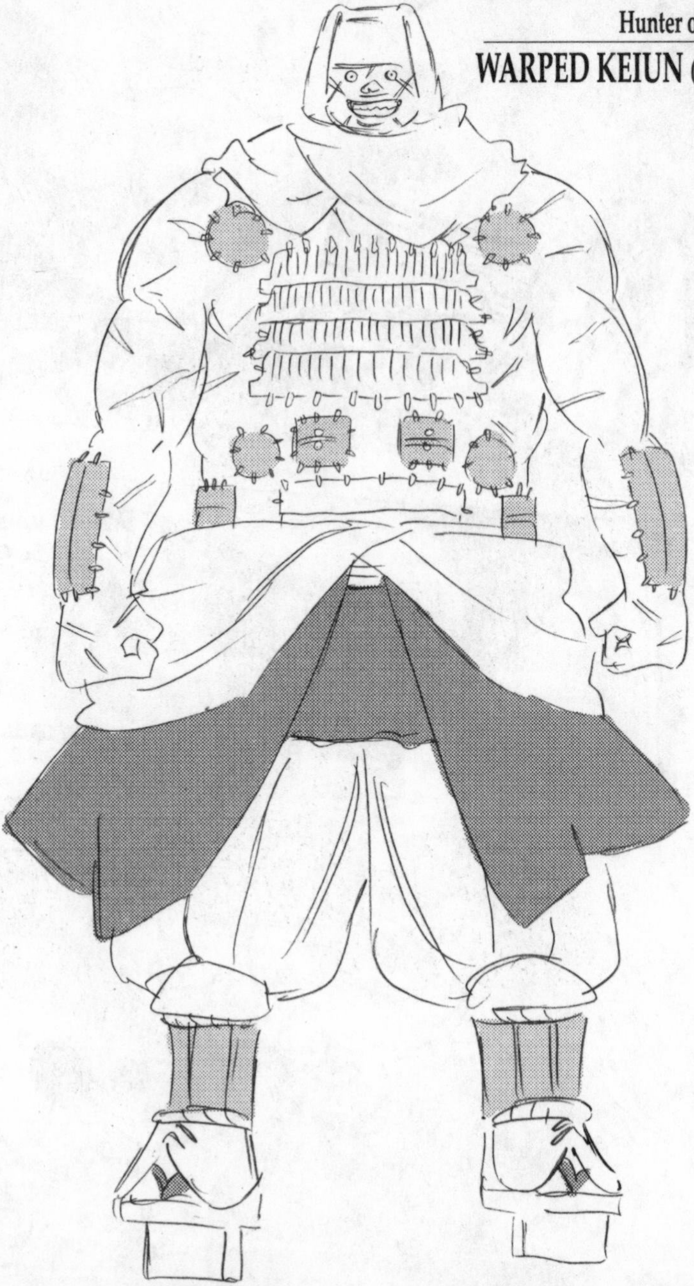

EVALUATION ► GOD OF STYLE ★×∞ PUT YOUR HANDS TOGETHER FOR THE GUY WHO BECAME ONE WITH HIS OWN FASHION!

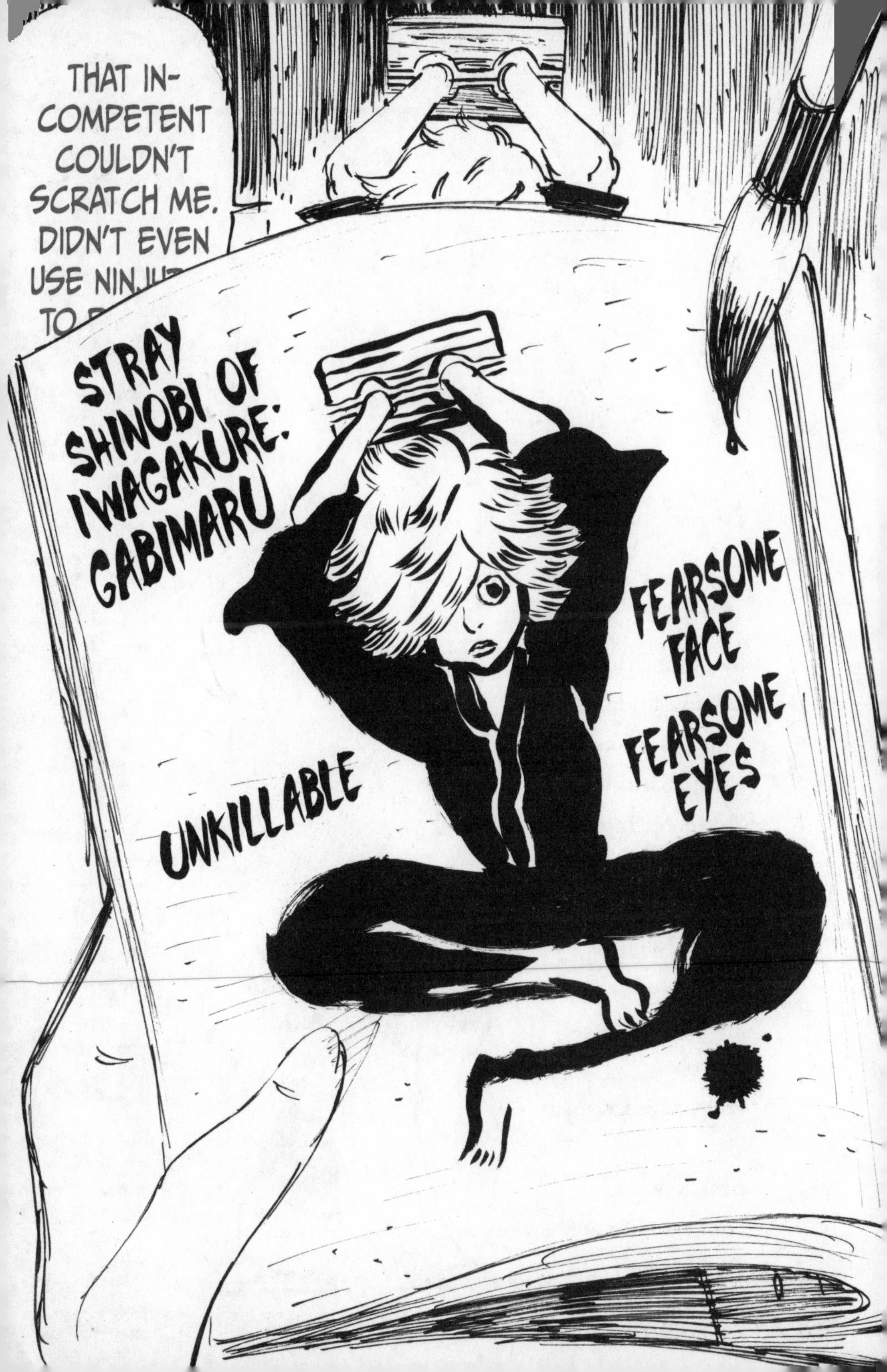

THAT IN-COMPETENT COULDN'T SCRATCH ME. DIDN'T EVEN USE NINJU... TO...
STRAY SHINOBI OF IWAGAKURE: GABIMARU
FEARSOME FACE
FEARSOME EYES
UNKILLABLE

PRODUCED WITH HELP FROM

Akane Arimoto

Megumi Uriu

Tatsuya Endo

Chu Kawasaki

Norito Sasaki

Yukinobu Tatsu

Midori Nishizawa

Aya Nakamura

Takuo Nagoya

Jung-Hyu Park

Thank you so much.

EDITOR

Hideaki Sakakibara

DESIGNERS

Hideaki Shimada

Daiki Asami

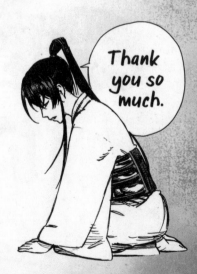

YUJI KAKU

Greetings.

They're mostly letting me draw whatever the heck I want for this, so I feel very lucky if people are enjoying it.

YUJI KAKU debuted as a mangaka in 2009 with the one-shot "Omoide Zeikan" (Memory Customs), which won honorable mention in the 14th Jump SQ Comic Grand Prix. He went on to write several other one-shots before beginning his first series, *Fantasma*, which ran in *Jump SQ* from 2013 to 2014. *Hell's Paradise: Jigokuraku* is his second series.

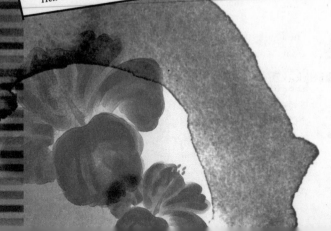

"Jigokuraku" is effectively a portmanteau of the Japanese words *jigoku* and *gokuraku*, which mean "hell" and "heaven," respectively. That said, the *goku* kanji in the title is the one corresponding to hell, giving us two parts hell to one part heaven.

p.25

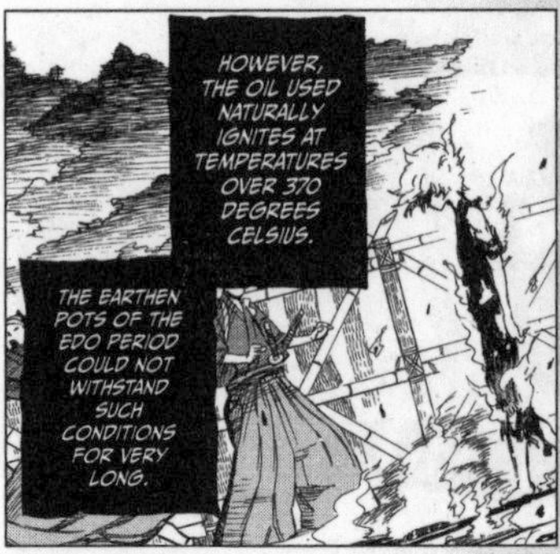
HOWEVER, THE OIL USED NATURALLY IGNITES AT TEMPERATURES OVER 370 DEGREES CELSIUS.
THE EARTHEN POTS OF THE EDO PERIOD COULD NOT WITHSTAND SUCH CONDITIONS FOR VERY LONG.

The Edo/Tokugawa period lasted from 1603 to 1868 and was defined by feudalism and relative peace (after the period of Warring States, before the Meiji era). Edo was the capital, and the Tokugawa were the ruling line of shogun. During this time, the value of a feudal domain was measured by how many *koku* of rice it could produce.

p.30

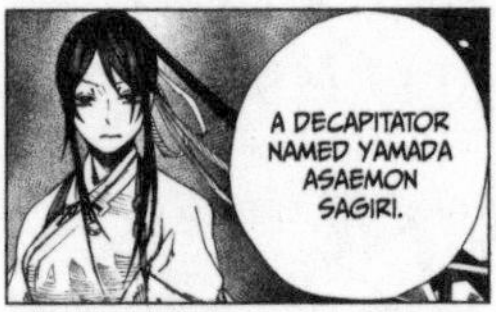
A DECAPITATOR NAMED YAMADA ASAEMON SAGIRI.

Sword testers and executioners from the Yamada clan who went by "Asaemon" really existed in the Edo period. A 1970s manga by Kazuo Koike and Goseki Kojima called *Kubikiri Asa* ("Neckchopper Asa," localized as *Samurai Executioner*) starred a skilled ronin named Yamada Asaemon. In this story, Sagiri is one of many who holds this title.

p.53

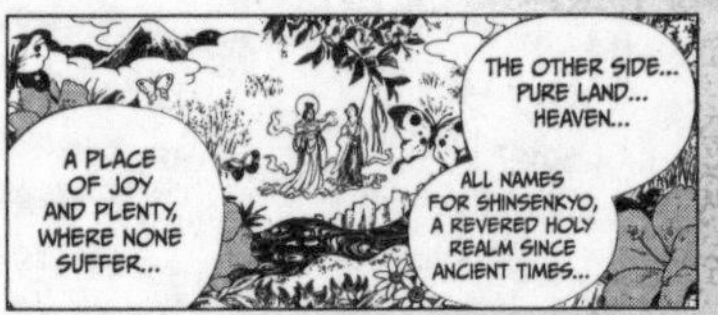
THE OTHER SIDE... PURE LAND... HEAVEN...
ALL NAMES FOR SHINSENKYO, A REVERED HOLY REALM SINCE ANCIENT TIMES...
A PLACE OF JOY AND PLENTY, WHERE NONE SUFFER...

"Shinsenkyo" is the Japanese name for the ancient Chinese version of paradise, populated by immortal gods and mountain hermits called *sennin*. Buddhism calls this realm Pure Land. A generic word for this paradise is the aforementioned *gokuraku*.

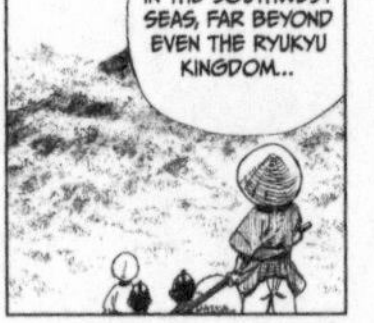
IN THE SOUTHWEST SEAS, FAR BEYOND EVEN THE RYUKYU KINGDOM...

p.53

The Ryukyu Kingdom covered what we know today as the Okinawa Islands. It was independent (not ruled by Japan) and controlled maritime trade in East and Southeast Asia. The story's key island is even farther southwest, towards Taiwan and mainland China.

p.78

THE GREAT 11TH SHOGUN, LORD TOKUGAWA NARIYOSHI, SITS BEFORE YOU!
NORMALLY, THE LIKES OF YOU WOULD BE UNFIT TO BE IN HIS PRESENCE.

There was never a Tokugawa Nariyoshi, historically, but him being the fictional 11th shogun would place this story between 1773 and 1841. The actual 11th Tokugawa shogun was Ienari.

Moro Makiya's epithet in Japanese is *korobibateran*, referring to Christian missionaries who were forced to convert to Buddhism and take Japanese names during the Edo period. In a word, apostates.

MORO MAKIYA THE APOSTATE.

p.123

p.127

IT EXISTS.
THE ELIXIR THAT GRANTS EVER-LASTING LIFE— TOKIJIKU NO KAGUNOMI.

Gabimaru calls the elixir of life *tokijiku no kagunomi*, which is a magical quest item found in the Kojiki (Japan's oldest recorded collection of myths, which tell of Izanami, Izanagi, Amaterasu, Susano'o and others). As the story has it, Tajimamori (the god of sweets) was ordered by the emperor to find a magical fruit in the mystical land of Toyo no Kuni (yet another nickname for the island in *Hell's Paradise: Jigokuraku*). He succeeded, but the emperor died anyway.

"Warped Keiun" is a clear allusion to the legendary 12th-century warrior monk Benkei, who wandered around Kyoto attempting to steal 1,000 weapons from their owners. The *kei* in Keiun is the same kanji as the *kei* in Benkei. Benkei analogues pop up in plenty of modern media, such as *Yu-Gi-Oh!*, *Okami* and *Nioh*.

HUFF
ONE OF THE OTHER CRIMINALS SENT TO THIS ISLAND.
HUFF
WARPED KEIUN.

p.136

Hell's Paradise 7

JIGOKURAKU

VIZ SIGNATURE Edition

STORY AND ART BY YUJI KAKU

TRANSLATION Caleb Cook
RETOUCH + LETTERING Mark McMurray
DESIGN Shawn Carrico
EDITOR David Brothers

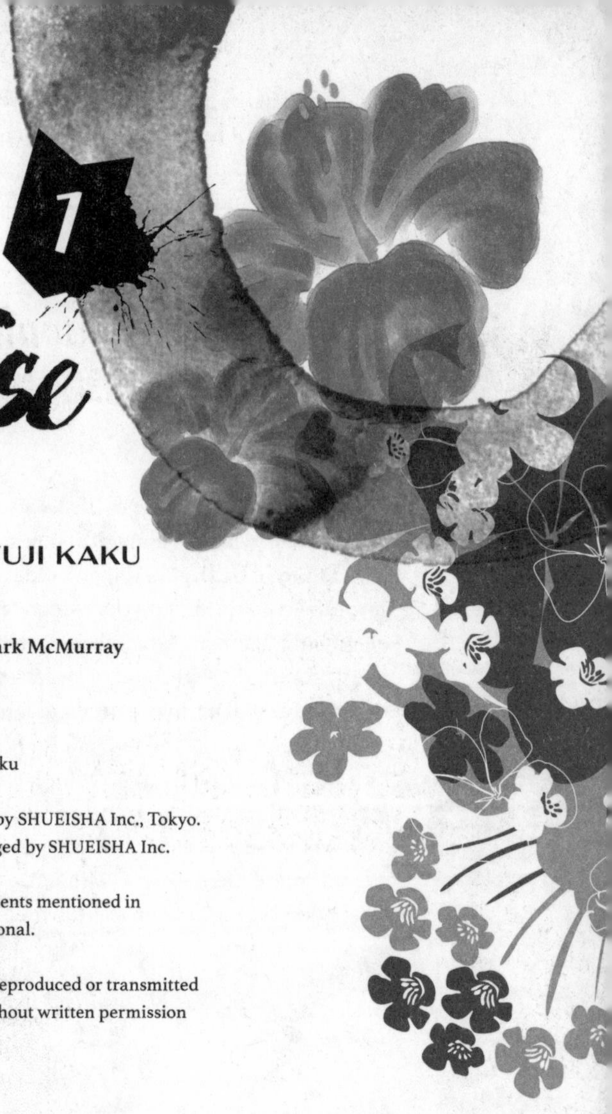

Printed in Canada

Published by VIZ Media, LLC
P.O. Box 77010
San Francisco, CA 94107

10 9 8 7 6 5 4
First printing, March 2020
Fourth printing, September 2021

VIZ MEDIA
viz.com

VIZ SIGNATURE
vizsignature.com

ratings.viz.com RATED M MATURE

PARENTAL ADVISORY
HELL'S PARADISE: JIGOKURAKU is rated M for Mature and is recommended for mature readers. This volume contains graphic violence, brief nudity and sexual situations.

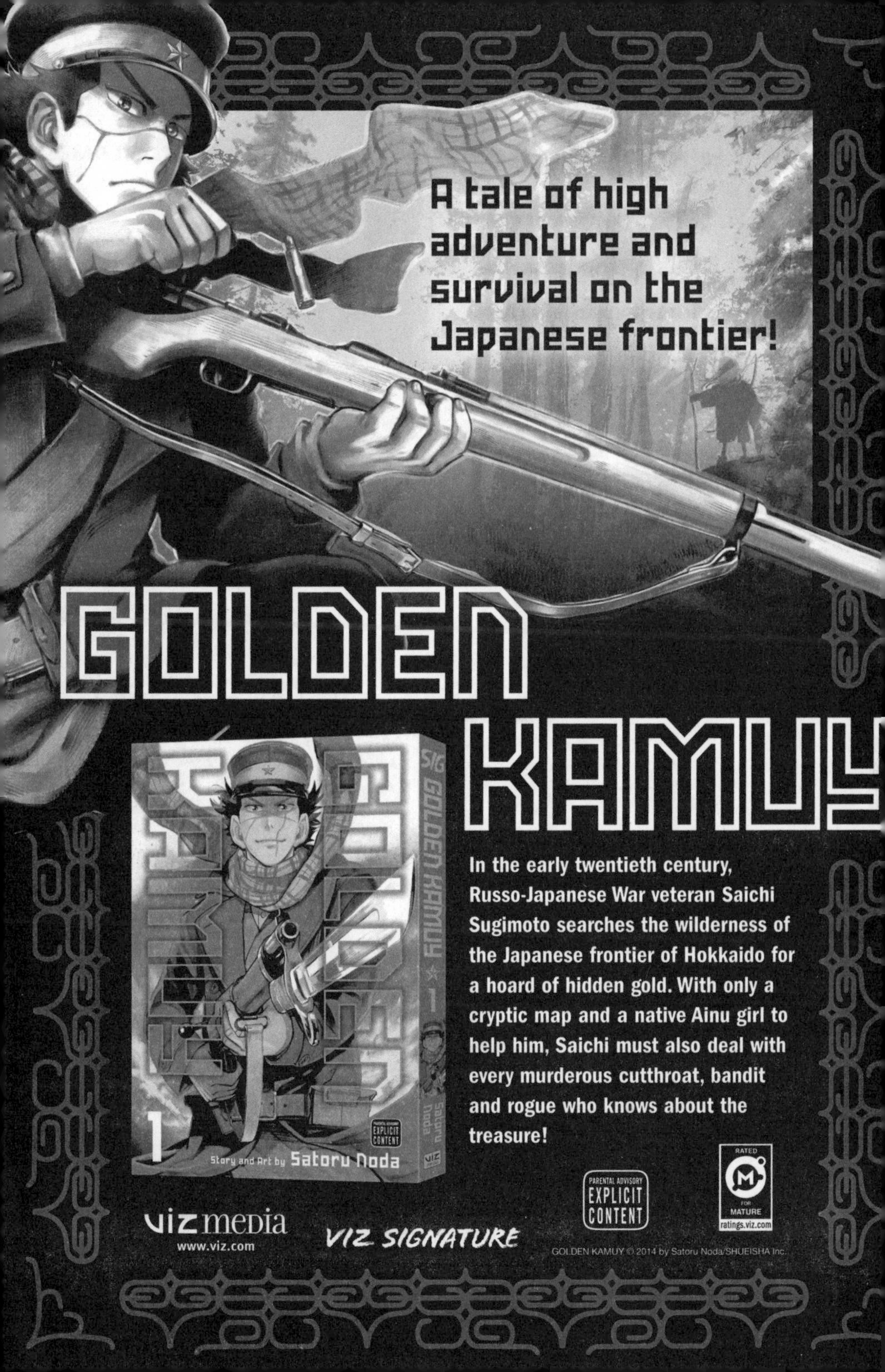
A tale of high adventure and survival on the Japanese frontier!
GOLDEN KAMUY
SIG GOLDEN KAMUY 1 Satoru Noda
1
Story and Art by Satoru Noda
PARENTAL ADVISORY EXPLICIT CONTENT
In the early twentieth century, Russo-Japanese War veteran Saichi Sugimoto searches the wilderness of the Japanese frontier of Hokkaido for a hoard of hidden gold. With only a cryptic map and a native Ainu girl to help him, Saichi must also deal with every murderous cutthroat, bandit and rogue who knows about the treasure!
PARENTAL ADVISORY EXPLICIT CONTENT
RATED M FOR MATURE ratings.viz.com
viz media
www.viz.com
VIZ SIGNATURE
GOLDEN KAMUY © 2014 by Satoru Noda/SHUEISHA Inc.

ABARA
COMPLETE DELUXE EDITION
TSUTOMU NIHEI

A visually stunning work of sci-fi horror from the creator of **BIOMEGA** and **BLAME!**

A vast city lies under the shadow of colossal, ancient tombs, the identity of their builders lost to time. In the streets of the city something is preying on the inhabitants, something that moves faster than the human eye can see and leaves unimaginable horror in its wake.

Tsutomu Nihei's dazzling, harrowing dystopian thriller is presented here in a single-volume hardcover edition featuring full-color pages and foldout illustrations. This volume also includes the early short story "Digimortal."

RATED T+ FOR OLDER TEEN

VIZ

TOKYO GHOUL

C O M P L E T E   B O X   S E T

STORY AND ART BY **SUI ISHIDA**

KEN KANEKI is an ordinary college student until a violent encounter turns him into the first half-human, half-Ghoul hybrid. Trapped between two worlds, he must survive Ghoul turf wars, learn more about Ghoul society and master his new powers.

Box set collects all fourteen volumes of the original *Tokyo Ghoul* series. Includes an exclusive double-sided poster.

COLLECT THE COMPLETE SERIES

THIS IS THE LAST PAGE.

Hell's Paradise: Jigokuraku reads from right to left, starting in the upper-right corner. Japanese is read from right to left, meaning that action, sound effects and word-balloon order are completely reversed from English order.

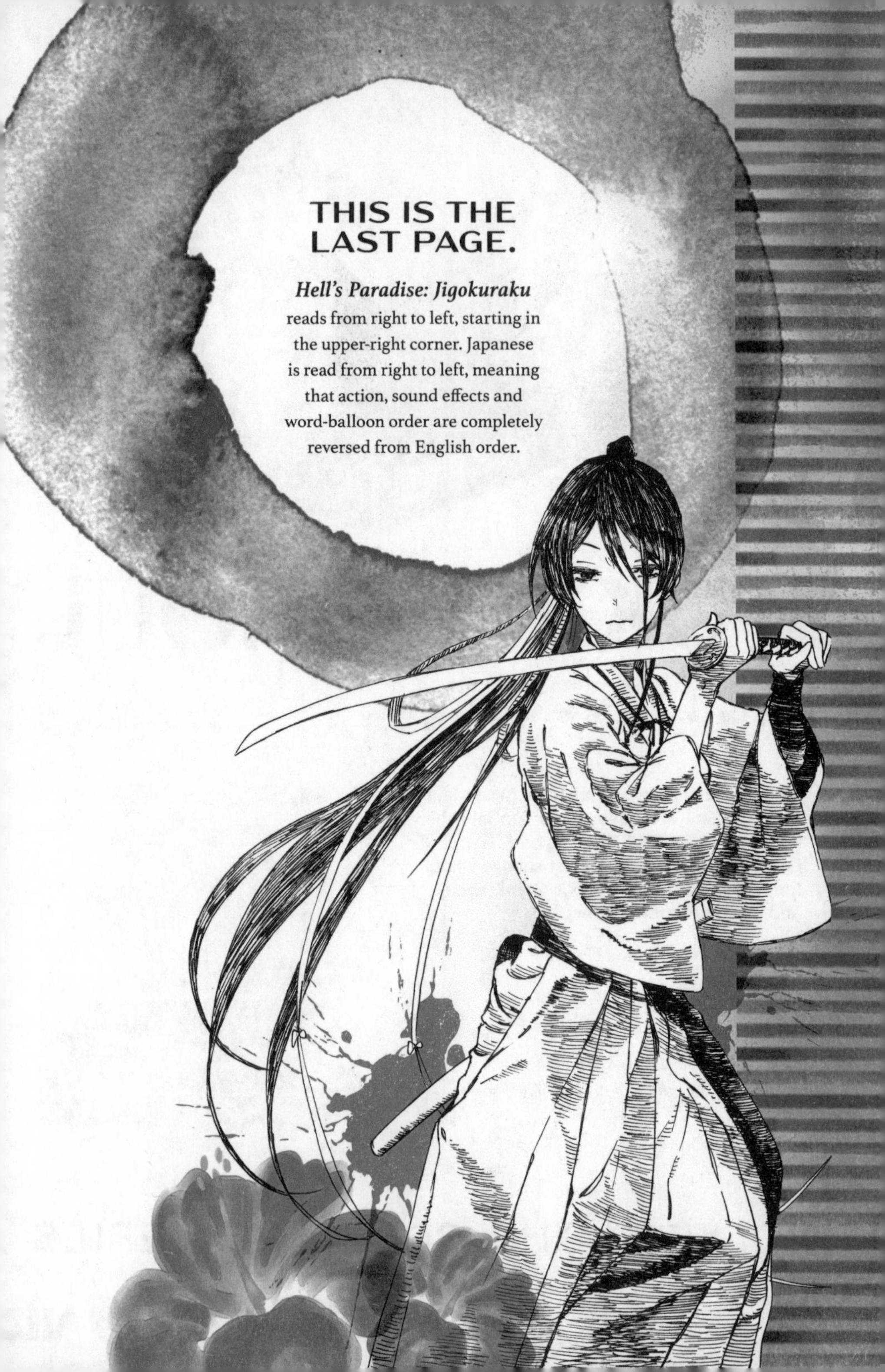